I0109453

Advance Praise for

KNOWLEDGE UNDER SIEGE

"In an age when universities stand surrounded—besieged by political opportunists, hemmed in by market logics, and shadowed by the rising specter of authoritarianism—*Knowledge Under Siege* emerges as both an unflinching reckoning and a defiant call to arms. This is no elegy for a dying institution but a passionate excavation of the university's soul—its contradictions, its responsibilities, and its untapped possibilities."

—**PETER MCLAREN**, Emeritus Professor, Graduate School of Education and Information Studies, University of California, Los Angeles

"Totalitarian rule is on the rise, and education is not some random collateral damage—it's an early and fundamental target. Those of us resisting the siege must grasp the dimensions of the crisis we're facing—its roots and its reach, its power and also its vulnerabilities. Marc Spooner and James McNinch have assembled an esteemed group of scholars, activists, and organizers who can help us do just that. They not only illuminate the crisis, but they also help us plot a path forward. This is an essential text for this fierce and urgent moment."

—**BILL AYERS**, author of *When Freedom Is the Question, Abolition Is the Answer*

"Around the world, universities are key battlegrounds in the fight against fascism. But as the contributors to this volume understand, we have to do more than aspire for a restoration of the previous, broken academic status quo. This expansive and insightful collection helps clarify the stakes of the current crisis and its antecedents as it also explores possible solutions and more life- and learning-affirming futures."

—**ASTRA TAYLOR**, co-founder of the Debt Collective and author of *The Age of Insecurity*

"Lively and timely, the chapters in this volume remind us that universities are worthwhile places for learning, meaning-making, and struggle, especially to confront fascism and settler colonialism. But if they can't do this, we need to create spaces that can."

—**EVE TUCK**, James Weldon Johnson Professor of Indigenous Studies at Steinhardt and Gallatin, New York University

"Marc Spooner and James McNinch have done it again, this time turning a critical but hopeful eye on the future of universities. Based on a series of symposia, this collection engages a range of topics from critical university studies to Indigenous studies. Its collaborators dare to argue that universities may emerge on the other side of new forms of authoritarianism not only intact but also with a new sense of purpose. Spooner, McNinch, and their international collective provide an unflinching courage in the face of global fears, a sense of direction amidst the feeling of dread. This book will lift your spirits and remind you that the university remains a central place for debate and open dialogue critical for any democracy worth the name."

—ZEUS LEONARDO, author of *Race Frameworks*

Knowledge Under Siege tells the eye-opening story of the many ways universities in Canada and around the world are in serious trouble. From the impact of neo-liberalism to the authoritarian assault on expertise and knowledge, the contributors make a compelling case for what's gone wrong and issue an urgent call for collective action to reimagine and remake universities that serve the common good."

—DAVID ROBINSON, Executive Director, Canadian Association of University Teachers

"A rigorous, urgent call to reframe higher education as a public good worth defending and reimagining."

—JESSICA RIDDELL, Stephen A. Jarislowsky Chair of Undergraduate Teaching Excellence at Bishop's University and founder of Hope Circuits Institute

"*Knowledge Under Siege* confronts the escalating attacks on universities— defunding, censorship, and the corporatization of learning—and shows why defending higher education is essential to democracy itself. Far from being businesses, universities are vital public institutions where truth is pursued, dissent is fostered, and hope is kept alive. This book is a call to protect the university as a space of critical inquiry, civic courage, justice, and imagination at a moment when its very future hangs in the balance."

—HENRY GIROUX, McMaster University Chair for Scholarship in the Public Interest and The Paulo Freire Distinguished Scholar in Critical Pedagogy

KNOWLEDGE UNDER SIEGE

Charting a Future
for Universities

EDITED BY
MARC SPOONER AND JAMES McNINCH

University of Regina Press

Copyright © Marc Spooner and James McNinch, 2026

All rights reserved. No part of this work covered by the copyrights hereon may be reproduced or used in any form or by any means—graphic, electronic, or mechanical—without the prior written permission of the publisher. Any request for photocopying, recording, taping, or placement in information storage and retrieval systems of any sort shall be directed in writing to Access Copyright. All efforts have been made to contact the rightful owners and attain permissions for the materials reproduced within the text. Please contact University of Regina Press should you have any questions about our use of these materials.

Printed and bound in Canada. The text of this book is printed on 100% post-consumer recycled paper with earth-friendly vegetable-based inks.

Cover design: Martyn Schmoll
Cover art: Michael Krahn, Unsplash
Interior layout design: John van der Woude, JVDW Designs
Copyeditor: Rachel Ironstone
Indexer: Patricia Furdek

Library and Archives Canada Cataloguing in Publication

Title: Knowledge under siege : charting a future for universities / edited by Marc Spooner and James McNinch.
Names: Spooner, Marc, 1969- editor | McNinch, James, 1947- editor
Description: Includes bibliographical references and index.
Identifiers: Canadiana (print) 2025025347x | Canadiana (ebook) 20250253755 | ISBN 9781779401274 (hardcover) | ISBN 9781779401243 (softcover) | ISBN 9781779401267 (PDF)
Subjects: LCSH: Education, Higher—Aims and objectives. | LCSH: Universities and colleges—Philosophy. | LCSH: Education, Higher—Forecasting. | LCSH: Higher education and state.
Classification: LCC LB2322.2 .K56 2026 | DDC 378/.01—dc23

10 9 8 7 6 5 4 3 2 1

University of Regina Press, University of Regina
Regina, Saskatchewan, Canada, S4S 0A2
TEL: (306) 585-4758 FAX: (306) 585-4699
U OF R PRESS   WEB: www.uofrpress.ca

We acknowledge the support of the Canada Council for the Arts for our publishing program. We acknowledge the financial support of the Government of Canada. / Nous reconnaissons l'appui financier du gouvernement du Canada. This publication was made possible with support from Creative Saskatchewan's Book Publishing Production Grant Program.

Canada Council for the Arts   Conseil des Arts du Canada   Canadä   creative SASKATCHEWAN   ONTARIO ARTS COUNCIL CONSEIL DES ARTS DE L'ONTARIO   An Ontario government agency un organisme du gouvernement de l'Ontario

This collection is dedicated to all the defiantly
hopeful lighthouse keepers and tree planters.

CONTENTS

LIST OF FIGURES AND TABLES

FIGURES

TABLES

FOREWORD

Gloria Ladson-Billings

At the time of the symposium coordinated by Professor Marc Spooner at the University of Regina (Saskatchewan) titled *What Are Universities For?* (May 2023), I offered a presentation called "Closing the Marketplace: Restriction, Repression, and Retrenchment in U.S. Higher Education," in which I argued the narrowing and limiting of academic ideas in the university are moving us toward an instrumental, technical, transactional, anti-intellectual institution that was once the font of inquiry, new ideas, inventions, theories, and methodologies. I will not claim clairvoyance, because all of the indicators in the United States were that higher education would be on the front line of the rightist culture wars. I was merely being observant.

I began my presentation by asking the question the conference posed—what is the purpose of the University?—and while I offered no definitive answer, I did suggest there were at least two different but not necessarily competing ideas helping to shape what we consider the modern university. One idea suggests that the university is "an arena where truth is sought, discovered, and explored" (Haidt, 2013). Another idea argues that the purpose of the university is not truth but rather inquiry (Khalid & Snyder, 2022). This debate about the university's purpose is not new. In 1644, John Milton (and John Stuart Mill in 1859) posited that the university should be a "marketplace of ideas" where competing ideas and robust debate underscore the notion that free speech should be tolerated because it would lead toward truth. Thus, the university was supposed to be the marketplace of ideas with freedom of expression that was analogous to the economic concept of a free market. This marketplace of ideas posits that the truth will emerge from the competition of ideas in transparent, free public discourse.

These European ideas clearly laid the foundation for Euro-American, Canadian, Australian, and other Anglo-dominant nations. However, they regularly failed to acknowledge the long history of higher learning that existed in non-European cultures and nations: In the third century, Egyptians established temple libraries and learning centres called the "Per-ankh," which means "House of Life." In the fourth century, the Axumite imperial church served as an organization of higher learning in Ethiopia. Asian institutions of higher education were established in the fifth century. By the seventh century, Tunisia established institutions of higher learning. In the eighth century, higher learning institutions were evident in Fez, Morrocco. By the twelfth century, the University of Sankore was established in Timbuktu, Mali, housing one of the largest libraries in the world. The European institutions of higher education began to appear in the twelfth century in places such as Bologna, Paris, Oxford, Cambridge, Toulouse, and Sienna.

Most European universities began as "church schools" or places where religion was codified and established. During the Middle Ages, the scholastics became more concerned with a critical organic method predicated on Aristotelian thinking, moving away from Latin Catholicism and trinitarianism toward more philosophical and scientific thinking. Harvard, as the earliest university established in the American colonies, in 1636, sought to replicate the European universities and offered what was considered a "classical" curriculum of Greek, Latin, rhetoric, and theology. However, by the nineteenth century, the liberal arts college model (which included science and the arts) took root in U.S. institutions of higher education. The first Black college opened on a farm outside of Philadelphia, Pennsylvania, in 1837 to promote literacy among Black people who would endure legal, chattel slavery until the ratification of the Constitution's Thirteenth Amendment on December 6, 1865.

Higher Education as a Tool for Social Good

I share this brief history in contrast to the fact that the university has often been at the centre of social conflict and change. Throughout the twentieth century, U.S. universities were the site of war (Vietnam), civil rights, and women's rights protests. However, at the same moment universities were a place of social change and championing the rights of the oppressed, they were also sites of elitism and exclusion. In the United States, failure to admit Black students into state-funded institutions of higher education was a major issue. Two significant cases adjudicated before the historic *Brown v. Board of Education* (1954) case declared that separate facilities were inherently unequal were *Sweatt v. Painter* (1950) and *McLaurin v. Oklahoma Board of Regents* (1950).

Heman Sweatt was an African American man who was denied admission to the University of Texas Law School in 1946 because of his race. Sweatt argued that there was no equivalent law school for Black students in the state. While the case was being adjudicated, the state of Texas built a law school at all-Black Texas Southern University in Houston, which at the time was known as Texas State University for Negroes. While the lower courts upheld the state's move to create an all-Black law school, NAACP attorneys Thurgood Marshall and Robert Carter successfully argued before the Supreme Court that the Texas two-schools remedy was not equal.

On the same day that the *Sweatt v. Painter* ruling was handed down, the Supreme Court also ruled on the *McLaurin v. Oklahoma Board of Regents* case. George McLaurin, who had a master's degree in education, was denied admission to a doctoral program at the University of Oklahoma because of his race. Mr. McLaurin successfully won a judgement from the US District Court of Western Oklahoma. He argued that he was being denied his Fourteenth Amendment rights—equal protection under the law. The state's remedy was to admit McLaurin to graduate school but to insist that he sit at a separate cafeteria table, a designated desk in the library, a desk outside the classroom doorway, or in a classroom closet. They sometimes demanded that he eat at separate times from the other students. McLaurin returned to district court regarding his unfair treatment, but the court denied his petition. He then appealed to the U.S. Supreme Court and on June 5, 1950, the Supreme Court ruled that a public institution of higher learning could not provide different treatment to a student based on his or her race.

Black students also publicly fought to enter institutions such as the University of Georgia, the University of Alabama, and the University of Mississippi. In 1978, the post-*Brown* era witnessed the case of *Regents of the University of California v. Bakke*. Allan Bakke, a white male student, argued that five African American students were admitted into the University of

California, Davis med school with a lower academic profile than his. The Supreme Court ruled that while affirmative action was legal, schools could not use quotas (a designated number) to admit non-white students. Over the next twenty-five years, the case against affirmative action would prevail.

In 2003 two cases brought against the University of Michigan (*Gratz v. Bollinger* and *Grutter v. Bollinger*) would deal another blow to the principle of affirmative action, which in the United States is designed to remedy past discrimination based on race or gender. The *Gratz* decision did away with the University of Michigan's "point system" in its undergraduate admissions. The system awarded points to students from "under-represented racial/ethnic groups." The court indicated that this process was unconstitutional. Interestingly, the ruling did not apply to the nation's military academies (i.e., West Point, Annapolis, and the Airforce Academy), where it was argued that it would be difficult to recruit armed service members of colour without military officers of colour.

The *Grutter* decision upheld Michigan's affirmative action policies for its law school, but it was clear that affirmative action's days as a tool for improving access to higher education were numbered. By 2013, the forces arrayed against affirmative action tried another strategy that resulted in the *Fisher v. University of Texas* (2013, 2016) cases. The state of Texas passed legislation that stated any student who graduated in the top 10 percent of their Texas high school class was eligible for admission into the University of Texas system of higher education (i.e., University of Texas branches, Texas A&M, Texas Tech, etc.). This meant that Black and Latinx students who may have attended inferior high schools were eligible for the state's universities if they were among the top 10 percent of their graduating class. Abigail Fisher was in the top 12 percent of her class and had an SAT score in the 25th percentile. The Supreme Court upheld the lower court ruling that Fisher did not suffer discrimination based on her race. When the case was reheard in 2016, the results were the same. Fisher eventually went on to attend and graduate from Louisiana State University.

In 2023, the case known as *Students for Fair Admissions v. Harvard* represented the demise of affirmative action as we know it. This suit, funded by Edward Blum, the same financier behind the *Fisher* case, asserted that Asian American students were being discriminated against in favour of non-Asian applicants with lower academic profiles. A six-to-three conservative majority of justices on the Supreme Court assured the victory for Students for Fair Admissions (SFFA), a group of Asian American students who preferred to remain anonymous. This decision has forced colleges and universities throughout the United States to rethink race-conscious admissions policies.

The Hard Right Turn

The 2016 election of Donald Trump and Republican majorities in the House of Representatives and the Senate allowed the executive branch to stack the US Supreme Court with conservative justices and left little room for liberal perspectives at the federal level. At the same time, state-level government was also becoming increasingly conservative. In 2022, twenty-seven states had Republican governors and twenty-three had Democratic governors. Likewise, twenty-three state legislatures were held by Democrats and twenty-six were Republican led. One state, Alaska, had a Republican majority but required a coalition of Democrats and Independents to conduct business. Two states—Florida and Texas—have become the most aggressive in adopting far right policies that impact higher education and serve as bellwethers for the closing of the academic marketplace.

In May 2023, the Florida Board of Education, under the direction of the state's governor, Ron DeSantis, enacted legislation that banned the use of any federal funds to promote any efforts toward diversity, equity, and inclusion (DEI). The state's Commissioner of Education Manny Diaz declared, "Higher education must return to its essential foundations of academic integrity and the pursuit of knowledge instead of being corrupted by destructive ideologies" (Brown, 2024).

A month later, Texas Governor Greg Abbott signed a very similar piece of legislation that banned that state's colleges and universities from using federal funds to advance DEI-related activities (Ibid.). Interestingly, these DEI bans do not exempt Historically Black Colleges and Universities (HBCUs), institutions whose very founding was premised on the need to provide opportunities for traditionally marginalized students, especially Black students. Under the legislation, HBCUs may not spend federal money to promote DEI efforts.

According to Kamola (2024) five trends characterize what is currently occurring in U.S. institutions of higher education. Citing work from the Center for the Defense of Academic Freedom, Kamola identifies over 150 bills in thirty-five states aimed at curtailing academic freedom on university campuses. Twenty-one of the bills had been signed into law at the time of his article. The trends in the legislation include academic gag orders, bans on DEI programs, weakening tenure protections, mandating content, and weakening accreditation (Brown, 2014).

1. Academic gag orders: Legislators introduced ninety-nine academic gag orders between 2021 and 2023. The bills claim that teaching about structural racism, gender identity, or views of American history that challenge mainstream ideologies harms students. The state legislatures (all Republican in the ten states that instituted them) termed the legislation "divisive concepts" or "anti-CRT" bills. Critical race theory (or CRT) became the whipping boy for concepts or ideas that conservatives found objectionable and was primarily a response to the 2020 Black Lives Matter protests that materialized across the country and around the world as a result of the murder of George Floyd, a Black man, in Minneapolis, Minnesota, who died as a result of local police officers restraining him in an aggressive and unsafe manner despite his pleas for relief. In Florida, Governor Ron DeSantis signed House Bill 7, the "Stop Woke Act" in 2022. This law vaguely defines as divisive concepts and prohibits the teaching of any "such virtues as merit, excellence, hard work, fairness, neutrality, objectivity, and racial colorblindness as racist or sexist."

2. Bans on DEI programs: Despite hundreds of educators and citizens testifying to speak against Texas Senate Bill 17, the state followed through on its decision to ban diversity statements and considerations in hiring along with restricting campus diversity training and defunding campus DEI offices at all of the state's public universities. The aftermath of the bill's passage has resulted in the closing of DEI programs, reduced services for students from marginalized communities, and the laying off of employees who provided services in DEI offices.

3. Weakening tenure protections: Tenure was developed in institutions of higher education to protect faculty members from external political pressures. The notion of tenure is designed to allow faculty to teach, research, and speak publicly without fear of losing their positions. Tenure allows faculty to teach ideas and

concepts that may not be popular without fear of reprisal. During legislative sessions from 2021 to 2023, twenty bills impacting tenure were introduced. Two such bills weakening tenure protections were signed into law in Florida and Texas. In Florida, Senate Bill 7044 required a system of post-tenure review allowing administrators to "review" tenured faculty every five years. The law also allows administrators to dismiss tenured faculty and requires faculty to post their course content (e.g., syllabi) in a searchable public database.

4. Mandating content: In several states, legislators passed laws requiring "viewpoint diversity," establishing new academic programs and centres to teach conservative content and shifting curriculum decision-making away from the faculty. Florida's Senate Bill 266 expanded the Hamilton Center for Classical and Civic Education at the University of Florida, without faculty input. In its original proposal, the Hamilton Center stated that its goal was to advance "a conservative agenda" within the curriculum. This bill also gave the state's governing boards the authority to determine which classes counted toward the core curriculum. In November 2023 the campus's introduction to sociology course was deemed by the Commissioner of Education to be a course "hijacked by left-wing activists" and one that "no longer serves the purpose as a general knowledge course for students."

5. Weakening accreditation: Finally, Kamola argues that the trend toward weakening accreditation is a way to subvert the process of external peer review to which most universities subject themselves. These institutional performance reviews provide a benchmark by which institutions can judge their strengths and weaknesses. Increasingly, conservative legislators reject accreditation agencies that criticize their stands toward establishing academic entities without the input or oversight of faculty. In North Carolina, through Senate Bill 680, the governing board required universities to choose a different accreditor each accreditation cycle. This would allow schools to search for accrediting agencies who would not object to political interference in the curriculum.

Because of the global nature of knowledge and information, these trends that are taking hold in the United States are unlikely to be limited to the geopolitical borders of the nation. The rightist turn throughout Europe—in the United Kingdom, France, Italy, Germany, etc.—portends the adoption of similar conservative and ultra-conservative strategies to limit the exercise of free speech and the ability to resist dogmatic and fascistic policies. The chapters contained in this volume raise important questions about the purpose of universities as well as their viability in a world of rapid technological change and the generation of information beyond the boundaries of the university. These chapters ask us to think about the university's role in continuing to create elites and further contributing to inequality as opposed to serving as a vehicle for social mobility and broader opportunities for creating equitable societies. In an ideal world, this volume's readers will come away with clearer understandings of the purpose of the university and will advocate for those purposes that lead us toward more just and liberating societies.

References

Brown, R. (2024, March 18). "A trend is clear": A national expert discusses DEI legislation. *Open Campus*. https://www.opencampusmedia. org/2024/03/18/a-trend-is-clear-national-expert-discusses-dei-legislation/

Haidt, J. (2013). *The righteous mind: Why good people are divided by politics and religion*. Vintage Books.

Kamola, I. (2024, May 29). State laws threaten to erode academic freedom in US higher Education. *The Conversation*. https://theconversation.com/state-laws-threaten-to-erode-academic-freedom-in-us-higher-education-230186

Khalid, A., & Snyder, J.A. (2022, February 10). The purpose of a university isn't truth. It's inquiry. *The Chronicle of Higher Education*. https://www.chronicle.com/article/the-purpose-of-a-university-isnt-truth-its-inquiry

PREFACE

Marc Spooner and James McNinch

This edited collection follows the *What Are Universities For? Exploring Roles, Challenges, Conflicting Tensions and Promising Re-Imaginings* symposium held at the University of Regina, Regina, Saskatchewan, Canada, on May 4 through 6, 2023.

Each generation must revisit the fundamental question "What are universities for?" and, perhaps more importantly, *"Whom* are universities for?" And yet, perhaps ironically, few spaces exist to address these fundamental questions. Through disparate and overlapping disciplinary approaches, in consensus and dissensus, the symposium conversations broke new terrain and opened up old discourses as they sought to map an inclusive path forward.

Questions that guided the discussions included

- What is the real value and responsibility of the university in 2023 and beyond?
- What makes universities unique in society?
- What is the university's contribution to democracy?
- What is the university's role in discovery?
- What does the university fight to preserve or place in hospice?
- What is the future of work?
- How does the university survive?
- What people, knowledge, and discourses are regularly excluded in both teaching and research?

- Can the university reconcile its own colonial, patriarchal, and elitist past with its current aims toward inclusivity, decoloniality, cultural responsiveness, and community engagement? And moreover, will the public be willing to accept such a reconciliation?

The symposium gathered national and international scholars to explore these questions and more. It featured a variety of locations, presentations, and sessions, including three special panels.

The first, a public panel, moderated by **Nahlah Ayed**, host/producer of CBC's *Ideas*, was held at Darke Hall, provided a general overview of the symposium theme, and included the following speakers:

- Dr. **Jonathan R. Cole**, John Mitchell Mason Professor of the University and Provost and Dean of Faculties, Emeritus at Columbia University;
- Dr. **Malinda Smith**, Vice-Provost and Associate Vice-President Research (Equity, Diversity and Inclusion) at the University of Calgary;
- Dr. **Linda Tuhiwai Smith**, former Pro-Vice Chancellor Māori University of Waikato and current Distinguished Professor at Te Whare Wānanga o Awanuiārangi; and
- Dr. **Joel Westheimer**, University Research Chair in Democracy and Education at the University of Ottawa.

This panel later became a top five CBC news story and a podcast for the award-winning scholarly program on CBC's *Ideas*, "What Are Universities For?" (Carty, 2023).

The second panel, moderated by Dr. **Shannon Dea**, dean of the URegina Faculty of Arts, was held at the University of Regina main campus and examined "The Changing (Canadian) Post-Secondary Context," featuring a never before assembled, in person, group of presidents:

- Dr. **Michael Strong**, President, Canadian Institutes of Health Research (CIHR);
- Dr. **Alejandro Adem**, President, Natural Sciences and Engineering Research Council (NSERC);
- Dr. **Ted Hewitt**, President, Social Sciences and Humanities Research Council (SSHRC);

- Dr. **Peter McInnis**, President, Canadian Association of University Teachers (CAUT); and
- Mr. **Paul Davidson**, President, Universities Canada.

The third panel, on the importance of Indigenous-led, and culturally responsive, higher education, was held at the First Nations University of Canada, with the following speakers:

- **Lori Campbell**, Associate Vice-President (Indigenous Engagement), University of Regina;
- **Cadmus Delorme**, former Chief of Cowessess First Nation and Chair, federal Residential School Documents Advisory Committee;
- **Tammy Joan Ratt**, doctoral student at the University of Regina and lecturer in the Indigenous language department, First Nations University; and
- Dr. **Blair Stonechild**, Professor of Indigenous Studies, First Nations University.

It was moderated by Dr. **Angelina Weenie**, program coordinator, Indigenous Education—Undergraduate Programs and associate professor, First Nations University.

In addition to the panels, the following world-renowned scholars presented a variety of perspectives on the symposium theme:

- Dr. **Consuelo ("Coni") Chapela**, Professor, Departamento de Atención a la Salud, Universidad Autónoma Metropolitana Xochimilco;
- Dr. **Piya Chatterjee**, Professor and Dorothy Cruickshank Backstrand Chair of Gender and Women's Studies and Chair, Department of Feminist, Gender, and Sexuality Studies, Scripps College;
- Dr. **Sheila Cote-Meek**, Director of Indigenous Educational Studies Programs, Brock University;
- Dr. **Sajeev John**, Professor of Physics at the University of Toronto and recipient of the NSERC Gerhard Herzberg Canada Gold Medal (2021);
- Dr. **Kevin Kumashiro**, former Dean of Education, University of San Francisco;

xxiv • Spooner and McNinch

- Dr. **Gloria Ladson-Billings**, Professor Emerita and former Kellner Family Distinguished Professor in Urban Education in the Department of Curriculum & Instruction, University of Wisconsin–Madison;
- Dr. **Simon Marginson**, Professor of Higher Education, Director of the ESRC/OFSRE Centre for Global Higher Education (CGHE), and editor-in-chief of the journal *Higher Education*, University of Oxford;
- Dr. **Liz Morrish**, independent scholar and honorary visiting fellow at York St John University, UK;
- Dr. **Morgan Ndlovu**, Professor, Department of Anthropology and Development Studies, University of Zululand (unfortunately he was unable to receive a Canadian visa in time);
- Dr. **Christopher Newfield**, Professor, Department of English, University of California, Santa Barbara;
- Dr. **Linda Tuhiwai Smith**, former Pro-Vice Chancellor Māori University of Waikato and current Distinguished Professor at Te Whare Wānanga o Awanuiārangi; and
- Prof. **Tom Sperlinger**, Professor of Literature and Engaged Pedagogy, Department of English, University of Bristol.

It should be noted that all symposium presenters were given the opportunity to contribute to this collection; however, for several, busy schedules and previous commitments did not allow for their participation. The good news is the entire symposium was recorded and may be accessed free of charge online at whatareuniversitiesfor.ca.

Thanks to Professor Stefan Collini, author of *What Are Universities For?* (2012). This book raised the fundamental question that the symposium and present collection have broadened with additional and diverse voices. As Professor Collini put it, future historians will ponder why governments "took the decisive steps in helping to turn some first-rate universities into third-rate companies" (2013).

Readers should note that although this current edited volume, *Knowledge Under Siege: Charting a Future for Universities*, was published in 2026, it is in many ways more appropriately read before our previously published award-winning edited collection released in 2018, *Dissident Knowledge in Higher Education*. That first book aspired to help academics better understand the histories of and threats and challenges to the modern academy, as well as to learn they are not alone in their struggles with and in the university. It was a call to action.

This second edited collection now asks us to question and reaffirm our raison-d'être as our very values and worth are questioned by politicians, the public, and ourselves. As this current book demonstrates, while there are many proposed answers to the question about what universities are for, there is a consensus that universities must continue to be autonomous, self-reflexive institutions that strive to better understand and thrive in the worlds we live in and aspire to.

References

Carty, M. (2023, September 11). What's the point of university? CBC Radio. https://www.cbc.ca/radio/ideas/universities-moderated-discussion-university-of-regina-1.6946951

Collini, S. (2012). *What are universities for?* Penguin UK.

Collini, S. (2013, October 24). Sold out. *London Review of Books*, 35(20). https://www.lrb.co.uk/the-paper/v35/n20/stefan-collini/sold-out

INTRODUCTION
A DEFIANT HOPE

Marc Spooner and James McNinch

> *It is certain, in any case, that ignorance, allied with power, is the most ferocious enemy justice can have.*
>
> —JAMES BALDWIN, *No Name in the Street*

In the many months since the symposium was held at the University of Regina which prompted this collective musing on the question "what are universities for?," the world continues to be a complex, complicated, and highly contested space particularly with the global rise of authoritarianism and democratic backsliding (Darian-Smith, 2025; Haggard & Kaufman, 2021; Stanley, 2024). The role of universities has been under greater scrutiny, from within the institutions themselves but to an even greater degree from those who live, work, and think outside its borders.

This exterior agitation poses the same question—"what are universities for?"—but it does not start with the assumption that a university is an institution whose purpose is to seek (research) and disseminate (teach) the truth (in all its contested meanings). This brings us to our current collection, *Knowledge Under Siege: Charting a Future for Universities*. Those working inside the university understand its fundamental values: freedom of inquiry and expression, academic freedom and intellectual integrity, and the equality and dignity of all people (Turpin & Bailey, 2024). How those values play out in the everyday is constantly being tested.

The university's biggest threats are not only occurring in fascist and authoritarian countries, but also in traditionally regarded liberal democracies[1] where these attacks follow a similar playbook:

> Undermine public trust in institutions that question power, and reward those that remain loyal. The goal is not just to control universities, but to reshape the civic imagination—to erode the idea that higher education should nurture questioning, complexity, and dissent. (Spooner & Westheimer, 2025)

This is most evident in the United States in the current administration of Donald J. Trump's targeted assaults on "the law, higher education, medical research, ethical standards, America's foreign alliances, free speech, the civil service, religion, the media and much more" (Edsall, 2025)—all of which parallel a well-worn trajectory to fascism.

The contributors to this book trouble both the internal and external assumptions about what universities have been in the past, what they are like currently, and what they might, could, or should be in the future.

A medieval institution at once steeped in tradition and yet ever-evolving to respond to current pressures and demands, the university is an entity like no other in society. Perhaps best described as a "multiversity" (Kerr, 1963/2001, p. 5). Kerr explains its ever-evolving nature:

> "The Modern University" was as nearly dead in 1930 when Flexner wrote about it as the old Oxford was in 1852 when Newman idealized it. History moves faster than the observer's pen. Neither the ancient classics and theology nor the German philosophers and scientists could set the tone for the really modern university—the Multiversity....Newman's "Idea of the University" still has its devotees—chiefly the humanists and the generalists and the undergraduates. Flexner's "Idea of the Modern University" still has its supporters—chiefly the scientists and the specialists and the graduate students. "The Idea of a Multiversity" has its practitioners—chiefly the administrators....These several competing visions of true purpose, each relating to a different layer of history, a different web of forces....The university is so many things to so many people that it must, of necessity, be partially at war with itself. (pp. 5-7)

Universities have adapted, and continue to adapt, in response to the demands, constraints, and needs placed upon them by the governments, societies, and communities in which they reside and indeed serve. One argument we wish to make explicit here is that universities operating in a liberal democracy have a special role to play, one that sets them apart from universities in totalitarian regimes and authoritarian and illiberal states.

In addition to seeking truth, making discoveries, and passing on knowledge and wisdom, the university in a democracy has as its unique purpose that of asking difficult questions of governments, of other power structures, and of society itself. Its role includes ensuring that public policy is informed by the best available evidence as well as helping to foster critical and creative citizens whose formation prepares them for a lifetime of meaningful employment, community engagement, and democratic participation. When a society and a university are operating in an optimal fashion, these processes are occurring both inside and outside of campus. The university is in the service of our current society but also, more importantly, to the aspirational one on the horizon.

Though this collection is not intended as another "academia in crisis book," it is imperative to acknowledge the moment we are in as well as the trajectories of our near past that affect and inform our present and future.

In the last hundred years or so, the modern public universities of North America have experienced a variety of watershed moments and crises. This can be observed from the first Red Scare, which led to the creation of the Association of American University Professors (AAUP) in 1915, to the Second World War and the advent of the second Red Scare and the creation of the House Un-American Activities Committee (HUAC) that eventually devolved into full-blown McCarthyism of the early 1950s (Cole, 2009). The turbulent 1960s witnessed student unrest and calls to end the Vietnam War, as well as many disruptions from a variety of social movements demanding equity and greater inclusion. The mid-1980s saw growing boycott, divestment, and sanctions (BDS) calls in an effort to end South African apartheid. Recently, encampments have dotted campuses throughout the United States and Canada, joining similar worldwide calls to action and denunciations of the ongoing atrocities and human rights violations that several organizations have identified as genocide in Palestine, including United Nations officials and Amnesty International. Many of these camps and protests were met with judicial injunctions and in several instances the use of state force to remove them.

Among a variety of developments of concern, our current moment features the outright banning of entire areas of study, the abolishment of tenure, and the curtailment of academic freedom, as well as a near ubiquitous push toward performance-based funding (Spooner, 2024). It also features chronic underfunding, international student quotas, and anti-woke sentiment with pushback against equity, diversity, and inclusion initiatives meant to permit greater participation in increasingly conservative and authoritarian interventionist states.

Still other developments include the widespread use and advancement of artificial intelligence and the uncertain ground upon which universities have based their diverse responses to it. It is a time of audit culture, anti-intellectualism, and disinformation (Spooner 2018, 2024).

It can be stated with little hyperbole that from our fields of study to our campus greens, academies and academics are under attack, just as our global democracies equally find themselves so challenged.

A common outsider's view of higher education is baldly expressed by American journalist Gus Carlson. In praising the get-tough actions of Tulane University administrators in dispersing and blocking anti-war protestors, he leads with the headline "Facing Pro-Palestinian Protests, Universities Must Realize They Are Businesses—and Act Like It" and continues:

> Their customers are the students and families who buy the product; their investors are the donors and taxpayers who fund the operations. Free expression may be a guiding principle, but it is not a one-way street if it threatens an enterprise's viability....In many respects, Tulane's commencement was the equivalent of a corporate annual meeting. It was a chance for the administration to show the school's skill in manufacturing its core product—brilliant young minds—and how its steady hand at the helm refuses to be blown off course by the strong winds of current events. A sad commentary on the current state of campus life? Perhaps, but Tulane's hard-line posture is a teaching moment for the craven chief administrators in so many ivory towers across academia, as well as in corporate C-suites. (Carlson, 2024)

Presuming that the product of a university is the preparation of "brilliant young minds" (without reference to Tulane University's research intensive agenda) is a common misrepresentation of what universities are for, if only because teaching students is a visible and quite public activity.

But assuming that a university should be run like a free enterprise business ("my way or the highway, buddy") is a serious neoliberal misunderstanding and misrepresentation of "what universities are for" even if Tulane is an elite and private institution.

As Jessica Riddell (2024) points out in *Hope Circuits: Rewiring Universities and Other Organizations for Human Flourishing,*

> universities are not businesses. They operate under different rules and governance structures. In Canada, universities are publicly funded social institutions. The logic of revenues, products, and customers in the business world does not seamlessly apply to universities, which are—at their core—values-driven centres of knowledge sharing and knowledge creation. Why would we cede the ground and play by a set of rules where students are customers, grades are transactions, degrees are bought and paid for, and research must have practical application in industry to be funded? (p. 230)

The week before Carlson's opinion piece appeared, a valedictory speech at the convocation of graduate students of the Max Rady College of Medicine at the University of Manitoba proved that mixing political issues with the business of appeasing wealthy donors can create highly charged situations, controversy, and ultimately compromise the university's mission. The valediction urged medical professionals and their associations to call for an "immediate cease-fire to the genocidal war" being waged by Israel against Hamas in Palestine.

Ernest Rady—who donated $30 million to the university in the name of his father (a Jewish émigré from nineteenth-century Russia), who graduated from the U of M's school of medicine at a time when there were strict quotas on Jewish students—accused the valedictorian of hate speech and said the university allowed him "to spew these hateful lies to a captive audience…dishonoured the memory of my father…but also disrespected and disparaged Jewish people as a whole." Rady demanded the video of the speech be removed from the university website (and it was). He then called on the medical college dean and the university president to "condemn, in no uncertain terms, the valediction as not only inaccurate, but [as] flat-out lies" (Rady, 2024).

The valedictorian, Dr. Gem Newman, speaking later to the media responded:

Criticism of the actions of the Israeli government does not in and of itself constitute antisemitism. That accusation (which has been levelled not only at me but at countless others) is not only unserious, but it also serves to trivialize the regrettably very real instances of antisemitism that do occur. (Buffie, 2024)

The question then is: "Wherein lies the truth or truths found in these two news stories?" In early 2024, the Canadian National Arts Centre Orchestra released *Truth in Our Time*, an album that includes the world premiere recording of Philip Glass's Symphony No. 13. The orchestra's musical director and conductor, Alexander Shelley, spoke of the origins of the idea for the album:

The question of where we get our information and how we judge its veracity and how we interact with that information and what is the truth, it seemed to underscore all of these issues…such as identity and the polarization of politics. We have different perceptions of what is happening with climate and our environment, for example, and different ways of acquiring information and which prism is it perceived through. (Wheeler, 2024)

The music director aptly underscores the difficulty in assessing the legitimacy of information. In this regard, the university plays a central role by curating what counts as knowledge, as truth, as legitimate, albeit ideally under constant and robust contestation. However, in order to optimally fulfill this role, diversity of viewpoints and knowledges must be present and held in concert. When interrogating this process, as explained in UNESCO's *Toward a Better World for All: Decoding, Deconstructing and Decolonizing Higher Education in Canada and Beyond*, it is important to recognize

open access to data and publications doesn't mean we have access to diverse knowledge systems. The question becomes: Whose knowledge are we accessing? Who is at the table making up the rules about what constitutes legitimate knowledge in the first place? And why do certain things get published and recognized while considerable knowledge from around the world continues to be sidelined? (UNESCO, 2024, p. 16)

Several contributions to this collection discuss the origins of universities across civilizations and how their roles have significantly broadened and increased in complexity as they attempt to know and understand the world and the universe from many different perspectives and adopt various standpoints on what is deemed to be true.

University of Toronto professor of philosophy Mark Kingwell (2024), in referencing the nineteenth-century British theologian Cardinal Newman, notes that universities "exert tremendous social and cultural influence, and control vast resources. They confer status and vouchsafe expertise. They also foster critical thinking, good citizenship, and human curiosity." Kingwell elaborates, "Education is always political, and too often in the service of dominant ideas, not novel ones....Intellectual inquiry should not offer comfort or affirmation of what we already believe" (Kingwell, 2024).

There is no question that universities have had, and do have, a wide variety of purposes and serve many constituencies, some discrete and diverse and some closely overlapping and entwined. We have seen, particularly in the United States (but also in Canada and the United Kingdom), how national and local legislators can deny or even erase academic freedom and intervene in the business of university governance. We have witnessed the influence of partisan funding of right-wing attacks on higher education. The chilling findings of a systematic analysis undertaken by the AAUP is detailed in their 2024 report entitled *Manufacturing Backlash: Right-Wing Think Tanks and Legislative Attacks on Higher Education, 2021–2023*. The report reveals that

> since 2021 more than one hundred and fifty bills have been introduced in state legislatures seeking to actively undermine academic freedom and university governance. This includes nearly one hundred academic gag orders seeking to ban the teaching of "critical race theory" (CRT) or other so-called "divisive concepts." (Kamola, 2024, p. 3)

According to the report, these efforts are being led by a network of groups and donors seeking to drive legislative attacks on diversity offices, tenure, and race- and gender-based instructional topics.

Inevitably conflict arises because higher education relies on a variety of sources of funding to maintain and support its operations. Increasingly, the business of running the enterprise has been centralized and managed by non-academic personnel. Gone are the days when department heads

xxxiv • Spooner and McNinch

and deans had a degree of autonomy in making decisions that might impact the overall budget of the institution. As governments' share of university funding has declined, academia has depended more and more on benefactors and donors to fund not just scholarships and bursaries, but to help with operations just to keep the lights on, as the saying goes.

The volatility of student enrolments and the dependency of universities on tuition dollars, particularly from international students, have led to difficult decisions being taken on many campuses that have impacted program restructuring, amalgamations, and unit closures. In April 2024, for example, Simon Fraser University, a year after ending its football program, cut the sports and information department. Many academics view such programs as peripheral to the core academic mission, but the next month SFU announced the termination of its Interpretation and Translation and its English Language and Culture programs leading to the laying off of "dozens of employees." Union leaders accused SFU of "withholding critical financial information," and in a release to the media, the administration cited budgetary challenges as the motivation for these cuts, stating that "declining international student enrolment has had an impact on our financial situation, as have other current cost pressures" (Matassa-Fung, 2024).

An emphasis on the need to compete for students coincides with an increasing emphasis on post-secondary institutions preparing students for the job market and, increasingly, being in direct training partnerships with business and industry.

Under pressure from provincial Ministries of Advanced Education, universities are expected to prove their worth as engines and drivers of the Canadian economy. The University of Alberta presented an impressive array of statistics to showcase this; "as we grow our student body to 60,000 students by 2030 [an increase of 20,000], the future impact of UofA alumni will only multiply," pronounced its president. According to a 2023 Ernst & Young survey commissioned by the university, "UofA alumni have founded more than 75,000 companies that contribute $250 billion to the global economy and employ 922,000 people worldwide" (Alumni Impact, 2024).

While business and industry targeted research is useful and serves an important function, too great a focus on it inevitably leads to a narrowing of scholarship, of what is possible, both in teaching and research, and inevitably harms society by robbing us of opportunities for risky yet innovative breakthroughs, as well as valuable areas of research and training that cannot easily be measured by a simple financial calculus. In short, we start to focus on what counts and what is rewarded over what matters.

That being said, universities have also learned to reach out and respond to community needs with new programs. In this we see how the values of universities are embodied and reflected in their actions and activities. In this sense, there is no such thing as a value-neutral education or institution. What is good and what is right and what is true? Universities across Canada, for example, make special efforts to acknowledge the Truth and Reconciliation Commission's findings and the harms of residential schools, as well as to celebrate and honour the resilient cultures and contributions to society by First Nations, Inuit, and Métis Peoples on National Indigenous Peoples Day, June 21, the summer solstice. As well, throughout June, also known as Pride Month, universities celebrate the journey of 2SLGBTQ+ people fighting for their human rights. This culture of encouragement is also a truth of what universities hope for and aspire toward, all while recognizing the dangers of tokenism and superficial change. Such programs and celebrations illustrate a new role for universities: their desire to respond to societal needs and to build knowledge through action.

In so doing they may offer us another truth: our need more than ever for a sense of hope. Such hope is embodied in the concluding "Section IV: Imagining Our Collective Future and the Future of Universities," in defiance of Sophocles's phrase, "How dreadful knowledge of the truth can be / When there's no help in truth!" (*Oedipus Rex*, line 316). The explosion of artificial intelligence (AI) and the intense efforts by some companies to accelerate the adaptation to AI before we have even had a chance to better understand it and its far-reaching implications for humanity and our planet is just the latest challenge to universities and society. Universities must fight to remain houses of sober second thought and careful, deliberate reflection as well as places of hope.

Journalist Ian Brown in his essay "Reading My Way Through a World Gone Mad" cites American writer and activist Rebecca Solnit:

Hope is an embrace of the unknown and the unknowable, an alternative to the certainty of both optimists and pessimists....It's the belief that what we do matters even though how and when it may matter, who and what it may impact, are not things we can know beforehand." (Brown, 2024)

In its aspirational ideal, the university is a place of hope and of our collective futurity. In deliberative truth seeking, there is hope. Every society and each generation of scholars must revisit the fundamental question "What are universities for?" and defend its ideals such as they are and are always becoming.

Against this backdrop, we ask, what kind of society do we want universities to serve and to aspire to become? The following collection will shed light on these issues and much more.

Section 1: University and Its Roles

This first section provides an overview of the university in all its multiple functions and spaces as well as the various pressures that constrain it.

Jonathan R. Cole's chapter "What Are Universities For?" highlights the ever-evolving role universities have and continue to play in serving society. He emphasizes, as jewels in a nation's crown, the importance of defending their vital work in fostering independent thought and skepticism, supporting research and discovery, and helping to create an active citizenry. In closing, Cole points out that "modern research universities are arguably the greatest mechanism for innovation that the world has known" and universities must never become pawns in political wars.

In a poetic narrative, "Universities are Playspaces," Whitney Blaisdell takes us on a tour of a current mid-size Canadian university campus. What she describes is a complex multiplicity of spaces and activities through both utopian and dystopian lenses. Blaisdell emphasizes that in the university fostering creativity is "paramount," as important as recognizing "the forces that threaten to shatter it: tendencies to overly objectify our individual and collective work,...[or claiming] certainty that the institution has any singular purpose at all."

Joel Westheimer's contribution, "Universities in a Democratic Society," draws a stark contrast between the roles universities play in a democratic society compared to those in a totalitarian regime. He then elaborates on three goals for universities to support democracy: encouraging the free exchange of ideas, nurturing student activism and community engagement, and orienting students to ideas of the public good. Westheimer underscores the "need to transform the increasingly market-driven goals of a university education into public goals—reconnecting education to the broader society."

Section II: Critical University Studies

In the second section, contributors examine hegemonic geopolitics, neoliberalism, and the effects of increasingly authoritarian governments on the university's ability to fulfill its multiple roles and aspirations.

In the chapter "Relations of Power in Worldwide University Science," Simon Marginson examines the relationship between global science and national government and national science as well as who and what are dominant and who and what are excluded. Marginson's citation research reveals a dramatic reversal: in the past five years, Chinese universities have overtaken American universities in physical sciences and engineering citation counts. He observes that "geo-politics threatens to subtract the autonomy of science, lock it into national silos, weaken or fragment the global system" and urges us to "defend the autonomy of global science...from technological nationalism and from commercial publishers."

Consuelo "Coni" Chapela provides "A Latinoamerican Perspective" in "For What and For Whom Are Universities?" She starts with a historical overview of the growth of the world's first universities. Despite the imposition of a hierarchical and elite university system, under Spanish colonization, Latin American universities emerged as the home of critical emancipatory education and philosophies of liberation, critical geography, and environmental activism. Chapela laments universities now, in the twenty-first century, "immersed in a context of neoliberal productivity." She concludes that to learn to fight and to love, "we need public, free, inclusive, autonomous, critical...universities for all, providing spacialities of hope."

Liz Morrish's chapter, "From Neoliberalism to Authoritarianism: Universities, Metrics, Regulation, and Surrender to Governmental Control," meticulously documents how UK "universities have been forced into a neoliberal straitjacket in which academic endeavour has been subordinated to the ethos of business" via powerful metrics and authoritarian performance management systems. The essay illustrates the resulting decline of the Humanities in comparison to funding for STEM, and the "purge of critical scholarship." Morrish concludes by reminding us that critical university studies provide a "vital framework" against which to fight the well-funded "enemies of critique and democracy."

In "Resistance and Redirection in the Managerial University," Peter S. McInnis warns that "Canadian post-secondary institutions are the locus for a multi-pronged attempt to limit academic freedom severely, undermine collegial governance, and hamper independent curiosity-driven research." From his vantage point as a scholar and a Canadian Association of University Teachers (caut) president, he makes clear that faculty and staff unions must continue to defend academic freedom, tenure, and collegial governance. He implores us not to "make the erroneous assumption that the triumph of the neoliberal university is well nigh when opportunities for progressive redirection are within our grasp."

Section III: Reframing the Responsive University

The third section provides an examination and a critique of the complexity and shortfalls of contemporary universities and offers potential new directions for the future.

Kevin Kumashiro proposes we "reframe" higher education by troubling commonly held assumptions of what should be "the central role of educational institutions in a democracy." His chapter, "Higher Education and Academics Must 'Step Up'" draws on the US context to explore: university mission, governance, curriculum and empire, and how universities advance the common good and justice movements. Kumashiro concludes that universities must do more than just prepare individuals for today's world; they must help us struggle "to build our capacity to imagine the world as it is not yet—the world as it could be."

In "Reimagining the Pedagogy of Truth," Sheila Cote-Meek deliberates on "considerations for difficult learning" and what she has come to understand as "Debwewin," the Anishinaabe word for "speaking from your heart" and "being as truthful as you can." Across much of the earth, the colonial foundations of the university have meant that Indigenous knowledges have been diminished, denied, ignored, or forgotten, creating tension, division, and conflict. Cote-Meek concludes that we must work collectively to reimagine the university of the future: "one where many truths are valued, understood, discussed, researched, and integrated."

Piya Chatterjee, in "Complicities, Margins, Resistance: Colleges, Plantations, and Bearing Witness," tracks the position of academics who, like her, "negotiate our complicities and bear witness to flickers of resistance." She details student activism on a private US college campus during the covid-19 pandemic, in contrast to Freirean-style literacy initiatives with female workers on tea plantations in northern India. Chatterjee asks us to appreciate, despite radical differences in locale, economies, class and culture, the "mutual aid" extended in both circumstances and asks how individuals and our universities are implicated in both perpetuating injustice and fostering "radical hope."

"When Should Universities Take a Stand?" asks Shannon Dea in a chapter that queries the complexity of the university's mission and argues that institutional neutrality "is at best a useful fiction and at worst a way of concealing universities' commitments and reinscribing the status quo." Dea first distinguishes between academic freedom and freedom of expression, noting that core values vary from institution to institution and "there is no 'view from nowhere.'" If duty of care is a core university value, it follows that universities should take a stand on matters in which they are implicated. She concludes that taking such "responsibility is less about achieving perfection than it is about moral repair."

Section IV: Imagining Our Collective Future and the Future of Universities

In this last section, authors detail creative new departures and reimaginings for the university of tomorrow.

In "The University's Four Futures; or, the Real Humanities Crisis and Its Cures," Christopher Newfield extrapolates the consequences of the Four Ds: "Decline (in learning and research that have no monetary return), Defence (as in 'defending the humanities,' where we focus on not getting any worse rather than on building something great), Deference (so defence stays within the narrow parameters of appeasement of our funding masters), and Denial (of the fact that the current model, no matter how repeatedly tweaked, locks in decline)." He then dares us to look beyond the rhetoric of crisis, to embrace decolonized philosophies and the public good, and to imagine and conceptualize the post-crisis university where a fully democratic commons and high levels of mass knowledge thrive.

Tom Sperlinger, in "Is Hope Practical? Remaking Universities in an Era of Climate Crisis," invites us to ask what voices are still not heard within the university. He then reflects on two hopeful experiments in rethinking the current model of higher education. The first case study details his experience working on a new campus development at the University of Bristol. The second, dedicated specifically to education at a time of climate emergency, encapsulates his work to create a new institution altogether:

Black Mountains College (BMC) in Wales. Sperlinger observes, "There is a real space and need for alternative forms of higher education to provoke and challenge conventional universities and to offer alternatives in themselves."

Linda Tuhiwai Smith, in her chapter, "Te Whare Wānanga o Awanuiārangi: What Are Universities For," draws on more than thirty years of experience retrieving and reclaiming Māori knowledge starting with her own family history. She has spent a lifetime advocating for Indigenous knowledge recognition and legitimation within the Western context. In building Māori educational centres, she reflects on how the university can be both a place of "great hope and possibility where you meet, if you're lucky, wonderful teachers who inspire you. But it can also be a place that is the exact opposite: a place full of denigration and hopelessness and exclusion."

Tammy Ratt, in "sîpâ waskwâhk (Underneath the Birch Tree): ê-iskocêsihkêhk (Creating Sparks for a Fire)—The Need for Indigenous Knowledge in Universities," reflects on the many and varied sessions that comprised the *What Are Universities For?* symposium. She passionately shares her engagement with the content and knowledge contained in each presentation. In doing so, she confirms "that the way forward on my own path is to articulate, live, and teach from a perspective of nêhiyaw [Cree] onto-epistemologies."

References

Alumni Impact. (2024). More than 100 years of impact. University of Alberta. https://www.ualberta.ca/en/alumni/alumni-impact.html

Brown, I. (2024, June 25). Reading my way through a world gone mad. *The Globe and Mail.* https://www.theglobeandmail.com/arts/article-reading-my-way-through-a-world-gone-mad

Buffie, N. (2024, May 21). U of M medical grad lashes out over "deafening silence" on Gaza crisis. *The Free Press.* https://www.winnipegfreepress.com/local/2024/05/20/u-of-m-medical-grad-lashes-out-over-deafening-silence-on-gaza-crisis

Carlson, G. (2024, May 24). Facing pro-Palestinian protests, universities must realize they are businesses—and act like it. *The Globe and Mail.* https://www.theglobeandmail.com/business/commentary/article-facing-pro-palestinian-protests-universities-must-realize-they-are

Cole, J.R. (2009). *The great American university: Its rise to preeminence, its indispensable national role, why it must be protected.* PublicAffairs.

Darian-Smith, E. (2025). *Policing higher education: The antidemocratic attack on scholars and why it matters.* Johns Hopkins University Press.

Edsall, T.B. (2025, May 20). I even believe he is destroying the American presidency. *New York Times.* https://www.nytimes.com/2025/05/20/opinion/trump-musk-doge-government.html

Haggard, S., & Kaufman, R. (2021). *Backsliding: Democratic regress in the contemporary world.* Cambridge University Press. https://doi.org/10.1017/9781108957809

Kamola, I. (2024). *Manufacturing backlash: Right-wing think tanks and legislative attacks on higher education, 2021–2023.* American Association of University Professors.

Kerr, C. (2001). *The uses of the university* (5th ed.). Harvard University Press. (Original work published 1963)

Kingwell, M. (2024, January 5). There was no halcyon age of university excellence. *The Globe and Mail.* https://www.theglobeandmail.com/opinion/article-there-was-no-halcyon-age-of-university-excellence

Matassa-Fung, D. (2024, May 18). Union shocked SFU ending English, interpretation and translation programs. Global News. https://globalnews.ca/news/10497817/sfu-end-english-translation-programs

Rady, E. (2024, May 22). Philanthropist who gave $30M to U Manitoba condemns "hateful" valedictory speech, university for allowing it. CBC News. https://www.cbc.ca/news/canada/manitoba/ernest-rady-letter-valedictorian-speech-university-manitoba-1.7211096

Riddell, J. (2024). *Hope circuits: Rewiring universities and other organizations for human flourishing.* McGill-Queen's University Press.

Spooner, M. (2018). Qualitative research and global audit culture: The politics of productivity, accountability, and possibility. In N.K. Denzin & Y.S. Lincoln (Eds.), *The SAGE handbook of qualitative research* (5th ed., pp. 894–914). SAGE.

Spooner, M. (2024). Backsliding toward illiberalism and authoritarianism: Qualitative inquiry, academic freedom, and technologies of governance. In N.K. Denzin, Y.S. Lincoln, M.D. Giardina, & G.S. Cannella (Eds.), *The SAGE handbook of qualitative research* (6th ed., pp. 567–93). SAGE.

Spooner, M., & Westheimer, J. (2025, May 14). Opinion: Canadian democracy needs universities—now more than ever. *Edmonton Journal.* https://edmontonjournal.com/opinion/columnists/opinion-canadian-democracy-needs-universities-now-more-than-ever.

Stanley, S. (2024). *Erasing history: How fascists rewrite the past to control the future.* One Signal Publishers.

Turpin, D.H., & Bailey, A. (2024, June 21). When the values of a university clash, seismic events occur. *The Globe and Mail.* https://www.theglobeandmail.com/opinion/article-when-the-values-of-a-university-clash-seismic-events-occur

UNESCO. (2024). *Toward a better world for all: Decoding, deconstructing and decolonizing higher education in Canada and beyond.* Canadian Commission for UNESCO.

Wheeler, B. (2024, February 26). NAC Orchestra's Alexander Shelley discusses new album and tribute to Canadian journalist Peter Jennings. *The Globe and Mail*. https://www.theglobeandmail.com/arts/music/article-nac-orchestras-alexander-shelley-discusses-new-album-and-tribute-to-a

Notes

1   We agree with Darian-Smith (2025): "…that attacks on higher education in the United States are connected to similar battles over higher education occurring around the world in other democracies such as Brazil, Germany, Britain, Thailand, Hungary, Australia, Canada, India, Israel, Poland, the Philippines, and Argentina. And I argue these attacks are related to a global rise in extreme politics and authoritarian-leaning governments that includes the United States." (2)

SECTION I
UNIVERSITY AND ITS ROLES

This first section provides an overview of the university in all its multiple functions and spaces as well as the various pressures that constrain it.

CHAPTER 1
WHAT ARE UNIVERSITIES FOR?

Jonathan R. Cole

W HAT ARE UNIVERSITIES FOR? IT SEEMS LIKE A STRAIGHT-forward question. Yet, there is not only current disagreement about the answer, but there has been an evolution of answers over the history of both the United States and Canada. I will address the question from the point of view of a student of American universities. We are facing a crisis in higher education. It is a time when government is trying to exercise control over our universities in terms of what can be taught, who can teach, and who can lead great places of higher learning. This threat, of course, reappears roughly every twenty years in the United States. It certainly did after the attacks on of the World Trade Center and the passage of the "anti-terrorism" legislation; it did during the war in Vietnam some decades earlier. Efforts by governments to intrude and repress different features of our universities has a long history of simmering just below the surface only to reach a boiling point every generation or so.

Whether we call this the New McCarthyism or not, the idea of the university and what it is for is under attack. Consequently, we must come to its defence. Before we can, there must be a clear idea of what we are defending. There is a lot at stake. Not enough people inside or outside of higher education have a clear idea of what that is.[1]

I shall try to state my views in sharp and hopefully clear terms. My views may seem extreme to some; to others they may not seem sharp enough.

There is much room for debate. I believe the very essence of what a university is for was outlined with brilliant simplicity and terseness during the time of riots by students over America's unfortunate involvement in Vietnam. It can be found in the recently rediscovered statement from a group of faculty members who took up the question that we address in this volume. In the Kalven Committee report of 1967, Harry Kalven (a leading law professor of his day) and a group of very distinguished colleagues, addressed the question and issued a three-page statement, which it seems to me is as relevant today as it was over fifty years ago. I shall quote at some length from it because I can't do better in stating the fundamental position.

> A university has a great and unique role to play in fostering the development of social and political values in a society. The role is defined by the distinctive mission of the university and defined too by the distinctive characteristics of the university as a community. It is a role for the long term.
>
> The mission of the university is the discovery, improvement, and dissemination of knowledge. Its domain of inquiry and scrutiny includes all aspects and all values of society. A university faithful to its mission will provide enduring challenges to social values, policies, practices, and institutions. By design and by effect, it is the institution which creates discontent with the existing social arrangements and proposes new ones. In brief, a good university, like Socrates, will be upsetting.
>
> The instrument of dissent and criticism is the individual faculty member or the individual student. The university is the home and sponsor of critics; it is not itself the critic....To perform its mission in the society, a university must sustain an extraordinary environment of freedom of inquiry and maintain an independence from political fashions, passions, and pressures.[2]

In pursuing its mission of educating everyone at the university on all manner of substantive matters, it must also make an effort for students and faculty to develop true independence of thought, high levels of skepticism about what is fact or fiction, and an evolving point of view, but it must also protect and embrace research efforts; resist attempts by government to impose prior restraint on the publication of research results or on the content of a curriculum; and make inquiries that at the time may seem to run contrary to the existing dogma of disciplines, to fashion new ways for discoveries to be made, and to make our students better and more active citizens of the nation. Except for matters of educational policy, no one speaks for the university—not its president, provost, or trustees.

This view of the university makes people uncomfortable because it relegates to *individual* faculty members and students to take a stand on a wide variety of issues where near consensus exists on deeply important political, economic, and social questions. For example, when apartheid was of paramount concern on university and college campuses and when Nelson Mandela and other South Africans asked for the support of outsider organizations and nations to censure and boycott South Africa, the University of Chicago, even though probably more than 99 percent of its faculty members and students strongly opposed the South African apartheid regime, would not sign petitions condemning it. That was not easily done; yet Chicago has demonstrated that independence on many occasions since Kalven's publication—although there are some who claim that the fundamental principles of Kalven have eroded even at Chicago—and many would argue that it should be altered.

Does this stance on speech and behaviour at Chicago and others who have adopted this basic framework make leadership at the top less important? It makes it more important. The university *must* protect its community against violence or overt acts of aggression—from forms of physical harm. There cannot be any wavering on that. Not only must they protect their students and faculty from external and internal physical abuse, but leaders must also set the example, through words and deeds, of what is meant by the Kalven principles, and articulate where the lines between protected speech and imminent behavioural action lie. The leadership, along with the faculty, is responsible for guiding a large, often unwieldy ship to safe harbour and to consider and quite possibly implement broad structural changes in the university. If there are new values that become part of the substructure of the university, it's the leadership through the faculty that must articulate these new values and oversee their adoption and institutionalization within the community. Helping the university to evolve in ways that allow it to continue to be great in new ways of teaching, in new combinations of disciplines, and in adopting new forms of scientific and humanistic inquiry are daunting tasks. Few do it exceptionally well. Presidents, provosts, deans—and trustees—play a key role defending the principles of education at the university and in responding to the need for change within the framework of a set of core values—some of which are articulated in Kalven.

Recently, I asked a group of undergraduate students in one of my Columbia seminars whether they felt safe on campus. Almost all said they did, but a few did not feel intellectually safe. I asked them whether they thought that a university should be designed to make them feel safe intellectually, or whether in fact it should be an instrument that will cause them to question their presuppositions and biases, their preexisting point of view. This became a teaching moment in the undergraduate seminar Law, Science, and Society. We could address the history of First Amendment, free-speech jurisprudence; we could examine the ideas of John Stuart Mill in *On Liberty* (1859), and his ideas about harm; we could move to Sir Isaiah Berlin's "Two Concepts of Liberty" (1958), positive and negative; we could parse the basic premises in John Rawls's *A Theory of Justice* (1971), and could extend the discussion with reference to Supreme Court dogma on free speech from *Schenck* to the brilliant opinion of Justice Holmes in *Abrams*, to a much later revision of "clear and present danger" ideas in *Brandenburg*. We discussed high-value and low-value speech and hate speech. In each case, students were part of a discussion about where *they* would draw the line between protected and unprotected speech—and why. This sharpened, I believe, the way they thought about free speech. We also discussed, toward the end of the session, how seriously they took Tim Wu's relatively recent argument that First Amendment jurisprudence may be obsolete, given the emergence of social media (Wu, 2017).

Let's take this argument down to a more concrete level. Three keen observers of universities have articulated their five or so primary goals for an outstanding student education. Columbia's professor of English and Comparative Literature Andrew Delbanco, who has also had an abiding interest in higher education, suggests, and I paraphrase and quote here, that a good liberal-arts education includes instilling in students "a skeptical discontent with the present, informed by a sense of the past"; an ability "to make connections among seemingly disparate phenomena"; an appreciation of the natural world through the acquaintance with science and the arts; an ability to imagine experience from alternative perspectives other than one's own"; and "a sense of ethical responsibly" (Cole, 2016, p. 46).

Harvard psychologist Howard Gardner, best known for his formulation of the concept of multiple intelligences, waded into this subject, suggesting, and again I quote and paraphrase here: (1) that students should have "the opportunity to spend extensive time with scholars from different disciplines and perspectives"; (2) have a chance to begin "to master...one subject and sample other areas of knowledge that will broaden their perspective"; (3) have the opportunity to live among others with very different backgrounds from their own; (4) have the opportunity "to receive intelligent, personalized feedback" on their work from their instructors; (5) "have the chance to have fun through participation in activities that also serve the local communities that embodies the best of human values—intellectual, social and ethical" (Cole, 2016, pp. 47–48).

The former president of the University of Chicago, historian Hanna Holborn Gray, in her 2009 Clark Kerr Lectures, added these compatible elements of the valuable components of a liberal arts education:

> The modern view sees the liberal arts as, literally, liberating, as freeing the mind from unexamined opinions and assumptions to think independently and exercise critical judgement, to question conventional doctrines and inherited claims to truth, to gain some skill in analysis and capacity to deal with complexity and embrace certain skepticism in the face of dogma, and to be open to many points of view. (Holborn Gray, 2012, p. 48)

I would include a few additional axioms for an exceptional undergraduate education:

- All students must think for themselves in a highly skeptical and critical way.
- The curriculum should be far more integrated than currently exists in most places; for example, in studying climate change, a program needs to integrate various sciences with economics, sociology, psychology, and law. Such problems cannot be studied in disciplinary isolation.
- Students should not only read extensively the works produced by their own culture but should have experience reading works of all kinds from other cultures.
- More of the undergraduate curriculum should be active rather than passive. Students should become actively involved in some research work at their university or projects that they develop on their own.

- Every student should become familiar with the core values of their institution and how the "house" was built (Cole, 2016, pp. 48–49).

Plainly, the values expressed by these educators dovetail well with the basic values and norms of science.[3] When you add, as they would, of course, the value of good expository writing and the ability to formulate a thesis or hypothesis and to apply a point of view to written work, we have a good set of imperatives for an extraordinary education. These priorities will continue to be part of a gold standard for undergraduate education. Regardless of structural and program differences in each of our colleges and universities, undergraduate education should require work that focuses on these values and norms.

The easiest way in the future to achieve these goals for a broad segment of the student population is by tearing down many of the walls between disciplines and schools—and perhaps to rearrange the university's structure, including its budget structure, and the geography and architecture of the university campus. Part of the structural change will come from continuing technological revolutions, including artificial intelligence and others that we do not foresee now. One of the challenges will be to construct an online experience for young people throughout the world so they can receive a very high-quality education that embodies the above values—and that matches or exceeds in measurable and demonstrable ways our current modes of teaching and learning.

One of the remarkable aspects of current attacks by outsiders on our great universities and colleges is the almost exclusive focus on undergraduate education. In fact, when I used to talk to alumni groups, they almost never asked a question about the state and aspirations for graduate education and, most particularly, about the research discoveries being made at Columbia and other universities. The government attacks on universities often take different forms. Research and curricula of graduate programs is one of these—as seen during the second Bush administration when it used, for example, the USA Patriot Act (2001) as a basis for searching scientists' laboratories, indicting scientists, monitoring scientific papers prior to their publication, and trying to modify and monitor the curriculum of graduate schools of foreign affairs.[4]

The investments in universities by the federal and state governments, following the ideas articulated by Vannevar Bush in his post–World War II policy statement, *Science, the Endless Frontier* (1945/1960), which successfully argued that the platform for discovery after the war should be the nation's universities, supported by federal taxpayer dollars, have borne much good fruit. This compact, which also has been under attack from time to time—and modified to the harm of universities—has been successful beyond measure or earlier imagination.[5] We've had Senator William Proxmire of Wisconsin awarding the "golden fleece of the month award."[6] Things got so bizarre that there were government attacks on chemistry project proposals that used the word "radical" as in "radical ions." Researchers were warned not to use the term in the titles of their grant proposals. There have been attacks on the peer review grant system as being nothing but an "old boy's network,"[7] and there have been efforts to limit or end research on stem cell research among other topics of importance. Ronald Reagan's administration ended, at one point, all National Science Foundation funding for the social and behavioural sciences. All of this sounds absurd, if not amusing. There is, in fact, a huge amount of evidence that federal funding of university-based research has changed our world.

Consider just a handful of discoveries that have been produced at universities over the past sixty years or so that have altered our lives. The development of computer technology grows exponentially every several years—with quantum computing about to revolutionize our current capabilities; the algorithm for Google searches; the cure for childhood leukemia; the Global Positioning System; DNA fingerprinting; the developments in artificial intelligence; fetal monitoring; scientific cattle breeding and food production; CRISPR technology; the development of antibiotics; the human genome project; stem cell research; methods of using the autoimmune system to treat various forms of cancer; new water source technology to draw water from the atmosphere; revolutionary vaccines to prevent disease and millions of deaths from pandemic viruses, which includes the most recent revolution in RNA knowledge and technology to create vaccines that are efficacious in treating COVID and other viral infections; results from cognitive neuroscience in a better understanding of how the brain works; the discovery of drugs that control HIV, transforming the virus from a death sentence to a livable condition; the discovery of prions as a cause of disease, and to mention just one more, the development of carbon sequestration. These are but a few of the extraordinary discoveries made at our universities.[8] When universities are under attack from outside sources, the productivity and creativity of our scientists and engineers decline as does the greatness of our institutions of higher learning.

The media often refer to public skepticism about higher education today. In fact, these data are quite misleading. For example, Research!America's annual survey of public attitudes toward federal funding of research found widespread support for financing university-based research.

A majority of Americans from the political spectrum say it is important for candidates this year [2024] to promote faster medical progress...94% agree it's important for the US to be a leader in medical and health research. The survey findings show robust bipartisan agreement that US global leadership in science and technology (S&T) is important, with 84% believing we should set a higher spending goal for research and development. (Woolley, 2024)

Throughout most of the twentieth and the twenty-first centuries, the challenges to the university and how it functions have come from government sources at one level or another. But recently, we have seen new characters entering the drama—the billionaire class who believe that through threats of withholding their financial support for their alma mater or some other university have tried to dictate university policy—and most particularly the hiring and firing of individuals, suggesting that if students don't toe the line on matters of foreign or domestic policy they will blacklist them from being hired at their myriad businesses. Harvard has recently had this experience with one of the plutocrats, as has the University of Pennsylvania. They are bullies and often hypocrites. Although the details of the efforts by these alums to fire presidents who they perceive hold values that are anathema to them are not entirely public knowledge; the very fact that the boards of trustees have not publicly chastised and openly rejected these threats, while reaffirming the fundamental values of these great universities, suggests that there is a lack of confidence at even the wealthiest, oldest, and most prestigious universities. Perhaps the worst consequence of this intrusion is that faculty members place their ideas and views in their back pocket to be used another day. For now, they are afraid of being cancelled or worse. Early in the twentieth century, similar efforts were made by "outsiders" and some who became "insiders" because of their money. These "captains of erudition," as Thorstein Veblen (1918, p. 85) called them, also included leaders of universities who were strongly connected to and influenced by a set of wealthy benefactors and wealthy trustees, whose boards the academic administrators also sat on.

If there are three legs to the academic stool, one is not getting sufficient attention and yet its role in society is of enormous importance. That is the role of colleges and universities in creating more civic-minded adults who understand some of our history, some of the ethical and moral dilemmas that they will face after college, and their role as active participants in a civil society. Too few of our students know much of the history of their country, or of the world, before they were born. This includes the history of their art and their literature. Few of my very bright Columbia students can correctly identify, much less speak about, Senator Joseph McCarthy or about Paul Robeson, as examples. They know little about American reconstruction after the Civil War. Few of our students are given the opportunity to read slowly and study the US Constitution.[9] Most could not tell you what is in it or how the Amendments came to pass. I'm not sure that many Americans today could do any better if asked about any specific aspects of the Constitution. Nor would they be able to say anything about some of the most important cases decided by the courts. They know almost nothing about Indigenous peoples and cultures; their laws and customs; and perhaps most shockingly about the history of slavery beyond the idea that it was an evil thing and may be the albatross about the neck of America.

One could go on ad nauseam. Thus, it is difficult for them to make connections, to produce analogues, to place current events in perspective—in short, to reason as well as they might without some rigorous training in history and the humanities. This is not their fault. We don't require them to dig into their own history and the humanities and examine it with skepticism and a critical eye. Few are taught to analyze a text closely. What they may have learned in secondary school is not enough to produce the perspective needed to be active citizens. Universities and colleges have an obligation to give their students a healthy dose of what is required for good citizenship. This leg in the stool is currently broken.

Despite the continual criticism of and current harm being done to our universities, we do have, I believe, the greatest system of higher education in the world (and that includes Canadian colleges and universities). That said, the idea of the university and its structure must be continually re-examined, and the structure of the colleges and universities must evolve as any organism with the hope of survival must do. In the final thoughts of this essay, let me suggest a few of the ways in which our universities and colleges, even the most elite of them, should change over the next thirty years or so. Some of that change is already underway.

Consider first the organization and structure of our universities. For one, they look too much alike. There is a need for differentiation and various emphases within our universities. Places like MIT and Caltech, or the Rockefeller University[10] offer one form of differentiation—focusing on the sciences and engineering while offering exceptional educations in fields like economics. But as the number of college-age students rises, and the need for advanced knowledge and training increases in the labour force, we need a different point of view realized in some of our universities. Not all universities should be full-service institutions. Arizona State University (ASU) is an excellent example of a distinguished university with an alternative mission compared with, for example, the Ivy Plus institutions. ASU offers a new way of designing a great research university with new, creative structures and methods of learning for all members of its community of over a hundred thousand students and faculty. Its mantra is "inclusion" not exclusion. It is proud of the numbers that it educates and what these graduates achieve after they finish their degrees. It aims to educate and conduct research at scale. Why should any college or university be proud of admitting only 5 percent of its undergraduate applicants? Obviously, getting in becomes much more of a crapshoot or lottery. Whether or not the very highly selective colleges expand is less important than to develop alternative models and designs where the goals of education referred to above are achieved.

Beyond issues of admissions, the old universities operate within an architecture that has existed a century or more. This architecture fetters the advancement of knowledge. I doubt that we will again see campus buildings that have engraved on their stone exteriors "Philosophy" or "Physics." We are not apt to see grand palaces built where libraries rest. Knowledge has grown beyond such traditional boundaries that we call disciplines. Seeing the rapidly growing interdisciplinarity of knowledge and its creation, we must rethink our campuses—both their intellectual and physical properties. Not only must we integrate knowledge and learning across disciplines but across schools as well. Biologists these days need computer scientists to do their work, mathematics and physics are more closely linked than ever, psychology and economics are similarly growing mutually dependent, and studies of global climate change cannot find solutions without multidisciplinary collaborations. To use ASU again as an example, the university under Michael Crow's leadership has almost completely redesigned itself—in terms of intellectual questions that need answers, research on the most important scientific and technical problems of the day, and the way it trains students—some undergraduates participate in pathfinding research.

But we must take the modern university to a still different position. It is time for our universities to create academic rather than sports leagues. The idea is simple to articulate but harder to implement because universities tend to be very territorial. Two examples should suffice. One is to envisage an Earth League, which in fact has been created. Here universities with common and complementary interests in global climate change and other geological issues begin to integrate their activities in this specific area of knowledge and discovery. Faculty members collaborate with each other (many already do); they share knowledge, their graduate and post-doctoral students would interact and become part of a small community or an "invisible college," and courses on related subjects could be taken by students at any university in the league for credit. The creation of academic leagues has a multiplier effect, expanding the range and talent of students interested in broad areas of important study as well as expanding the number of exceptional faculty members working on similar research projects. It may also allow for new combinations of researchers—one of exceptional quality at one university in one specialty of research, another with a different set of exceptional talents at another university.

The other example is the study of social and economic inequality. This is currently the focus of intellectual attention at many universities in the world. Its study is of quintessential importance. Suppose you could link the best minds at our universities in an "Inequality League."[11] Think of what might be produced through interactions of people like Thomas Piketty, Emmanual Saez, Joseph Stiglitz, and Paul Krugman.[12] These well-known economists represent just a few among many who could join this league. Their students could take courses with any member of the league, they would receive credit for those studies, and they could collaborate with members of the league located at different universities. The proposition is that the leagues would have value added, would make the education of students stronger, and would lead to important insights, theories, and empirical studies—as well as policy proposals that address ways of dealing with societal and international inequalities.

There are numerous other purposes for our universities. One that is often overlooked is the university as a source of "soft power." American universities, without being hegemonic, have a role to play in the education of peoples in less developed countries, particularly young women who are often being excluded from those educational assets that developing nations have. If we are to create new allies around the world, we are more likely to do so using soft power rather than military force. But we have not organized the universities as a source of such power as would come from scientific and engineering collaborations or the education of millions of able young people who do not as yet have access to quality higher learning nor to the technology that can now deliver it. We must also learn from their cultures and embrace their ideas into our curriculum development. We need to encourage undergraduate and graduate study in the United States. These will be our ambassadors later in their lives. Many of the very talented will also remain in the States and become part of our university faculties. And we must begin to be viewed as a safe harbour for scholars who are at risk in their own societies. We can do this by a well-funded government program that supports intellectual migration. Attracting foreign students and faculty increases what Georg Simmel called a "web of affiliations" that brings our nations closer together—if we don't pursue this in an old, imperialist way. When we think of the tens of billions of government funds spent on new aircraft or other weapons, the price of employing soft power through our universities is far less expensive and more efficient than the continual use of military force. If there was a Peace Corps, why not an Education Corps?

Our universities should be the site for more "blue sky" research—the type of research often sponsored by the Defense Advanced Research Projects Agency (DARPA). This is research that often conflicts with established dogma and is prematurely discarded by the authorities in a field of work as outside the possible. The probability that these research ideas will bear extraordinary fruit is low, but each of the discoveries that pans out may change the world. Stanley Prusiner's discovery of prions is one such example. There ought to be funding through our universities for such projects, and universities ought to be more receptive to housing and supporting such research. The federal government ought to create the equivalent of the Howard Hughes Medical Institute's Investigator Program, which fully funds biological scientists and their entire labs for five years. No proposals are written for continued funding during that period; periodical reports must be made to the foundation of discoveries and progress toward discoveries; serious reviews for continued funding take place roughly every five years. But the concentration is on scientists doing research and training the next generation of scientists, engineers, and leaders of industrial science. The federal government needs to expand its research support for social and behavioural scientists in the form of Investigator Program grants, and particularly for cross-disciplinary research, such as cognitive neuroscience. Fundamental problems of inequality of wealth, of a broken system of incarceration, of the forces at play undermining civil society and liberal democracies, are worthy of much more focused and extended support.

There is much discussion and debate at American universities about whether the university has an important role to play in seeking to educate all qualified and interested students regardless of their race, nationality, socio-economic status, gender, and sexual orientation. Affirmative action policies in higher education have been struck down by the US Supreme Court. What kind of restriction by the court will be next is hard to fathom. Let us remember, however, that political scientist Ira Katznelson is right when he argues that for more than two hundred years in the United States affirmative action has been white. The privileged white men who had the means to attend boarding schools, who had a father or grandfather who attended Harvard or Yale or Princeton, have a very large head start as compared to the brilliant person of colour who grew up near the plantations of the pre–Civil War years. And of course, women had few opportunities to attend these most prestigious colleges until quite recently. Few flag this when they discuss diversity, equity, and inclusion. Universities are for education for all of those who are qualified for admission without regard for their background status, and it would seem just and fair to flag these students in the admissions process who have been historically suppressed and excluded from "the club" and to consider the weights that they have had on their backs before they began the race to college admissions. When a great research university like ASU admits those who are qualified rather than excludes many who could achieve success at the most prestigious and exclusive academic clubs, that changes the angle of vision on whom universities are for and for the goals of a university's education.

Yet, as I write here of ways that the work of universities can be and should be expanded, we must first defend the universities from banners of books, censors of curricula, and opponents of open and critical thinking. This is the job of all of us at universities; it is the time for courage and voice. While the older private universities get most of the press, most of the consequential attacks on academic freedom and free inquiry come from leaders of state governments. They have the bully pulpit, and often they have the power to appoint public university presidents and select individuals for the university's board. These appointees often lack any real knowledge of what a university is for, or of the guiding principles that our institutions of higher learning live by. Trustees or regents of public universities ought to be selected as guardians of university values—they should be knowledgeable about the treasures that they guard. Part of their role is to protect the universities from politically based ideological attacks.

In closing, I want to reinforce the point that our universities are jewels in our nation's crown. Without them we would not be world leaders in producing the superb transmission of knowledge that currently exists at most of our institutions of higher learning. Our modern research universities are arguably the greatest mechanism for innovation that the world has known. We must adequately represent our universities as sites for the transformative research that is continually improving the lives of citizens of the world lest we fail to adequately educate a labour force for a job world that requires far more skills than in the past. Citizens of the United States, Canada, and others around the world will benefit enormously in the future, perhaps more than in the past, from what we at these universities can achieve collectively. If we fail to realize that, if our universities become pawns in political wars, if we undermine our core values, we will lose our edge.

Coda

This essay was completed for publication prior to Donald Trump's election in November 2024 and before he had assumed office in January of 2025. Trump's subsequent ignorant, vindictive, and ill-advised assaults on the American research university takes us back to the McCarthy attack on universities. His Executive Orders, which may well be illegal, have been aimed at the very core values of universities. The threat to academic freedom and free inquiry strikes at the heart of what a university is for. To submit to the government's coercive effort to halt research grants that were already made—totally in the tens of billions of dollars—if you include his holds on both state and private universities—would cripple the greatest sources of innovation and discovery that the world has ever known. We must not capitulate to his wrongheaded demands. (See Cole, 2025) The cost for research designed to cure disease, to improve the quality of life of people around the world, to discover new therapies and drugs, to provide aid to the poor around the world, is beyond measure. Many essays could focus on various aspects of these ill-conceived, punitive and irrational actions and their consequences. This essay was limited, however, to the pre–Trump second term.

References

Allen, D. (2015). *Our declaration: A reading of the Declaration of Independence in defense of equality*. Liveright.

Abrams v. United States, 250 US 616 (1919)

American Academy of Arts & Sciences. (n.d.). "Project: Humanities Indicators. https://www.amacad.org/humanities-indicators

Berlin, I. (1958). *Two concepts of liberty*. Clarendon Press.

Brandenburg v. Ohio, 395 US 444 (1969)

Bush, V. (1960). *Science, the endless frontier: A report to the President on a program for postwar scientific research*. National Science Foundation. (Original work published 1945)

Cole, J.R. (2009). *The great American university: Its rise to preeminence, its indispensable national role, why it must be protected*. PublicAffairs.

Cole, J.R. (2016). *Toward a more perfect university*. PublicAffairs.

Cole, J.R. (2025, March 24). Columbia's capitulation will hurt us all. *New York Times*. https://www.nytimes.com/2025/03/24/opinion/universities-inventions-funding.html

Holborn Gray, H. (2012). *Searching for utopia: Universities and their histories*. University of California Press.

Merton, R.K. (1979). The norms of science. In R.K. Merton, *The sociology of science: Theoretical and empirical investigations* (Norman W. Storer, Ed.). University of Chicago Press.

Mill, J.S. (1859/1978). *On liberty* (Elizabeth Rappaport, Ed.). Hackett.

Rawls, J. (1971). *A theory of justice*. Belknap Press.

Schenk v. United States, 249 US 47 (1919)

Veblen, T. (1918). *The higher learning in America: A memorandum on the conduct of universities by business men*. B.W. Huebsch.

Woolley, M. (2024, February 8). America speaks. Mary Woolley's weekly letter. Research!America: Discovery, Innovation, Health. https://www.researchamerica.org/marys-letters/america-speaks

Wu, T. (2017, September 1). Is the First Amendment obsolete? Knight First Amendment Institute, Columbia University. https://knightcolumbia.org/content/tim-wu-first-amendment-obsolete

Notes

1   In this essay I will not address the economics of higher education, as important a topic as it is. I only will point out that there is substantial empirical evidence of the economic rewards of a college or higher degree; that, except for engineering, there are only relatively small differences in the salaries of students who majored in the humanities versus the sciences, and after a decade beyond the degree, those who held humanities degrees were as "happy" as were those who majored in other fields. For those interested, see the American Academy of Arts & Sciences' Humanities Indicators project. The results can be found on its website (https://www.amacad.org/humanities-indicators).

2   Source: University of Chicago Faculty Committee. (1967, November 11). "Kalven Committee: Report on the university's role in political and social action. *Record*, 1(1). https://provost.uchicago.edu/sites/default/files/documents/reports/KalvenRprt_0.pdf. Among the relatively small number of faculty on the committee were John Hope Franklin and George Stigler.

3   The five core values that I allude to here are academic freedom, which is an enabling value without which the force of other norms and values are diminished; universalism; organized skepticism; communism; and disinterestedness. Here, we are not referring to "communism" as a political ideology or movement; it refers instead to a shared set of values within a given community. For a full discussion of four of these values, see Merton (1979) and Cole (2009).

4   Not enough attention is focused on the creativity and work of graduate and post-doctoral students in the sciences. They make up the bulk of members of great laboratories, and it is often their ideas and work for their senior mentor that makes a large difference in whether discoveries are made. More support for these students ought to be the object of research and ultimately greater funding.

5   The other side of the compact was, of course, granting universities autonomy and the freedom to make choices about its students, its faculty, and the way it conducted research with the aim of advancing pure knowledge or ideas that could reach the marketplace.

6   Proxmire claimed that there was wasteful spending in the science budgets and that he was trying to rid the National Science Foundation and the National Institutes of Health of such waste. Much of it was political posturing.

7   The claim was that prominent scientists would all scratch each other's backs in the peer review process, closing off opportunities for scholars and scientists who were not in the network.

8   Here I have limited the list to discoveries in the sciences and engineering, but there have also been advances in the social sciences and humanities as a result of federal government funding—even if on a much smaller scale than what exists for the more expensive sciences.

9   For a brilliant book about "slow reading" and close textual analysis, see Allen (2015).

10   Rockefeller, which is truly one of the great sites of learning and discovery, is almost totally limited to the biological sciences, although it also has small programs in other fields.

11   Note that the two examples I've given intentionally focus on subject matters, not disciplines. Leagues can have a unit of analysis on a substantive topic. We are not talking here about leagues of entire universities and colleges; nor are we speaking about a collective of disciplinary members at a variety of universities. The leagues' focuses would be on on major social and scientific, as well as historical and ethical, problems.

12   Of course, these distinguished economists in all likelihood do interact with each other, but other extremely talented economists working on this problem would now have access to their own collaboration with these "stars" and others.

CHAPTER 2
UNIVERSITIES ARE PLAYSPACES

Whitney Blaisdell

Utopias

N A PAPER CALLED "WHAT IS A SCHOOL FOR?" JOHN DEWEY (1923/ 2021b) declares, "The public school must exist to serve the purposes of the community as a whole, to develop good citizens in the most comprehensive sense of that term" (p. 118). Ten years later, however, he writes a creative piece in which he visits a utopia where rather than contained within classrooms and buildings, schools are integrated into daily public life. During his visit, Dewey (1933/2021a) asks what the purposes of school are and is met with utter confusion. As he describes, "The whole concept of the school, of teachers, and pupils and lessons, had so completely disappeared that when I asked after the special objectives of the activity of these centres, my Utopian friends thought I was asking why children should live at all" (p. 123).

A Campus Visit

What are universities for? Beginning to write without knowing the end of this chapter, I opt to explore a university's tangible, material qualities. This exploration, on foot and on page, does several things: it complicates distinctions of universities from their communities and reveals how their purposes occupy both public and personal spaces. Whereas the immediate physical environment of universities may sometimes appear utopian and good, further inquiry undoes such ideal images of the institution. Sitting with the ways that universities are less-than-ideal invites examination of what their ideals, or purposes, might be. Finally, wandering the institution reveals how, in many ways, the university is a playspace, ultimately evading the assignment of a purpose at all.

To orient readers to the chapter, I visit a university and welcome the reader along in a sort of collective daydream. According to Gaston Bachelard (1958/2014), this necessitates that readers flee the objects of their surroundings and land *elsewhere*, in this case, a university campus, in search of answers to the immense question at hand: *What are universities for?* Thus, though we each occupy unique bodies, positions, experiences, and perhaps universities, I commence with a visit to a university campus that we will share throughout the chapter.

A cycling path takes me directly to campus, where I lock my bicycle alongside a half dozen others. I open the doors and walk straight across the hall into the university library. The first floor has computers with access to countless academic journals spanning every discipline. One can search published peer-reviewed reports of research ranging from methods for increasing the harvesting efficiency of solar energy (Zhang & John, 2021) to explorations of women's self-organized activism in North Bengal tea plantations (Chatterjee, 2008) to developing rapid and systematic methods for identifying lactic acid bacteria in meat (Yost & Nattress, 2000) to explorations of self, language, land, and Indigenous identity reclamation (Ratt, 2022). Perhaps universities are for research and exploration; scholars make groundbreaking discoveries that contribute to scientific advancement and nuanced understandings of the world.

There is a display of books, thoughtfully curated around a timely theme by staff. There are multiple floors lined with colourful spines, any of which might possess the prose to change a perspective, which can be to change a life. There are lifetimes of readings one could do in the library. Centuries of scholars have used universities to read, write, strengthen their reading and writing skills, and produce these texts, layering on top of one another, overtly constructing knowledge and hiding subtle references for close readers to delightfully seek. Perhaps universities are for reading and writing these texts, in all disciplines, contributing to understandings of love (hooks, 2000), sex and gender (Dea, 2016), power (Alexis, 2015), posthuman imaginings (Logan, 2021), and the human condition and its multitudes (Whitman, 1855/2014). Perhaps universities are for reading, writing, and contemplation.

I venture the staircase to the top floor, pull out a dark emerald volume of poetry, and look out at the campus green. Through the bare branches of varied trees, one can glimpse where the student-run community garden ripens and matures in the warm months and where hammocks stretch, drooping with cloud-gazers and readers on their backs. I view an outdoor classroom area. I hear music swell—during Welcome Week, in the fall, bands are commissioned to play on the well-manicured green. I see posters around the library inviting students to involve themselves in serious matters they care about, including student elections and public interest research groups. More posters welcome students to trivia nights, book clubs, conversation groups, film screenings, and craft clubs. Posters in the university pub inform viewers on consent, bystander intervention, and alternatives to drinking and driving. Perhaps universities are for intellectual expansion. Undergraduates, some having moved from home for the first time, are granted opportunities to open and change their minds, learn new languages, and kindle curiosities.

I picture convocation, when the university overflows with joyous graduates in caps and gowns, taking photos with their proud loved ones. Students meet people who will become lifelong companions. Today it is winter, and someone has used their body to push snow and draw an anatomical picture. Perhaps universities are a time of fleeting self-indulgence; they provide a decadent experience of playfulness and effort, wilful encounters, and vibrant emergence.

I take the elevator back to the main floor, turn left, and wander the halls through different buildings. They are architecturally spectacular. The science buildings strike a balance of convention and innovation, and the humanities buildings, a balance between wear and warmth. A bulletin board alerts graduate students and faculty to an opportunity to present research to city council that may be relevant for local policy. Large photographs are on display in a sunny hallway; it is a photovoice research project on Black joy and wellness (Mudzongo et al., 2024) with a guestbook signed by dozens of visitors. I have witnessed this atrium filled with people sitting in chairs in structured rows. The university hosts clinics with health-care workers on campus to administer vaccines. Perhaps universities are for facilitating knowledge dissemination; they ensure scholars have opportunities to impact public policy, perceptions, and health. Perhaps aside from publishing papers, universities are for pushing scholars to, as Linda Tuhiwai Smith reminds, remember the public (Cole et al., 2023) and as Cindy Blackstock encourages, *do* things with their scholarship, to express it in ways people can understand, listen to, and get behind (Rynor, 2023).

I continue to walk down the hallway. I know that up the stairs is the Saskatchewan Urban Native Teacher Education Program (SUNTEP); the university partners with the provincial government and Gabriel Dumont Institute to provide a pre-service teacher training program with an emphasis on Métis ways of knowing and being. The program involves a Michif language camp to nurture language revitalization and prepares graduates with culturally relevant pedagogy so they may enter the teaching profession prepared to support students' learning, cultural competence, and critical consciousness (Ladson-Billings, 1995). Soon, I hear soft, high voices; through a large window, I see that educators at one of the campus childcare centres have taken children outside. Their breath is visible in the cold air as they play. I wander past a bookstore where staff are buying back used books from students. The smell of coffee and food fills the air as I approach a restaurant area with a student-staffed pub. Perhaps universities are for teaching and employment. They not only provide job training across many fields but enable the betterment and transformation of the disciplines in which they teach. Additionally, they are employers themselves to a vast array of employees.

There are stairs, and if I take them, I will find a student union office, a women's centre, a centre for sexuality and gender diversity, a student newspaper, a writing centre, and several offices where one can access free mental health services. If I go straight ahead, I will find the campus theatre on the left, where I hear more children in the distance; a local elementary school class is attending a matinee play with residents from a local senior centre. If I leave the main doors on the right, there will be a row of more cafés, restaurants, and pubs, hoping to capture the attention of students who park off-campus and walk to avoid parking fees. Within walking distance is a public art gallery featuring a solo exhibition by a university alumna (Murray, 2024). This week, a colleague is touring the exhibit with their graduate class on creativity. I turn left toward a glass atrium filled with flourishing plants in large terracotta pots. Someone is playing a piano. The university art gallery is tucked nearby and hosts an exhibit of multiple staff, faculty, and student ceramics; all pieces were fired in the campus outdoor fire kiln (Chaithanya et al., 2023). Perhaps the university is for collaborating with public partners to enrich community members' daily experiences and well-being through creativity and the arts.

Lately, during these walks, I encounter groups of students, staff, and faculty. Student-organized demonstrations are frequent on campus. As they move through the hall, bodies join their assemblage and voices join their chorus. I pick up a student newspaper. Most of the articles are written by students in the university's journalism program, who have used the campus environment to connect directly with specialists across the university faculties. They weave expert voices and research into their work, including on local climate change (King, 2022; Schneider, 2019) and harm reduction policies (O'Connor, 2021). As mentioned by Joel Westheimer, Maxine Greene argues the purpose of education is to "comfort the troubled and trouble the comfortable" (Cole et al., 2023). I attend a lecture where a union representative is present to address questions, listen to debate, invite ideas, and receive critique regarding how the union navigates new government policy. The university exhibits a high tolerance for public dispute, and dominant narratives are "troubled and informed, contested, and disrupted" (Spooner, 2024, p. 573). Perhaps universities are for nurturing a healthy democracy.

After my lecture, I make my way back to the bicycle path. Framed art, often by recognizable names of university alumni, adorns the walls. The piano reverberates, students flow in and out of various support offices, books open and close, and the show goes on. There are therapy dogs on campus, and I pause to visit one briefly before I leave. I feel a thrill when I spot my red bicycle waiting for me. I use my afternoon commute to consider the possibilities of my own research project. Perhaps universities are for cultivating hope, imagining better futures, and shaping dreams into reality. I think back to the therapy dogs on campus. Why are there therapy dogs on campus?

Dystopias

Virginia Woolf noticed that "intellectual freedom depends upon material things" (Woolf, 1928/2004, p. 125). The material qualities of universities deserve attention if we are to examine their purpose. Campuses often boast multiple libraries, gardens, child-care centres, bookstores, cafés, theatres, studios, galleries, and lecture halls with public lectures that serve students, faculty, staff, and the public. They are home to students and provide hospitality to visiting scholars and evacuees, forced to leave their own homes and communities because of increasing disasters such as forest fires (Mandes, 2023). Plants thrive, architecture dazzles, and furniture welcomes. Campuses are playful, multi-age, and multispecies gathering spaces. Cities materialize around them; bus routes and multi-use pathways create a network of access to universities. Politicians campaign on campuses, aware that universities have the tools to support civic engagement in students who are thereby more likely to be politically savvy (Hillygus, 2005), and to volunteer and organize (Barber et al., 2013), discuss politics with loved ones, and vote in elections (Fernandez, 2021; Stewart, 2023). Community and arts organizations flourish in university cities; educational attainment is associated with attendance at art events (Falk & Katz-Gerro, 2016; Fluharty et al., 2021) and support for community-based organizations (Gong & Hong, 2021; Perna, 2005). Coffee shops, pubs, galleries, and theatres sprout up near campuses, delighting not only students, staff, and faculty, but neighbourhood residents. The very presence of a university campus cultivates a blossoming population and nourishes a city's economy, democracy, arts, food, culture, and connectivity. Getting a university education is associated with higher life expectancy (Balaj et al., 2024), higher income (Zhang et al., 2024), higher civic engagement (Doyle & Skinner, 2017; Malin et al., 2017), and lower rates of depression (Gaydosh et al., 2018).

What even are universities? Do such spaces bracket the real world? Do they mimic it? Do they serve it? Are they part of it? Are they utopias, with their accessible transportation, libraries, child-care centres, art galleries, and therapy dogs? The university appears to have many purposes: it provides opportunities for research and exploration, contemplation of the human condition, self-discovery, teaching, service, employment, well-being, and protection of democracy. The physical campus offers clues that can lead us to pull back some curtains. Affrica Taylor (2013) prompts children to ask "what else is going on here" when they are confronted with paradoxically mundane yet unusual details of daily happenings. What happens if one begins to look at the *what else is going on here* of the university?

The bike lane that leads straight from my home to campus is inaccessible from the most impoverished areas in the city. This is not unique to the city in which I live; connectivity in urban spaces, including to universities (Guzman et al., 2017), is associated with higher wealth (Carpenter &

Peponis, 2010), meaning that disconnectivity to universities is associated with lower wealth. The closer one lives to a university campus, the likelier one is to enrol in higher education (Sá et al., 2006; White & Lee, 2020), meaning the farther one lives from a university campus, the less likely one is to enrol in higher education. Furthermore, university access is often divided along racial lines (Lipsitz, 2011).

Physical access to campus, however, is only one barrier. Once arrived, there is a culture of whiteness that permeates higher education (Gusa, 2011). Eve Tuck (2018) notices that

> when we look at the origin stories of many academic disciplines, we see that they are entangled with the projects of settler colonialism: justifying the theft of Indigenous land and the demolition of Indigenous life, and establishing racial hierarchies to justify the enslavement of Africans. (p. 151)

Students and faculty are disproportionately likely to experience gender and sexual harassment during their university careers depending on their race, sex, gender, and positions within power hierarchies in the academy (Hango, 2021). Those who do are often poised to leave university altogether (Molstad et al., 2023). A factor in some students' academic incompletion is the betraying realization of the institution's enablement and indifference to their abuse (Ahmed, 2021; Cipriano et al., 2022; Smith & Freyd, 2013). Although many universities pride themselves on being "safe spaces," as noted on their websites and strategic plans, students, staff, and faculty who take steps to document and confide, in detail, their experiences with harassment and bullying at the university are most often silenced by the institution (Ahmed, 2021; Cipriano et al., 2022). So, those therapy dogs; what is it that we touch when we touch them (Haraway, 2007)? Though they may sense cortisol and understand that their furry bodies offer comfort, do they know what troubles those they comfort?

Behind the flourishing potted plants, impressive art collections, mid-century furniture, and admirable strategic plans is a dizzying paradox, both responding to and enabling violence. As Jonathan Cole stresses, universities are not the radical spaces many consider them to be but are rather fundamentally conservative ones (Cole et al., 2023). If universities are for fulfilling dreams, then what happens to the dreams of dreamers who leave the institution for their own well-being? If universities serve the purpose of protecting democracy, but the institution excludes, mistreats, and pushes people out based on intersections of race, gender, and sexuality, then whose democracy is protected? If "grandeur progresses in the world in proportion to the deepening of intimacy" (Bachelard, 1958/2014, p. 212), then how could institutions that act, in such intimate and vulnerable moments, so egregiously, ever fully realize the grandeur of their many purposes? Dwelling with the destructive tendencies of the university, surprisingly, is a worthwhile exercise for revealing its purposes. Examining wounds inflicted by institutional betrayal provides important hints at what is betrayed: the institution's unique potential for creating more just and kind worlds.

It seems that universities' ability to create more just and kind worlds is tied to their relationships with the public. Walking through this university has revealed neither a beginning nor an ending to it; any binary between the university and the public was artificial. Universities are tentacular things, extending and travelling far beyond their campuses. Students, graduates, university staff, and faculty *are* the public. They live in neighbourhoods and make choices around things like whether to see a doctor, participate or not in mutual aid, email their city councillor their thoughts on a civic issue, and run for office. They decide what speed to drive in a school zone, when and if they shovel their walk, and how to solve neighbourly disputes. The health-care system, social supports, and local policies, too, are entangled with the university, as are an endless number of issues that collectively comprise neighbourhoods, communities, cities, and public life. The university is not contained within a campus: the university and the public co-emerge.

However, over the past few decades, the funding composition for universities has crept further away from public and closer toward private support (Stein et al., 2019). The less public funding universities receive, the more they must rely on private funding and increased tuition fees, including exorbitant tuition fees for international students (Stein & Oliveira de Andreotti, 2016). The gaps in well-being and privilege that advantage some groups while disadvantaging others to attend universities widen. Furthermore, the students who do attend want a return on their degree, received at an extensive monetary, time, and opportunity cost to them and which is therefore often and justifiably positioned as an investment. This model transfers power from the public to corporations, who hire graduates based on the skills and knowledge they consider most hireable and thereby pressure the university to produce in students. The increasing demands on students and faculty to outshine their peers and colleagues in a "cycle of individualized inducements" (Grande, 2018, p. 183) conditions graduates to appease and serve industry standards as they are instead of collectively imagining and transforming them into what they could be. Furthermore, scholars face increasing pressures to produce measurable research outputs, an effect of "audit culture" in the neoliberal academy (Gill, 2018; Sparkes, 2021; Spooner, 2018). Universities deliver on their demands; higher education attainment continues to be associated with skills training for jobs and higher salaries for graduates (Zhang et al., 2024), and scholarship outputs become narrowly focused on the proliferation of journal articles and grants. However, proficiency does not equate to purpose.

Rather than being creative, critical, community-engaged spaces host to creative, critical, community-engaged students and scholars, universities become a market. Such a model seems to carry great potential to lose public trust in universities, which, rather than contribute to better and more just worlds and systems, are reduced to instruments for widening gaps in wealth, success, happiness, well-being, and privilege based on who can attend and thrive in the institution. Brilliant minds and dreams are considered trespassers on campuses, based on the bodies that hold them (Woolf, 1928/2004). The public co-emerges with this neoliberal academy. At the risk of sounding dramatic, the gap between what universities could do and what they actually do, is devastating. The university is a beautiful dystopia. To write this chapter, it became necessary to separate what universities do from what they ought to do.

The marketized university is imitative; it is uninspired and uninspiring. Grande (2018) encourages readers to view one's university experience as not an individualist project but rather a disruption of the structures that form the university as a self-promoting project in the first place. She asks readers to commit to collectivity, reciprocity, and mutuality. Rather than prime graduates to succeed in the current world at the expense of the failure of their peers, the university should be a space of collective transformation. It does not serve industry and society; it improves them. Perhaps *this* is what universities are for.

That's not entirely it, though. While, yes, one principal purpose of universities is to not only serve but transform societies and systems, I remain interested in how universities do serve micro, individual purposes too. It is an impossibility that universities only affect public and not private space, or that the degrees of the private space they affect could be controlled. I think the university is integrated into minor and mundane moments. Is the university not evoked in how one settles an argument with a spouse, how they calm a child's distress, how they evaluate friendships, listen to the news, look at art, and select a novel? Study, real study, as Harney and Moten (2013) describe it, does not respect the boundaries of the institution, nor does it only inflict the student. The university makes grand romantic gestures; it provides the means for climate crisis research, good teachers, public policy, and democracy. It also offers whimsy and wonder to ordinary life. The two spaces, immense and intimate, "keep encouraging one another, as it were, in their growth" (Bachelard, 1958/2014, p. 218).

Universities as Heterotopias

> *Does the university contradict itself? Very well, it contradicts itself. It is large…it contains multitudes (paraphrasing Whitman, 1855/2014).*

Foucault (1986) discusses what he calls *heterotopias*, which I think are useful for examining universities. Unlike utopias, which for Foucault do not exist in real life, heterotopias *do* exist, as counter-sites. They are real places in which all other real places are found, reflected, contested, and referenced. Heterotopias have six principles: they are constituted in every culture; they have specific functions that society can alter; they can juxtapose several sites onto themselves, even if such sites once appeared incompatible; they are linked to slices in time; entry is either compulsory or requires certain permissions or gestures; and finally, they serve a function for all the space outside of themselves.

Foucault (1986) offers examples of heterotopias that satisfy all six principles, including cemeteries, prisons, gardens, and theatres. Theatres, for example, are found in every culture; they have been used to maintain order, assert democracy, educate, entertain, and contemplate; they bring countless worlds into small rooms; they host activities that unfold live, yet reference and evoke pasts and futures; they require some exchange or gesture to enter; and they serve multiple functions for society outside of themselves. Universities, too, are heterotopias. They exist in all cultures in some form; have been used for a wide variety of purposes that society actively controls; evoke endless places, pasts, and futures; have admission processes; and I suppose we are struggling with what function they serve for the space outside of themselves.

To help me write this chapter, someone asked me to consider what kind of university I want to inherit. This prompt seemed to imply a distant heir, watching as others form something I will later obtain. (This seems like a good place for a joke about how, judging by the academic job market, I am very unlikely to obtain much of anything.) However, playing with writing this chapter has revealed the university's tentacular tendencies. It extends far beyond campuses, forming and formed by everyone and everything. As a student, therefore, I wonder if I am not inheriting a university, but rather, constantly co-creating one. I wonder if students refuse to realize their power, and refuse to participate in the future of universities, we give them up (Lorde, 1982/1984).

As students, what kind of courses do we choose to take? What efforts do we make? What contributions do we offer? What relationships do we open, nurture, and sustain? What kinds of scholarship do we engage with and in? When we talk about universities, what do we talk about? What and who do we read? What and who do we cite? What do we *do* about the things we learn and discover, and who do we do them alongside? What kinds of behaviour do we accept? Which do we emulate? Which do we refuse? Who do we become alongside the institution that we make and that makes us? What are our dreams, and how do we execute them?

Audre Lorde (1978) describes the power of the erotic, which is to crave and desire a world that pleases and satisfies through its goodness and justice. Although the university may make grand romantic gestures and nestle into cozy, intimate spaces, it is unclear whether the institution is up to the task of satiating erotic desires for a more good and just world. Is this institution what we have been craving? Are our dreams contained in journal articles, behind paywalls? Is this *satisfying*? We are all complicit in whatever the university is, and our attention seems to be a strong currency, forming a current that gently but surely erodes and forms the institution.

By now, I hardly know what a university is, let alone what its purposes are. I even feel a protective urge to argue that we shall never know. However, there is great value in grappling with this question, which allows us to practise hope in universities and to hold high expectations of them. Perhaps we *are* in a utopia, as Dewey (1933/2021a) described, in the sense that universities are simply part of, and impossible to untangle from, daily life. Universities are a lot like play. One key component of play is its *pur-poselessness*: It resists submission to outcomes and prioritizes process over production. Play is the prize of play. I wonder if this is not how universities are meant to be.

For Huizinga (1938/2016), play is about intellectual prowess, machoism, and competition among men. Some people treat universities this way too. Universities have a bad habit of rousing arrogance (Machado de Oliveira, 2021). Just like universities, though, play can be otherwise. Both univer-sities and play invite confusion and deliberation on their definitions and purposes. It is part of the fun. Both can welcome vulnerability. What is this book, if not an invitation to play? Rather than make spectacles of ourselves, producing and promoting our individual outputs to satisfy audit culture demands (Sparkes, 2021), we chapter authors make fools of ourselves, alongside one another. The project—*What Are Universities For?*—rekindles "the idea of universities as places where scholars may take intellectual risk" and challenges the reproduction of "nothing but success and certainty" (Morrish & Sauntson, 2016, p. 3). Surely no one can answer this question successfully or certainly, but the point seems to be that we attempt to answer the question, not that we actually answer it. In the *process*, though, we evaluate universities. We explore, and examine, and discuss them. We figure out all sorts of things that are wrong with them, and right with them, and together we develop higher expectations of universities and make them better through this playful exercise.

Play is ubiquitous; it, too, reveals itself in immense and intimate ways. Play is also transformative (Sutton-Smith, 1997; Vygotsky, 1933/1967). Similar to universities, play is not exempt from the harms of racist, sexist, colonial, and oppressive forces (Trammell, 2023), nor is it always joyful and pleasurable. Similar to scholarship, play is challenging: creating, shar-ing, and suspending worlds while resisting the forces that attempt to shat-ter them is difficult and gritty work.

Scholarship is play. Through play, often another world, affected by and affecting the real world, is enacted and carried by those brought into it. Scholarship, similarly, is deeply imaginative, involving the carrying of a world that, like play, "[fabricates] another world that lives alongside the first one and carries on its own kind of life, a life often much more emo-tionally vivid than mundane reality" (Sutton-Smith, 1997, p. 158). To me, this is how higher education should feel: research, teaching, and service make new worlds possible that begin to live alongside and emerge with everyday reality. Chris Richards (2013) found that children experienced a school playground as "mundane and real and institutionally defined but also a place of fantasy and possible transgression" (p. 388). Universities are playspaces.

I welcome the reader to consider how universities and play worlds are both heterotopias. Both are found in some form in every culture; societies assign both fluidly changing purposes; and both are proficient at inviting and suspending other places within themselves, absorbed in and referencing pasts and futures. Further, whereas universities more clearly require exchange, often financial, or at least an admission process, play worlds are also complex to enter, sometimes requiring a third party or personal ritual. Analyzing universities and play through the lens of heterotopias invites readers to see their similarities, even in the difficulty of describing a function for how they serve the spaces around them.

I wonder if play might be useful for helping universities to be *disarmed* spaces (Machado de Oliveira, 2021) by encouraging them to be more process-based. In ceasing the obsessive attempt to produce the image of a safe, productive space, perhaps the university can open possibilities for students, staff, and faculty to admit that the university is unsafe, that they do not always have answers, that sometimes they get nervous, that they fear they do not belong, that a reviewer's comments were hurtful, that they have failed at something, or that something has failed them. Vulnerability is required for universities to confront a multitude of truths, many of which are uncomfortable, but necessary, nevertheless, for universities to be transformative (Cote-Meek, 2023). Such vulnerability is not only interior, but exterior. Universities that accept vulnerability and openness, open the public to the true possibilities of understanding the vulnerability of being human or being alive at any time. That stars, air, water, animals, plants, architecture, and ideas are all unstable. There is a precariousness to *everything*. Play may help the university to become a disarmed space where it acknowledges that it, alongside the world, is not yet as good as it could be, but is dedicated to caring and acting and trying to make things better.

Perhaps dancing between universities as utopias and dystopias, acknowledging the pain of knowing the university as both friend and foe, can affirm that it inflicts not only personal but collective injuries (Gill, 2018). Perhaps a playful and disarmed university might release pressure on scholars to produce, and offer them time to learn, get smarter, and change their minds (Lincoln et al., 2018). Perhaps playfulness is necessary if the university has hope in facilitating wide-awakeness (Greene, 1977) amongst so much anti-wokeness (Crenshaw, 2024; Ladson-Billings, 2023).

Conclusion

Exploring universities through this work has revealed that the whole concept of the university, of its teaching, research, and service, is so intertwined with daily public and private life that it is difficult to grasp and understand what a university even is, or to locate its beginnings and endings. If nothing else, the playful act of exploring and writing this chapter has allowed me to further make sense and lose sense of the purposes of universities. I have attempted to wander a university, realized the blurred lines between the public and the university, and how the university extends into magnificent and minute moments. I have examined a singular university that demonstrated itself to be at once for research and exploration, contemplation, self-discovery, knowledge dissemination, job training and employment, enriching daily life, and nurturing democracy. I have explored how the institution, with its sweet intimate moments and its grand romantic gestures, fails to satisfy its purposes, even if it is unclear what those may be. The university sprawls and seeps into all spaces. Universities do things that are not their purpose and have purposes that remain unfulfilled.

I have begun to wonder, how are universities *not* playspaces, and how is scholarship *not* play? As I wander back through campus, I see play: it is in the books in the library and the discoveries made. I wonder how many insights and innovations were accidental, euphoric, and playful. In a way, the arts, music, and theatre, the nonsense and absurdity, the relationships, the stimulating intellectual debate, and the personal and systemic transformation afforded by universities are all elements of design in an intimate and immense playspace. Play is in the symposium that preceded this book and tightly woven into the tapestry of its pages. Contributors and readers play with, dwell with, grapple with, and transform alongside universities. Play, with its ways of thinking, knowing, and being that rouse curiosity, unknowing, and imagination, is what universities are for. As scholars, students, faculty, staff, and the public, it is paramount that we preserve such playfulness in the academy. It is imperative that we recognize the forces that threaten to shatter it: tendencies to overly objectify our individual and collective work, efforts to thread apart or elevate any one of the university purposes above others, and assertions of certainty that the institution has any singular purpose at all.

References

Ahmed, S. (2021). *Complaint!* Duke University Press.

Alexis, A. (2015). *Fifteen dogs.* Coach House Books.

Bachelard, G. (2014). *The poetics of space* (M. Jolas, Trans.). Penguin Group. (Original work published 1958)

Balaj, M., Henson, C.A., Aronsson, A., Aravkin, A., Beck, K., Degail, C., Donadello, L., Eikemo, K., Friedman, J., Giouleka, A., Gradeci, I., Hay, S.I., Jensen, M.R., Mclaughlin, S.A., Mullany, E.C., O'Connell, E.M., Sripada, K., Stonkute, D., Sorensen, R.J.D., & Gakidou, E. (2024). Effects of education on adult mortality: A global systematic review and meta-analysis. *The Lancet Public Health, 9*(3), e155–65. https://doi.org/10.1016/S2468-2667(23)00306-7.

Barber, C., Mueller, C.T.,...Ogata, S. (2013). Volunteerism as purpose: Examining the long-term predictors of continued community engagement. *Educational Psychology, 33*(3), 314–33. https://doi.org/10.1080/01443410.2013.772775

Carpenter, A., & Peponis, J. (2010). Poverty and connectivity: Crossing the tracks. *The Journal of Space Syntax, 1*(1), 108–20.

Chaithanya, A., Chambers, S., De Lugt, J., Demchuk, L., Heinrichs, A., Kequahtooway, L., Lang, H., McLeod, L., Ortman, M., Ramsay, C., Schentag, P., Vincent, J., Wecker, S., & Tagseth, M. (2023). *Forged in flame: Clay, wood kilns & community* [Woodfired ceramic]. Fifth Parallel Gallery, Regina, SK, Canada.

Chatterjee, P. (2008). Hungering for power: Borders and contradictions in Indian tea plantation women's organizing. *Signs: Journal of Women in Culture and Society, 33*(3), 497–505. https://doi.org/10.1086/523820

Cipriano, A.E., Holland, K.J., Bedera, N., Eagan, S.R., & Diede, A.S. (2022). Severe and pervasive? Consequences of sexual harassment for graduate students and their Title IX report outcomes. *Feminist Criminology, 17*(3), 343–67. https://doi.org/10.1177/15570851211062579

Cole, J. R., Smith, M., Tuhiwai Smith, L., & Westheimer, J. (2023, May 3). In N. Ayed (Chair), *What are universities for? Pre-symposium, expert panel* [Panel]. https://www.youtube.com/watch?v=DgnwIO4DVGM

Cote-Meek, S. (2023, May). *Reimagining the pedagogy of truth.* [Presentation]. What Are Universities For? International Symposium. Regina, SK, Canada. https://www.youtube.com/watch?v=dwVFGodvjfU

Crenshaw, K. (2024, April 11). *Fighting back to move forward: Defending the freedom to learn in the war against woke.* [Opening Plenary Address]. American Educational Research Association Annual Meeting, Philadelphia, USA.

Dea, S. (2016). *Beyond the binary: Thinking about sex and gender*. Broadview Press.

Dewey, J. (2021a). Dewey outlines utopian schools. In E.T. Weber (Ed.), *America's public philosopher: Essays on social justice, economics, education, and the future of democracy* (pp. 121–26). Columbia University Press. (Original work published 1933)

Dewey, J. (2021b). What is a school for? In E.T. Weber (Ed.), *America's public philosopher: Essays on social justice, economics, education, and the future of democracy* (pp. 117–20). Columbia University Press. (Original work published 1923)

Doyle, W.R., & Skinner, B.T. (2017). Does postsecondary education result in civic benefits? *The Journal of Higher Education*, 88(6), 863–93. https://doi.org/10.10 80/00221546.2017.1291258

Falk, M., & Katz-Gerro, T. (2016). Cultural participation in Europe: Can we identify common determinants? *Journal of Cultural Economics*, 40(2), 127–62. https://doi.org/10.1007/s10824-015-9242-9

Fernandez, F. (2021). Turnout for what? Do colleges prepare informed voters? *Educational Researcher*, 50(9), 677–78. https://doi.org/10.3102/0013189X211045982

Fluharty, M., Paul, E., Bone, J., Bu, F., Sonke, J., & Fancourt, D. (2021). Difference in predictors and barriers to arts and cultural engagement with age in the United States: A cross-sectional analysis using the Health and Retirement Study. *PLoS ONE*, 16(12), e0261532. https://doi.org/10.1371/journal.pone.0261532.

Foucault, M. (1986). Of other spaces (J. Miskowiec, Trans.). *Diacritics*, 16(1), 22–27. https://doi.org/10.2307/464648

Gaydosh, L., Schorpp, K.M., Chen, E., Miller, G.E., & Harris, K.M. (2018). College completion predicts lower depression but higher metabolic syndrome among disadvantaged minorities in young adulthood. *Proceedings of the National Academy of Sciences of the United States of America*, 115(1), 109–14. https://doi.org/10.1073/pnas.1714616114

Gill, R. (2018). Beyond individualism: The psychosocial life of the neoliberal university. In M. Spooner & J. McNinch (Eds.), *Dissident knowledge in higher education* (pp. 193–216). University of Regina Press.

Gong, H.J., & Hong, J.E. (2021). Does postsecondary education attainment matter in community service engagement? Evidence from across 18 OECD countries. *Education Sciences*, 11(3), Article 3. https://doi.org/10.3390/educsci11030096

Grande, S. (2018). Refusing the university. In M. Spooner & J. McNinch (Eds.), *Dissident knowledge in higher education* (pp. 168–89). University of Regina Press.

Greene, M. (1977). Toward wide-awakeness: An argument for the arts and humanities in education. *Humanities and the Curriculum*, 79(1), 119–24.

Gusa, D.L. (2011). White institutional presence: The impact of whiteness on campus climate. *Harvard Educational Review*, 80(4), 464–90. https://doi.org/10.17763/haer.80.4.p5j483825u110002

Guzman, L.A., Oviedo, D., & Rivera, C. (2017). Assessing equity in transport accessibility to work and study: The Bogotá region. *Journal of Transport Geography*, 58, 236–46. https://doi.org/10.1016/j.jtrangeo.2016.12.016

Hango, D. (2021, July 16). *Harassment and discrimination among faculty and researchers in Canada's postsecondary institutions*. Statistics Canada, Government of Canada. https://www150.statcan.gc.ca/n1/pub/75-006-x/2021001/article/00006-eng.htm

Haraway, D. (2007). *When species meet*. University of Minnesota Press.

Harney, S., & Moten, F. (2013). *The undercommons: Fugitive planning & Black study*. Minor Compositions.

Hillygus, D.S. (2005). The missing link: Exploring the relationship between higher education and political engagement. *Political Behavior*, 27(1), 25–47. https://doi.org/10.1007/s11109-005-3075-8

hooks, b. (2000). *All about love: New visions*. William Morrow.

Huizinga, J. (2016). *Homo ludens: A study of the play-element in culture*. Angelico Press. (Original work published 1938)

King, J. (2022, November 17). New report puts the spotlight on Regina's climate policy. *The Carillon*. https://carillonregina.com/new-report-puts-the-spotlight-on-reginas-climate-policy/

Ladson-Billings, G. (1995). Toward a theory of culturally relevant pedagogy. *American Educational Research Journal*, 32(3), 465–91. https://doi.org/10.2307/1163320

Ladson-Billings, G. (2023, May 3–6). *Closing the marketplace: Restriction, repression, & retrenchment in US higher education*. [Presentation]. What Are Universities For? International Symposium, Regina, SK, Canada. https://www.youtube.com/watch?v=wKBF_Oondqo

Lincoln, Y., Lynham, S., & Guba, E. (2018). Paradigmatic controversies, contradictions, and emerging confluences, revisited. In N.K. Denzin & Y.S. Lincoln (Eds.), *The SAGE handbook of qualitative research* (5th ed., pp. 213–63). SAGE.

Lipsitz, G. (2011). *How racism takes place*. Temple University Press.

Logan, Z. (2021). *A natural history of unnatural things*. Radiant Press.

Lorde, A. (1978, August 25). *The uses of the erotic: The erotic as power*. [Paper presentation]. Fourth Berkshire Conference on the History of Women, Mount Holyoke College.

Lorde, A. (1984). Learning from the 60s. In *Sister outsider* (pp. 134–44). Crossing Press. (Talk delivered at the Malcolm X Weekend, Harvard University, February 1982)

Machado de Oliveira, V. (2021). *Hospicing modernity: Facing humanity's wrongs and the implications for social activism*. North Atlantic Books.

Malin, H., Han, H., & Liauw, I. (2017). Civic purpose in late adolescence: Factors that prevent decline in civic engagement after high school. *Developmental Psychology*, 53(7), 1384–97. https://doi.org/10.1037/dev0000322

Mandes, J. (2023, May 18). University of Regina welcomes evacuees from northern Sask. communities. Global News. https://globalnews.ca/news/9708343/university-of-regina-evacuees-northern-saskatchewan-wildfires/

Molstad, T.D., Weinhardt, J.M., & Jones, R. (2023). Sexual assault as a contributor to academic outcomes in university: A systematic review. *Trauma, Violence, & Abuse*, 24(1), 218–30. https://doi.org/10.1177/15248380211030247

Morrish, L., & Sauntson, H. (2016). Performance management and the stifling of academic freedom and knowledge production. *Journal of Historical Sociology*, 29(1), 42–64. https://doi.org/10.1111/johs.12122

Mudzongo, F., Saskatchewan Association of Black Social Workers, & Danish, U. (2024). *The mosaic of Black joy and wellness* [Photovoice Exhibit]. University of Saskatchewan Student Wellness Centre.

Murray, A. (2024). *To make smoke* [Exhibition]. MacKenzie Art Gallery, Regina, SK, Canada. https://mackenzie.art/exhibition/audie-murray-to-make-smoke/

O'Connor, L. (2021, September 16). Regina takes steps towards harm reduction for drug users. *The Carillon*. https://carillonregina.com/regina-takes-steps-towards-harm-reduction-for-drug-users/

Perna, L.W. (2005). The benefits of higher education: Sex, racial/ethnic, and socioeconomic group differences. *Review of Higher Education*, 29(1), 23–52. https://doi.org/10.1353/rhe.2005.0073

Ratt, T. (2022). Miskasowin askîhk: Coming to know oneself on the land. *In Education*, 27(2b), 37–51. https://doi.org/10.37119/ojs2022.v27i2b.615

Richards, C. (2013). "If you ever see this video, we're probably dead"—A boy's own heterotopia (notes from an inner London playground). *Journal of Children and Media*, 7(3), 383–98. https://doi.org/10.1080/17482798.2012.755635

Rynor, B. (2023, April 5). "Don't just publish another paper. Let's do something," says scholar-advocate Cindy Blackstock. *University Affairs*. https://www.universityaffairs.ca/features/feature-article/dont-just-publish-another-paper-lets-do-something-says-scholar-advocate-cindy-blackstock/

Sá, C., Florax, R.J.G.M., & Rietveld, P. (2006). Does accessibility to higher education matter? Choice behaviour of high school graduates in the Netherlands. *Spatial Economic Analysis*, 1(2), 155–74. https://doi.org/10.1080/17421770601009791

Schneider, B. (2019, July 31). Newest U of R Canada Research Chair offers insight to Sask. climate change policy. *The Carillon*. https://carillonregina.com/newest-u-of-r-canada-research-chair-offers-insight-to-sask-climate-change-policy/

Smith, C.P., & Freyd, J.J. (2013). Dangerous safe havens: Institutional betrayal exacerbates sexual trauma. *Journal of Traumatic Stress*, 26(1), 119–24. https://doi.org/10.1002/jts.21778

Sparkes, A.C. (2021). Making a spectacle of oneself in the academy using the H-Index: From becoming an artificial person to laughing at absurdities. *Qualitative Inquiry*, 27(8–9), 1027–39. https://doi.org/10.1177/10778004211003519

Spooner, M. (2018). Qualitative research and global audit culture: The politics of productivity, accountability, and possibility. In N.K. Denzin & Y.S. Lincoln (Eds.), *The SAGE handbook of qualitative research* (5th ed., pp. 894–914). SAGE.

Spooner, M. (2024). Backsliding toward illiberal democracy and authoritarianism: Qualitative inquiry, academic freedom, and technologies of governance. In N.K. Denzin, Y.S. Lincoln, M.D. Giardina, & G.S. Cannella (Eds.), *The SAGE handbook of qualitative research* (6th ed., pp. 567–93). SAGE.

Stein, S., & Oliveira de Andreotti, V. (2016). Cash, competition, or charity: International students and the global imaginary. *Higher Education: The International Journal of Higher Education Research*, 72(2), 225–39. https://doi.org/10.1007/s10734-015-9949-8

Stein, S., Oliveira de Andreotti, V., & Boxall, R. (2019). The ethics of private funding for graduate students in the social sciences, arts, and humanities. *Critical Education*, 10(16), Article 16. https://doi.org/10.14288/ce.v10i16.186429

Stewart, D-L. (2023). Civic engagement and resisting "docile bodies" in postsecondary education. *Teachers College Record*, 125(5), 29–38. https://doi.org/10.1177/01614681231181795

Sutton-Smith, B. (1997). *The ambiguity of play*. Harvard University Press.

Taylor, A. (2013). *Reconfiguring the natures of childhood*. Routledge.

Trammell, A. (2023). *Repairing play: A Black phenomenology*. MIT Press.

Tuck, E. (2018). Biting the university that feeds us. In M. Spooner & J. McNinch (Eds.), *Dissident knowledge in higher education* (pp. 149–67). University of Regina Press.

Vygotsky, L. (1967). Play and its role in the mental development of the child (based on 1933 lecture). *Soviet Psychology*, 5(3), 6–18.

White, P.M., & Lee, D.M. (2020). Geographic inequalities and access to higher education: Is the proximity to higher education institution associated with the probability of attendance in England? *Research in Higher Education*, 61(7), 825–48. https://doi.org/10.1007/s11162-019-09563-x

Whitman, W. (2014). *Leaves of grass*. Penguin Books. (Original work published 1855)

Woolf, V. (2004). *A room of one's own*. Penguin Books (Original work published 1928)

Yost, C.K., & Nattress, F.M. (2000). The use of multiplex PCR reactions to characterize populations of lactic acid bacteria associated with meat spoilage. *Letters in Applied Microbiology*, 31(2), 129–33. https://doi.org/10.1046/j.1365-2672.2000.00776.x

Zhang, L., Liu, X., & Hu, Y. (2024). Degrees of return: Estimating internal rates of return for college majors using quantile regression. *American Educational Research Journal*, 61(3), 577–609. https://doi.org/10.3102/00028312241231512

Zhang, X., & John, S. (2021). Photonic crystal based photoelectrochemical cell for solar fuels. *Nano Select*, 2(6), 1218–24. https://doi.org/10.1002/nano.202000143

CHAPTER 3
UNIVERSITIES IN A DEMOCRATIC SOCIETY

Joel Westheimer

F YOU THINK ABOUT DIFFERENT UNIVERSITIES AROUND THE world—in a totalitarian dictatorship, in a religious theocracy, in a democracy—in any form of government—there are some things in common in all those places. In all those countries, leaders want students to learn mathematics. Maybe a foreign language. Maybe history. All those countries want students to learn how to be nice to one another. All those countries want citizens who are responsible and law abiding. They all want citizens not to litter, to help an old person across the street, and give blood when blood is needed.

When I consider these global commonalities in educational goals, I am drawn to an important question: If universities are implicated in educating "good" citizens—and they are—how should universities in a democratic society be different than those in, say, a totalitarian dictatorship? I will say, first and foremost, that democratic societies have different requirements of their citizens than other forms of government. In a dictatorship or a religious theocracy or a country led by a military junta, rules for how the society functions are issued by decree, from the top. The role of citizens in these societies is to follow those edicts, not to question them.

In contrast, democratic societies need citizens who actively participate in civic life and who are informed about policies and can make decisions about those policies and weigh in with opinions. Democratic societies need citizens who think critically, who ask tough questions about social policies of significance, who actively participate in decision-making, and who can examine multiple perspectives.

How do we nurture that kind of vision of a "good" citizen? The philosopher John Dewey said that democracy "must be born anew with every generation and education is its midwife" (1899/1980, p. 139). That should be a primary goal of universities: to be democracy's midwife. What should this midwife do? I'm going to suggest three goals for a democratic education. First, universities in democratic societies must nurture the free exchange of ideas; second, they should—to the extent possible—encourage community participation and political engagement, building community along the way; and finally, a university education in a democratic society should emphasize the importance of pursuing the public good.

Three Goals for Universities That Nurture Democracy

For universities to fulfill their role as democracy's midwife, they must, first, encourage the free exchange of ideas even when those ideas are contentious. They should see arguments and debates and the embrace of multiple perspectives as essential to a good education. It is important for students and for all of us to recognize that intelligent, well-meaning people differ on ideas of social significance and that we can have different opinions and still move forward with making decisions about self-governance. Should we raise taxes or lower them? Regulate telecommunications companies or let the market dictate best practices? Ban cell phones in schools or allow them? Lower the voting age to sixteen or keep it at eighteen? Universities play a crucial role in cultivating critical thinking and intellectual curiosity among their students. By encouraging open dialogue, debate, and the examination of different perspectives, universities foster a culture of intellectual curiosity, inquiry, and healthy skepticism. This serves to cultivate a citizenry able to evaluate information critically, question authority, and engage in meaningful civic discourse—cornerstones of any vibrant democracy.

Second, ideally, a university education that nurtures democracy would introduce students to community participation because democratic life requires active engagement. Through pedagogical approaches such as service learning and action civics, students can engage with these multiple perspectives and complex issues not only in their academic lives but also in the community, bringing community life back to their academics and bringing what they learn in their classrooms back to the community.

Collective action in the community also helps to build meaningful relationships; these relationships within communities are a large part of what strengthens democratic societies. The only way to enable healthy debate and work together for the benefit of all is to build a foundation of trust and mutual respect. This requires attention to fostering connections and relationships across diverse populations. Universities are sites where this can be best pursued because they are places where diverse communities come together in the common project of learning.

Building relationships also combats the loneliness and isolation that are now so pervasive among people and that threaten our ties with one another. We are living in an era where (especially) post-pandemic youth and young adults (but also those who grew up before the pandemic) are experiencing unprecedented levels of loneliness and alienation. When it comes to creating and sustaining a vibrant democratic community, relationships are important. I don't think there is anything more vital than bringing young people into a community of ideas and of creative expression where they can become the best version of themselves and can connect with others in common projects. That is the language we need to emphasize in public discourse when talking about the purposes of a university education.

It is also worth noting that community participation includes being politically active. Democracies require citizens to be politically engaged, and political activity is the vehicle for political engagement. Being active in gym class is a good thing; being active generally is seen as a good thing. Similarly, being politically active (activism) should be seen as a beneficial part of a democratic education. Not only is activism often viewed negatively, but even the work of being *political* is often viewed as something to be avoided. Politics is the domain in which we are active, and politics is the way we come together to work out our differences. Bernard Crick in his book *In Defense of Politics* (1962/1993) writes that politics is the way people in a democratic society come together to work out their differences and move forward toward policy. Especially in these polarized times, students need experiences in political discourse across differences. A university education should demonstrate that being active is important, being political is important, and that the academic curriculum is tied to community and civic engagement.

Third, a university education should be oriented toward nurturing ideas of the public good. For democracy to function, citizens must be concerned with the radical question "How should we live?" This question is radical because it implies that we have choices about how we interact with one another, how we distribute resources, and what should be allowed and disallowed in a robust democracy. Students should learn that those choices have consequences, and that all of us are meant to be a part of that conversation through dialogue and debate. Citizens of a dictatorship do not have these choices. Pursuing the public good means keeping in mind that the rules and laws we live by should benefit all and not just a powerful few.

Furthermore, universities themselves should be viewed as instruments of the public good. It's not just that each of us wants an education; we all have a stake in living in an educated society. Even without talking explicitly about the civic goals of university, we should acknowledge the importance of a broad education in and of itself: a democratic society is more robust if people are educated. Universities are themselves, therefore, a public good.

The Neoliberal University as an Obstacle to Education for Democracy

"There can be little doubt," writes Henry Giroux (2024), "that neoliberalism has undermined...the notion of higher education as a democratic public sphere—a protective and courageous space where students can speak, write and act from a position of agency and informed judgment." Over the past few decades, universities have been transformed to reflect the undeserved trust in market forces that have gripped other institutions and broad visions of how society should function. We have reframed universities now as solely job training institutions. This is an individualistic rather than a collective view of the function of a university. It is an emaciated view of the historic ideal of a university. Of course, everyone wants students to be able to find meaningful work after university. But that's just where it begins. A university education can simultaneously pursue the kind of education that prepares students for gainful employment *and* that prepares them for democratic life. We need universities that are concerned with more than individual training, that embrace goals of a better society for all.

The purpose of a university education has always included providing students with the knowledge, skills, and attitudes they need to succeed in the workplace. But a specific orientation to job training was traditionally the purview of businesses. They would pay new employees while they were training for their specific job; that is what corporations did. Now they have pulled off a sleight of hand—to their benefit—of downloading that training onto the university. And not only does that benefit them but it is also a disservice to the student who might well be in a different job later on. They should expect and have the right to be trained by that job. Universities should not be saddled with the task of job training.

This also means rejecting the growing influence of standardized testing and so-called value-added measures of university success that accompany the neoliberal remaking of the university's mission. Every institution in our society is now subjected to talk of standards and accountability and bean counting and value added. We lose a lot under this unchallenged neoliberal ideology of ubiquitous quantification and attempts at standardization.

There is nothing wrong with standards; we all have them. I have never met a professor who doesn't have standards and who doesn't feel accountable to the students and to the university and to the broader society. The problem is with the word "standardization," which literally means making everything the same. The university is not McDonald's, and we don't want to "Big Mac-asize" all our classrooms in the service of uniformity and predictability. The things that make university classes brim with passion and creativity are local things, what local professors and students are passionate about and feel creative about. This might include local political initiatives or community projects, for example. When students are actively immersed in that kind of eclectic and unpredictable environment, students gain experiences in democratic citizenship and learn the skills and dispositions that democracies need.

We are often told that students do not want that kind of education. Many students report that they want to go to university simply to train for their career; they want to be educated in the skills they need for employment but not for broader goals of an educated society; they want to get in and out of university as quickly as possible. It is important to note that students themselves have fallen prey to neoliberal ideas of market utility. We have lost the discourse about universities as anything other than job training institutions. We must recreate that language and create that space where students feel free to explore the pursuits that they care about, develop their own passions, and recognize their role in engaging in the task of improving society. Students also need the financial security that makes those pursuits possible. Perhaps an even greater obstacle to education beyond job training is the financial realities students face.

Who Should Pay for a University Education?

The neoliberal university advances the idea that, since an education is purely an individual good (so that each individual student can compete in the market economy), it should be up to each individual to pay for it. I think we should all pay for it. The public. It is one of the best investments we can make. For example, research shows that a better education results in better health outcomes (Goldman & Smith, 2011) and reduced incarceration rates (Hjalmarsson et al., 2015), among many other costs that we otherwise would have to pay down the line. So even though terms such as "investment" and "returns" are the language of neoliberalism and detract from the arguments at hand (and so, I am disinclined to accept that playing field), I will note that even on those terms, education is a sound investment with excellent returns.

In addition, the current reality of governments disinvesting in education means that the burden of paying for university is increasing as the share of university costs represented by tuition rises. Students do not currently have the freedom to pursue a richer, broader, and more vital education. The financial realities in the face of government underfunding means that students want to get in and out quickly and get a job. They are saddled with an enormous amount of debt when they leave university, and many cannot even afford to go to university in the first place. In my classes, I see a steep increase in the number of students who are working full-time while they are also in school full-time just to make ends meet. That means student desires about their education are shaped by their financial situations more than by the kind of education they would ideally like to receive.

Job pressures and other pressures students now face also result in some students preferring online education to in-person teaching and learning. This makes it more difficult to build the kinds of civic communities on which democracy thrives. As many of us know, in addition to traditional means of subject-matter teaching and learning, education takes place in the in-between spaces: during breaks in class, in hallways and campus quads, during all-night discussions about philosophy, science, literature, and politics. That type of education is the kind of education that binds us to one another and increases our sociality. Investing in students and their education is good for democracy.

Why does the public so often overlook these aspirations for a university education? The dominance of neoliberal framing drives the shift in education's perceived goals. Happily, the solution to shifting public understanding of the importance of education for democracy is education itself. Faculty, administrators, and all those who care about schooling's democratic mission must not only engage in public education but also in educating the public about these broader democratic goals of a university education.

A central mission of the university should be to improve society and nurture democracy. We need to transform the increasingly market-driven goals of a university education into public goals—reconnecting education to the broader society, nurturing the free exchange of ideas, encouraging participation and political engagement, building community, and directing teaching and learning to the common good. By fulfilling these roles, universities will contribute to the cultivation of an informed, engaged, and empowered citizenry—the kind of citizenry democracy requires.[1]

References

Crick, B. (1993). *In defense of politics* (4th ed.). University of Chicago Press. (Original work published 1962)

Dewey, J. (1980). The need of an industrial education in an industrial democracy. In J.A. Boydston (Ed.), *The middle works of John Dewey, 1899–1924, volume 10* (p. 137–143). Southern Illinois University Press. (Original work published 1899)

Giroux, H. (2024, June 8). The neoliberal university faces a crisis: This generation could change everything. *Salon.* https://www.salon.com/2024/06/08/the-neoliberal-university-faces-rebellion-this-generation-could-change-everything/

Goldman, D., & Smith, J.P. (2011). The increasing value of education to health. *Social Science & Medicine, 72*(10), 1728–37. https://doi.org/10.1016/j.socscimed.2011.02.047

Hjalmarsson, R., Holmlund, H., & Lindquist, M.J. (2015). The effect of education on criminal convictions and incarceration: Causal evidence from micro-data. *The Economic Journal, 125*(587), 1290–326. https://doi.org/10.1111/ecoj.12204

Notes

1   Adapted from my presentation and discussion at the special pre-symposium
     public panel, broadcast on CBC Ideas, and titled "What Are Universities For?"
     (May 3, 2023).

SECTION II
CRITICAL UNIVERSITY STUDIES

In this second section, contributors examine hegemonic geopolitics, neoliberalism, and the effects of increasingly authoritarian governments on the university's ability to fulfill its multiple roles and aspirations.

CHAPTER 4
RELATIONS OF POWER IN WORLDWIDE UNIVERSITY SCIENCE

Simon Marginson

Introduction

THIS CHAPTER FOCUSES ON GLOBAL SCIENCE, WHICH IN MANY disciplines has become the dominant part of scientific work in epistemic terms. Why talk about relations of power in global research and science in a book on higher education? Science and higher education are closely joined (Powell et al., 2017). Only a minority of higher education institutions conduct research, but those that do are important in science, and research is the marker of status in higher education worldwide. More than four-fifths of published science papers have at least one university author. And science matters, so relations of power in science also matter.

"Global science" is here defined as knowledge in the two main bibliometric collections, Web of Science (WoS, 2024) and Scopus (Elsevier, 2024). This includes some work in social sciences and a minority part of world scholarship in the humanities. As this suggests, global science, which is almost entirely published in the English language, is not equivalent to human knowledge as a whole. This is so even in the natural sciences. *"Global science" as structured by human action is not the whole of world knowledge, most of which is outside recognized global science.* This is a crucial issue in relations of power in science. The limits of the bibliometric collections as repositories of knowledge is expanded on below.

The chapter begins with the global science system and the relation between, on one hand, global science and, on the other hand, national government and national science. Then it moves to who and what are dominant in global science and who and what are excluded. This is followed by a discussion of changes in global science and the implications of these changes for relations of power. Global science is continually evolving (Marginson, 2022a).

Growth of Global Science

First, the growth of global science. This is an outcome of the spread of Internet-mediated communications. In *Theory of Society*, Luhmann (2012) notes that the decisive step toward world society was "the full discovery of the globe as a closed sphere of meaningful communication" (p. 85). After 1989 the Internet facilitated the rapid expansion of networked communications. Electronically mediated communication made possible the foundation and expansion of a new global science system driven not by technology but by human agents. North American universities had a large presence in the early Internet, and the early building of networked science was led by faculty in the United States.

This meant that the global science system became patterned by the expansionary dynamics of an open network, and also that it became closely shaped by American faculty norms. Fortunately, this included the robust practice of autonomous professional regulation in disciplinary communities with free bottom-up interaction between researchers that was independent of government. On the downside it meant from the beginning that global science embodied the equally robust Anglophone self-belief in its own cultural superiority.

Since 1996 the number of papers in the global literature has grown by over 5 percent per year. Published science has doubled every twelve years or so. There has also been rapid growth in the number and proportion of papers with international co-authors; and partly through this, active science has spread to many countries. In the STEM disciplines, though less so in other disciplines, most important new science starts in the global literature, not single nation literatures. As noted, global science has become epistemically primary.

Open Networks

There's much to be said for the open network in science. In networks, knowledge, messages, and information travel with lightning speed without respect for national borders. Innovations spread very rapidly. Networks become cheaper per connection as they grow (Castells, 2000). By joining the pre-existing network, new researchers and new national science systems readily gain access to immense resources. Established institutions and large countries cannot gatekeep in the global science system because researchers can freely form ties with any other researcher in the network, and do so.

> The organization may be more open to new members, since greater density of the network and the lowered in-betweenness measures suggest that fewer of the communications pass through the leading nodes or countries…international cooperation is particularly advantageous for less advanced countries.…With improved scanning of research and more effective communications, [researchers can] leverage foreign research, data, equipment, and know-how.…The global network is arguably now a more stable system that serves as a source of vitality and direction to R&D at all lower levels. (Wagner et al., 2015)

The fastest growth in collaborative relations in global science has been the growth in relations between researchers in different emerging science countries.

Figure 4.1 shows especially rapid growth since 1996 in science papers in China, India, and the rest of the world. Established science in the United States, the United Kingdom, Germany, and Japan grew more slowly. The Anglophone countries, Western Europe, Russia, and Japan once produced nearly all global science, but no longer. Countries generating 90 percent of science increased from twenty in 1987 to thirty-three in 2022. Their researchers produced over fifteen thousand papers in Scopus in 2022; fifty-nine countries produced over five thousand science papers (NSB, 2024): all of these countries had viable endogenous science systems, as indicated by local doctoral graduates in at least some disciplines, and all of these countries connected to the shared global science system.

Figure 4.1. Growth of science papers in Scopus by large country/world region, 1996–2022

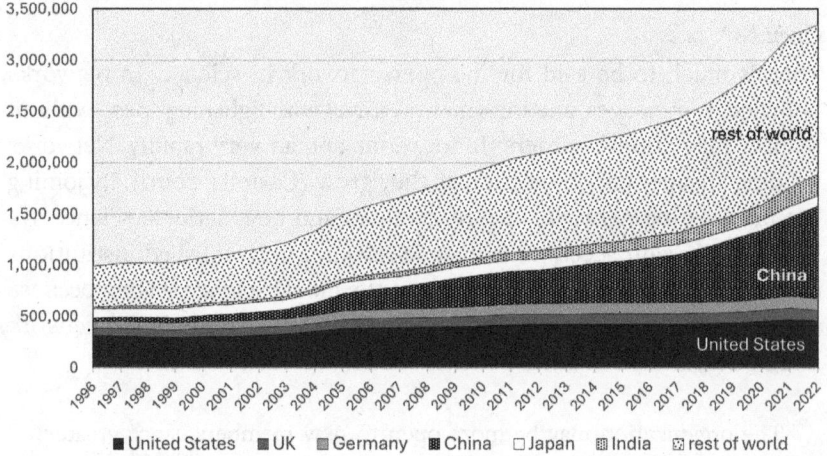

Source: NSB (2024)

Cross-Border Collaboration and Mobility

The number and proportion of papers co-authored in more than one institution in the same country has risen sharply, and papers co-authored in more than one country have risen faster. Figure 4.2 indicates the growth of cross-border papers in Scopus from 1996 to 2022. The proportion of all published science papers that entail authors from institutions in more than one country jumped from less than 2 percent of all Web of Science papers in 1970 (Olechnicka et al., 2019) to a high point of 23.2 percent of papers in Scopus in 2020. Figure 4.2 uses the Scopus data. Since 2020 there has been a slight falling away to 22.6 percent of all papers in 2022 (NSB, 2024), partly because of a decline in the volume of United States–China collaborations, but clearly collaborative science now has a major global component.

Mobile doctoral students play a large part in the globalization (meaning the cross-border convergence and integration) of science, though the proportion of doctoral students who come from another country varies between the national systems. In Canada in 2021, 35 percent of doctoral students were classified as foreign students in terms of citizenship compared to 24 percent in the United States. In the United Kingdom, 41 percent of doctoral students were classified as international in that they had crossed the border (OECD, 2023, p. 259).

Figure 4.2. Number and proportion (%) of papers in Scopus that were internationally co-authored, World: 1996–2022

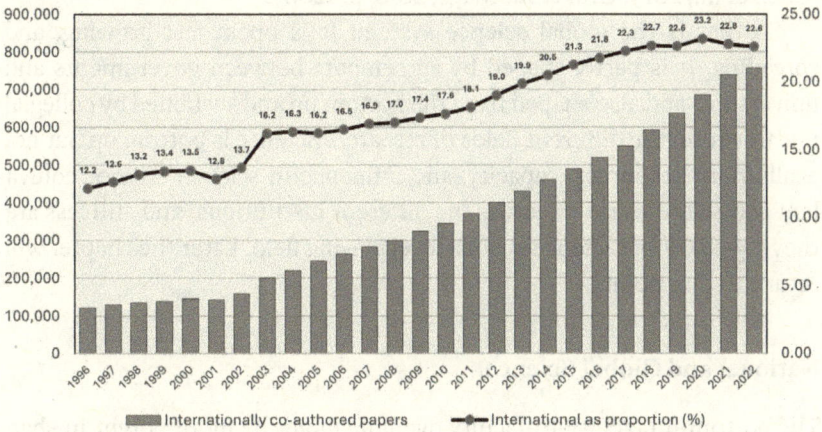

Source: NSB (2024). *A change to data compilation in 2003 disrupts comparison over the full period.*

Why do researchers collaborate internationally? Several answers are offered in the research literature on science (see, for example, Georghiou, 1998; Birnholtz, 2007; Winkler et al., 2015; Chen et al., 2019). Funding and program structures often incentivize cooperation. For example, in Europe the conditions of research funding often require cross-country teams. Government policies can also weaken collaboration, as will be discussed. But the intrinsic motives of researchers also matter. There can be career gains in going global: for example, partnerships between researchers in the Global North and emerging researchers in the Global South are common, often through the doctoral education of the Global South researchers. Career motivated collaboration is referred to as "preferential attachment" (Wagner & Leydesdorff, 2005). Interviews with scientists suggest that epistemic motivations are also often strong: most researchers want to make a significant contribution to discovery and many want to work with good researchers in their own research domain. The research literature mentions shared problems and factors such as respect and trust (Melin, 2000). Disciplinary ties are strong and often readily operate across borders.

Other affinities are also explanatory of cross-border patterns of co-authorship. All of linguistic, cultural, historical, geographic and political proximities can encourage scientific collaboration across national borders (Chen at al., 2019; Graf & Kalthaus, 2018, p. 1200).

So that is the global science system. It is open, fast growing, and spreading. It is partly shaped by agreements between governments and universities and also shaped from the bottom up and sustained by collegial norms within the different fields of research. Science is bottom up but not egalitarian. Resources, capacity, and influence in science are not equivalent across the world or across the different institutions, and still less are they equal. Global science is not a level playing field. Later the chapter will return to that point.

National and Global Science

The bottom-up faculty-to-faculty dynamic might be more potent in shaping the epistemic content of *global* science than the policies and actions of national governments. Yet in conventional descriptions of science it is seen to be organized in separated national systems, and its distinctive and separate global aspect is invisible. Data describing science often split intentionally collaborative papers on an arbitrary proportional basis between the countries concerned, which is highly misleading. It seems that "the only reality we are able to comprehensively describe statistically is national, or at best international" (Dale, 2005). Yet as the parent of comparative studies of science, Robert May, puts it, in the founding paper, data on "comparisons are to a degree confounded because a large and growing fraction of scientific work involves international collaborations" (May, 1997, p. 795).

Does it have to be either/or, though? Can science be global, local, and national simultaneously? What then are the relations between global and national science?

National governments and public research agencies are essential to science in the material sense. They provide the infrastructure of the institutions that house nearly all basic science: universities and government laboratories. They partly fund those institutions and largely fund their research projects. They often (though not always) provide a stable policy, legal, and regulatory framework for science. This might suggest that cross-border science, the global science system, is simply an outgrowth of national science. But this would miss the fact of global networking, collaboration, and creativity, where most of the discoveries in natural science are made. In global science, knowledge and its organization are grounded not in universities or in countries but in the disciplines and cross-disciplinary groups, in freely connecting research networks. The global science system is much more than the sum of the different national parts. It has its own networked relations and dynamics of growth. Its practical autonomy from national authorities creates challenges for governments. Table 4.1 distinguishes global and national science (see also Marginson, 2022b).

Table 4.1. Distinctions between global and national science systems

	Global Science System	National Science System
Core Components	codified, globally legitimated knowledge, people, networked communications, norms	institutional structure of science activity ordered and resourced primarily by nation-state
Enabling Conditions	global communications, resources, institutions, and (often national) agencies/policies/rules	sufficient political and economic stability and policy commitment to science activity
Main Functions	production, codification and legitimation, circulation of new shared knowledge in English (inclusion/exclusion function)	legal, political, financial conditions of science; new national knowledge, new applications of knowledge
Boundary	world society, but only some knowledge and knowledge producers are included	nation-state, limits of activity are set by state policies and willingness to fund
Normative Centre	no normative centre; diffuse disciplinary community of persons sharing knowledge	normatively centred on state and institutions

	Global Science System	National Science System
Growth Dynamics	continually expands to all possible networked connections, intensifies existing connections ("edges")	growth is less inherently dynamic, being determined by national policy and funding, and industry take-up of research
Social-Relational	collegial scientists in professional organizations, forums, and networks	government agencies, research organizations and institutions, networked scientists in national and local scales
Regulation	local self-regulation using global collegial scientific norms (norms of dominant science nations)	national law, official regulation, policy, financing systems, cultural norms
Division Of Labour	knowledge potential of global science stimulates national system-building and state funding	national science provides institutions, personnel, resources essential to global science

The global network has a culture, pathways, and norms of communication specific to its structure, and diverging from national, regional, or disciplinary norms. (Wagner et al., 2017, p. 1646)

Collaboration has grown for reasons independent of the needs and policies of the state....This dynamic system, operating orthogonally to national systems, is increasingly difficult to influence and even less amenable to governance as it grows...nations must learn to manage and benefit from a network. (Wagner et al., 2015, pp. 2 and 12)

Science is multi-scalar in the geographic sense (for more discussion, see Marginson 2022c). It operates at different levels—it is individual, it is locally collaborative, it is national, often regional, and global now in a very visible way, all at the same time. These levels of science differ from each other in fundamental ways. National science is firmly centred by the nation-state, by governments. Global science has no normative centre. It is bottom-up. It is regulated not by rules and funding allocations but by voluntary cooperation, shared understanding, and the protocols that govern scientific work. It is influenced by national governments but is partly outside them. To understand worldwide science, it is essential to recognize this heterogeneity of science in the different geographical scales.

At the same time, while global and national science are different, they also overlap in important ways and there is mostly a symbiotic relationship, a functional division of labour, between them. Much scientific activity takes place in both scales simultaneously. Scientists who lead their global discipline often also lead science at institutional and national levels. Knowledge generated originally for national government purposes can find its way into the global conversation. Reciprocally, globally sourced knowledge becomes part of national scientific, governmental, and industrial agendas. National governments mostly support global science and encourage international scientific collaboration because this is seen as beneficial for parties located at the national level and makes it possible for government itself to be in touching distance of innovations in science and technology.

> The sciences develop internationally, but the funding is mainly national. (Bornmann et al., 2018, p. 931)

> International and national networks may be shaping each other in a process of co-evolution between the national institutional structure and the global network. The relative influences of national and international networks appear to vary among nations. (Wagner et al., 2015, p. 11)

It is nevertheless a complex relationship. When nations treat science as a common human endeavour, focused on shared global problems such as climate change or epidemic diseases, the relationship is more seamless. However, nations often treat science as a tool of "technological nationalism," hoping to mobilize science to pursue competitive nation-bound agendas. Then global science and national science find themselves pulling different ways. The nation-bound outlook can limit what science can achieve. It leads to confusion about the nature of science and its relation with the national economy.

For example, governments hope that by investing in science within national universities and other agencies they thereby foster economic innovation. But the "knowledge economy" is a myth. On the balance of probability, national science that enters the global pool is more likely to be used by foreign not local capital. Innovations by national industry are mostly sourced in foreign science, except in the United States and China. In any case, the majority of research is "altruistic," not focused on economic development or national security at all (Klavans & Boyack, 2017).

So that's the relation between global science and national science. Nations have resource power and legal power. The global system has knowledge power. They often work together but are sometimes pulling apart. Now the chapter will unpack the earlier statement, "science is not a level playing field." Here the argument will draw on Gramsci's (1971) concept of "hegemony," dominance via consent, and the content of the hegemony.

Hegemony in Global Science

Table 4.2, derived from the Leiden ranking which uses Web of Science data on science output, lists the world's twenty-five leading research universities on the basis of production of highly cited science papers published between 2018 and 2021 inclusive (CWTS, 2023).

Citations measure recognition of research, not the quality of research, but an order based on recognition shows where authoritative science is concentrated. This list includes twelve universities from the United States, four from the United Kingdom, one from Canada, seven from China, and one from Singapore. In the top ten there are four from the United States, three from the United Kingdom, and three from China. There are no non-UK European universities in the top ten or top twenty-five because the measure is partly size dependent and European research universities are typically smaller than are Anglophone and Chinese universities.

The top twenty-five list is changing. Five years earlier there were seventeen from the United States, two from Canada, none from Singapore, and just two from China, which were in twentieth and twenty-fifth position. East Asia is coming on with a rush, especially the leading research universities in China. But the Anglophone countries were still somewhat stronger in 2018–2021, led by Harvard, which produces twice as much high-citation science as the number two university, Stanford, primarily because of the weight of the research output of Harvard Medical School.

This list explains much about global science. It is led from familiar universities where reputation, resources, and talents are concentrated. Nominally, the high-citation data capture the quantity of quality (science

Table 4.2. Leading universities in high-citation science, Web of Science papers, 2018–2021, inclusive

University	Country	Top 5% Papers	All Papers	% Papers in Top 5% in Field	Cross-Border Papers	% Papers Cross-Border
Harvard U	USA	4,256	36,355	11.7%	50,465	55.0%
Stanford U	USA	2,065	17,958	11.5%	21,421	48.1%
Zhejiang U	China	1,974	33,090	6.0%	17,878	31.1%
Tsinghua U	China	1,898	23,152	8.2%	17,882	37.4%
U Toronto	Canada	1,833	25,295	7.2%	32,136	60.1%
U Oxford	UK	1,763	17,065	10.3%	32,681	71.7%
Shanghai Jiao Tong U	China	1,716	31,789	5.4%	17,957	31.0%
Huazhong U Science & T	China	1,559	24,435	6.4%	10,866	27.0%
U Michigan	USA	1,488	20,120	7.4%	18,913	41.7%
U College London	UK	1,486	16,247	9.1%	30,997	69.3%
U Pennsylvania	USA	1,478	16,900	8.7%	16,160	39.7%
Johns Hopkins U	USA	1,457	18,416	7.9%	22,165	47.2%
MIT	USA	1,445	10,504	13.8%	18,235	59.1%
U Cambridge	UK	1,407	14,386	9.8%	27,091	72.1%

University	Country	Top 5% Papers	All Papers	% Papers in Top 5% in Field	Cross-Border Papers	% Papers Cross-Border
Central Southern U	China	1,332	23,497	5.7%	9,719	25.2%
Peking U	China	1,319	21,238	6.2%	16,491	36.5%
Cornell U	USA	1,299	13,673	9.5%	16,218	49.4%
U California, Los Angeles	USA	1,277	14,894	8.6%	17,857	47.8%
Imperial College London	UK	1,264	12,864	9.8%	26,012	72.4%
U Chinese Academy Sci	China	1,255	19,751	6.4%	23,889	26.9%
Columbia U	USA	1,241	13,295	9.3%	18,168	50.0%
National U Singapore	Singapore	1,238	13,855	8.9%	23,603	72.0%
U California San Diego	USA	1,236	13,308	9.3%	16,093	48.4%
Yale U	USA	1,227	12,474	9.8%	15,053	47.2%
U Washington, Seattle	USA	1,225	15,363	8.0%	18,487	44.8%

Source: Centre for Work and Technology Studies (CWTS, 2023).
Most papers have multiple authors. The data for total papers and top 5 percent papers are based on fractional count: a single unit value of one per paper is allocated between different institutions on the basis of the proportion of total authorship. The data for international collaboration papers are based on total paper count so that each authorship (regardless of the number of authors in the paper) equals one.

fire power) in these institutions so that performance is determined by a combination of scientific merit with size. However, "scientific merit" is here dominated by Western and especially English-speaking universities. Even the rising stars in China excel by being good at Western science. Does this mean that the West is the best and the rest are nowhere? It is not that simple. The universities that dominate the comparison house the leading scientists who shape the comparison. They determine what is legitimate as global science, interacting with the publishing companies that circulate global science, in journals edited by the same discipline leaders, and the two large bibliometric companies that are the repository for global science.

Through these processes, knowledge becomes rank ordered in terms of value and prestige. First, some knowledge is selected as legitimate and other knowledge is excluded. Second, there is a hierarchy within the selected global knowledge that is based on journal ranking and citation impact. Global science is real knowledge, but that knowledge, and the prestige attached to it, are socially constructed—and much other knowledge is excluded.

Publishing

Global science publishing is largely monopolized by five large companies: Elsevier, Springer Nature, Taylor & Francis, Wiley-Blackwell, and SAGE. Like science, they operate freely across national borders. Science is a public good, but the publishing companies turn it into something owned by them. They are capitalist corporations that seek profit and market share as ends in themselves, absorbing academic networks, growing and diversifying journals and users, and differentiating value in the manner of markets. Open access publishing has become another way of monetizing science, via author processing charges. The networked scientific world provides publishers with their essential conditions of operation. Publishers extract papers from the larger body of formal and informal knowledge for digital-based revenue creation, exercising proprietary control. The peer review systems that sanction and differentiate the value of published papers as science are managed digitally in publisher platforms and increasingly regulated by the publishers' systems.

The publishers actively encourage the publish-or-perish growth of science, regardless of content or originality, because this expands their market share and profitability. Is science thereby subsumed into capitalist production? Are scientists reduced to wage labour for publishers? There's a tendency to this at the margin, but, largely, no. Publishers do not create knowledge. They are parasitic on knowledge, a public good that is produced in non-profit universities and research institutes. But they also help to create the rhythms of production of that public good and closely affect its use as a tool of institutional, national, economic, and cultural power. Public goods are often captured and deployed by powerful social groups.

The Bibliometric Collections

The output of journals is fed into the two main bibliometric collections, Web of Science and Scopus, which are owned by companies specializing in scientific information and publishing: Clarivate Analytics and Elsevier, respectively. Books play a minor role in the bibliometric collections: journal papers are more amenable to rank ordering based on peer review, journal selectivity, and citation impact and are more readily accessed by users.

Table 4.3. *The role of the main bibliometric collections in the global ranking of universities*

Rankings	Publication-Related Indicators as Proportion %	Databases
Shanghai Jiaotong Academic Ranking of World Universities (China)	70.0	Clarivate Analytics's Web of Science
Times Higher Education (THE) World University Rankings (UK)	38.5*	Elsevier's Scopus
QS World University Rankings (UK)	20.0*	Elsevier's Scopus
Leiden Ranking (Netherlands)	100.0	Clarivate Analytics's Web of Science
Best Global Universities (USA)	72.5	Clarivate Analytics's Web of Science

Source: Author, based on university-ranking websites.
*Beyond bibliometrics, research performance has a further, indirect but important, effect through its impact on the surveys used by THE and QS, and in THE data on postgraduate studies and income—arguably, in total, research performance constitutes more than two-thirds of the THE index (Marginson, 2014).

Bibliometrics have enabled the creation of a quasi-economy of science in which all outputs are assigned shadow values. These metrics then regulate the value of individuals, academic units, institutions, and countries as assessed on a comparative basis in higher education. Here, value is differentiated on the basis of culture; 97 percent of items in the bibliometric collections are in English, and nearly all work in other languages is excluded.

This machinery has acquired its own momentum. Yet it still rests on decisions about inclusion and legitimacy made by faculty leaders and peer reviewers in the disciplines. The prime instruments of global hegemony are the faculty in those countries that exercise it.

A crucial part of this quasi-economy of science is global university rankings. The main component of the rankings is bibliometric data. Research metrics directly determine most of the Shanghai and Times Higher rankings, and the prestige effects of research metrics indirectly determine the surveys used by Times Higher and QS (Table 4.3). Rankings turn bibliometrics into the recognized hierarchy of universities, in which the Anglophone universities are dominant, and privileged social groups reproduce their inherited place in the world. This construction of science has moved a long way from the shared joys of grassroots scientific collaboration. The collegial decisions of peer reviewers have not only been monetized by publishers, they are also used to determine and reproduce university hierarchies.

Knowledge That Is Excluded

This is what global science has become. It is a multiple and contradictory beast. It remains a system of open collaborative knowledge creation grounded in disciplinary networks. It is also annexed to institutional and geopolitical power and serves as an instrument of power and control. It is reproduced in circular fashion by the combination of national science infrastructures, leading universities, leading scientists, publishing companies, bibliometric companies, and university rankings. It is neo-imperial. It reproduces a global cultural hierarchy, inherited from the colonial era, which nurtures notions that some cultures, some languages, countries, people, are more highly valued, more creative and scientific, more objective, than others. Global science is seen as universal science, and the rest of knowledge in whatever language is treated as "just local" with no larger contribution to make.

What falls outside the charmed circle? Everything else. Issues of exclusion are by no means limited to fake data, fake news, raw ideology, and propaganda. Much truth-oriented material is also excluded. There is the large body of research-based "grey literature" in government and commerce that does not figure. Most of the research that is for local or national use, including most of the social sciences and humanities, is outside the main bibliometric collections. And as noted, they omit nearly all knowledge in languages other than English, including all Indigenous knowledge. English is the first language (L1) of 4.7 percent of the world's population, the third L1 after Mandarin Chinese (11.6 percent) and Spanish (5.9 percent). English is the first or second language of 18.2 percent of people. Yet 98 percent of Web of Science and 96 percent of Scopus are in English.

It is telling that the divide between knowledge that is inside global science, and outside global science, is the old colonial divide between the dominant powers and the rest.

> The understanding of the world by far exceeds the Western understanding of the world and therefore our knowledge of globalization is much less global than globalization itself...the more non-Western understandings of the world are identified, the more evident it becomes that there are still many others to be identified and hybrid understandings, mixing Western and non-Western components, are virtually infinite. Post-abyssal thinking thus stems from the idea that the diversity of the world is inexhaustible and that such diversity still lacks an adequate epistemology. In other words, the epistemological diversity of the world does not yet have a form....Post-abyssal thinking confronts the monoculture of modern science with the ecology of knowledges. (de Sousa Santos, 2007, pp. 64–66)

The languages of the colonized are all excluded. Yet Anglophone and Western countries do not monopolize all wisdom or have all the answers. Quite the contrary—arguably the Western model of economic development, in which the base level freedom is the freedom to accumulate private capital and all else is organized on that basis, is destroying Earth. In the question of broadening the charmed circle of knowledge, there is much at stake.

Signs of Change

Fortunately, everything is always changing and no system of power is fixed in stone. In the last thirty years science and knowledge have evolved remarkably. In this lies the possibility of a more inclusive and diverse science conversation. There is also the possibility that science will increasingly close down, becoming more closely annexed to national interests as a tool of geopolitics, fracturing the global science system and stunting scientific creativity.

The paradox of global science is this: Open networking has fostered all-round capacity development, but global hegemony, and the associated social, economic, and institutional processes, have imposed hierarchy and closure on the network. Hegemonic power has not stopped broad-based scientific development, but it has imposed a hierarchy of value and forced new science players to conform to the content requirements of the leading players. These content requirements reproduce patterns of dominance. Nevertheless, across the world there is significant pushback against the Anglophone control of science.

Pushback Against Hegemony in Science

We see this in Latin America and Africa, and in the Chinese policy emphasis on moving beyond catching up to the West to develop higher education and research with "Chinese characteristics." Latin American scholars who focus on epistemic injustice point out that when science is defined as work in English, Latin America seems impoverished. But that is quite wrong. When work in Spanish and Portuguese is included, the picture looks different.

> The mainstream has been self built on the supposition that outside there is backwardness and lack of academic value....The publishing system has become determinant in the distribution of scientific recognition by reinforcing a hierarchy built on the basis of a triple principle: institutional development, discipline and proficiency in English. (Beigel, 2014)

> Visibility alone is not enough. Effective presence requires being in such a state of visibility that anyone neglecting it will be faulted for carelessness, incompetence or ignorance....While much good and even extraordinary science does exist in non-OECD countries, it needs to be integrated at its right place within (real) world science. (Vessuri et al., 2014)

Figure 4.3a. *Science output growing* slower *than world average rate (5.38 percent per annum) in 2003–2022*

Average annual growth in science papers in each country compared to GDP (PPP) per capita in each country. Dotted line is world average GDP per capita in 2022 (US$20,694 current prices). Total science papers in 2022 shown by size of ball.

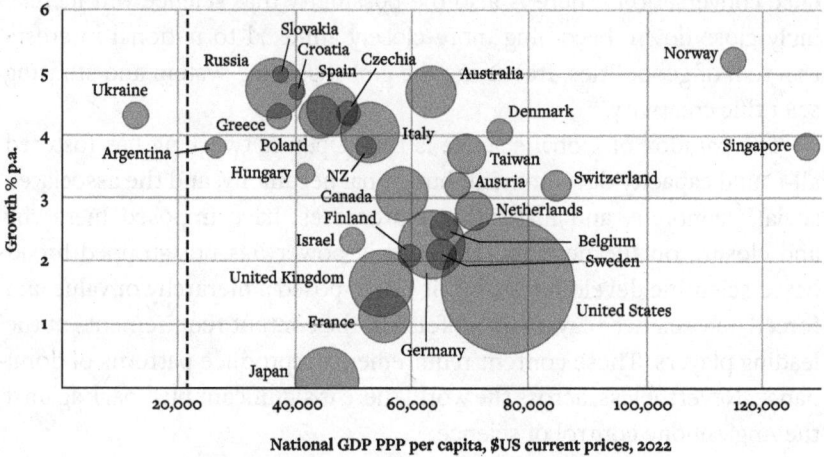

National GDP PPP per capita, $US current prices, 2022

Figure 4.3b. *Science output growing* faster *than world average rate (5.38 percent per annum) in 2003–2022*

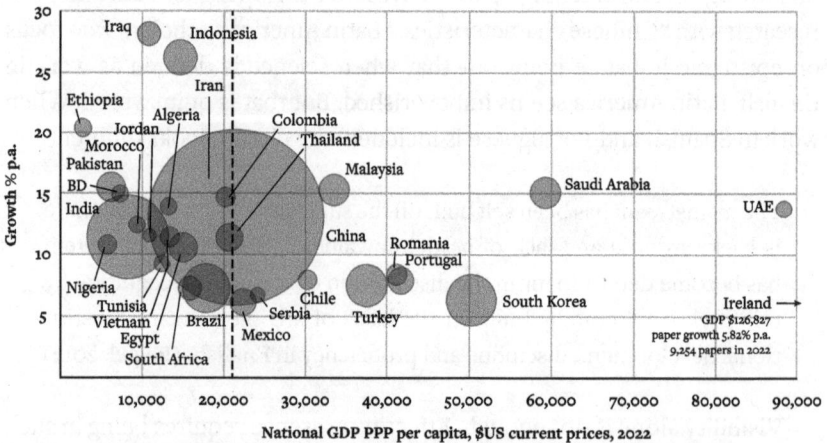

National GDP PPP per capita, $US current prices, 2022

Source: World Bank (2024); NSB (2024); Statistics Times (2024)
Countries producing more than 5,000 papers in 2022 only. NZ = New Zealand. UAE = United Arab Emirates. BD = Bangladesh.

Global Pluralization of Science Capacity

In the long run, all-round capacity development must foster a more inclusive and more diverse world of knowledge. Science output in China now massively exceeds that of the United States. India has passed Germany, the United Kingdom, and Japan to become third largest producer of science papers in Scopus. Brazil, Iran, Turkey, and South Korea—all operating outside the West—have achieved large-scale science infrastructure and output. But the pluralization goes further than this.

The growing diversity of scientific capacity is made clearer in Figures 4.3a and 4.3b. These present two contrasting groups of national science systems. In the two charts, the volume of national science output is indicated by the size of the ball. The vertical axis shows the rate of annual growth in the number of science papers between 2003 and 2022. The horizontal axis shows national income per head, which is a rough measure of the material capacity to provide scientific production. The dotted line is the world average income per head in 2022.

The first chart (Figure 4.3a) shows science systems that after 2003 grew *more slowly* than the world average rate of 5.38 percent per year. These systems were all established prior to 2003. They are mainly in Western countries with incomes well above the world average—in fact, only one of the slower-growing systems, Ukraine, had below-average GDP per head.

The second chart (Figure 4.3b) tells a different story. These are the national systems where science output is increasing *faster* than the world average rate. They are mostly relatively new science powers. Some of these countries have seen spectacular growth—almost 15.6 percent per year in Iran, one of the larger science systems, with 60,940 papers in 2022—not far short of France—and an incredible 26.2 percent in Indonesia, where the number of papers grew from just 387 in 2003 to 31,947 in 2022. Further, consider the diversification in terms of the economic indicator. Nearly half of these fast-growing science countries have incomes per head below the world average. The identifiable science systems include Ethiopia, with a GDP of only $2,813 per head in 2022, Nigeria ($5,862), Pakistan ($6,351) and Bangladesh ($7,398). Like mass higher education (Cantwell et al., 2018), global science has spread to middle-income countries and some low-income countries as well. This is empowering in the emerging countries, a process of democratization on the world scale.

Table 4.4. Top universities in STEM *research, Leiden ranking*

Papers in top 5 percent by citation rate, 2018–2021, in (1) physical sciences and engineering, (2) mathematics and computing, (3) biomedical and health sciences, (4) life and earth sciences.

University	System	(1) **Physical Sciences & Engineering**
Tsinghua U	China	1,054
Zhejiang U	China	783
Shanghai Jiao Tong U	China	736
Harbin IT	China	720
Huazhong U S&T	China	687
U Science & Technol	China	649
Tianjin U	China	635
U Chinese Acad Sci	China	621
MIT	USA	614
Xi'an Jiaotong U	China	593
Hunan U	China	582
Nanyang TU	Singapore	557
Central Southern U	China	551
National U Singapore	Singapore	538

University	System	(2) **Maths & Computing**
Tsinghua U	China	402
U Electron S&T	China	402
Harbin IT	China	265
Xidian U	China	263
Huazhong U S&T	China	259
Shanghai Jiao Tong U	China	228
Zhejiang U	China	228
Beihang U	China	228
Southeastern U	China	228
Nanyang TU	Singapore	220
Northwestern Poly U	China	219
Wuhan U	China	212
MIT	USA	193
Beijing IT	China	190

University	System	(3) Biomedical & Health Sciences
Harvard U	USA	3,027
U Toronto	Canada	1,154
Johns Hopkins U	USA	1,104
Stanford U	USA	1,017
U Pennsylvania	USA	1,009
U Calif, San Fran	USA	921
U Oxford	UK	829
U College London	UK	816
U Michigan	USA	792
Yale U	USA	732
U Calif San Diego	USA	709
U Texas HSC Hous	USA	699
Cornell U	USA	692
U Wash, Seattle	USA	675

University	System	(4) Life & Earth Sciences
China Agriculture U	China	343
Zhejiang U	China	335
U Chinese Acad Sci	China	288
Wageningen U	Netherlands	287
Northwest Ag & For U	China	285
China U Geoscience	China	261
Harvard U	USA	241
U Calif Davis	USA	236
Cornell U	USA	235
Nanjing Agricultural U	China	233
ETH Zurich	Switzerland	232
Tsinghua U	China	224
U Florida	USA	217
U Oxford	UK	215

Source: CWTS (2023)

Pluralization of Leading Science

There is another kind of pluralization at the top levels of science. This becomes clear when we look at universities that lead high-citation research, as measured by top 5 percent papers, in the science, technology, engineering, and mathematics (STEM) fields. Table 4.4 lists high-citation papers in four broad discipline clusters. The first page covers physical sciences and engineering, and the second page covers mathematics and computing. These lists are now absolutely dominated by China. The two leading Singapore universities also figure at the top of STEM research.

The top line of Table 4.4 represents a dramatic change in worldwide science power. Only five years earlier, eleven of the top universities in physical sciences and engineering were from the United States and one from China. Of the fourteen listed, eleven are now from China, two are from Singapore, and one is from the United States. It is not that American science has declined. What has happened is that Chinese science, fed by state investment, has developed quickly and moved past the United States. China is even more dominant in mathematics and the associated cluster of computing research.

These numbers have put the fear of God into the Trump and Biden administrations in the United States. It seems that previously it was acceptable in the United States for China's science to develop, a process long assisted by open mutually funded collaboration with US science, because it was expected that the collaborative contact would lead to the Westernization of China and it was never imagined that Chinese STEM research in the top universities would become stronger than in US universities. No doubt the reversal of the leadership table has been one key factor driving the American policy of decoupling in research in science and technology. In the United State, it is hoped that this decoupling will slow China's rise in STEM. However, while a weakening of collaboration tends to slow research development everywhere, China's science capacity is now well established, and the decoupling strategy is unlikely to achieve its goals.

However, China is by no means number one now in all research fields. As the second page of Table 4.4 shows, the story outside STEM is different. In biomedicine and health, Anglophone universities are still dominant. University of Toronto is number two in the world after Harvard. The first non-Anglophone European university is Copenhagen at twenty-seven and highest in China is Shanghai Jiao Tong at eighteen. Life and earth sciences are more geographically plural.

Geopolitics and Science

As the preceding discussion shows, in the last ten (and especially the last five) years governments have become more nation-bound and competitive about science. Haupt and Lee (2021) refer to a tension between collaborative global science, "scientific globalism," and "scientific nationalism," sometimes referred to as "technocratic nationalism," that is based on narrowly bordered interests. The geopolitical tensions between the United States and China, and the rise of national competitiveness in other countries which is often associated with nativism in identity, enhance technocratic or scientific nationalism. At its worst, this stance can translate into stigmatization of cross-border links simply because they are cross-border. Beyond that, the partial mental closure that is entailed in stigmatizing broader scientific links begins to shade into the pathologies of climate change denial and populist rejection of science and expertise.

In the United States, the China Initiative first established by the Trump government has entailed investigations shading into persecutions of some researchers with double scientific locations in the United States and China and has discouraged many others from establishing links. It has been associated with racial profiling of American citizens of Chinese heritage. Lee et al. (2021) show that a large minority of American scientists are now reluctant to work with Chinese scientists.

> Scientific discovery, fundamentally borderless, is being politically bordered. Geopolitical tensions between the US and China have spilled over into academic science, creating challenges for many scientists' ability to fully engage in research and innovation. (Lee et al., 2021)

Visas for doctoral students from China have been restricted, especially in research domains regarded as strategically significant, such as AI. The most recent data on research collaborations from the US National Science Board saw a decline in the number of joint China–United States papers, from 62,904 in 2020 to 58,546 in 2022, reversing a long pattern of growth (NSB, 2024). In many other Western countries, partly because of lobbying by US representatives, research links into China have been problematized and the policy emphasis has shifted from encouraging open collaboration to security politics and risk management. For example, in Australia there has been a sharp decline in the number of China-Australia projects funded by the Australian Research Council. All of this discourages collaborative projects and joint authorship and reduces university autonomy and academic freedom. Unregulated bottom-up cross-border relationships are less free to shape science.

From time to time, geopolitics have impacted science, but this is the first time since the advent of the Internet that the global science system has been compromised. The problems are not confined to relations between Euro-America and China. Scientific truth is the first casualty in war, whether it is a cold war or a hot war: The present hot war in Ukraine has generated an extraordinary level of Russian government-instigated disinformation, as well as breaking ties between Russian universities and their cross-border counterparts, driving some researchers out of Russia and halting much of the scientific investigation in Ukraine. The war between Israel and Palestine in Gaza has also touched academic conditions in many countries. Brexit took the United Kingdom out of the European Union and researchers in the United Kingdom had no access to the Horizon Europe research program. British participation has now resumed but has been weakened.

Conclusion: A More Truly Global Science

So, where does global science go from here?

The science debate has just begun. Much will depend on it. Global science has great potential but presently has both upsides and downsides. Scientific knowledge is collective, collaborative, and accumulative, a common good that crosses over the separated self-interests of individuals, institutions, companies, and nations. At best it looks beyond a nation-bound perspective and thinks at the level of the world as a whole. It is vital to defend and advance this potential. Since the Internet began at the end of the 1980s, global science has been open, largely free to evolve, and facilitated the emergence of diverse national nodes and scientific voices. Science can talk truth to power, cutting across all the rubbish in the political space and social media, the fake news and manipulative populism. The reflexivity of science, the mode of judging science, is the test of truth. This is tremendously valuable.

But global science is also culturally fixed; almost exclusively Western in its inherited traditions, language, and norms; neo-colonial in form and in the assumptions and relations and world views that it fosters. Science is steeply hierarchical inside the global system and has generated a large hinterland, its "non-scientific" other, of knowledge that is excluded. This "other" comprises the vast majority of human knowledge, including almost everything in languages other than English, and endogenous knowledge/ Indigenous knowledge from everywhere. This includes Indigenous under-standings of land, nature, and ecology, which are often more constructive than accumulative capitalism. We lose much by excluding this diversity.

In short, autonomous global science has been hegemonic and exclusive. Autonomous scientists have been the excluders, though aided and abetted by the publishing and bibliometric world. Now geopolitics threatens to subtract the autonomy of science, lock it into national silos, weaken or fragment the global system. So where do we go from here? We defend the autonomy of global science as best we can—from technological national-ism and from commercial publishers. We push for the further opening of science, not closure. We maintain open cooperation between scientists all over the world. No cold war in science.

The ways forward to more democratic relations of power in science are genuine open access publishing, not fake "gold open access" where the authors have to pay charges to the publisher, and a global conversation based on multiple languages. Publishers can use the emerging software to translate knowledge in languages other than English into English, and knowledge in English into other languages. There is no reason not to pub-lish all the leading disciplinary journals and books in multiple languages. In face of global problems, knowledge and cooperation are all we have. That makes it essential to bring all of the voices, all of the different ways of seeing, all of the insights and ideas, into the common conversation.[1]

References

Beigel, F. (2014). Introduction: Current tensions and trends in the World Scientific System. *Current Sociology*, 62(5), 617–25. https://doi. org/10.1177/0011392114548640

Birnholtz, J.P. (2007). When do researchers collaborate? Toward a model of collaboration propensity. *Journal of the American Society for Information Science and Technology*, 58(14), 2226–39. https://doi.org/10.1002/asi.20684

Bornmann, L., Adams, J., & Leydesdorff, L. (2018). The negative effects of citing with a national orientation in terms of recognition: National and international citations in natural-sciences papers from Germany, the Netherlands, and the UK. *Journal of Informetrics*, 12(3), 931–49. https://doi. org/10.1016/j.joi.2018.07.009

Cantwell, B., Marginson, S., & Smolentseva, A. (Eds.). (2018). *High participation systems of higher education*. Oxford University Press.

Castells, M. (2000). *The information age: Economy, society, and culture. Vol. 1. The rise of the network society* (2nd ed.). Blackwell.

Chen, K., Zhang, Y., & Fu, X. (2019). International research collaboration: An emerging domain of innovation studies? *Research Policy*, 48(1), 149–68. https://doi.org/10.1016/j.respol.2018.08.005

CWTS (Centre for Work and Technology Studies). (2023). CWTS *Leiden ranking 2023*. University of Leiden. https://www.leidenranking.com/ranking/2023/list

Dale, R. (2005). Globalisation, knowledge economy and comparative education. *Comparative Education*, 41(2), 117–49. http://www.jstor.org/stable/30044528

de Sousa Santos, B. (2007). Beyond abyssal thinking: From global lines to ecologies of knowledges. *Review (Fernand Braudel Center)*, 30(1), 45–89. https://www.jstor.org/stable/40241677

Elsevier. (2024). Scopus Content. https://www.elsevier.com/products/scopus/content

Georghiou, L. (1998). Global cooperation in research. *Research Policy*, 27(6), 611–26. https://doi.org/10.1016/S0048-7333(98)00054-7

Graf, H., & Kalthaus, M. (2018). International research networks: Determinants of country embeddedness. *Research Policy*, 47(7), 1198–214. https://doi.org/10.1016/j.respol.2018.04.001

Gramsci, A. (1971). *Selections from the prison notebooks*. (Q. Hoare and G. Nowell Smith, Ed. and Trans.).

Haupt, J.P., & Lee, J.J. (2021). Geopolitical tensions and global science: Understanding US-China scientific research collaboration through scientific nationalism and scientific globalism. In J.J. Lee (Ed.), *US power in international higher education*. Rutgers University Press.

Klavans, R., & Boyack, K. (2017). The research focus of nations: Economic vs. altruistic motivations. *PLoS ONE*, 12(1), Article e0169383. https://doi.org/10.1371/journal.pone.0169383

Lee, J.J., Li, X., & Staff of Committee of 100, (2021). Racial profiling among scientists of Chinese descent and consequences for the US scientific community. University of Arizona. https://www.committee100.org/wp-content/uploads/2021/10/C100-Lee-Li-White-Paper-FINAL-FINAL-10.28.pdf

Luhmann, N. (2012). *Theory of society*. Vol. 1 (Rhodes Barrett, Trans.). Stanford University Press.

Marginson, S. (2014). University rankings and social science. *European Journal of Education*, 49(1), 45–59. https://doi.org/10.1111/ejed.12061

Marginson, S. (2022a). What is global higher education? *Oxford Review of Education*, 48(4), 492–517. https://doi.org/10.1080/03054985.2022.2061438

Marginson, S. (2022b). What drives global science? The four competing narratives. *Studies in Higher Education*, 47(8), 1566–84. https://doi.org/10.1080/03075079.2021.1942822

Marginson, S. (2022c). Space and scale in higher education: The glonacal agency heuristic revisited. *Higher Education*, 84(6), 1365–95. https://doi.org/10.1007/s10734-022-00955-0

May, R.M. (1997). The scientific wealth of nations. *Science*, 275(5301), 793–96. https://doi.org/10.1126/science.275.5301.793

Melin, G. (2000). Pragmatism and self-organization: Research collaboration on the individual level. *Research Policy*, 29(1), 31–40. https://doi.org/10.1016/S0048-7333(99)00031-1

NSB (National Science Board). (2024). Publications output: US trends and international comparisons. *Science and engineering indicators 2024 report*. https://ncses.nsf.gov/pubs/nsb202333/downloads

OECD (Organisation for Economic Co-operation and Development). (2023). *Education at a glance 2023: OECD indicators*. OECD Publishing.

Olechnicka, A., Ploszaj, P., & Celińska-Janowicz, D. (2019). *The geography of scientific collaboration*. Routledge.

Powell, J.J.W., Baker, D.P., & Fernandez, F. (Eds.) (2017). *The century of science: Vol. 33. The global triumph of the research university*. International Perspectives on Education and Society. Emerald Publishing Limited. https://doi.org/10.1108/S1479-3679201733

Statistics Times (2024). List of Countries by GDP (PPP) per capita. https://statisticstimes.com/economy/countries-by-gdp-capita-ppp.php

Vessuri, H., Guédon, J.C., & Cetto, A.M. (2014). Excellence or quality? Impact of the current competition regime on science and scientific publishing in Latin America and its implications for development. *Current Sociology*, 62(5), 647–65. https://dx.doi.org/10.1177/0011392113512839

Wagner, C.S., & Leydesdorff, L. (2005). Network structure, self-organization, and the growth of international collaboration in science. *Research Policy*, 34(10), 1608–18. https://doi.org/10.1016/j.respol.2005.08.002

Wagner, C.S., Park, H.W., & Leydesdorff, L. (2015). The continuing growth of global cooperation networks in research: A conundrum for national governments. *PLoS ONE*, 10(7), Article e0131816. https://doi.org/10.1371/journal.pone.0131816

Wagner, C.S., Whetsell, T.A., & Leydesdorff, L. (2017). Growth of international collaboration in science: Revisiting six specialties. *Scientometrics*, 110(3), 1633–52. https://doi.org/10.1007/s11192-016-2230-9

Winkler, A.E., Glänzel, W., Levin, S., & Stephan, P. (2015). The diffusion of the internet and the increased propensity of teams to transcend institutional and national borders. *Revue économique*, 66(1), 115–42. https://doi.org/10.3917/reco.661.0115

WoS (Web of Science). (2024). Web of Science Core Collection. https://mjl.
clarivate.com/collection-list-downloads

World Bank (2024). *GDP per capita, ppp [purchasing power parity] (current
international $)*. [Data Set]. https://data.worldbank.org/indicator/ny.gdp.pcap
.pp.cd

Notes

1 This chapter is based on a paper delivered online to a conference at the
University of Regina, Canada, May 4, 2023.

CHAPTER 5
FOR WHAT AND FOR WHOM ARE UNIVERSITIES?
A LATINOAMERICAN PERSPECTIVE

Consuelo Chapela

> *Our fight is no longer just for freedom, justice and democracy,*
> *it is in fact for life itself…*
> *Because we are optimists we fight.*
> *Because we have hope in a destiny, we are critical.*
> *But we do not accept authoritarian optimism or hope*
> *without critical thinking…*
> *The new thing is coherence…*
> —**PABLO GONZÁLEZ CASANOVA** (in Mateos-Vega 2018;
> Hernández Navarro, 2020; Ortiz Tejeda, 2023)[1,2]

AT FIRST GLANCE, THE PRESENT STATE OF MANY LATINO-American universities shows common problems with other pre- and post-COVID universities in Europe and North America. Problems resulting from a historic turn materialized in agonizing neoliberal capitalism that crashed in circumstances of its own making. When lunatics run the asylum (Chomsky, 2017; Chomsky & Barsamian, 2023), they overexploit people and the planet, instrumentalizing a loud and relentless silencing of words where not even shouting can be heard. This static noise silences words and increasingly displaces meaning at all levels, from families and barrios to schools and universities, as social reproduction *dispositifs* or devices and technologies of the self (Agamben, 2015; Foucault, 1996). Agonistic capitalism materialized in an unleashed phantom of "artificial general intelligence" capable of creating Frankenstein-like software such as "generative pre-trained transformers" (GPT), for example, in cyber "social networks." The result stripped humanity of its core transcendental definitions such as dignity, collective life, and solidarity, resulting in sad individuals fearing a future without hope and a death without mercy. Just listen to the desperate screams of individuals uprooted from meaningful words through an endless machination of lies, forgeries, fictions, and intended and unintended errors. We are witnessing a historic turn where Julius Caesar's and Napoleon's "divide and conquer" rule has been replaced by neoliberals' "confuse and profit" tactic, even when the possibility of profiting at the expense of humans and the earth is coming to an end: "no planet = no profit." This is a world where, as Don Pablo González Casanova said, and I paraphrase here, today, far more revolutionary than choosing whether to "be" left, centre-left, centre-right, feminist, masculinist, anarchist, socialist, communist, post-post-meta modernist, critical, environmentalist, vegan, or other is *to choose coherence* (Ortiz Tejeda, 2023).

As Norbert Elías (1939/2016) and others propose, a coherent understanding of reality cannot be attained without tracing what happened to have us become what we now are. We do this by looking for "social configurations" built up in reciprocal relationships among individuals and social groups. Tracing such configurations is similar to what Bourdieu (Bourdieu & Passeron, 1990) described as pedagogic work followed by pedagogic action in social fields, and can be a step toward the possibility of defining, following Ernesto Laclau (2005), the limits of one's totality, one entire being, in order to find out what is beyond those limits, in the search for dialogue between insiders—those with symbolic power inside our totality—and outsiders—those with their own symbolic power inside their totality—where each considers the other an outsider.

If we do not travel on this trajectory, we cannot assure coherent or consistent analysis of the specific reality of Latinoamerican universities. These institutions are disregarded by universities in the Occidental North which set their limits, including language and racial criteria, as outsiders and are, sometimes, completely ignored. On the other side, from the Latinoamerican universities' perspective, due to power struggles in the academic, scientific, and economic fields, Occidental North universities are always-present outsiders.

In order to get some coherence in an attempt to address, from a Latinoamerican perspective, the question "What are universities for?" I have added a set of linked questions aided by Laclau (Butler et al., 2011): For whom do universities exist? Who sets their limits? What is the intentionality embedded in defining the limits of the university? Is there *a* university? Who belongs to the inside establishment, and who are the outsiders? How does the insider-outsider relationship work? With those questions in mind, I consider some socio-historical perspectives because, as we name it, the present is already in the past and subject to historical scrutiny. I do so with the final objective of finding an answer to the question that I consider should always be at the core of all human action: How does an action, or how does what we do, advance epistemological and hermeneutic justice? Specifically: How do public autonomous Latinoamerican universities advance or prevent epistemological and hermeneutic justice?

I propose that there is not such a thing as *the* university, but "*spatialities,*" as defined by critical geography (Santos, 2000): systems of objects, practices, and intentions conforming to place and territory. Spatialities are formed with the intent to understand and change the lived world through embodied historically situated practices. Those practices are determined by ongoing power struggles. Spatialities are capable of bringing about, or hindering, the possibility of searching for epistemologic and hermeneutic justice, which public, autonomous Latinoamerican universities, in one way or another, claim as their purpose.

Like other complete entities, the limits of such spatialities (and the site of the inside establishment versus those excluded, the outsiders) is determined by the power centres that decide the meaning of things of the world. Perhaps that is why Bologna is often identified as the beginning of all universities, but I will argue it is not. Here are the tasks assigned to current institutionalized universities: research, useful for whomever supports the institution; teaching, leading to the consecration of professionals through titles and canonries incarnated in professional bodies; and "culture-extension," often meaning the diffusion of selected bits of academic knowledge outside the institution's boundaries, never fully releasing their academic or scientific secrets. Such work had been done in different parts of the world well before the European invasions of the Americas.

For example, in his studies of the history of universities, Carlos Tünnermann Bernheim (1991) mentions the Brahmanical schools in India (fifth century BCE), the Academy and the Lyceum in Greece (fourth century BCE), the Alexandria School of Egypt (second century BCE), and the Roman Empire Juridic Schools (25 BCE to the third century CE). In the sixth century CE, China's higher education implemented examinations to award titles, and aspirants to a position in the public service needed to compete with other aspirants thorough public service examinations. Across the Pacific, the Mayans' Telpoxcalli (third century), the Aztecs' calmecac (fourteenth century), and the Incas' Yachaywasi (fifteenth century) also established and managed education ranging from basic schooling for children to specialized subjects for adults (León-Portilla, 1961; Mariátegui, 1993).

Universities developed alongside and around places where people were able to narrate and describe the world in written words.[3] For whom were those places where privileged knowledge accounted for prestige and for privileged spaces in society? Let's get a little closer to one of them: the Alexandria School of Egypt.

From the beginning, the Alexandria School of Egypt, constituted by the Alexandria Museum and including the attached largest library of antiquity, was declared to be "open to all." But what in this case was meant by "all"? What were the "limits of such totality"? Who were considered part of the establishment and who were the outsiders? The Alexandria Museum, a public temple of the Muses, was a place where nine highly specialized Muses inspired understanding of complex existential and practical problems of reality. Eight of them, Caliope (eloquence, beauty), Clio (history), Erata (poetry), Euterpe (music), Melpomene (tragedy), Polyhymnia (sacred songs, discretion, silence), Thalía (comedy), and Terpsichore (dance and oral poetry) specialized in what we probably could equate with the humanities and arts. It was only the ninth Muse, Urania, that represented the fields of science and technology.

The Museum, or temple, was a place to read, to think, to discuss, to confront ideas, to argue, and to teach and learn from the people who gathered there. It also contained many rolls of papyrus and parchments still tainted by blood since they were forcibly taken a few times for the knowledge they contained, but also many others were taken for greed or glory.

This temple of the Muses was a poetic place where, two centuries before Christ, the movement from speaking to writing was encouraged. Lacking a common grammar, oral reading, with pauses and using varying intonations, was the only way of making sense of what was written. Inspired by the Muses, the performance of reading aloud for others or for the same reader, was an open act of communication within this privileged space.

Similarly, reading required a high degree of interpretation by the reader, on top of copyists' interpretations, first on papyrus and later on parchments and then on books chained to shelves. In the Museum these documents held and told stories bringing together voices from distant parts of the world. But they also suffered the torture of continuous interpretation and eventually became unrecognizable in a kind of epistemicide of thought. Interpretation required consultation with whomever was around. So, the temple became a place of discussion, knowledge interchange, and construction; of investigation and teaching among teachers and students, with hierarchies and chains of command…thus, one ancient public institutionalized university, is it not?[4]

But, who can "all" mean in the Museum? Who was considered "all of us," or even a "person" capable of speaking and listening at the foot of the Muses? What was the meaning of "public" when to be part of "all" a person needed wealth? This restricted the gift of reading to those capable of conducting themselves as aristocrats, since the Museum was built in Alexandria's Bruquion, the neighbourhood of palaces. Such exclusive elitism is very much what has happened in other past and present institutions of higher education.

After many Ptolomean regencies, Roman war campaigns set fire to Alexandria, including the Museum, the library, statues of the Muses, books, papyrus and parchment scrolls, everything.[5] Later in history, other libraries were also set on fire: Constantinople (1204), Bebelplatz in Berlin (1933), Baghdad (2003), and today in Gaza (2024) among others.[6] Today, fire is no longer needed since in a war rage against meaning (that is, coherence and truth), words burn in other kinds of fires such as TikTok, Facebook, X (formerly Twitter), Netflix, YouTube, and other platforms of social media.

The Islamic higher education centre in Baghdad and the Al-Andalus in today's Spain in the ninth century had already accomplished the task of becoming institutionalized universities. According to Mejía-Ricart (1981), they were equipped with large libraries and astronomical observatories and provided examinations and awarded diplomas; however, they did not grant teaching authorization. According to Tünnermann Bernheim (1991), in Cairo, al-Azhar Mosque, founded in 988, was the oldest Islamic higher education institution. It became famous because of the quality of its teaching in theology, grammar, rhetoric, maths, literature, logic, and jurisprudence, and also for developing the art of medicine far beyond what existed at the time. Islamic institutionalized universities were also renowned for the sciences and humanities advanced by scientists such as Avicenna, Averröes, and Maimonides, who developed Aristotelean teachings trying to reach faith through reason and opening the way to Occidental philosophy. In the caliphate of Toledo, Arabs, Christians, and Jews worked together in the famous Toledo School of Translators. In this way, the Arabs absorbed Greek culture and, for about five centuries, cultivated it as well as the original Islamic advances in the Iberian Peninsula.

Who defined such limits? From all these historic developments of knowledge capital, experience, and educational institutions begins the story of the university, as told not by a Europe that still, at the time, was not Europe, but only centuries later, alongside the imperialistic invasions of America, Asia, Africa, and the Pacific.

As Arabs and Romans left, Europe was a collection of scattered towns, with abbeys and monasteries safeguarding and copying books. Carlomagno[7] conceived the school as a means to achieve homogeneity and unity from Italy to the Nordic tribes. This is the beginning of the Schola Palatina, meaning palace school. The Schola Palatina in the late eighth and early ninth centuries, adopted the Greek liberal arts *trivium* (of grammar, rhetoric, and dialectic) and *quadrivium* (arithmetic, geometry, astronomy, and music) which lasted a long time in European higher education. This school admitted royalty and also the *nutritii*, children of the nobility who ate and studied in the palace. The Schola was not a specific part of the palace; the teaching and learning happened throughout the building.

What was this university for? Even though the Schola Palatina did not last long, Carlomagno's use of teaching with specific political ends set an antecedent of the planned use of higher education as a *dispositive* or space of resolution for hegemonic power.

As urbanization occurred between the eleventh and fourteenth centuries in what we know now as Europe, artisans gathered in cities where their skills were required. To protect themselves and share problems, skills, and knowledge, they organized guilds and brotherhoods to fight their way among other similar organizations. As the rising bourgeoisie demanded more learning opportunities, some teaching moved from monks to secular teachers. A fever for knowledge grew in artisans, merchants, and their families, who were the unconscious heirs of the Islamic interest in learning. They were also outsiders willing to be accepted in this developing enterprise of education. The new mobility movement of young and older people allowed them the privilege of accessing books, meeting other people, and gaining new knowledge, learning to read, write, and do arithmetic. Some secular teachers had the benefit of having some noble or church relative; others belonged to a strong guild. Such advantages encouraged learning about whatever was available: thinking, questioning, and confronting many different ideas. The streets and other public spaces became places of knowledge exchange and development. Without the burden of being tied to a building, learning was informal, fluid, and mobile. Able to move from one place to another, without purpose-built structures, teachers and students relied on monastic spaces or private libraries, without access to tools or equipment to help in the observation of the world. Nevertheless, not to be confined to buildings gave teachers some autonomy; teaching became another skilled craft in high demand, with the same values and problems as other occupations. I think it is very important to recognize how the changes in teachers' autonomy vis-à-vis their dependence on monasteries and monks, influenced university development at this time.

As opposed to the Latin term *singuli*, which refers to individuals, at first, *universitas*[8] referred not to a totality of knowledges but to a collection of people—in this case, students and teachers bound by similar objectives, skills, and challenges—and as such as a space, as defined in previous paragraphs. Threats to their integrity could come from what they said or wrote, which could lead to them to be signalled, for example, as blasphemers, sorcerers with relations with the devil, or traitors, requiring them to build a community and seek immunity from the emperor or the Pope, which they frequently achieved. This protection increased until they gained exclusive prerogatives, such as exemptions from taxes, unlike other guilds. The intellectual guild could use their dispersion capability of moving elsewhere as a tool against other guilds, enhancing in this way their exclusive powers. Yet, these immunities worked also to attach such intellectual guilds to the politically and socially powerful. Ties to sources of such immunity and financial support remain to the present day, hindering and compromising the autonomy of what we now call academic freedom.

The intellectual guild, composed mostly of outsiders coming from different places and speaking Latin as the common language, needed to fight for survival and development; however, this fight was not a revolutionary fight, not as today's students struggle for the right to knowledge. The street functioned as an intellectual arena in which to realize the institutionalized university goals: teaching, investigating, and extending knowledge, probably in a democratic way. However, the guilds ignored the cultural capital of the students. It was assumed that common people lacked the necessary knowledge, language, thinking, and discursive skills to bridge the social limits of a nascent intellectual totality.

Most universities today remain aristocratic. From its etymological origin: *aristos* (the best) and *kratos* (power or force), ancient and current aristocrat institutionalized universities impose the meaning of what is best in order to shape its totality and safeguard its limits, defining who and what counts as the establishment and who and what remain outside. Outsiders may also refer to other university spatialities such as the Universities of Bologna and Paris. The Bologna model focused on the interests of students organized in "nations," which conformed to collegiate ways of decision-making and electing their student-rector (*universitas scholarium*). The Paris model, called by Francis Bacon a "teachers' jail," centred on teachers (*universitas magistrorum*) and theology, was born within the Notre-Dame Cathedral schools to attend to the doctrinal needs of the Catholic Church (Tünnermann Bernheim, 1991). The University of Salamanca adopted the Bologna model and later passed it on to Latinoamerican universities which, at that time, were founded to meet the academic necessities of people born to Spanish parents in Spanish Viceroyalties such as Mexico and Peru. Ever since then, knowledge control in universities has been political, as is every discourse, even empty discourses. So, university space is political.

After the time of the European invasions, and after the French Revolution and the beginning of capitalism following the creation of nation states, Napoleon completely reorganized France's educational system. In 1808, Napoleon's creation, the Imperial University, became the monopoly of an expansionist state that eliminated philosophy and literature from the curricula (Cobo, 1979). In the Imperial University, it was the state that decided ethics, curricula, and pedagogies as an explicit means to control the moral and political content of public thought and opinion,[9] resulting in a centralized, hierarchic, and, indeed, bureaucratic institution. This was formed by a constellation of separate professional schools without any cohesive nucleus. Here was another university breaking completely with Paris, Bologna, and other previous universities. This Napoleonic model was adopted by Latinoamerican universities after their independence movements in the nineteenth century and maintained partially until the student movements of the 1960s.

In Berlin, in the eighteenth century, the emperor asked Wilhelm von Humboldt to create a new model of the university capable of raising a renewed spirit of inquiry in a context of academic freedom. This included a close relationship between teaching and research as well as between objective science and subjective development through the use of maieutic or Socratic pedagogies (Tünnermann Bernheim, 1991). This model was designed to achieve a balance between the state and the institution.

North American universities, emerging during the capitalist boom of the nineteenth century, adopted von Humboldt's model in private schemes and included providing loans to students as well as Dewey's proposal of linking work and study. President Lincoln promoted agriculture and engineering. State colleges connected strongly to communities through university extension programs. Here, the introduction of the specialized department as a basic academic unit broke with the idea of interdependent knowledges to understand reality. After the Second World War, student enrolment grew, allowing for the expansion of the already profitable institutionalized universities, creating systems resembling corporate enterprises, and, as such, changing the overall scope of their limits. They became a kind of trampoline or springboard to catapult new outsiders into the establishment.

Turning to Latinoamerica we find that, during the imperialistic Spanish invasion (sixteenth through nineteenth centuries), universities were a major means of defining non-Spanish people as "used-and-disposed of" (dispossessed) outsiders. In the context of imperial reconfiguration, Latinoamerican universities became the new outsiders to Anglo colonialism. However, insiders and outsiders only exist in relationship to each other. In the twentieth century in some Latinoamerican university spaces, scholars became aware that we, academics, were now the establishment, and the former imperialists were now the outsiders.

The Latinoamerican University, thought of as one socio-historical entity, is a result of epistemicidal machinery that came into operation in the sixteenth century during the Spanish invasion and genocide in *Abya Yala*, which, in Dulegaya language in the Darién region of Panama, means "land of plenty," also named *Cemanahuac* in Nahuatl, meaning "near the water" or "between waters," corresponding to collective attachment to natural ontologies characteristic of original Mesoamerican nations. Abya Yala, Cemanahuac, were desecrated when named "America" after the explorer Amerigo Vespucci, marking this continent as an invader's asset, something to grab and use, something to clean of uncomfortable trash, including Indigenous language, philosophy, and other inconvenient markers of identity. This is very much part of the logic of nascent capitalism with tentacles extended, in the name of their own gods and kings, to other places in Asia, Africa, and the Pacific. In the twentieth century, now ascended to the gang of past and present imperialists, "Uncle Sam" grabbed for himself even the name of a whole continent: America. In this paper, when I use the signal "America" I am signifying Abya Yala, Cemenahuac, from Kanata (Canadian) to Mapuche (Chilean) territory, where struggles against imperialism, colonialism, and epistemicide are today in different stages of struggle and success.

In 1553, the first inland viceroyal universities were founded as Royal and Pontifical Universities in Peru and in Mexico, following the Salamanca model, for the *criollos*, Spanish children born in America who would be trained to reproduce colonial epistemologies in both colonizers and the colonized. The criollos at the time were outsiders both in relation to Spain as well as in relation to the invaded nations. However, in relation to the invaded nations, they were the establishment capable of killing and robbing what they constructed as the indigent outsiders. Perhaps because some criollos broke their links with their Spanish ancestry, they were finding and founding new identities. As a result, the colonial universities as a whole became different institutions. After independence, they evolved as national state universities, adopting the Napoleonic model. It is interesting to note here, that the criollos actively participated in Latinoamerican independence movements.

In 1918 in Córdoba, Argentina, a students' popular movement pushed the university in a new direction: giving identity to a free, public, autonomous, collegiate, Latinoamerican university. This movement involved students, parents, community members, and other former outsiders, who raised their voices and broke the spell that kept the various universities in the hands of the aristocracies, from the Brahmanical to the North American. The Córdoba movement called for a university that was to be for everyone. This time, the totality understood in the word "all" meant the expansion of limits through the inclusion of students from all economic and social classes, thus bringing to university all knowledges that led to new understandings of past and present problems and the spread of university knowledge to all of society.

However, at the beginning of the twentieth century, the unity of knowledge in the university was fragmented with the creation of departments as part of the North American university model, which also merged with an authoritarian Napoleonic model, already rooted for more than a century in Latinoamerica. This merger occurred in the context of a growing interest in Marxism, Gramsci, the Frankfurt school, existentialism, and revolutionary Latinoamerican thought and action. This situation lasted until the 1960s when student movements took place simultaneously in Latinoamerica and Europe. These movements reconstructed the idea of the university where the totality included teachers, students, and surrounding communities and their problems. The dark decade of coups and authoritarian governments caused academic migration within Latinoamerican countries and stimulated critical diverse and revolutionary thinking, including, for example, Mariátegui, Quijano, Paulo Freire, Che Guevara, Maoism, Cuban and Nicaraguan revolutionary movements, the Theology of Liberation, and the redefinition of the universities as diverse spatialities[10] mirroring a society on the one hand with an increasing access to critical higher education because of the strengthening of the public university to fulfil the needs of the state, and, on the other hand, nursing highly conservative private universities.

In the 1970s, the boom in university enrolment and the "technologies of education" filtered into the Latinoamerican university, heralding thirty years of neoliberal governments there and in most corners of the world (Tünnermann Bernheim, 2003). In contrast, but also in the seventies, a school of popular education emerged, using problem-based learning and linking the three university tasks, teaching, research, and service, to communities informed by pedagogic models in which teachers became companions and guides to students' construction of knowledge.[11]

During the decade of 1980, public universities maintained and strengthen links with communities. However, neoliberal agencies, such as the Organisation for Economic Co-operation for Development (OECD) and the International Monetary Fund, dictated technocratic economic and educational policies favourable to capitalist development. Again, new ways of curricular design, academic evaluation, and research topics were imposed by outsiders. Since individual academic productivity was tied to the salaries of researchers and teachers, collegiate academic discussion began to decline. This lack of academic dialogue led to fast research for the publication of papers that were increasingly less innovative, profound, critical, or committed to social problems. Obtaining funding began to be part of the researchers' regular activities, and, indeed, through financing, it is again the outsiders who define what is to be investigated in our countries. This worsened with the COVID-19 pandemic closures (2020–22) where new means of coloniality emerged, such as teaching through Zoom, Meet, or other platforms, and, indeed, the replacement of libraries and writing by easy information searches, cumulative information, and superficial essays where the use of "cut-and-paste" is easier than developing written language.

Perhaps because of the richness of our cultures, the strength of our sense of rebellion, and following our history of counterculture, Latinoamerican public universities' research, teaching, and social service outside the international mainstream aim at social and epistemological justice and the enforceability of rights, developing Latinoamerican epistemologies such as Critical Emancipatory Education (Freire, 2009), Philosophy of Liberation (Dussel, 2011), Social and Community Medicine (Laurell, 1981; Spinelli, 2004), Critical "Nuestroamericana" Pedagogy (Santos, 2017), and Critical Geography and the Nature of Space (Santos, 2000).

What we have now are universities immersed in a context of neoliberal productivity, where academic people are workers and "products"—such as a publication or a grant—are better valued than the understanding and incidence, for example, in human, social, or justice problems. Seminars, workshops, face-to-face debate, field work with people, or peer group study are often replaced by screen-teaching and the use of artificial intelligence, electronic aids, and social media. We are living a post-modern, post-truth colonization, where the result of lies, half-truths, and falsification materialize, for example, in lonely students attached to their selfies, needing "likes," fearful of digital exclusion, looking for comfort, fun, easy stuff, banalities, confused and lost in the digital network. Teachers are trapped by requirements for productivity, postposing retirement, and tied to computers. Highly qualified young people are unemployed. There is a lack of academic leadership and a lack of trust in administrative bureaucracy, which includes both rewards and penalties. All this in a perverted system of academic communication, information storage and retrieval, with AI increasingly filtering and defining the spatialities of public universities. One must concede that, as the colonizer is the same, this situation is turning "democratic," since, perhaps trespassing or merging totality limits, it is now widely spread in Anglo-Saxon and Latinoamerican academic life.

But at the same time, young people are eager for reason and illumination to wake them up. They have a great need for love and kindness, perhaps eagerly waiting for some help to unplug their desire for knowledge and to spring free their curiosity. Teachers are longing for the extraordinary feeling of teaching something relevant to human dignity, for reflection and debate in real time and real spaces. Perhaps everybody is longing for a library as the heart of a community of meaning, creating spatialities, where everyone's voice has a space on library shelves and in *scriptoriums* where normative knowledge and knowing fades in the light of virtue and coherence, dignifying internationalities, and where practices include oration and debate.

The Latinoamerican university strives to find its knowledge limits in dialogue with other knowledges, in the search of something that for millennia has been denied: the mutual inclusion of knowledges valid for understanding and solving present problems of reality; it is not possible anymore to understand them as individual problems or problems that will not affect everyone. To give human life a future, universities, institutionalized or not, have to stop looking at screens, to wake up, to revive forgotten words, and go to the other in the flesh, to build a common house for all: to move from the singular "I" to the inclusive "we." To make sure that we recognize the human being and humanity as a species different than AI, because humans can love the other and care for the other; because humans can live collectively, building up, searching, meeting, advancing together, fighting for utopias; can develop indignation and dignity, understanding as *verstehen*, sense and meaning of the world; because humans can cry when burying a loved one.

Perhaps aware of our physicality, as professor Sajeev John told us (during the 2023 University of Regina international symposium: *What Are Universities For?*) that there is no molecule without atoms sharing electrons, we know that we would be nothing without sharing electrons, we would not be molecules, not cells, not tissues, not brains, not words: nothing. We need to share electrons and words to create a space where all exclusions join and fight together for life and living, no race exclusions, no gender exclusions, no body-size exclusions, no nationality exclusions. We need to gather all exclusions and work together for life and living.

This is the hermeneutic and epistemological task for university spatialities, unavoidable in the search for epistemic and hermeneutic justice. Above all, it is necessary to learn again, and again, what Don Pablo Gonázlez Casanova taught us: The key to living a meaningful life is "to fight and love...We are facing an unprecedented period in the history of humanity. Our fight is no longer just for freedom, justice and democracy, it is in fact for life itself" (Mateos-Vega, 2018).

To coherently learn to fight and love, we need public, free, inclusive, autonomous, critical, committed to social problems, close to people, sensitive to suffering, responsible, articulated interdisciplinary, networked, high-quality universities for all, providing spacialities of hope.

References

Agamben, G. (2015). ¿Qué es un dispositivo? [What is a dispositive?]. Anagrama.

Bourdieu, P., & Passeron, J.C. (1990). Reproduction in education, society and culture (2nd ed.) SAGE.

Bourdieu, P. (1992). La opinión pública no existe [Public opinion does not exist]. Debates en sociología, 17, 301–11. https://doi.org/10.18800/debatesensociologia .199201.013

Butler, J., Laclau, E., & Zizek, S. (2003). Contingencia, hegemonía, universalidad. Diálogos contemporáneos en la izquierda [Contingency, hegemony, universality: Contemporary dialogues on the left] (Cristina Sardoy & Craciela Homs, Trans.). Fondo de Cultura Económica.

Chomsky, N. (2017). Réquiem por el sueño americano. Los diez principios de la concentración de la riqueza y el poder [Requiem for the American dream: The ten principles of concentration of richness and power] (Magdalena Palmer, Trans.). Sexto Piso.

Chomsky, N., & Barsamian, D. (2023, April 6). When lunatics run the asylum: Noam Chomsky interviewed by David Barsamian. Tom Dispatch. https:// chomsky.info/20230406-2/

Cobo, J.M. (1979). La enseñanza superior en el mundo. Estudio comparativo e hipótesis [Higher education in the world: Comparative study and hypothesis]. Narcea.

Desai, C. (2024, February 8). The war in Gaza is wiping out Palestine's education and knowledge systems. The Conversation. https://theconversation.com/the-war-in-gaza-is-wiping-out-palestines-education-and-knowledge-systems-222055

Dussel, E. (2011). Filosofía de la liberación [Philosophy of liberation]. Fondo de Cultura Económica.

Elía, R.H. (2013). El incendio de la biblioteca de Alejandría por los árabes: una historia falsificada [The burning of the Library of Alexandria by the Arabs: A falsified history]. *Byzantion Nea Hellás*, 32, 37–69.

Elías, N. (2016). *El proceso de la civilización* [*The civilizing process*]. Fondo de Cultura Económica. (Original work published 1939)

Foucault, M. (1996). *Tecnologías del yo* [*Technologies of the self*]. Editorial Paidós Ibérica.

Freire, P. (2009). *La educación como práctica de la libertad* [*Education as practice of freedom*] (Lilién Ronzoni, Trans.). Siglo XXI.

Hernández Navarro, L. (2020, February 18). Pablo González Casanova: el amor y la lucha [Love and fight]. *La Jornada*. https://www.jornada.com.mx/2020/02/18/opinion/012a1pol

Laclau, E. (2005). *La razón populista* [*The populist reason*]. Fondo de Cultura Económica.

Laurell, A.C. (1981). La salud-enfermedad como proceso social [Health and disease as social process]. *Revista Latinoamericana de Salud*, 12, 7–28.

León-Portilla, M. (1961). *Los antiguos mexicanos a través de sus crónicas y cantares* [*The ancient Mexicans through their chronicles and songs*]. Fondo de Cultura Económica.

Mariátegui, J.C. (1993). *Siete ensayos de interpretación de la realidad peruana* [*Seven interpretive essays on Peruvian reality*]. Ediciones Era.

Mateos-Vega, M. (2018, March 5). La pelea ya no es por la justicia, es por la vida: González Casanova [Our fight is not for justice anymore, it is for life: González Casanova]. *La Jornada*. https://www.jornada.com.mx/2018/03/05/cultura/a06n1cul

Mejía-Ricart, T. (1981). *La universidad en la historia universal* [*The univerity in universal history*]. Editorial de la Universidad Autónoma de Santo Domingo.

Ortiz Tejeda, C. (2023, April 24). Nosotros ya no somos los mismos [We are not the same anymore]. *La Jornada*. https://www.jornada.com.mx/2023/04/24/opinion/01001pol

Santos, J.A. (2017). Aportes para una pedagogía crítica nuestroamericana: identificando el núcleo conceptual del pensamiento político-pedagógico de Paulo Freire [Contributions to a critical pedagogy in Latin America: Identifying the conceptual core of Paulo Freire's political-pedagogical thought]. *Revista Pedagógica*, 19(41), 80–95.

Santos, M. (2000). *La naturaleza del espacio. Técnica y tiempo. Razón y emoción* [*The nature of space: Technique and time. Reason and emotion*]. Editorial Ariel.

Spinelli, H. (2004). *Salud colectiva: Cultura, instituciones y subjetividad* [*Collective health: Culture, institutions and subjectivity*]. Lugar Editorial.

Tünnermann Bernheim, C. (1991). *Historia de la universidad en América Latina. De la época colonial a la Reforma de Córdoba* [*History of the university in Latin*

America: From colonial times to the Córdoba Reform]. Editorial Universitaria Centroamericana, EDUCA.

Tünnermann Bernheim, C. (2003). *La Universidad necesaria para el siglo XXI* [*The necessary university for the twenty-first century*]. HISPAMER.

UAM. (1974). *Documento Xochimilco*. Universidad Autónoma Metropolitana.

University of Regina (1963, December 13–15). *The Regina Beach Manifesto.* University of Saskatchewan—Regina Campus Committee on Educational Policy for Liberal Arts.

Vallejo, I. (2021). *El infinito en un junco* [*The infinite in a reed*]. Siruela.

Vallejo, I. (2022). *Papyrus: The Invention of Books in the Ancient World* (Charlotte Whittle, Trans.). Knopf.

Notes

1   I dedicate this paper in memoriam of Pablo González Casanova (1922–2023), ex-rector of the National Autonomous University of México (UNAM). A sociologist, philosopher, writer, citizen, life artist who walked side by side with people, students, and colleagues. A human—very, very human—and an essential.

2   I'm grateful to James McNinch for his kind notes and gentle corrections during the final draft of this chapter.

3   At this point, I must pause to recommend, to those who haven't read it yet, a great and very well-informed book inspiring some aspects of what I am saying here: *El infinito en un junco* [*The Infinite in a Reed*] by the young Spanish philologist and writer Irene Vallejo (2021; 2022).

4   James McNinch, professor emeritus and former dean of the Faculty of Education at the University of Regina, accurately points out that the 2023 Regina symposium, which was the catalyst for this collection of essays, recalls the activities of Alexandria Museum.

5   Elía (2013) denies the assumption that it was the Arabs who set fire in Alexandria's library.

6   Constantinople, Berlin, and Baghdad are examples of hatred of books leading to specific searches to burn them as means of exclusion, menace, and punishment. Netanyahu's massacre in Gaza intends to wipe out not only books, but every Palestinian word and knowledge system (Desai, 2024): a complete epistemicide, whether words are said or written by Palestinian people, or of Palestinian buildings and mosques, songs, schools, medical knowledge, paintings, dance, dress, pictures, toys…books are only one among many other targets.

7   Carlomagno (Carolus-Magnus, Charlemagne, 748–814), emperor of the Franks and Romans in the ninth century, establisher of the Carolingian Empire in the early Middle Ages, which expanded to Italy and other parts of what we know now as Europe.

8   University etymology: uni = "one," versus = "turned"; thus, it does not mean "everything" but "one and what surrounds one."

9   Bourdieu (1992) does not believe public opinion exists.
10   It is important to note that in Canada, the Regina Campus of the University
     Saskatchewan's *Regina Beach Manifesto* (1963), in seeking institutional autonomy
     and for other reasons, also pursued a more justice-seeking institution and a
     stronger commitment to the liberal arts.
11   See for example, UAM (1974), *Documento Xochimilco*.

CHAPTER 6

FROM NEOLIBERALISM TO AUTHORITARIANISM
UNIVERSITIES, METRICS, REGULATION, AND SURRENDER TO GOVERNMENTAL CONTROL

Liz Morrish

Ignoring the Early Signs

BACK IN THE 1990S, AT A REMOTE BENEDICTINE MONASTERY in Devon, UK, a lone monk called Brother Adam tended his bees with religious devotion. His purpose was to save colonies from a plague that had wiped out most strains and build new apiaries at the monastery. In doing so, he became a world class authority and published three books on bees and their genetics. Alongside this project, the monastery developed a healthy sideline in selling honey. Brother Adam studied, wrote, and worked well into his nineties until, in 1992, a new abbot decided that he was spending too much time on building the apiaries and not enough time on maximizing the monastery's income from honey. He was an obedient but sad monk as he laid down his research and henceforth confined himself solely to his spiritual devotions. Meanwhile, what the press quickly dubbed "FastBuck Abbey" continued to serve Mammon (Associated Press, 1996).

The Discipline of the Market

This episode, while it may have passed us by, should have been a prescient lesson to all in higher education. What is significant is not just the banality and tawdriness of capitalism but the extent of neoliberal penetration even into those sectors we might have considered immune from financialization. As Brown (2015) tells us, neoliberalism has been far more successful as an ideology than as an economic formula. Over and above government, this in itself has become a governmentality—a strategy for rendering subjects and states governable, even while those subjects believe they have autonomy. It should be no surprise that in their turn, universities have been forced into a neoliberal straitjacket in which academic endeavour has been subordinated to the ethos of business.

In 1992, UK universities underwent a process known as incorporation as a result of the Jarratt Review of higher education (Jarratt, 1985). Designed to increase "efficiency," the recommendations were largely aimed at centralizing decision-making among the senior management teams. This was a new lexicon at the time. We started to hear about chief executives, cost centres, best practice, value for money, and line managers. There were strategic plans and performance-related pay for those who fulfilled their aims and objectives. University councils, made up of lay members often with business and industry backgrounds, were imposed at the expense of academic senates. Although Jarratt was still committed to the idea that academic freedom must be protected if universities were to function (Greatrix, 2015), I will argue that the structures he initiated are incompatible with that aim. Neoliberalism—the rule of free markets, privatization, and competition—has transformed the day to day of universities to the extent that their existence and subsidy from the public purse must be justified entirely in economic terms. This exigency has become the overriding impetus for all strategic decision-making in universities. It has truly given shape to the Thatcherite mantra of "there is no alternative." Meanwhile, the important academic conversations of scholars are shifted temporally, spatially, and culturally to the margins.

Once academics had been sidelined, vice-chancellors were free to enforce managerial practices of top-down autocracy verging on authoritarianism. In the place of faculty democracy and discussion stand sham "consultations" repurposed as relay stations for reactive policy-making in the name of "agility." As a result, there are regimes of enforced compliance with restructurings, curriculum reviews, and, of course, frequent audits of research to make sure academics are continuing to work within "areas of excellence and selectivity" prescribed by research-funding councils at the behest of a government in pursuit of a "world-class, dynamic and responsive research base" (REF 2029, 2025). This has amounted to an epidemic of bullying—officially prohibited by institutional policies, but its tolerance derives legitimacy from those who believe that autocracy is a leaner, more efficient mode of governance.

The Jarrett revolution has found apostles and imitators across the world. We have witnessed a slide from *dirigisme* (state intervention in policy making) to authoritarianism whereby governments have felt empowered to pressure universities to conform to unpopular ideological stances. In some countries, universities are subject to state control, but in many more, autonomy is granted in name only. We see this most clearly now in certain American states like Florida, where there has been a declared "war on wokeness" and a campaign to outlaw critical race theory. New College of Florida, part of the state university system, was known for its liberal orientation in terms of curriculum and assessment. Such was the threat from this college of free thinkers that Governor Ron DeSantis imposed a new board of trustees and removed the president in order to refashion it in the mould of a fundamentalist Christian college (Wallace-Wells, 2023). This has been presented as a necessary intervention to protect academic freedom when, in reality, it is a targeted assault on precisely that.

It now seems as if the success of certain states in legislating against DEI initiatives or curricular offerings in gender studies or race studies has emboldened members of the US Congress to campaign for the removal of the presidents of both Harvard and the University of Pennsylvania (Matza, 2024).

Worldwide, the rap sheet of offenders against academic freedom and autonomy grows. In 2015, the Japanese government required universities to reform and divert resources away from arts and humanities toward sciences (Dean, 2015). In Greece, a special police force has been assigned to universities to surveil and counter left-wing activism (Kitsantonis, 2022). In Hungary, Viktor Orbán closed the Central European University precisely because of the growing influence and reputation of its courses in social science and gender studies (Walker, 2019). Brazil, Turkey, and Hong Kong have all seen the state extend its control into university curriculum, freedom of expression, and suppression of dissent.

Metrics and Authoritarian Performance Management

The neoliberal agenda and managerialism have led to an emphasis on calculability. What can be measured is measured and becomes the priority. Beer (2016) writes that metrics measure us in new and powerful ways such that they order the social world and shape our lives. The original sin in the United Kingdom was the inauguration of research selectivity exercises—the Research Assessment Exercise (RAE) followed by the Research Excellence Framework (REF). It was justified as offering accountability for public expenditure on university research, to provide a picture of the quality of research in the United Kingdom, and to ensure that monies gravitate to the best research centres. This required each university department to identify areas of excellence so that research funding councils could respond by selecting for areas of priority in research. If your work is interdisciplinary or veers away from the departmental orthodoxy, your "outputs" may not be submitted to the REF, an outcome which is career-limiting at best. There is now evidence (Jones, 2022) that this has resulted in the scope of research in the social sciences being narrowed in the direction of orthodoxy.

With each iteration of the REF, the assessment formula has expanded. "Outputs" in the form of published research will now only count for 50 percent of the unit score in the 2029 exercise. There will be a requirement, weighted at 25 percent, to demonstrate that research has economic or social "impact" (Jisc, n.d.). The result will be that universities and individual scholars will be asked to demonstrate international excellence in research as well as national influence and local salience. That is quite a difficult balance of priorities to achieve. Although this accounting and surveillance bureaucracy has in some ways elevated the previously marginalized institutions that did applied research, the REF has nevertheless been successful in upholding existing hierarchies of academic status; the top ten universities has largely remained stable over the various iterations of the RAE/REF, even while the top one hundred has proved more porous.

Despite claims of problems with assessment methodology and validity (Sayer, 2015), the REF has never been resisted by managers because it offers them an invaluable tool—apparently objective measurement together with the threat of job insecurity. Staff are subject to performance management mechanisms in the form of research metrics: number of publications, citations, journal impact factors, H-index, impact, and, of course, grant capture. There has been a cultural change in which staff are treated as overheads who can only redeem their indentured servitude if they bring in external income via research grants or industry contracts.

Bonfire of the Humanities

The metric of grant capture has not worked to the advantage of arts and humanities subjects. Work in literature or philosophy, for example, is unlikely to be awarded the headline-grabbing amounts boasted by bioscience, data science, or engineering. It is not unknown, however, for large grants to be awarded for projects in "digital humanities" (Berry, 2019)—another contested designation—but these projects tend to be utilitarian rather than theoretical in nature.

Nor does teaching escape quantification. Its value is now assessed in terms of a set of shifting "outcomes"—drop-out rates, student satisfaction, and graduate progression to professional and managerial jobs—which allow universities to be compared and ranked. This concern with outcomes has been driven by an expensive funding regime since 2012, which burdens students with loans that the government wants paid back. They have consequently sought to steer students toward higher-paying subjects (economics, medicine) at the expense of socially necessary programs like nursing, teaching, and social work, or even university lecturing.

The result of all this has been a bonfire of arts and humanities, even though they are cheaper to teach and lead to "better outcomes" in the long term by the government's preferred measure of graduate salaries. This carnage is entirely unnecessary, if only politicians and university managers were willing to take a look at the evidence. Robson and colleagues (2023), examining the career destinations of nine thousand Oxford humanities graduates, found their careers benefit from qualities of resilience, flexibility, and skills to adapt to challenging and changing labour markets. A British Academy study found the employability of humanities graduates to be robust, with eight of the ten fastest-growing sectors of the economy employing more graduates of the arts, humanities, and social sciences than graduates of other disciplines (British Academy, 2020). A recent report for the United Kingdom's Higher Education Policy Institute offers convincing evidence that STEM graduates may move into higher paying jobs initially, but this evens out over five to ten years, and the wider range of skills and attributes possessed by the arts and humanities graduate prove to be popular with most employers who, in any case, do not demand particular degree subjects. These soft skills offer a more resilient pathway through career changes in the long term (Thain et al., 2023).

Despite this plentiful evidence, vice-chancellors in the United Kingdom have piled on to dispense with entire disciplines in clusters, following each other in a carousel of panicked imitation. The year 2020 saw a cull of creative arts and modern languages courses. In 2021 it was the turn of history and archaeology, while 2022 saw more linguistics courses axed. And yet, even when we consult the metric of graduate salaries, we find evidence that these abandoned subjects deliver well on what the government calls its *Start for Success* measure. Take the case of linguistics at the University of Huddersfield, which was cancelled in 2022. There is some easily available data from the Higher Education Statistics Agency comparing the scores for BA (Hons) Linguistics at Huddersfield (8.5 out of a possible 10), and BA (Hons) Applied English Language Studies, BA (Hons) English Language, and BA (Hons) English Language and Linguistics, which all score 9.025. By contrast, courses in Linguistics at the University of Leeds (Russell Group) score between 7.2 and 8.5 (Figure 6.1.).

Figure 6.1. UK *Government* Start to Success

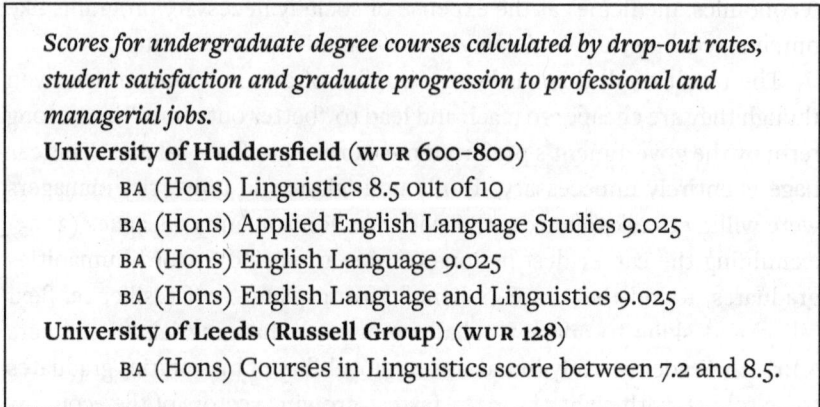

Scores for undergraduate degree courses calculated by drop-out rates, student satisfaction and graduate progression to professional and managerial jobs.

University of Huddersfield (WUR 600–800)
    BA (Hons) Linguistics 8.5 out of 10
    BA (Hons) Applied English Language Studies 9.025
    BA (Hons) English Language 9.025
    BA (Hons) English Language and Linguistics 9.025
University of Leeds (**Russell Group**) (WUR 128)
    BA (Hons) Courses in Linguistics score between 7.2 and 8.5.

Source: *Higher Education Statistics Agency Unistats 2020–2021.*

If a student applicant is concerned about outcomes and careers after graduation, there would be no reason to prefer to study Linguistics at Leeds (World University Ranking 128) over Huddersfield (World University Ranking between 600 and 800), other than concern over perceived prestige—a metric that has only myth as its basis, not even qualitative measures. I would argue that the way to make gains on that front would be to invest in those courses which lead to enhanced opportunities rather than cancelling the university's strongest programs.

There are also problems with measuring the success of a course or its graduates solely by arbitrary measures like employability and salary. An apt assessment comes from Simon Marginson, who was recently quoted as saying

> the adoption of employability as a "universal measure of value" is forcing "the square peg" of higher education into "a round economic hole," overlooking its "intrinsic" purposes of educating students and disseminating knowledge—the "classical inner core" of higher education, which is about learning and knowledge for their "own sake." (Ross, 2023)

I accept that the marketization of universities has presented us with some contradictions, and these must be difficult for any leader to manage effectively. The reactive strategy of the marketized university suggests prioritizing student applicant choice in courses, but this requires constant revision of the course portfolio in order to accommodate shifting popularity. The proactive strategy is to identify the university's strengths in teaching, research, and outcomes and support their development. I imagine a university employs a marketing team in order to persuade students to enrol in such proven high-quality courses. You have to ask, if marketing fails to persuade, what is marketing for?

When I asked that question of the University of Huddersfield vice-chancellor, I didn't get a reply. And so, we have arrived at a situation in which a university is unwilling to defend its highest-quality courses because the government prefers them to be eliminated. How can a university fulfill its mission to be a custodian and producer of knowledge under such circumstances? Why should academics spend years in study and writing only for their contributions to be squandered by a system that rewards the basest form of value?

Post-Pandemic Control Opportunity

Disaster capitalism never misses an opportunity, and this was spectacularly true in the UK academic sector. In July 2020, the government seized the chance for what they actually called a Restructuring Regime (Morrish, 2020), which postured as a mechanism to access financial support during the pandemic—but it came with a cost. Government expected universities to "undergo their own restructuring to ensure they are better suited for the post-Covid world," understood as code for a demand they would reorient university courses toward STEM (Team Wonkhe, 2020). The much-needed new source of funding was appropriated to coerce universities into more closely serving the technical and vocational needs of their localities. Somehow, this is always envisioned as technology, even as the urgent needs of the tourism or agricultural industries are neglected.

As well as financial mechanisms, there has been pressure from the demand-side of potential applicants. High schools have faithfully delivered the message that the only thing that counts is science and technology. This is nudge theory in action, and it gives the appearance that curricular changes are being driven by student choice. The discourse of personal and societal benefit has emerged in lockstep with the levers of persuasion: government discourse about the supposed economic benefit of university courses has been mirrored in choices of evaluative terms in the semantic field of appreciation (worthwhile, effective, world-class, valuable, innovative, etc.), displacing any affectual responses in terms of emotion (love, passion, inspiration) or mental process or behavioural transformation (changed my life, made me challenge my previous views, trained me to think critically).

Purge of Critical Scholarship

And so, almost by stealth, areas of critical scholarship have been eliminated or marginalized; typically, cultural studies has been absorbed into sociology, whose scope has been narrowed to social work, social policy, or criminology. You would think the business school might be exempt from much restructuring by an agenda of real-life learning, vocational relevance, and high earnings. But there is the troublesome area of critical management studies (CMS) to reckon with and its implied critique of managerialism and performance-based outcomes. In 2021, at the University of Leicester, scholars of CMS in the business school were selected for redundancy simply by dint of having the word "critical" in a title of a journal article, or by submitting to a journal with "critical" in the title (https://ulsb16.com/chronology-documents/). The same fate was visited on scholars in political economy. The purge was not due to weakness in research or disappointing REF scores. This was evident in the fact that the Univeristy of Leicester School of Business was known internationally for CMS.

The wanton destruction at Leicester was memorialized in a paper entitled "Crawling from the Wreckage" (Fleming et al., 2022), written while four of the five editors were threatened with redundancy. The wreckage is "neoliberal reforms, market orientation, performance regimes, and increased precarity." They write: "engagement in critical scholarship at Leicester University effectively became a dismissible offence" (7) and with it the expectation that non-orthodoxy, disciplinary or institutional critique might be afforded academic freedom.

This is the most egregious example of ideological intrusion and a breach of academic freedom by a UK university that has not apparently perturbed a government currently pushing through parliament a very heavy-handed bill designed to legislate on this issue.

Another example of institutional hostility to scholarship that university management deems oppositional lies in the case of Dr. Susanne Täuber. She was dismissed by the University of Groningen (Netherlands) for publishing a critique of a program designed to offer opportunities to women researchers in the university but whose outcomes delivered the reverse (Gulland, 2023). The article (Täuber, 2019) was in a prestigious journal and peer reviewed, but the university felt her opposition to the program made a working relationship impossible. This suppression of critical voices is beginning to look like a global campaign that also targets liberal democracies.

Unfortunately, university faculty, staff, and students mount very little resistance. Rarely are there strikes or walkouts over the colleague who is silenced or made redundant over their dissident views. In a recent interview, Steven Salaita (who was fired en route to his new, tenured job at University of Illinois in a controversy over the content of an essay) said that for university managers, critical thinking is merely a brand signifier.

> The moment it becomes an avocation—that is, a practice trained on identifying and undermining systems of power—it becomes unwelcome. Administrators and many faculty like to think of critical thinking in the abstract, as a command of theoretical material, say, and not as a practice that intervenes in systems of injustice—least of all those on the campus itself. Critical thinking is tamed precisely at the point that it threatens to deliver on its promise. (Salaita, 2023)

Culture Wars and Equality Agendas

The anti-humanities, anti-critical, anti-theory stance is not just directed toward research; it also has teaching and learning methods and regulatory compliance in its grasp. The years 2022 and 2023 saw a number of UK media reports (Harding & Henry, 2022; Standley, 2023) stating that universities are "still using remote learning." The disturbing implication is that face-to-face is the only valid mode of teaching and that the pandemic exigencies could not have uncovered new and valuable hybrid pedagogies. This invited a frenzy of recrimination from government ministers who for the past several years have been scolding universities for using the same teaching methods as a hundred years ago. When higher education is on the front line of the culture wars, you really cannot win.

In the same vein, in May 2022, the UK government again provoked conflict with the sector when it criticized Advance HE—a higher education charity specializing in professional development programs—of imposing a woke agenda on universities after publication of their Race Equality Charter (Malnick, 2022). Advance HE responded: "Activism plays no part in our work. We have no particular ideological stance or agenda that we are seeking to promote," and affirmed that the intent was to act against racial harassment and encourage universities to incorporate race equality within course content (Advance HE, 2022).

This is a dignified response, but it fails to call out the irrationality of contradictory government instructions. The Department for Education, in February 2019, charged universities with tackling racial disparity in degree outcomes: "Universities will now be held to account on how they will improve outcomes for underrepresented students, including those from ethnic minority backgrounds, through powers of the Office for Students, who will scrutinise institutions' Access and Participation plans," insisting that the race gap in degree outcomes be eliminated (Department for Education, 2019). To this end, they explicitly required Advance HE to review its Race Equality Charter to ensure it is robust enough to support better outcomes for both ethnic minority staff and students.

It is the very definition of gaslighting when the government obliges the higher education sector to comply with equalities legislation and then castigates it for its efforts. However, in order to undermine the trust of the populace in higher education, it is expedient for those in power to conflate equality and inclusion legislation with critical race theory, which the right wing in the United Kingdom and in North America has sought to outlaw. Similarly, some American states are already seeing the effects of "don't say gay" legislation in schools. Teaching about race and the civil rights struggle is now contentious. In Florida, schools are attempting to teach the story of Rosa Parks without mentioning her race. The purpose is to deflect questions about inequality, power, and representation in America. Alarmingly, the British right wing has learned to follow suit in an equally unprincipled way.

The dislike of the higher education sector by the UK government is so entrenched that they are even ready to sacrifice its hard-earned international reputation for quality. The higher education regulator, which bears the Orwellian name of the Office for Students (OfS) has been weaponized as an instrument of anti-academic coercion. When the much-vaunted OfS student panel failed to agree with the list of issues that the chair and CEO had decreed were student priorities, the members were silenced. While the chair and CEO had been appointed with a "freedom of speech" mission to make universities safe for right-wing academics and politicians to speak at universities without being disturbed by protest, the student panellists felt that the cost of living and value for money were more important themes. These issues were not considered nearly populist enough and unlikely to mobilize suspicion against universities to the extent desired by the Conservative government. It would have been unimaginable, just ten years ago, to envisage the slide into authoritarianism and partiality taken by what is supposed to be an independent regulator, i.e., positioned at a distance from government. The chair of the Office for Students is Lord James Wharton, a friend and appointee of former prime minister Boris Johnson. A year ago, Wharton was discovered sharing a platform with racists, anti-democratic Trump sympathizers, and Orbánistas at the world Conservative Political Action Conference in Budapest 2022. Presumably he went there to find out how best to shut down any of the other leading European arts and social science universities as Orbán has done with Central European University.

In September 2023, the House of Lords Industry and Regulators Committee delivered an excoriating condemnation of the conduct and organization of the Office for Students. Particularly damning was their verdict on the politicization of the chair's role (2023, para. 417): "During our inquiry, we heard widespread concerns that Lord Wharton's appointment as Chair of the OfS, and in particular the fact that he continues to retain the Conservative whip, had contributed to the perception that the

OfS lacks independence from the Government." Similarly, the OfS has allowed the media to displace policy setting according to academic needs (para. 405): In giving evidence, "the University of Huddersfield said that 'political headlines are very quickly translated into OfS policy which places additional burden/responsibility on the university sector.' They cited in particular a case where parts of the media and some MPs raised concerns, 'without clear evidence,' over competence in written English, which 'quickly translated into an OfS edict imposed on the sector requiring spelling and grammar assessment, without any investigation of what was common practice or the rationale for the sector position.'"

The House of Lords committee recognized a clear and present danger that UK higher education risks sliding into authoritarian control and also risks losing credibility as a result of this cozy affiliation between regulator and a government easily cowed by the right-wing press.

Conclusion

Anne Applebaum writes in her recent book that steps one and two of an authoritarian takeover are to establish control of the media and the universities (Applebaum, 2020). It is now clear that universities have ceded too much control to government to the extent that ministers now feel empowered to intervene on course provision, curriculum, modes of teaching delivery, and student admissions. Academic freedom and areas of critical scholarship are not best defended when scholars don't know from one year to the next whether their high-quality programs will satisfy whatever shifting metrics government and university management are setting. This corrosion must be opposed if universities are to function as pillars of liberal democracy. It calls for a stronger response from academics and sector-wide bodies in order to preserve the autonomy of universities and academic freedom enshrined in the UK's *Higher Education and Research Act 2017* (UK Government, 2017, para. 36) and UNESCO's statement on academic freedom. The latter's provision is explicit:

> Higher-education teaching personnel are entitled to the maintaining of academic freedom, that is to say, the right, without constriction by prescribed doctrine, to freedom of teaching and discussion, freedom in carrying out research and disseminating and publishing the results thereof, freedom to express freely their opinion about the institution

or system in which they work, freedom from institutional censorship and freedom to participate in professional or representative academic bodies. (UNESCO, 1997, para. 27)

This invites a question of how do we get beyond the contradictions and the corrosion of purpose, to reclaim a narrative, purpose, and reputation for higher education? As the Irish saying goes, if you want to get to there, I wouldn't start from here. Unhappily, we are very far from where we would want to be in higher education because, as we have learned from the tale of Brother Adam, function and value exceed mere monetary measure. This opinion will be refused and silenced if raised in front of university management. It will be derided as a utopian fantasy.

But we continue to imagine a different future because the present is too painful, especially for younger and contingent colleagues who must contemplate building their careers and advancing knowledge within the current systems. This chapter emerged from a presentation at a conference on what universities are for. I was enlivened by the presence of others who shared my critique and offered their own stories of revision and resistance. Primarily we are informed by critical university studies, which is a vital framework to allow us to identify what it is we don't want. What doesn't work. What is inimical to our understanding of a university. With that understanding, we can at least start to marshal our efforts in the right direction, even if we find ourselves in hostile territory when we try and apply our critical lens to internal processes.

Some years ago, a scholar working in South Africa, Paul Prinsloo, offered the term "hospicing" to refer to that sense of powerlessness—of being headed off at every resistant turn—all the while feeling the need to record what is happening and announce one's despair at it (Prinsloo, 2016). We can, as the editors of that recent paper in the journal *Ephemera* recommend, consider what it means to work in the wreckage (Fleming et al., 2022). But we should also remind ourselves that universities have been around for millennia and have survived many attacks on their operation and purpose. The enemies of critique and democracy are very well-funded. What *we* have is intellectual rigour and a committed constituency. Where we let ourselves down is in solidarity, organization, and a tendency to think the public are as inimical to academic values as the press and politicians often are. We must act to defend our autonomy in the classroom, and we must act in solidarity if we are to allow universities to work as they are designed to.

References

Advance HE. (2022, May 31). Advance HE statement about tackling inequalities. https://www.advance-he.ac.uk/news-and-views/advance-he-statement-about-tackling-inequalities

Applebaum, A. (2020). *Twilight of democracy: The seductive lure of authoritarianism.* Knopf Doubleday.

Associated Press. (1996, September 4). Brother Adam, 98, bee breeder who developed new varieties. *New York Times.* https://www.nytimes.com/1996/09/04/world/brother-adam-98-bee-breeder-who-developed-new-varieties.html

Beer, D. (2016). *Metric power.* Palgrave Macmillan.

Berry, D.M. (2019, February 13). What are digital humanities? *The British Academy Blog.* https://www.thebritishacademy.ac.uk/blog/what-are-digital-humanities/

British Academy. (2020). *Qualified for the future: Quantifying demand for arts, humanities and social science skills.* https://www.thebritishacademy.ac.uk/publications/skills-qualified-future-quantifying-demand-arts-humanities-social-science/

Brown, W. (2015). *Undoing the demos: Neoliberalism's stealth revolution.* Zone Books.

Dean, A. (2015, September 26). Japan's humanities chop sends shivers down academic spines. *The Guardian.* https://www.theguardian.com/higher-education-network/2015/sep/25/japans-humanities-chop-sends-shivers-down-academic-spines

Department for Education. (2019, February 1). Universities must do more to tackle ethnic disparity. UK Government. https://www.gov.uk/government/news/universities-must-do-more-to-tackle-ethnic-disparity

Fleming, P., Olaison, L., Plotnikof, M., Grønbæk Pors, J., & Pullen, A. (2022). Crawling from the wreckage. *Ephemera,* 22(3), 1–20. https://ephemerajournal.org/contribution/crawling-wreckage

Greatrix, P. (2015, September 8). The imperfect university: The Jarratt Report 30 years on. *Wonkhe.* https://wonkhe.com/blogs/the-imperfect-university-the-jarratt-report-30-years-on/

Gulland, A. (2023, April 13). University of Groningen faces growing calls to reinstate sacked gender-equality researcher. *Nature.* https://www.nature.com/articles/d41586-023-01286-5

Harding, E., & Henry, J. (2022, May 16). More than half of elite universities are *still* teaching online—as bosses are told to justify £28,000 fees for remote learning. *Daily Mail.* https://www.dailymail.co.uk/news/article-10814559/Some-elite-universities-teaching-online.html

House of Lords Industry and Regulators Committee. (2023, September 13). Must do better: The Office for Students and the looming crisis facing higher education. HL paper 246. https://publications.parliament.uk/pa/ld5803/ldselect/ldindreg/246/24602.htm

Jarratt, A. (1985). Report of the steering committee for efficiency studies in universities. *Education in the UK*. https://education-uk.org/documents/jarratt1985/index.html

Jisc. (n.d.). Research excellence framework 2029: Initial decisions and issues for further consultation. https://beta.jisc.ac.uk/future-research-assessment-programme/initial-decisions

Jones, S. (2022). *Universities under fire: Hostile disources and integrity deficits in higher education*. Palgrave Macmillan.

Kitsantonis, N. (2022, October 9). Greece tries stationing police on campus, and students fight back. *New York Times*. https://www.nytimes.com/2022/10/09/world/europe/greece-universities-campus-police.html

Malnick, E. (2022, May 14). Universities' racial equality scheme branded "egregious wokery." *Sunday Telegraph*. https://www.telegraph.co.uk/news/2022/05/14/government-denounces-egregious-wokery-mps-question-worth-university/

Matza, M. (2024, January 2). Claudine Gay resigns as Harvard University president. *BBC News*. https://www.bbc.co.uk/news/world-us-canada-67868280

Morrish, L. (2020, August 9). From regulation to regime: Are we seeing a government takeover of universities? *Academic Irregularities*. https://academicirregularities.wordpress.com/2020/08/09/from-regulation-to-regime-are-we-seeing-a-government-takeover-of-universities/

Prinsloo, P. (2016). Curricula as contested and contesting spaces: Geographies of identity, resistance and desire. Working paper. https://doi.org/10.13140/RG.2.1.4943.7208

REF 2029 (2025). What is the REF? Research Excellence Framework. https://www.ref.ac.uk/about/what-is-the-ref/

Robson, J., Murphy, E., Nuseibeh, N., Tawell, A., Hart, B., Stewart, J., Keep, E., & Marginson, S. (2023, June). *The value of the humanities: Understanding the career destinations of Oxford humanities graduates*. Oxford University's Humanities Division. https://www.ox.ac.uk/sites/files/oxford/media_wysiwyg/Oxford%20U%20Value%20of%20Humanities%20report.pdf

Ross, J. (2023, March 27). Employability "mantra" supplanting higher education's "inner core." *Times Higher Education*. https://www.timeshighereducation.com/news/employability-mantra-supplanting-higher-educations-inner-core

Salaita, S. (2023, April 19). When critical thinking becomes undesirable: Ivana Perić interviews Steven Salaita. *No Flags, No Slogans*. https://stevesalaita.com/when-critical-thinking-becomes-undesirable-ivana-peric-interviews-steven-salaita/

Sayer, D. (2015). *Rank hypocrisies: The insult of the REF*. SAGE.

Standley, N. (2023, January 6). Nearly a third of university courses still have hybrid teaching. *BBC News*. https://www.bbc.co.uk/news/education-64130367

Täuber, S.J. (2019). Undoing gender in academia: Personal reflections on equal opportunity schemes. *Journal of Management Studies*, 57(8), 1718–24. https://doi.org/10.1111/joms.12516

Team Wonkhe. (2020, July 16). The restructuring regime: Money, but at a cost. *Wonkhe*. https://wonkhe.com/blogs/money-but-at-a-cost/

Thain, M., Fitzmaurice, S., Gill, J., Gregory, J., Harkness, N., Marshall, G., Pittock, M., & Thorpe, A. (2023). *The humanities in the uk today: What's going on?* HEPI *Report 159*. Higher Education Policy Institute. https://www.hepi.ac.uk/wp-content/uploads/2023/03/The-Humanities-in-the-UK-Today-Whats-Going-On.pdf

UK Government. (2017) *Higher Education and Research Act 2017*, c. 29. https://www.legislation.gov.uk/ukpga/2017/29/contents/enacted

UNESCO (1997, November 11). Recommendation concerning the status of higher-education teaching personnel. https://en.unesco.org/about-us/legal-affairs/recommendation-concerning-status-higher-education-teaching-personnel

Walker, S. (2019, November 16). Classes move to Vienna as Hungary makes rare decision to oust university. *The Guardian*. https://www.theguardian.com/world/2019/nov/16/ceu-classes-move-to-vienna-orban-hungary-ousts-university

Wallace-Wells, B. (2023, February 22). What is Ron DeSantis doing to Florida's public liberal-arts colleges? *The New Yorker*. https://www.newyorker.com/news/the-political-scene/what-is-ron-desantis-doing-to-floridas-public-liberal-arts-college

CHAPTER 7
RESISTANCE AND REDIRECTION IN THE MANAGERIAL UNIVERSITY

Peter S. McInnis

T HE DEBATE CONCERNING "WHAT UNIVERSITIES ARE FOR" IS
apt as we enter the second quarter of the twenty-first century. To
speak knowledgeably of the contemporary situation, some historical perspective is imperative. Arguably, the two foundational
innovations for Canada from the 1960s were the advent of public health care and a significant expansion of post-secondary education.
The massive public investments made by the federal and provincial governments in these two areas have been crucial as social determinants
of health for postwar generations. Access to basic health care through
adopting Medicare has vastly improved the quality of life and extended
longevity. Health care alone, however, is insufficient for maintaining and
expanding outcomes if not teamed with access to quality post-secondary
education. Citizens lacking the necessary training and career pathways
cannot achieve the desired social mobility and participate actively in a
robust democracy. The question now arises why have we largely failed
to sustain our collective commitments to quality health care and post-
secondary education?

The dramatic postwar demographic growth during the 1960s and 1970s also spurred rapid educational development. New universities were constructed from the ground up on greenfield sites while existing campuses were consolidated or expanded. A partial list of such universities from west to east would include Victoria, Simon Fraser, Calgary, Lethbridge, Regina, Winnipeg, Guelph, Laurier, York, Trent, Carleton, Université du Québec à Montréal, Sherbrooke, Moncton, Prince Edward Island, Cape Breton, and Memorial. Established universities were expanded to adopt emerging fields of research and teaching while admitting a broader spectrum of students, eventually including Indigenous and other equity-deserving groups. The establishment of numerous colleges and institutes further augmented educational options.

In Quebec, the notable report of the provincial Royal Commission of Inquiry on Education led by Monseigneur Alphonse-Marie Parent, and in Ontario, the Hall-Dennis Report, both proposed radical reforms to all levels of education (Bibliothèque, 1963–1966; Connexions, 1965–1968). This was an era of risk-taking and experimentation with the laudable goal of making education more relevant. Other provinces were similarly engaged in revisioning post-secondary education from a comparatively elitist and exclusive enclave of the privileged to institutions that embraced broad access to the lifelong benefits of knowledge. Thus, dating from the 1960s onward, Canadians came to expect reasonable delivery of health care (from prenatal to geriatric) and that they, and their children, could be educated in comprehensive areas of interest and expertise without incurring massive personal debt for either service.[1]

It comes as no surprise to scholars and social activists that we are presently experiencing a concerted effort to roll back or eliminate decades of progressive reform in the public sector. The Canadian experience mirrors that of the United States, the United Kingdom, Australia, and New Zealand as targets for neoliberal transformation under the aegis of a new public management schema. In the international context, changes came slowly only to advance suddenly. Incremental adoptions of campus managerialism initiatives led to major concessions placing faculty and students in disarray. This golden age of post-secondary expansion has left us with a far different contemporary educational landscape. The core activities of research, teaching, and service are now under considerable duress as the managed neoliberal university becomes the ubiquitous mode of operation.

Canadian post-secondary institutions are the locus for a multi-pronged attempt to limit academic freedom severely, undermine collegial governance, and hamper independent curiosity-driven research.[2] The delegitimization of dissent in universities is notable as administrations contort their mandates from proponents of critical inquiry to become streamlined job-accreditation facilities at the behest of corporate interests. This is especially true of regions experiencing protracted decline.

On the national level, the Canadian Association of University Teachers (CAUT) developed specialized training and analysis to encourage a "mobilization model" of grassroots activism for faculty associations seeking to defend educational core values (CAUT, n.d.-a). In the last several years there has been a notable uprising in faculty associations, and especially graduate or postgraduate unions in the United States and Canada. This mobilization offers hope for the future, yet the overall trend to disempower academic staff continues. A salient example is the decline of tenure-track appointments replaced by precarious contract academic staff.

Universities and Academic Tenure

Too often the concept of tenure is reduced to merely a guarantee of job protection. That oversimplification leads to critiques that such continuing appointments obstruct the implementation of discredited performance-based metrics or related administration-driven initiatives to introduce perpetual faculty reassessments. Some argue that tenure should be rescinded or, at least, be subject to ongoing post-tenure reviews with the intent to reduce faculty complement. Unsupported allegations that tenured faculty pose an obstruction to institutional innovation frequently surface. This perspective obscures the core value of tenure, which is to ensure workplace permanency and provide the necessary stability to perform our core professional duties of advancing and communicating knowledge. Quite directly, this baseline is necessary to accomplish the full range of the academic job.

Canadian institutions still fare well when contrasted with international post-secondary employment where tenure is often unavailable or comparatively restricted. The United Kingdom lost tenure altogether in 1988 when it was replaced with fixed-term contracts, themselves subject to incessant metrics-driven demands of the Research and Teaching Excellence Frameworks. Similar limited-term contractual employment may be found in a broad range of countries including Sweden, Finland,

Italy, Denmark, Germany, the Netherlands, Australia, and New Zealand. The lack of job stability is frequently identified as a leading factor in workplace stress and declining career satisfaction (Xu & Wang, 2023).

The contemporary vulnerabilities of tenure and academic freedom have become embroiled in the broader culture wars in the United States. The precipitous decline of tenured positions began in the 1970s, and 2023 data from the American Association of University Professors (AAUP) indicates that an astonishing 70 percent of undergraduate instruction is performed by precariously employed faculty (AAUP, n.d.). As well, approximately 10 percent of new appointments will be "tenure-eligible" in this just-in-time delivery model whereby faculty are simply couriers of educational products. The AAUP report concludes the "overreliance on contingent appointments, which lack the protection of tenure for academic freedom and the economic security of continuing appointments, threatens the success of institutions in fulfilling their obligations to students, and to society" (Colby, 2023, p. 2).

While not as extreme as in the United States, the situation in Canada is concerning as the expansion of contractual appointments now constitutes most undergraduate course instruction, especially at large urban campuses. Gender disparity remains a persistent obstacle as Statistics Canada data indicates that 60 percent of tenured positions are male appointments. Contact academic staff are disproportionately women and/or members of equity-seeking groups. This lack of balance is more pronounced in science, technology, engineering, and mathematics (STEM) disciplines (Uppal & Hango, 2022). In 2018, two reports prepared by CAUT and the Canadian Centre for Policy Alternatives noted that 54 percent of academic appointments were limited-term positions. Of those, the majority were short-term contracts of four to eight months. While considering chronic underfunding of post-secondary education, shifting student demographics, and differing demands in subject disciplines, these surveys observe that precarity cannot be deemed a temporary aberration but an ensconced structural reality and a conscious administrative choice to opt for workplace insecurity.

It should come as no revelation that in this unstable working environment, concomitant moves to sharply restrict or eliminate academic freedom have escalated in some states, including Georgia, Iowa, South Carolina, and Wisconsin. Academics engaged with subjects involving critical race theory, gender, sexuality, and environmental science are now especially vulnerable to swaying political currents. The quandary is how to engage in intramural and extramural academic freedom if one's employment is subject to the animus of powerful opponents (Ruth, 2023). Widespread use of social media has exacerbated this susceptibility, and an errant post on X (formerly Twitter) may lead to doxing or mobbing forms of cyberbullying and concerted demands for workplace termination.

Reductions in tenured appointments reveal weaknesses in the academic model of collegial contributions to peer-reviewed scholarship. Those willing to serve as adjudicators for funding agencies, to join editorial boards, review submissions for journals, act as assessors for external department reviews, as well as rank and tenure committees have been less forthcoming in recent years. Fundamental service of this nature generally falls to tenured faculty and these numbers are diminishing.

So, is academic tenure destined to gradually disappear? Complacency is the enemy of collective action. Those with tenure or tenure-track appointments should be aware of the inherent inequities for the ever-growing ranks of contract academic staff (CAS). This not only entails ensuring fair treatment for CAS appointments but also pushing for a clear conversion process for contractual faculty to tenure-stream permanency. Certification and inclusive collective agreements offer an avenue of legal protection. Faculty complement language, that is mutually agreed definitions of faculty positions with minimum quotas, may be negotiated along with related protections for contingent academics. It is in the best interests of everyone to resist the insidious bifurcation of academia.

It has long been recognized that the erosion of collegial governance within post-secondary education must be countered with coordinated efforts to reassert the voices of academic staff and students on our campuses, and more broadly within our communities.[3] Less analyzed are specific prescriptions for mobilizing effective resistance to neoliberalism. This chapter suggests that the tools for such activism are often hidden in plain sight and that recognition of latent potential may offer the best approach to the long-term protection of academic freedom in our universities and colleges.

Universities Advance Research

Original research forms the basis for professional practice in Canadian universities and colleges and is a core activity for most of our careers. Across all academic disciplines, projects involving human subjects must pass the scrutiny of research ethics boards (REBS). In principle, such oversight is justified to ensure research participants are protected appropriately. The Tri-Council (CIHR, NSERC, SSHRC) Policy Statement, *Ethical Conduct for Research Involving Humans*, or TCPS 2,[4] explains in detail the principles and procedures required for approval. Few would contest the obligation for ethical research; however, fealty to acceptable conduct has, with the actions of some REBs, transformed it into an onerous and excessively bureaucratic barrier to timely and innovative projects.

Researchers at many universities and colleges report that approval of projects is subject to prolonged delay, repeated demands to revise and resubmit, and even queries of the rationale for the projects themselves—applications of the TCPS 2 that go far beyond the stated terms of reference. Recently, the Syndicat des professeurs et professeures de l'Université Laval (SPUL) published a survey of faculty experiences of their obligatory REB process.[5] The results are alarming. Requesting anonymity to avoid administrative reprisal, Laval researchers spoke of the "zeal" of reviewers who questioned the expertise of widely published faculty, demanded capricious alterations in methodology, and whose "rigid and fussy" requests routinely delayed approval to the point that projects became conceptually or financially unviable. Active researchers with years of productivity and sustained peer-reviewed funding deliberated on whether it was worth continuing to submit projects for approval in the face of increasing administrative interference.

Beyond the technical specifics of research proposals, some approvals were withheld seemingly due to administrative fears of reputational damage to the university or concerns that projects might stray into controversy and incur the wrath of provincial governments. When REBs assume the role of political or ideological filter, the humane principles of TCPS 2 have been distorted out of all proportion. Instead of a case-by-case assessment of proposals, frustrated researchers report the broad, unilateral application of expectations that undermine exploratory or innovative approaches, even where anticipated risks to participants are minor. This stop-loss, risk-averse formulation of research ethics has increasingly less to do with protecting human subjects and more with brand management of the workplace. The implication for academic freedom is as concerning as the societal costs of research foregone.

Recognizing that research of human subjects has widely diverse applications and variable levels of risk, the TCPS 2 emphasizes nuance and suggests "tailoring the level of scrutiny" when assessing projects. Yet, such flexibility appears to erode in practice. In some instances, assessments are performed by colleagues without sufficient expertise or, worse, by administrative staff intent on minimizing broadly perceived risks to their institutions. This lack of proportionate risk assessment has various dimensions. Indigenous researchers comment that risk assessments interfere with the analysis of the legacy of colonial oppression. Others say that they deliberately exclude Indigenous participants from their research design lest the review process be unreasonably complicated. Similarly, some researchers avoid inquiries into gender/sexual identity as barriers to ethics approval prove too onerous. In this climate of mistrust, proposals are modified and crafted to steer clear of anticipated objections. Such exclusions exacerbate existing social injustice as research objectives are curtailed or abandoned.

Researchers report that students at all levels, but especially graduate and post-doctoral candidates, are dissuaded from undertaking certain types of investigations as the approval timeline delays fieldwork while consuming scholarships. Ethics assessment must remain a core dimension of good research rather than an obligation to superficially fulfill. The viable timeline for student projects is always narrow and REBS must take this into consideration. Research boards not convening regularly, or at all during summer months, compound the problem. The lack of uniformity in ethics assessments amongst Canadian institutions serves to disadvantage researchers at rigidly risk-averse universities and colleges compared to those with a more streamlined process.

Research involving international cooperation may complicate outcomes and deter collaborative ventures. Research ethics approval is ostensibly conducted by academic colleagues as part of the accepted process of peer review, but often the policies and final administrative vetting are directed by offices of research that in practice diverge from the altruistic principles of collegial oversight. Concerns related to "foreign interference" and broadly defined national security further complicate research ethics and may pose major obstacles to collaborative projects if they are deemed to have "dual-purpose" applications for military or commercial applications (Government of Canada, n.d.b; Public Safety Canada, 2023).

Academic research with human subjects must be conducted with due respect for participants. Ethical considerations must be proportionate and assessed in a coherent, timely process for a diverse range of disciplines. One size for all should never form the evaluative framework. REBS must start from the positive obligation to advance research rather than negatively through a lens that overemphasizes liability. The fundamental academic freedom to research in one's discipline must be upheld and not subject to inappropriate supervision and control by a university or college. TCPS 2 has much to commend to all researchers striving for altruistic standards of comportment. Let us not allow the misapplication of ethical principles and processes to unfairly encumber researchers.

Universities Service Multiple Communities

In the calculus of academic performance, service is often relegated to a distinctly minor role behind research and teaching. The oft-cited workload ratio of 40/40/20 (service) is invoked to suggest some clear rationale for these artificial divisions and that, by implication, professional careers may be so neatly subdivided. The term service itself should be scrutinized for its connotations as a form of domestic service, and the often-gendered implications of such framing, as a way of dismissing its importance. Is academic service simply something to dispense with quickly as tertiary labour dutifully or reluctantly offered to then focus on activities that are more highly valued in career metrics? Too often we read listserv emails pleading for committee nominations as vacancies remain unfilled. Should we then resort to roving press gangs to recruit faculty for service?

Service and collegial governance have recently become topics of intense debate between academic staff and employers. The CAUT policy statement *Nature of Academic Work* emphasizes the importance of the all-inclusive academic job: "Central to academic work is service to the profession, internal and external to post-secondary institutions including collegial governance, academic staff association work, the defence and promotion of academic work, activities in provincial and national academic staff associations, community engagement, and public discourse" (CAUT, 2016, para. 1).

The overreliance on precarious contract academic staff undermines the service component of the academic job. These positions are sufficiently demanding and poorly compensated to make additional contributions onerous. One of the lessons of the last three years of the COVID pandemic (2020–2023) suggests service should be emphasized if we are to ensure the progressive future of post-secondary education. Citing the need for expediency during the public health emergency, many universities and colleges sought to bypass existing channels for routine decision-making. This truncated collegial consultation continues as many collective forums for faculties and senates have retained online formats. While this technology allows for easy access to meetings, should one click the provided links, this may discourage active engagement. In many instances, the adoption of a passive acceptance model defaults to administrative acquiescence unless challenged from the virtual floor. Arguably, it is much easier to rush through an agenda online than in person. A simulacrum of collegial engagement is of no benefit to our campus communities. Service must become a priority for the survival of the campus collective as traditionally defined.

The linkage between service and effective collegial governance is important. The pernicious trend to retain outside consultants to advise on "streamlining" governance to ostensibly improve "efficiency" may ultimately diminish the service component of faculty activities. Fortunately, these initiatives are not universal. Some enlightened administrators have stated they are willing to embrace collegial governance provided there is mutual commitment. It's a fair point. This would entail more faculty volunteering for committees, reading the relevant advance documents, and coming prepared to make substantive contributions to the debates. In return, this service must be foregrounded as a crucial component of rank and tenure decisions.

Academic staff associations also struggle with service. Faculty members with a history of long-term commitment to their associations comment on the challenges of recruiting colleagues. Further, there is often a discernible generational gap among union activists that skews toward older members. Association executives may show evidence of stagnant electoral renewal and lag in encouraging the participation of members who have only limited investment in their unions. New tenure-stream faculty are frequently advised to shy away from active association service until their careers are well established. Such delayed interaction often leads to ongoing patterns of disengagement.

The neoliberal university defines successful academics more as private entrepreneurs, intent on maximizing individual gain, rather than members of the collective collegium with a broader civic mission. Academic staff associations in this restricted sense merely function on a transactional basis to negotiate a collective agreement and address grievances rather than as part of a broader project to support collegial governance and the academic job: *the* union as opposed to *our* union.

It should be obvious to all that Canada's post-secondary educational system has weathered the last few years with tenacity, but our public institutions face considerable challenges. Service, to our specific institutions and our profession, is vital to overcoming adversity. Collegial governance, sometimes derided as an illegitimate effort at "co-management," is long overdue for constructive renewal. To support this goal, academic staff associations must make concerted efforts to attract and encourage their members to see this work as crucial to the broadly defined profession. University and college administrators must similarly value all aspects of service and ensure this continues to inform their future actions.

Universities Support Equity and Social Justice

Often campus-led efforts to support equity-deserving groups elicit an enthusiasm for specific and general projects to advance equity, but also frustration that the objectives for equity too often involve extended timelines and many obstacles. We know from history that waiting out such moments will not suffice. The mere passage of time does not assuage barriers to equity, and only focused activism will yield the desired results. Members of equity-deserving groups and their allies confront the sheer breadth of equity issues, ranging from gender, race, sexual orientation, age, and manifestations of physical or mental health challenges. The intersectionality of these issues and the importance of developing language for our collective agreements that advance equity are vital objectives. This language must also be, when necessary, effectively protected through the grievance and arbitration process. The term "accommodation" is often raised, both in its technical framing as a statutory and contractual obligation and as a moral demand for due consideration. Given the extended struggle to achieve objectives, there are times when it may be poignantly asked, how long must we accommodate those who do not wish to accommodate the equity-deserving in our midst?

CAUT has developed an online Equity Toolkit as a multi-faceted resource to educate allies of equity-deserving groups and a detailed guide to addressing specific issues arising from this process. An overview explains the centrality of equity in all its manifestations, not just with the intent of reiterating these topics among equity advocates but to make the cogent argument that equity must be a broader concern for everyone. Frequently, we are informed by administrators that sufficient data is lacking on equity-related challenges. Faculty are told the collection of such data is too complicated or time-consuming to assemble, and that existing policies already address equity concerns. Again, the Equity Toolkit provides an effective rejoinder to such dismissive responses.

We all benefit from the achievements in equity and we all must join this campaign. Beyond specific guidance to pursue equity issues, the Equity Toolkit articulates why this larger project is necessary: "Realizing equity is both an individual and a collective responsibility. Academic staff associations must take a leadership role. Equity is more than a particular set of issues. It is a lens through which all issues should be considered. It is not about balancing different, competing interests. It is about achieving justice for all" (CAUT, n.d.-b.)

Universities and Progressive Governance

The advent of formal union certification in Canadian post-secondary education gained momentum in the 1970s and continues apace. This move to embrace collective bargaining was also adopted when the American Association of University Professors contributed by 1975 to the peak of tenured academic positions in the United States at 37 percent (Reichman, 2015; AAUP, 2013). Statistics Canada lists "educational services" as having among the highest union density, at 68 percent, in 2012, of all public- and private-sector unions in Canada, and this compares to 27 percent total union membership in the private sector (Galarneau & Sohn, 2013; Government of Canada, n.d.-a; Katchanovski et al., 2011).[6] The segment for post-secondary education is even further concentrated, more than 80 percent, as university workers have placed significant confidence in the collective bargaining process (Heron, 2015). The large majority of these unions are, in turn, active members of CAUT. A rise in periodic militancy leading to strike action is notable over the last decade as the consequences of the neoliberal agenda are more sharply defined.[7]

It is also clear that North American post-secondary union membership has been subject to a massive anti-labour campaign, involving education-focused foundations and think tanks, provincial/state/federal governments, and the courts, as part of an intensive scheme to defund and demobilize this sector. Key adversaries include the Manning Centre for Building Democracy, Working Canadians, The Fraser Institute, the Atlantic Institute for Market Studies, the Higher Education Quality Council of Ontario, and, in the United States, the American Legislative Exchange Council and the National Right to Work Committee. Harvard sociologist Theda Skocpol's recent research into conservative ideologues and "dark money" identifies Americans for Prosperity (AFP), the Koch Foundation's primary vehicle for neoliberal strategy, as particularly intent on destroying the union movement in all its capacities as a champion of equity-seeking groups and other causes for social justice.[8] AFP funding is at the root of the 2018 Supreme Court of the United States challenge against "agency fees" in *Janus v. AFSCME* (*American Federation of State, County, and Municipal Employees*), a ruling that has implemented de facto right-to-work regulations for all American public-sector unions.[9]

The Canadian equivalent to agency or "fair share" union deductions is the landmark Rand Formula (1946) that established automatic check-off of dues as an attainable bargaining goal and remains the foundation of contemporary union stability. While there have been efforts to curtail or eliminate Rand this drastic course of action has yet to gain sufficient political traction in Canada.[10] Several provinces have, however, introduced highly restrictive legislation limiting the activities of certified unions. Some of these measures have been challenged successfully through the courts, but the process has proven time-consuming and costly. For example, egregious anti-union legislation that arguably established a form of right-to-work by broadly defining "essential" workers, introduced in Saskatchewan in 2008, was only partially struck down by the Supreme Court of Canada in 2015.[11] The Saskatchewan experience suggests how the battles of one province's public-sector unions may soon become the struggle for workers nationally, and therefore activists need to think beyond the narrow confines of their specific workplaces.[12]

The education profession generally, and post-secondary divisions in particular, may not be known as hotbeds of militant industrial unrest, but events of the last months challenge notions of quiescence. In Britain, the University and College Union (UCU) has staged walkouts over poor wages and conditions, and in 2022 48,000 academic workers in the University of California system launched the largest-ever strike in this sector. The right to support collective bargaining through the use of strikes raises numerous questions. How a union reaches the position of authorizing a strike, and what constitutes a legal strike, have been highlighted across Canada and internationally. The answer is both simple and complex.

Simple, in that withholding labour to achieve an acceptable negotiated contract is one of the most democratic actions unions may undertake.

Before formal negotiations, unions poll their membership on the issues they wish to bring forward. Actual bargaining is undertaken by a smaller group of colleagues representing the broader collective. Hence the term "collective bargaining." Expectations for constructive interchange between a union and administration may not unfold as expected, and an impasse is declared. A strike vote may be undertaken at any point, but the question is always direct: Do the members of a certified bargaining unit support a cessation of their professional activities to bolster their team's position at the negotiating table? Complex, with variations for differing provincial laws, a successful strike vote is a high bar to clear. The union must usually achieve not only a majority of those casting votes but also the majority of the entire membership, an impressive level of engagement, one not even expected for political elections. Provinces may also differ on the timeline required to reach a legal strike. A government-appointed conciliator will try to forge a late settlement, but failing this, there may be a "no board" report to the minister of labour indicating a stalemate. This is followed by a mandatory "cooling off" period, after which a strike or lockout may be declared.

In Canada, legal strikes are rarely spontaneous events instigated by a small cadre of exuberant activists but rather a deliberative action of the entire collective. Some have described this multi-stage process as ponderous and bound by "industrial legality," but it is the system we've inherited to protest workplace inequalities and strive for progressive reform. Having reached the point of a strike, why commence a workplace stoppage if, as critics claim, it's disruptive? The intention is that disruption, for without this extraordinary leverage many university/college administrators will not agree to most union proposals. Without the potential of strikes, the workplace is less democratic and less collegial. Sometimes constructive progress is born of strife, and, surprisingly, many picket line experiences are positive as faculty/staff learn of each other's research, teaching, and a shared commitment to quality education. Students also have an opportunity to engage in vital debates on the educational mission as they represent a crucial element of the campus community.

While strikes are comparatively rare, there have been efforts to stifle even the potential for job action. During the fractious negotiations for primary school educational support workers, the government of Ontario attempted to impose a multi-year contract and shield this unilateral action with the audacious application of the notwithstanding clause to exempt bad faith bargaining from legal challenges under the Charter of

Rights and Freedoms. If implemented, this pre-emptive use of section 33 of the Charter would have not only quashed the constitutional rights of these workers but also had the potential to render all collective bargaining rights effectively moot. The collective protests of the labour movement were swift, the legislation was repealed, and the negotiations eventually concluded with a ratified agreement.

When post-secondary faculty/staff vote to certify a union to be their sole representative for the purpose of negotiating a collective agreement, and to support that legal agreement through grievance and other procedures of redress, they are also accepting that some instances may compel adversarial confrontation. For contemporary Canadians, the constitutional right to strike, however, encumbered with multiple procedural tests and limitations, forms the keystone for all collective agreements that in turn buttress collegial governance and academic freedom. Therefore, we should strike when necessary and then strike to win for the benefit of our profession and our democracy. If there is "power in the union," then it is to be found in the collective voice of our colleagues. To those who have witnessed this directly, it is a persuasive argument to continue this project of mobilization. A vibrant union culture on our campuses is the most effective form of applied governance we have as our collective resource.

Universities and the Academic Job

All these recent Canadian cases of dysfunctional governance find parallels in disputes at American and British universities as publicly funded institutions shroud with secrecy their increasingly corporatized and neoliberal decisions. This part of the story is not new, but what is encouraging is the concerted efforts to rebuff this administrative culture of control. For this, campus progressives have forged broad alliances among faculty, staff, students, and alumni to hold universities accountable and protect principles of academic freedom. Yet too often faculty unions do not participate actively in recruiting suitable candidates for board appointments nor do these union councils monitor closely the actions of their putative faculty representatives. Such lackadaisical actions leave clear the path for the routinization of administrative practices that are increasingly unaccountable for publicly funded institutions.[13]

Several observations are worth noting. Most of those who work and learn in a post-secondary educational setting remain unclear as to the definition of academic freedom, why these principles are crucial to a robust intellectual culture, and how these connect with matters of governance. Therefore, these explanations must be offered to all concerned and must lead to concrete steps to ensure responsible, transparent governance structures are erected and protected. In deciding what defines "good governance" we need to be explicit about what constitutes "bad governance" in a manner that wrests these descriptors away from senior administrators who are all too willing to casually invoke abstract terms such as "best practices" and "openness and transparency" with the cynical intent of offering none of the above. Collegial governance of universities is, and will remain, a struggle, but it has not been decided against those with the better interests of the civic university in mind.

The necessary focus on the intersectionality of academic freedom, tenure, and collegial governance is key. These are pillars from which to develop an effective resistance, yet for many in academe they are invoked sporadically or defined too narrowly. Efforts to impose a highly restrictive definition of academic freedom (as in the 2011 Universities Canada statement) are effectively countered by a focus on the historical understanding of these concepts.[14] The insidious diminution of academic freedom (intramural/extramural) to the severely truncated definition of so-called "employee speech"—thou shalt not speak ill of administrators—as encapsulated in Robert Dickeson's "The Four Facets of Academic Freedom," is an obvious distortion of this concept (Dickeson, 2014, pp. 23–25). In *An Introduction to University Governance*, Cheryl Foy offers a cantankerously dismissive notion of faculty rights that all but eliminates collegial governance (Foy, 2021; Eastman et al., 2022). This calls for active rebuttal precisely because many university workers are confused or ambivalent about what may appear as abstractions. Tenure is similarly under assault and a rigorous defence will not only protect full-time faculty but should be extended to a principled effort to bring precariat just-in-time contract academic staff under its aegis of the union and, in so doing, address the issues of workplace casualization and post-tenure review.

Collegial governance is too often relegated to the complacent acquiescence of academics unwilling to act on the protections and implicit responsibilities afforded by academic freedom and tenure. University senates or other governing bodies may be reformed, if not transformed, if sufficient faculty and students seek to exercise democratic process and informed debate. These reforms are challenging to implement and require concerted coordination and stamina. That the governance systems of academe are too often distorted and dysfunctional is insufficient reason to abandon the latent potential afforded by collegial governance and to activate the very egalitarian "regimes of trust" so despised by administrators. In so doing, the limitations of administrative control are exposed as well as the vacuity of descriptive language used to cloak their true intent: when top-down managerialism is packaged as ersatz bottom-up populism (Simpson, 2014).

Faculty and staff unions must take the initiative to protect the conditions of their working environment in a manner that highlights activism. In a recent policy statement, CAUT has issued an important definition of the nature of the academic job to explicitly include "service to the profession including collegial governance, academic staff association work, the defence and promotion of academic work, activities in provincial and national staff associations, community engagement, and public discourse" (CAUT, 2016 , para. 1). This policy, if implemented in some form as a model clause in future collective agreements, will address ambiguous definitions of service that are vulnerable to constrictive administrative practice. We cannot, and should not, concede that the issue of post-secondary education governance and managerial fundamentalism is a foregone conclusion; for when scrutinized these many administrative projects remain inchoate and incoherent. British sociologist Paul Thompson long ago observed that many of the managerial approaches presently used to secure greater control of the educational sector are, in fact, not novel and not without limitations (Thompson & McHugh, 1990; Ackroyd & Thompson, 1999). This being the case, the real potential for effective resistance remains within the grasp of those who teach, work, and learn at these institutions of higher learning. Too often we make the erroneous assumption that the triumph of the neoliberal university is well nigh when opportunities for progressive redirection are within our grasp.

References

AAUP. (n.d.) *Background facts on contingent faculty positions*. https://www.aaup.org/issues/contingency/background-facts

AAUP. (2013). *Trends in faculty employment status, 1975–2011*. https://www.aaup.org/sites/default/files/Faculty_Trends_0.pdf

Ackroyd, S., & Thompson, P. (1999). *Organizational misbehaviour*. Sage.

Bibliothèque. (1963–1966). *Rapport Parent: Rapport de la Commission royale d'enquête sur l'enseignement dans la province de Québec*. Commissions d'enquête au Québec depuis 1867. https://www.bibliotheque.assnat.qc.ca/guides/fr/les-commissions-d-enquete-au-quebec-depuis-1867/7548-commission-parent-1963-66

Brownlee, J. (2015). *Academia, inc.: How corporatization is transforming Canadian universities*. Fernwood Publishing.

CAUT (Canadian Association of University Teachers). (n.d.-a). *Campaigns*. https://www.caut.ca/campaigns

CAUT. (n.d.-b). The importance of equity. Equity toolkit. https://www.caut.ca/publication/importance-equity

CAUT. (2016). *Nature of academic work: Policy statement*. https://www.caut.ca/about-us/caut-policy/lists/caut-policy-statements/policy-statement-on-the-nature-of-academic-work

CAUT. (2023). *Interview with Madeleine Pastinelli*. https://www.caut.ca/bulletin/interview-madeleine-pastinelli

Colby, G. (2023). *Data snapshot: Tenure and contingency in US higher education*. American Association of University Professors. https://www.aaup.org/sites/default/files/AAUP%20Data%20Snapshot.pdf

Connexions. (1965–1968). *Living and learning: The report of the provincial committee on aims and objectives of education in the schools of Ontario*. https://www.connexions.org/CxLibrary/Docs/cx5636-HallDennis.htm

Côté, J.E., & Allahar, A.L. (2011). *Lowering higher education: The rise of the corporate university and the fall of liberal education*. University of Toronto Press.

Dickeson, R.C. (2014). The four facets of "academic freedom." *How to engage faculty in academic program prioritization*. Academic Impressions. http://webmedia.jcu.edu/president/files/2019/04/howtoengage.pdf

Eastman, J., Jones, G.A., Trottier, C., & Bégin-Caouette, O. (2022). *University governance in Canada: Navigating complexity*. McGill-Queen's University Press.

Foy, C. (2022). *An introduction to university governance*. Irwin Law.

Galarneau, D., & Sohn, T. (2013). Long-term trends in unionization. *Insights on Canadian Society*. Statistics Canada. https://www150.statcan.gc.ca/n1/pub/75-006-x/2013001/article/11878-eng.pdf

Ginsberg, B. (2013). *The fall of the faculty: The rise of the all-administrative university and why it matters* (2nd ed.). Oxford University Press.

Giroux, H.A. (2014). *Neoliberalism's war on higher education*. Haymarket Books.

Government of Canada. (n.d.-a). *Labour program*. https://www.canada.ca/en/employment-social-development/corporate/portfolio/labour.html

Government of Canada. (n.d.-b). *Policy on sensitive technology research and affiliations of concern*. https://science.gc.ca/site/science/en/safeguarding-your-research/guidelines-and-tools-implement-research-security/sensitive-technology-research-and-affiliations-concern/policy-sensitive-technology-research-and-affiliations-concern

Heron, C. (2015). From deference to defiance: The evolution of Ontario faculty associations. *Academic Matters*. http://www.academicmatters.ca/2015/06/from-deference-to-defiance-the-evolution-of-ontario-faculty-associations

Katchanovski, I., Rothman, S., & Nevitte, N. (2011). Attitudes towards faculty unions and collective bargaining in American and Canadian universities. *Relations industrielles/Industrial Relations*, 66(3), 349–73. https://doi.org/10.7202/1006343ar

Liptak, A. (2018, June 27). Supreme Court ruling delivers a sharp blow to labor unions. *New York Times*. https://www.nytimes.com/2018/06/27/us/politics/supreme-court-unions-organized-labor.html

MacKinnon, P. (2014). *University leadership and public policy in the twenty-first century*. University of Toronto Press.

MacKinnon, P. (2018). *University commons divided: Exploring debate & dissent on campus*. University of Toronto Press.

MacLean, N. (2017). *Democracy in chains: The deep history of the radical right's stealth plan for America*. Viking Press.

Newson, J., & Polster, C. (2015). *A penny for your thoughts: How corporatization devalues teaching, research, and public service in Canadian universities*. Canadian Centre for Policy Alternatives.

Public Safety Canada. (2023). *What we heard report: Consulting Canadians on the merits of a foreign influence transparency registry*. Government of Canada. https://www.publicsafety.gc.ca/cnt/rsrcs/pblctns/2023-nhncng-frgn-nflnc-wwh/index-en.aspx

Reichman, H. (2015). Professionalism and unionism: Academic freedom, collective bargaining, and the American Association of University Professors. *Journal of Academic Freedom*, 6, 1–18. https://www.aaup.org/sites/default/files/Reichman_0.pdf

Ruth, J. (2023). Subnational authoritarianism and the campaign to control higher education. *Academe Magazine*, 109(4). https://www.aaup.org/article/subnational-authoritarianism-and-campaign-control-higher-education

Stan, A.M. (2015). Funding from the Koch network. PSC-CUNY. https://psc-cuny.org/clarion/2015/october/whos-behind-anti-union-scotus-case

Skocpol, T. (2016, February 3). Who owns the GOP? Review of Jane Mayer's *Dark money: The hidden history of the billionaires behind the rise of the radical right*. Dissent. https://www.dissentmagazine.org/online_articles/jane-mayer-dark-money-review-koch-brothers-gop

Skocpol, T., & Hertel-Fernandez, A. (2016). The Koch effect: The impact of a cadre-led network on American politics (unpublished paper, 27 January 2016). https://scholars.org/sites/scholars/files/the_koch_effect_for_spsa_w_apps_skocpol_and_hertel-fernandez-corrected_1-4-16.pdf

Simpson, J.S. (2014). *Longing for justice: Higher education and democracy's agenda*. University of Toronto Press.

Thompson, P., & McHugh, D. (1990). *Work organisations: A critical introduction.* Palgrave Macmillan.

Tuchman, G. (2009). *Wannabe U: Inside the corporate university.* University of Chicago Press.

Uppal, S., & Hango, D. (2022). Differences in tenure status and feelings of fairness in hiring and promotions among male and female faculty in Canadian universities. *Insights on Canadian Society.* Statistics Canada. https://www150.statcan.gc.ca/n1/pub/75-006-x/2022001/article/00007-eng.htm

Washburn, J. (2005). *University, inc.: The corporate corruption of higher education.* Basic Books.

Xu, Y., & Wang, Y. (2023). Job stress and university faculty members' life satisfaction: The mediating role of emotional burnout. *Frontiers in Psychology,* 14, Article 1111434. https://doi.org/10.3389/fpsyg.2023.1111434

Notes

1   We are, of course, mindful that not all of us had (nor still have) proper access to health care and education, such as members of First Nations and other equity-deserving groups.

2   Indicative of this contemptuous administrative approach is MacKinnon (2014 & 2018). Peter MacKinnon was president of the University of Saskatchewan and later served brief terms at Athabasca and Dalhousie universities.

3   Analysis of the consequences of corporatized post-secondary education is extensive and includes: Washburn (2005); Tuchman (2009); Côté & Allahar (2011); Ginsberg (2013); Giroux (2014); Newson & Polster (2015); Brownlee (2015).

4   The Panel on Research Ethics's TCPS 2 (2022) can be found on the Government of Canada website. https://ethics.gc.ca/eng/policy-politique_tcps2-eptc2_2022.html

5   SPUL. (2022, August 24). Remettre les CÉRUL au service du bien commun, https://spul.ca/wp-content/uploads/2022/08/CERUL-et-liberte-academique-1.pdf. See also, CAUT (2023).

6   This union density has remained consistent over longitudinal indices. The most recent reliable statistics are from the 2011 census.

7   Strikes occurred recently at University of Manitoba (2021); Lethbridge University, Acadia, Université Sainte-Anne, Concordia University of Edmonton (2022); Université Laval, University of Prince Edward Island, Memorial University, Cape Breton (2023).

8   Skocpol, & Hertel-Fernandez (2016); Skocpol (2016); MacLean (2017). Other US-based anti-union foundations include Olin Foundation, Bradley Foundation, Cato Institute, and Mackinac Center for Public Policy. Further details of Koch infiltration of North American universities can be found at http://www.unkochmycampus.org/.

9 Liptak (2018); scotusblog, https://www.scotusblog.com/case-files/cases/
janus-v-american-federation-state-county-municipal-employees-council-31/.
Professional Staff Congress-City University of New York, The anti-union group
Center for Individual Rights has received funding and other support from the
AFP in the campaign to target public-sector unions. The February 2016 death of
Justice Antonin Scalia raises further questions on an earlier ruling in Friedrichs.
See https://academeblog.org/2016/02/16/the-future-of-friedrichs-in-the-supreme-
court/. With Justice Scalia's death, the Court was split 4-4 on Friedrichs, thus
upholding the Court of Appeals for the Ninth Circuit Court, decision per curium,
to dismiss the challenge to agency fees. A further attempt to appeal the ruling
was denied in June 2016.

10 In a decision with some parallels to Friedrichs, the 1990–1991 Supreme Court of
Canada ruling on Lavigne v. Ontario Public Sector Employees Union (OPSEU), [1991]
2 SCR 211, upheld the principles of the Rand Formula. See Christopher Schenk,
(2012, September), Unions in a democratic society: A response to the
consultation paper on the renewal of labour legislation in Saskatchewan, CCPA.
https://www.policyalternatives.ca/news-research/unions-in-a-democratic-society/

11 In 2015's Saskatchewan Federation of Labour v. Saskatchewan, 2015 SCC 4, the
Supreme Court of Canada struck down 2008 legislation that imposed severe
restrictions of union activities as a violation of the Charter of Rights and
Freedoms. See also details of the Charter implication in the BC Health Services
in Michael Lynk, (2007, November), "Supreme Court boldly affirms labour
rights," CAUT Bulletin 54/9, https://bulletin-archives.caut.ca/bulletin/articles/
2007/11/supreme-court-boldly-affirms-labour-rights-.

12 The American experience with charter schools is another pertinent example
of corporate wealth introduced to undermine teachers' unions and the civic
mission of public schools.

13 The efforts to reform senates at several universities are notable. These include
the University of British Columbia with its innovative "UBclean" campaign;
Dalhousie University was compelled to expand student representation and
diversity in the wake of the Faculty of Dentistry scandal in 2014; Carleton
University is subject to an ongoing campaign to free senators from imposed
confidentiality policies.

14 Universities Canada (formerly the Association of Universities and Colleges
of Canada) issued its 2011 Statement on Academic Freedom, which sharply
restricted the traditional definitions of the concept (http://www.univcan.ca/
media-room/media-releases/statement-on-academic-freedom/). CAUT responded
with an open letter detailing the significant problems posed by the UC statement
(http://www.caut.ca/docs/default-document-library/caut_to_aucc_academic_
freedom.pdf?sfvrsn=0). See also the CAUT Policy Statement on Academic
Freedom (http://www.caut.ca/about-us/caut-policy/lists/caut-policy-statements/
policy-statement-on-academic-freedom).

SECTION III
REFRAMING
THE RESPONSIVE
UNIVERSITY

*The third section provides an examination and a critique of
the complexity and shortfalls of contemporary universities
and offers potential new directions for the future.*

CHAPTER 8
HIGHER EDUCATION AND ACADEMICS MUST "STEP UP"

Kevin K. Kumashiro

GUIDED BY THE FRAMING QUESTION OF THE SYMPOSIUM, *What Are Universities For?*, I would like to explore what it means to "reframe" higher education—that is, to use a different metaphor to describe a problem, or to rattle or shake the assumptions or underlying story behind whatever question we are grappling with, or simply to ask a different kind of question—as a way to broaden our understanding of the problem and the solution. This chapter will do so by looking at five topic areas, drawing primarily on US contexts and scholarship but with the invitation to apply elsewhere: university mission, university governance, universities advancing the commons, universities advancing justice movements intersectionally, and university curriculum and empire.

Why "Reframe"?

A central theme of this chapter is to shift our analytical focus from the level of the individual to the level of systems. Two examples from my experiences are illustrative. First, when I was living in Chicago, Illinois, a dozen years ago, lawmakers were debating how public school teachers should be evaluated. They were asking questions like, "Should student test scores count for 25 percent of a teacher's evaluation or 45 percent?" If we accepted that framing of the question, the most that we could debate is what percentage of the teacher evaluation should be constituted by student test scores. But if we understood the problem differently—for example, not as a question of whether teachers are raising test scores, but rather of whether test scores are valid measures of teacher quality—then we might want to pose a different question altogether, as my colleagues and I did when we held a press conference and asked: "Should student test scores count at all in the evaluation of teachers?"

A second example points to where even education scholars can remain stuck in problematic frames. In 2015 the administration of then-president Obama proposed a set of regulations that would have applied to the over twenty thousand university-based teacher-preparation programs in the United States. Relying heavily on value-added modelling (by aiming to determine the value or impact of one factor alone), the federal Department of Education not only presumed that we can determine how effective a teacher is by looking at how well they raised their students' test scores, but also, in turn, presumed that we can determine how effective a teacher-preparation program is by looking at how well their graduates raised their students' test scores. Programs were to track their graduates for three years after graduation, and if in those three years their students' test scores went up, the department would conclude that the teachers were effective and the programs that prepared those teachers were too.

Assessment experts had long been arguing that standardized tests are neither valid nor reliable for making such claims. Some teacher educators similarly argued that it would be problematic to rely solely on student test scores because they capture only a small slice of what students know and can do. But what some scholars offered as an alternative was to replace standardized tests with more robust assessments such as portfolio assessments to determine student learning, which in turn would be used to determine teacher effectiveness and again, in turn, program effectiveness. Such a response remained within the logic of value-added modelling and, in particular, continued to focus predominantly on trying to determine the impact of a teacher alone (or a program alone). We needed to tell a different story. One way to reframe this narrative would have been to shift the focus from the individual to the system. As reflected in the notion that "it takes a village to raise a child," the educational village or system needs to work effectively *as a system* in order to educate, which means that the goal of evaluating teachers should involve trying to determine not the impact of the teacher irrespective of other factors or variables but how that teacher contributes to and works synergistically within the multi-factor system in which teaching and learning occur.

There are a number of resources that are helpful for understanding and imagining the transformative potential of reframing so-called "reforms" in education. At least five come to mind. The first is Brazilian educator Paulo Freire's book *Pedagogy of the Oppressed* (1970/2018). One of the arguments he makes is that we should not race too quickly down a path to solve a problem until we first more deeply understand what that problem is. We need to do our homework by "reading the world"—that is, by critically examining and then telling our own story of what the problem is—because if we do not, we might end up accepting someone else's story of what the problem is and, in so doing, pursue a solution that does not make things better and might even be counterproductive.

The second resource is a video published in 2020 on The Intercept's YouTube channel called "Coronavirus Capitalism—and How to Beat It" (https://www.youtube.com/watch?v=niwNTI9Nqd8), featuring Canadian scholar and journalist Naomi Klein, who reminds us that how a society responds in a moment of crisis depends on the stories available to us. For example, in a situation like the global financial crisis of 2008–09, or the global coronavirus pandemic that started in 2020, if all we hear is that resources are limited and spending must be cut—that is, if all we hear are stories of scarcity and austerity—then the only thing to debate is how much to cut and where. But as we know, in the midst of both of those crises, not all sectors of society were characterized by scarcity and austerity: during the financial crisis, the military and prison industrial complexes continued to grow, and throughout the latest pandemic, many multinational corporations saw record profits and concentration of wealth. The dominating frames of scarcity and austerity served to mask the whole story, and in so doing, rationalized only certain responses.

The third resource, published and circulated worldwide at around the same time as Klein's video, is the essay by Indian writer Arundhati Roy entitled "The Pandemic Is a Portal" (2020), which cautions against rushing to "return to normal." Such is what schools all over the world were trying to do at the start of the coronavirus pandemic—either return to how things used to be as quickly as possible or, in the short term, try to mimic normalcy as much as possible, as when trying to make online instruction look as much as possible like in-person classrooms. The problem with such moves is that they end up dragging with them all the problems that came with the status quo; after all, normalcy was not such a great thing to begin with. Crises give us the opportunity to hit the pause button and to ask whether there is a better way forward. The pandemic, Roy argues, can serve as a portal, a gateway to a different future. Did we really take that opportunity? Many would argue, at least in the United States when it came to education, that we did not: we rushed to "return," and in so doing, doubled down on some of the most harmful aspects of schooling.

The fourth resource is a book by Jack Halberstam, *The Queer Art of Failure* (2011; published under a former name), that draws on the paradigm shift inaugurated by the queer activism of the 1980s. Beginning around the 1950s in the United States, much of the civil rights activism regarding lesbian, gay, bisexual, and transgender (LGBT) people centred on narratives that "we" are as "normal" as everyone else. But not all agreed with that strategy, and by the 1980s, more activists were pushing back on the assimilationist demand of such narratives by arguing that we should not be insisting that we are as normal as others because there is something wrong with how society defines normalcy. Queerness became a standpoint from which to question the hegemonic or oppressive nature of normalcy. Halberstam makes a parallel argument about success and failure. Conventional wisdom tells us that failure can be helpful because it eventually helps us to succeed: we say that "failing builds character," "we learn from our mistakes," and "try and try again." But perhaps that is not the only value of failure. As with queerness, sites of failure can serve as standpoints from which to critique success, which like normalcy is not always a good thing and can instead demand assimilation and deny the value of difference.

This reminds me of the late gay activist and scholar Eric Rofes who, in a lecture that he delivered at a conference that I organized two decades ago, argued that academia is, at its core, assimilationist. Just think about what we value most in academia: Writing articles primarily for a scholarly audience that the general public sometimes cannot easily understand because of the jargon and cannot easily access because they are published in small and often paywalled journals. Simultaneously, the processes of hiring, tenuring, and promoting faculty often devalue and even discourage public scholarship or in other ways leveraging our scholarship to change policy, practice, and public awareness. As long as we continue to privilege only certain forms of scholarship, we hinder our ability to have public impact.

Both Rofes and Halberstam raise questions about what it means to succeed in education. As educational historians point out, the earliest US public schools and universities were not created to level the playing field; that was not their original intention. Educational institutions, especially those that serve the masses, were created to socialize and sort. This means that success in educational institutions is not necessarily a sign of being smarter or more accomplished but, at least in some ways, is a sign of learning to play the game better than most people. Success, in this way, is not so much what distinguishes one from the norm but rather is a measure of just how well one has conformed.

The fifth resource is my book *Surrendered: Why Progressives Are Losing the Biggest Battles in Education* (2020), in which I try to think through a lot of what I am arguing here, particularly the acknowledgement that the reason progressives have often acted in counterproductive ways in public and higher education is that we failed to reframe the debate. Such will be the theme that echoes throughout this chapter, starting with perhaps the most fundamental of questions for universities: What is our mission?

University Mission

In June 2023, the US Supreme Court effectively ended affirmative action in university admissions by finding unconstitutional the race-conscious practices within the holistic (whole-student) review process used by Harvard University and the University of North Carolina. Also that summer, through protests, letter-writing and media campaigns, and other organizing initiatives, activists were increasing pressure on President Biden's administration to expand student debt relief and to make public higher education more affordable as court decisions and expiring policies accelerated the debt cliff that many borrowers faced. Expanding access through admissions and affordability has long faced opposition by those who argue that such initiatives are unfair and make university enrolments less about merit and more about social status, and in contrast, has long been supported by those who argue that such initiatives remedy historical and structural barriers and trouble what we think does or should count as merit.

I strongly support affirmative action, student debt relief, and free tuition, but I also argue that these do not go far enough because they focus on individual access rather than system change and, in so doing, can function to increase access to what is in many ways a problematic system. This is not unlike debates about health care: "single payer" (which, in the United States, would be like expanding the Medicare system to all) would publicly fund how we access the health-care system, but the health-care system itself remains primarily privatized; hospitals and medical providers, for example, would not transform into public industries and employees. So, too, with increasing access to a higher education system that functions, in some ways, to socialize and sort us into a vastly inequitable society and does so, at least in part, by teaching us narrowly to "succeed" or, even more narrowly, to compete. The mission of the university often focuses on the individual—and this is what needs to change.

What would it mean for the mission of universities to centre more squarely on building the capacity of communities and society to advance democracy and justice? A helpful model already exists at the K–12 level where social movements are transforming traditional schools into "community schools." These schools offer wraparound services and serve as hubs for community capacity building. In a highly coordinated way, the school runs or houses a range of public and private services and resources that support not only individual student academic success but student wellness, family wellness, and community wellness too. The National Education Policy Center offers a range of resources regarding community schools (https://www.nepc.colorado.edu).

Too often, educational institutions are quite the opposite of community schools. At the start of the COVID pandemic in 2020, for example, what did many universities do? They shrank in scope: they offered fewer services and resources and, in so doing, actually exacerbated the swelling ranks of the un- or underemployed and underinsured, the housing- and food-insecure, and so on. Universities were even offering less educational programming just when we needed to broaden our skill sets in order to pursue different kinds of work and different kinds of relationships. This is where the title of this chapter comes from: rather than scaling back, if they pursued a different mission, universities would have felt called upon to step up.

So long as the focus of universities is narrowly on preparing individuals to compete or succeed, our admissions cannot help but to be narrowed in what counts as merit. A broader mission will reshape the admissions criteria, looking beyond merit—for example, beyond considering what you have accomplished so far and what you can accomplish in the future as an individual—to the university's ultimate mission, leading us to ask: Which applicants for admission will, if they come here, help to advance the university's mission of building the capacity of communities to advance justice?

Reframing the university mission changes everything about the university. To illustrate: I recently consulted for a university that wanted to increase student diversity. When I asked what they were doing already, they pointed to changes in recruitment and admissions strategies. I did not disagree with such changes, but I urged them to consider how the demographics of a student population is influenced by pretty much everything that happens at a university: how you govern and make decisions; your strategic plan; how you spend money; your student services; the demographics of your faculty, staff, and leaders; the partnerships you have, what kind of public voice you have—all of these come to bear on your ability to recruit, retain, and graduate a more diverse student body because all play an integrated role in making universities function as they do (they are all part of the problem and solution). A helpful resource for tackling the many domains of a university is the Framework for Assessment and Transformation, created a few years ago by a group of us in the nationwide network Education Deans for Justice and Equity (EDJE, 2019).

University Governance

What does it mean to reframe governance so that it can more forcefully pursue democracy and justice? Perhaps the most common approach to democratizing university governance is to increase the diversity and representativeness of those in leadership roles. But as with the previous examples of increasing access to a problematic system, adding more diversity to a leadership structure does not necessarily mean that the structure itself is changing or that it will function differently. To see this, it is helpful to see how governance structures typically fall in four categories, all of which are limited.

First is the internally appointed governing body (for example, a board of trustees appointed by the university president), which exists in many US private colleges and universities. A common problem with such boards is that they are making the major decisions for and about the institution but do not consist primarily of educational experts; rather, they tend to comprise wealthy business leaders who were chosen because of their capacity to help with major fundraising. Second is the publicly appointed body (appointed by a public official), which exists in many public institutions, as when state governors appoint public university trustees or city mayors appoint public school-board members. A common problem with such boards is that they are not directly accountable to the public, which is why, for decades, communities have been organizing to end mayoral control of K–12 school boards and transition to elected boards.

Third is the publicly elected board, such as college trustees or school-board members who are elected by their city or county constituents. While theoretically more democratic than the first two structures, such boards (particularly school boards) have come to be dominated by the religious and political right, which strategized how to take control through elections starting in the 1980s. Even among more liberal or progressive candidates, educational boards are often dominated not by education experts but by individuals who treat such positions as stepping stones into electoral politics because such positions are typically far less competitive to win. Fourth is the publicly rotated body, such as juries in courts that are selected by lottery and in which most members of the public are subject to participate. Again, such bodies are theoretically more democratic than the first two categories but, as exemplified by court juries, they are often diminished in their role as decision-makers because so much effort is spent beforehand to limit who can serve, what gets presented to them, and how they are to deliberate. While more inclusive, both the third and fourth categories have significant problems, and while they provide necessary steps toward inclusion, they are not sufficient to democratize.

What else, then, is needed? I see at least four organizing priorities that can point the way.

First, involving more people in decision-making must be accompanied by critical consciousness-raising. One of the key strategies of progressive social movements is increasing political awareness, namely, by engaging both the key stakeholders and the general public in collective inquiry to historicize how we got here, connect the dots between issues and communities, follow the money to understand power and priorities, and so on. Such forms of political education must accompany initiatives like elections and lotteries that increase access because without such education the elected or selected leaders are more likely to defer to those who are the most persuasive or to what common sense tells us that we should do (which is a problem because, like normalcy and success, "common sense" is not always the best guide for making decisions).

Some of the groups engaging in such political education are progressive unions, which leads to my second point: involving more people in unions must be accompanied by structural change. Unions provide an important intervention toward increased involvement in governance. But ironically, a strong union, as is the case with any social or political grouping, can also increase a sense of separation between us and them when unions rally together in opposition to or distinct from other groups. Alongside self-advocacy, then, must come systemic change and a far more expansive vision of the economy. Such expansive visions are offered when, say, engaging in cross-sector organizing and bargaining in ways that coordinate with and support other unions, as well as in bargaining for the common good— that is, for not just what is good for members but also what is good for the broader public. An expansive vision also comes with calls for the abolition of capitalist structures, the creation of an economy where the production of goods is not at odds with the people producing or consuming them, and the formation of workplaces where management interests are not antithetical to labour's.

Another contradiction inherent in collective bargaining is when advocacy results in even less involvement in governance than before, which leads to my third point: empowering and humanizing labour must involve blurring the labour-management divide. Some people think that organized labour will help to rattle leadership and decision-making and advance democracy, but a structural barrier can become even more impermeable as traditional unionization strengthens: namely, the delineation between what counts as labour and what counts as management (and who is eligible to do what). Fortunately, there exist alternative governance structures that allow for management and labour to be one and the same, such as worker-owned cooperatives. What are lessons learned from such cooperatives—what has worked well and what has not, or what might apply to universities and what might not? We can look at places like Mondragon University (https://www.mondragon.edu/en/home) in Spain, a private not-for-profit community-based, worker-owned and governed, cooperative university as we consider what it means to truly share or distribute what typically falls under management.

As with the division of management from labour, and the evolution of a factory-mode of production in education, universities often compartmentalize work, which leads to my fourth point: advancing diversity and justice must be a collective commitment and endeavour. Since the 1990s, many universities have been creating offices or units that focus on diversity, equity, and inclusion (DEI), such as the chief diversity officer (CDO) or Office of DEI. These initiatives can be impactful in some ways, but when they operate in a highly compartmentalized way, as is sometimes the case, other units may not feel the responsibility to advance such initiatives or, for that matter, to assess how their current operations are antithetical to such goals. Rather than maintaining a traditional organizational structure and adding a separate position, what if every member of a leadership team were required to hold the qualifications of a CDO and to integrate that vision in everything that they do—that is, to centre DEI in every aspect of finance, of academic affairs, of student services, of development, of communications, and so on? The EDJE Framework for Assessment and Transformation that I mentioned earlier can help with such systemwide distribution of justice work.

Universities Advancing the Commons

In the United States under the Obama administration, we experienced what was known as the Race to the Top initiative, a $4.35 billion US Department of Education competitive grant program created to spur and reward innovation and reforms in schools across the country, but which resulted in fuelling privatization and profiteering in public education because much of the work that was funded ended up being outsourced. Turning to the private sector to save us is a tendency of both Democrat and Republican administrations. Take the more recent example of billions in federal COVID relief funds that, within the educational sector, were funnelled toward the educational technology sector. As schools transitioned to online instruction, and as some students had less or insufficient access to necessary technologies, more and more people were calling to increase access by subsidizing the cost of hardware and the provision of Wi-Fi, which helps to explain the record profits of tech companies.

Fortunately, not all were proposing that public funds get funnelled to private companies. Instead, some were calling for the ed tech sector to become public industries: the federal government, for example, could have taken control of private industries for the public good (via, for instance, something like the *Defense Production Act* to publicly fund the production of hardware for all students), or more state and city governments could have done what was indeed happening in some places with the creation or expansion of publicly funded "municipal broadband." The California Alliance of Researchers for Equity in Education (CARE-ED) made precisely these reframings in our 2020 brief on online education (https://www.care-ed.org): the problem is not merely that hardware is too expensive and should be subsidized; no, the problem is that hardware production is a for-profit industry, and when it comes to public education, this is a mismatch. In fact, regarding all needs of schools, from the production of technology and the provision of food and transportation to the preparation of teachers and leaders and the provision of health services—all of these should be public industries in support of public education.

Universities Advancing Justice Movements Intersectionally

To do this, universities must advance justice movements intersectionally. That is, to reimagine universities, we must connect the dots. School lunches provide a helpful example. Recently, Minnesota became the fourth state to pass legislation providing for universal free school lunches in public schools. This is a good thing: schools should be feeding every student breakfast and lunch, and universities should too. But what exactly are we feeding students, and how are these meals being provided?

Marcus Weaver-Hightower, in his book *Unpacking School Lunch* (2022), connects the dots between the early roots of the national school lunch program and US imperialism. His book reveals the racialized rationale and rhetoric behind the debates and policies for school lunch programs. He reveals how school lunch programs are incredibly expensive and, as such, provide opportunities for privatization and substantial profiteering. And yet, school lunch programs continue to burden economically struggling families, and payment policies and practices often involve debt-shaming of young children and their families. The types of food we serve, along with the forms of production of such food, have had a highly destructive impact on the environment. Students often complain that the food is not tasty, but even or especially when it is the food is often irresponsibly unhealthy (not only lacking in nutritious value but harmful as well), which we have known for decades can negatively impact not only the long-term health of students but their academic outcomes as well. For these reasons, increasing access to the school lunch system is one small part of the solution; we must change the entire system of school lunch and the many problems with which it intersects—from financial access and nutrition to economic and environmental justice to racism and, yes, even imperialism.

University Curriculum and Empire

In the United States, the most recent wave of legislation to censor any discussion in schools of controversial issues like racism (or to block any support structures for targeted groups like trans students) kicked off with a bang in 2020 when then-president Trump and other far-right pundits began to demonize and grossly mischaracterize curriculum or initiatives that raised awareness of or attempted to remedy injustice, such as the *New York Times Magazine* 1619 Project (Hannah-Jones & *The New York Times Magazine*, 2021) and critical race theory. As with explosive controversies over ethnic studies curriculum a decade earlier, or multicultural curriculum several decades earlier, the critics blended psychological-sounding rhetoric (teaching about controversial topics is harmful to children) with nationalist and imperialist rhetoric (teaching about injustice is anti-patriotic and will hurt our standing as a world superpower).

The links between curriculum and US empire-building have long permeated schools. During the Cold War, for example, the federal government pushed the teaching of science, technology, engineering, and mathematics (the STEM subjects) so that we could compete with Russia, who had just beat us in the space race with the launch of the Sputnik 1 satellite. Employees in some public sectors, including teachers, were required to swear oaths of loyalty to the United States and were demonized via red-baiting (harassment of suspected communist-leaning groups or individuals) if they were deemed sympathetic to the enemy. Books were being banned if they were deemed to promote communism. In these ways, public schools have long been positioned to serve and protect the security of the state.

So, too, with universities, and not only during the Cold War. Just ten years ago, I attended a national conference about federal grants programs for Minority-Serving Institutions, which includes Historically Black Colleges and Universities, Hispanic-Serving Institutions, Asian American and Native American Pacific Islander–Serving Institutions, and several more. The goal of these grants programs was to increase the numbers of students of colour going into higher education, but one of the main sessions offered a troubling reason why: with higher education, people of colour could serve within the national security-state apparatus as inter-preters and interlopers who could work across racial, national, cultural, and linguistic differences to increase our national security.

Empire building is an ideological and identity-building project; it builds not only a nation, but the nationalism that fuels it. And educational insti-tutions, as arms of the state, will always be implicated in that process, even when we do not realize it, and even when we are actively countering it.

Conclusion: What Are Universities For?

In May 2023 the US Department of Education released its biennial National Assessment of Educational Progress (NAEP)—what is often called the Nation's Report Card. For decades it has shown nationwide test scores from different subjects and grade levels: starting in 1969 the assessment focused on scores in math and reading, and starting in the 1990s, on his-tory and civics. The most recent report shows that history and civics test scores, particularly for eighth graders, plummeted during the four years since the coronavirus pandemic began. This was not surprising: the 2022 Report Card (https://www.nationsreportcard.gov/) already showed that math and readings scores had plummeted. This was, after all, a time when much in schooling changed: we shifted to online instruction, less contact with teachers, less coverage of curriculum content, less support services and resources, and so on.

But what was most interesting to me about the data was not the scores related to civics but the students' perspectives about civics education. Students with higher proficiency in civics were between one-and-a-half and three times more likely to say that (a) it is important to understand the political process and government; (b) it is important to be involved in the political process; (c) they feel they better understand the world and its problems; and (d) they feel that they can make a difference in their com-munities—that is, they feel that they can be part of the solution.

These tasks—of troubling and reframing the problems we face and the solutions that we can create—constitute the central role of educational institutions in a democracy. Education should aim not merely to prepare us to succeed in the world as it is but rather to build our capacity to imag-ine the world as it is not yet—the world as it could be—and then to work toward creating that world if we so choose. What are universities for? They are for raising critical consciousness about the kinds of intersectional and global issues raised throughout this chapter and book. Let's create universities that embody these goals.[1]

References

Education Deans for Justice and Equity (EDJE). (2019). Education colleges for justice & equity: A framework for assessment and transformation ("The EDJE Framework"). Version 6.20.2019. https://sites.ehe.osu.edu/edje/publications

Freire, P. (2018). *Pedagogy of the oppressed*. Bloomsbury. (Original work published in English in 1970)

Halberstam, J. (2011). *The queer art of failure*. Duke University Press.

Hannah-Jones, H., & *The New York Times Magazine*. (2021). *The 1619 project: A new origin story*. One World.

Kumashiro, K.K. (2020). *Surrendered: Why progressives are losing the biggest battles in education*. Teachers College Press.

Roy, A. (2020, April 3). The pandemic is a portal. *Financial Times*. https://www.ft.com/content/10d8f5e8-74eb-11ea-95fe-fcd274e920ca

Weaver-Hightower, M.B. (2022). *Unpacking school lunch: Understanding the hidden politics of school food*. Palgrave Macmillan.

Notes

1   This chapter is an edited version of a keynote address delivered on May 5, 2023.

CHAPTER 9
REIMAGINING THE PEDAGOGY OF TRUTH

Sheila Cote-Meek

Situating Self

I T IS IMPORTANT FOR ME TO TELL THE READER WHO I AM, WHERE I come from, and how I approach my work. This is important because who I am is directly linked to how I view and understand the world around me as well as my relationship to all things. I also draw on my cultural understandings in the work I do as an educator, administrator, and leader in higher education. I do this because systems like universities have continually worked to erase our identities as Indigenous people from our work. This is especially true of research where Indigenous knowledges, ways of being, and ways of knowing have been devalued.

Boozhoo, Kwe Kwe, Semaa-Kwe ndishnikaaz, Mukwaa dodem, Teme-Augama Anishnabai. My name is Tobacco woman, I come from the Bear Clan and belong to the Temagami Anishnabai—the people of the deep water—where I am a member of the Temagami First Nation. If you have an understanding of First Nations people and relationality, I have actually shared with you much about who I am and my path in this world. My identity is rooted in my ties to the lands and kin of my mother's home community. I am also of Irish/Scottish descent on my father's side. I was largely disconnected from my father's family while growing up as a consequence of classism and racism. My world view is deeply informed and influenced by my mother and her family. Today I live and work in the traditional territory of the Anishinaabe and Haudenosaunee, in the Niagara area of Ontario. I am grateful to live and be able to work in this territory.

This chapter weaves personal narratives and learnings from my personal experiences and work in higher education along with research. I cannot compartmentalize my learning into a tidy box labelled "academic research" but rather recognize that who I am and the experiences I have also form the basis of my work and academic writing. I also draw on some of my earlier work (Cote-Meek, 2014) on pedagogical considerations for difficult learning and what I have come to understand as Debwewin (truth). My hope is that my offering of a perspective on the fundamental question of the *What Are Universities For?* symposium held in Regina, Saskatchewan, in 2023 will stimulate critical thought and conversations about what we do in institutions of higher learning, how this impacts Indigenous peoples, and, importantly, how we can reimagine the pedagogy of truth in universities.

Troubling Sites of Higher Learning

I started reflecting on the role of the university relative to Indigenous Peoples several decades ago when I first started working in institutes of higher learning. I recognized very early in my educational journey and in the various roles I held that universities were places that were not always welcoming or inclusive. I felt this when I embarked on my own undergraduate education when another student, upon finding out I was Indigenous, literally exclaimed to the whole class, "Wow, a real live Indian! I never met one before." I struggled to maintain any kind of dignity and wished I could have crawled under my desk and disappeared. Later, when I found myself teaching in higher education, I started on a journey of exploring how classrooms and institutions more broadly could be more welcoming, supportive environments and what I could do to help achieve this specifically in the classroom. In fact, the question of pedagogy and classrooms is at the centre of *Colonized Classrooms: Racism, Trauma and Resistance in Post-Secondary Education* (Cote-Meek, 2014). One of the key findings in the research that informed this book was that Indigenous students, professors, and programs such as Indigenous studies "are viewed as out of place in the academy" (p. 143). This sense of not belonging in spaces of higher learning also includes how we as Indigenous people articulate and understand our tribal knowledges. Rather as Linda Tuhiwai Smith (2012) points out, the West has extracted our knowledges under the guise of modernity, reinterpreted our knowledges through their lens, leaving "fragments of ourselves" that were redistributed through various disciplines and left unrecognizable to Indigenous Peoples (p. 61). As Smith (2012) points out, colonization was not just about the land and the resources but also about the colonization of knowledge and culture. This perpetuates the notion that the West and the academy know Indigenous Peoples, their knowledges, and their cultures better than they know themselves. This results in a tension where Indigenous Peoples are constantly negotiating their right to exist with their knowledges and flourish in spaces of higher education as well as "confronting and challenging ongoing hegemonic and racial constructions that work to keep them in a place of inferiority and/or out of the academy in the first instance" (Cote-Meek, 2014, p. 143).

This context leads to critical questions about the purpose of universities and who they continue to operate for. Deeper questions also include whether we should be introducing Indigenous knowledges into the academy when there is so much resistance and, if so, how they should be introduced. Over the years, both as a faculty member and an administrator, I have found myself in many situations of having to defend the place of Indigenous Peoples and Indigenous knowledges in the academy. Despite some changes to the system over the last thirty years or so I still remain at times ambivalent and always cautious about how Indigenous Peoples and knowledges are viewed, positioned, and taken up in the academy. Like many Indigenous scholars, I have these concerns as well as concerns around appropriation and who is transmitting Indigenous ways of knowing. It is abundantly clear there are contradictions in the professed role of the university system and the context in which Indigenous people find themselves when entering such sites.

Debwewin, Truth

In an article that appeared in *University Affairs*, Bird (2020) argues that the purpose of the university has narrowed to focus on attaining credentials, finding a career, and essentially getting a job. However, he reminds us that the central purpose of a university is "to discover and impart knowledge" citing Harvard University's motto of "Truth."

> Universities nourish the innate longing of humans to obtain knowledge and to reshape our ways of living and thinking according to the knowledge we obtain. We intuitively recognize knowledge as an intrinsic good that cultivates the flourishing of individuals and, in turn, the betterment of societies in which they live. It is awe-inspiring to consider the countless achievements for humanity that stem from research and study at universities. (Bird, 2020)

Essentially, the definition of truth is akin to seeking knowledge and imparting knowledge, research, and teaching for the benefit of society. While Bird (2020) goes on to describe how the pursuit of truth necessitates open inquiry, academic freedom, and debate, there is little attention to what truth is. Nor is there a sense of whose truth we are talking about or of what truths are valued. Further, how do universities confront difficult truths? Can we reimagine truth as more inclusive? Shouldn't the search for truth be about broadening our lens to include a variety of ways of viewing the world? In other words, if the purpose of the university is the *pursuit of truth*, in essence the pursuit of knowledge, how can we reimagine a university that confronts multiple truths that are inclusive of Indigenous Peoples as well as the multiplicity of world views?

It is difficult for me to think about the pursuit of truth and knowledge without thinking about what Debwewin means to me as an Anishinaabekwe. Reimagining the pedagogy of truth as Debwewin is about speaking your truth, from your heart and all that life encompasses. I question whether everyone has heard the truth. Are the truths of Indigenous Peoples represented in the academy?

While I am not a fluent speaker nor an expert of Anishinaabemowin, I have long recognized the importance of Indigenous languages in describing and understanding Indigenous world views. Poitras Pratt & Gladue (2022) note the importance of drawing on our Indigenous languages to understand world views, otherwise described as ontological and epistemological foundations:

> We engage with our ancestors through the learning, and revitalization, of Cree and Michif (Cree-Métis) words to ground our Indigenous

ontological and epistemological locations. The use of ancestral languages, in both traditional and contemporary forms, provides a precision of meaning which we believe honours both the sacred purpose and the ideals of academic integrity. (p. 104)

The meaning of words expressed in Anishinaabemowin provide a deeper level of understanding and the way we see ourselves and the world around us. My own personal journey of language reclamation has been slow but steady. To assist me on this journey, I reach out to friends who are fluent speakers who so willingly give of their time and knowledge. In the Anishinaabe language we speak of Debwewin, truth. While I understood Debwewin to mean truth, I lacked the deeper understanding and meaning. Dominic Beaudry, a fluent speaker, historian, former Education Director and now the Associate Vice-President, Indigenous at Laurentian University, was kind enough to share the following with me:

Debwewin
- De—meaning the heart and speaking from the heart
- Ishkode—meaning new fire, first fire and also refers to that first spark of life. When a human comes into life, that is the first spark of life from a heartbeat.
- Debwe—meaning the sound of truth. The first sound of truth of the world.
- Debwewin—meaning the act of being as truthful as you can. (Beaudry, 2023)

Clearly the depths of Debwewin are deeper than simply saying "truth." I personally understand Anishinaabe truth as connected to a holistic understanding of the world. In that truth, the sound of truth becomes a reflection of the world around us. Speaking from the heart means we must be in touch with our heart, our spirit, mind, and body, and then we can speak from that place as opposed to speaking only from our cognitive being. I have heard Elders relay a similar story about talking heads and how many of us in academia are talking heads. That is, we only speak from what we spew out of our brain, and there is a disconnect between the heart and mind. Speaking one's truth requires us to connect mind, body, and spirit. Further, the search for truth would naturally encompass a holistic approach, one that embraces multiple ways of knowing and understanding the world. This then informs how the search for truth is undertaken in terms of methodology.

If one of the purposes of universities is pursuit of truth or in being as truthful as we can be, we also need to be attentive to how we ensure inclusivity of voice(s). How can we be as truthful as we can when so many voices are excluded or missed in teaching, in research, and in the governance of the university? The system is set up to value Western approaches to teaching, research, and governance. Relative to this I rarely see a connection between the heart and the mind except in a very few instances.

We can also extend this understanding of truth to teaching. For example, who decides what truth gets taught, who gets to teach? Research is essentially about the search for truth(s), and it begs the question of who decides which methodologies are deemed valid and appropriate. How are other methodologies recognized in the university system? And how is governance based on alternate ways of viewing the world? For example, who is represented in university governance? In the administration? It is well documented that there is a lack of representation of Indigenous and racialized people in the academy, including the governance system (Smith, 2013). I have been at countless administrative tables over the last thirty years and often find myself as the lone Indigenous voice, which comes with a whole host of expectations around what I should know, how I should contribute, and how I should be. These are all forms of truths about how universities operate and how colonialism remains deeply embedded in the structures and systems of the university.

Colonial Foundations of the University

Christensen Hughes (2022), in a chapter on academic integrity, provides a brief tracing of Western higher education's development from medieval times in Europe to North America. She argues

> that the academy has paradoxically been both a dominating and liberating force since its inception, imposing conceptions of morality and truth that have shifted over time, behaving itself in unethical ways, while elevating its largely privileged graduates to positions of influence within society and advancing national aims. (pp. 25–26)

In Canada, the context for education remains deeply embedded within its colonial origins. For example, Battiste & Henderson (2000) note that education "has been used as a means to perpetuate damaging myths about Indigenous knowledge and heritage, languages, beliefs and ways of life. It has established Eurocentric science as the dominant mode of thought" (p. 86). Objectifying and reducing Indigenous Peoples to an inferior status was essential for the advancement of colonization (Cote-Meek, 2014; Fanon, 1952/1967; LaRocque, 2004; Paul, 1993). However, as noted by Christensen Hughes (2022), the devaluing of Indigenous Peoples and their respective knowledges is inconsistent with the values of morality and truth. Educational systems, like the residential schools, are one of the primary tools of colonization and where ongoing stereotypical narratives about Indigenous Peoples are perpetuated (Cote-Meek, 2014, p. 49). It's important to note that while there is a lot of focus on residential schools as being highly problematic and violent, we have to keep in mind that the underlying beliefs of how Indigenous Peoples were viewed and subsequently treated was, and continues to be, threaded through all education systems and society in general. These underlying beliefs were supported by the policies of assimilation and integration. There can be no doubt that "[e]ducation for Aboriginal peoples has always been part of the colonial regime—one wrought with violence, abuse and processes that have had devastating effects" (Cote-Meek, 2014, p. 46). At the University of Regina symposium, Linda Tuhiwai Smith (2023) also commented that universities are institutions and places of contractions and contestations—on the one hand professing and aspiring to notions of being places of open exchanges of ideas and imaginings of the future, places where good things are created for the betterment of society, and at the same time remaining deeply colonial and violent. In the pursuit of truth, of being as truthful as we can (Debwewin), universities must grapple with the contradictions of their longstanding and ongoing history of colonialism and with the contradiction of reconciling lofty goals of the pursuit of truth with being institutions that create space for ensuring differing world views and forms of coming to know are valued and included. Instead, the current system is one where "scholars are expected to conquer, possess, and dominate knowledge within hierarchical structures that reward those who replicate and uphold the status quo" (Poitras Pratt & Gladue, 2023, p. 108). In a sense, the machinery of the institution becomes a self-regulating system that makes change challenging.

Reimagining the Pedagogy of Truth

As we are reimagining the future of the universities, we must also grapple with how universities can become institutions where the pursuit of truth embodies a multiplicity of truths. First, there must be acknowledgement and dialogue about these deeper systemic issues; unpacking what it means to be a colonial institution is critical if we are to make any real headway in the process of decolonization. However, what often happens is after a conference we go back to our respective universities and the academic machinery seems to take over again and we get caught up in all its messiness and contradictions.

Moeke-Pickering and colleagues (2006) discuss the notion of "white amnesia" and define it as a

> disease rooted in racism, [that] is a common strategy used to ignore the historical and ongoing injustices perpetrated on Indigenous peoples. These learned behaviors and associated attitudes stem from a lack of acceptance and continued denial among non-Indigenous academics about their potential roles as colonisers and oppressors. White amnesia allows non-Indigenous peoples to continue in their day to day world without seeing or involving themselves in other worldviews that would challenge their understanding of their oppressive practices.

Second, in order to reimagine the pedagogy of truth, the pursuit of truth, we must confront some difficult truths about how institutions are operating now. For example, I have to wonder with all the emphasis on reconciliation, decolonization, Indigenization, and the broader emphasis on equity, diversity, and inclusion, whether what is operating is another form of white amnesia, a process of ignoring the historical and, importantly, ongoing injustices perpetrated on Indigenous Peoples. We have a lot of nice words to couch the ugliness of ongoing colonization. I have a strong view that if we do not talk about the Debwewin (truth) more deeply and how we arrive at those truths, universities will remain as colonial, patriarchal, and elitist as they have always been.

Further, the pedagogy of "truth is in the difficult stories, the harder ones to speak aloud. They are the more difficult ones to hear and listen to because they are stories about injustices, abuse and genocide" (Cote-Meek, 2020, p. xviii). As I have noted previously these difficult stories are not only rooted in pain but importantly "these stories also lay the basis for understanding why we have much work to do and why reconciliation is not a feel-good process or an easy one. They are the stories that are easily forgotten by white amnesia as we barrel ahead" (p. xviii) and as we busy ourselves with ensuring we uphold standards and quality of what counts as excellence in teaching and research.

When I reflect on the role of the university, I think about how complicit universities are in ensuring the spaces within the institution are actually places where Indigenous Peoples feel valued, included, and have a real sense of belonging...*the truth* is that many Indigenous learners express experiences with navigating racism and violence in the classroom and in broader society. I have described (2014) how Indigenous students find themselves contending with how difficult stories/histories such as those associated with ongoing colonization are narrated in the classroom as well as finding themselves in positions where they are witness to how these narratives are received and consumed by their peers. The complexity and challenges of encountering difficult stories are exacerbated for Indigenous learners "when one is the casualty in the narrative" of ongoing colonial violence (p. 149). In the same vein, there are also likely non-Indigenous learners in the classroom who may or may not be impacted by the same stories and as a result may experience feelings of resistance to undertake critical analysis of the content (Schick & St. Denis, 2005), denial (Cote-Meek, 2014), various microagressions (Brant, 2023), or as settler moves to innocence (Mawhinney, 1998; Tuck & Yang, 2012). Inevitably there are also racist discourses that are operating and perpetuated consciously or unconsciously in the classroom and other spaces that further exacerbate the experiences of Indigenous learners. As Brant (2023) notes it can be particularly unsettling for students to be "called to reckon with their complicities with troubling narratives. This can mark the classroom as an uncomfortable site and in turn produce student resistance" (p. 246).

As we reimagine a pedagogy of truth and confront difficult truths, I continue to contend that we must also think critically through our individual and collective pedagogical and ethical responsibilities as we engage learners and call them to engage in difficult knowledges of materials such as residential schools. While I stress the importance of inclusion of difficult truths and knowledges, I also ask that we think about how this knowledge is portrayed and taken up in the classroom (Cote-Meek, 2014). For example, Brant (2023) and Dion (2009) both discuss how traumatic histories and difficult knowledges call for a different kind of pedagogy, one that may call for staying with one's vulnerability as both a learner and a teacher.

In reimaging a pedagogy of truth, consideration must also be given to Indigenous peoples of these lands. *The truth of the matter* is that despite being Indigenous to this land there are still many instances where erasure of our existence is prominent. Reimagining a pedagogy of truth requires confronting this and many other difficult truths and asking why and how are universities perpetuating the erasure of Indigenous Peoples and knowledges?

In closing, there is no doubt that the Truth and Reconciliation Commission (TRC, 2015) has caused many post-secondary institutions to re-examine how they are providing education to Indigenous and non-Indigenous students. The report calls on post-secondary education to engage in the reconciliation process and essentially lead change in education that promotes *awareness and understanding and, importantly, integrates Indigenous histories, knowledges, and pedagogies in the classroom.* We must continue this work collectively if we are to reimagine a university of the future, one where many truths are valued, understood, discussed, researched, and integrated within the system.

References

Battiste, M., & Henderson, J.Y. (2000). *Protecting Indigenous knowledge and heritage: A global challenge.* Purich.

Beaudry, D. (2023, April 28). Personal Communication, shared with permission.

Bird, B. (2020, October 29). Rediscovering the truth-seeking mission of universities. *University Affairs.* https://www.universityaffairs.ca/opinion/in-my-opinion/rediscovering-the-truth-seeking-mission-of-universities/

Brant, J. (2023). Confronting colonial violences in and out of the classroom: Advancing curricular moves toward justice through Indigenous Maternal Pedagogies. *Curriculum Inquiry,* 53(3), 244–67. https://doi.org/10.1080/03626784.2023.2200809

Christensen Hughes, J. (2022). Academic integrity across time and place: Higher education's questionable moral calling. In S.E. Eaton & J. Christensen Hughes (Eds.), *Academic integrity in Canada: An enduring and essential challenge* (pp. 25–59). Springer.

Cote-Meek, S. (2014). *Colonized classrooms: Racism, trauma and resistance in post-secondary education.* Fernwood Publishing.

Cote-Meek, S. (2020). Introduction: From colonized classrooms to transformative change in the academy: We can and must do better! In S.

Cote-Meek and T. Moeke-Pickering (Eds.), *Decolonizing and Indigenizing education in Canada* (pp. xi–xxiii). Canadian Scholars.

Dion, S.D. (2009). *Braiding histories: Learning from Aboriginal peoples' experiences and perspectives*. UBC Press.

Fanon, F. (1967). *Black skin, white masks* (C.L. Markmann, Trans.) Grove Press. (Original work published in 1952)

LaRocque, E. (2004). When the "wild west" is me: Re-viewing cowboys and Indians. In L. Felske & B. Rasporich (Eds.), *Challenging frontiers: The Canadian west* (pp. 136–53). University of Calgary Press.

Mawhinney, J. (1998). *Giving up the ghost: Disrupting the (re)production of white privilege in anti-racist pedagogy and organizational change* [Masters thesis, University of Toronto]. T-space. https://tspace.library.utoronto.ca/handle/1807/12096

Moeke-Pickering, T., Hardy, S., Manitowabi, S., Mawhiney, A.M., Faries, E., Gibson-van Marrewijk, K., Tobias, N., & Taitoko, M. (2006). Keeping our fires alive: Towards decolonizing research in the academic setting. *World Indigenous Nations Higher Education Consortium Journal*.

Paul, D.N. (1993). *We were not the savages: A Mi'kmaq perspective on the collision of European and Aboriginal civilization*. Nimbus.

Poitras Pratt, Y., & Gladue, K. (2022). Re-defining academic integrity: Embracing Indigenous truths. In S.E. Eaton & J. Christensen Hughes (Eds.), *Academic integrity in Canada: An enduring and essential challenge* (pp 103–23). Springer.

Schick, C., & St. Denis, V. (2005). Troubling national discourses in anti-racist curricular planning. *Canadian Journal of Education*, 28(3), 295–317. https://doi.org/10.2307/4126472

Smith, L.T. (2012). *Decolonizing methodologies: Research and Indigenous peoples* (2nd ed.). Zed Books.

Smith, L.T. (2023, May 3–6). *What we can learn from developing different institutions in higher education?* [Presentation]. What Are Universities For? International Symposium. Regina, SK, Canada.

Smith, M. (2013). Situating Indigenous education in Canada. In M. Smith (Ed.), *Transforming the academy: Essays on Indigenous education, knowledges and relations* (pp. 10–13). Federation for the Humanities and Social Sciences.

Truth and Reconciliation Commission (TRC). (2015). *Honouring the truth, Reconciling for the future: Summary report of the final Report of the Truth and Reconciliation Commission of Canada*. Truth and Reconciliation Commission of Canada. https://publications.gc.ca/collections/collection_2015/trc/IR4-7-2015-eng.pdf

Tuck, E., & Yang, K.W. (2012). Decolonization is not a metaphor. *Decolonization, Indigeneity, Education & Society*, 1(1), 1–40. https://jps.library.utoronto.ca/index.php/des/article/view/18630

CHAPTER 10
COMPLICITIES, MARGINS, RESISTANCE
COLLEGES, PLANTATIONS, AND BEARING WITNESS

Piya Chatterjee

> *The plot of her undoing begins with his dominion. It begins in the fifteenth century with a papal bull, with a philosopher at his desk, pen in hand, as he sorts the world into categories of genus and species....The plot of her undoing begins with a man in his study writing a tome about the Americas, the species, the fauna, the races, it is a compendium illustrated with botanical drawings, architectural plans, sketches of farm buildings, and a microscopic view of her scarf skin....The plot of her undoing begins with the violence of reason. It begins with an entry into the ledger that itemizes her as number 71, a meager girl, and forever erases her name.*
>
> —SAIDIYA HARTMAN, "The Plot of Her Undoing"

N HER ESSAY "THE PLOT OF HER UNDOING," SAIDIYA HARTMAN asks us to consider the living pasts, and the afterlives, of slavery and conquest through a distilled, brilliant lyricism which brings us, almost immediately, to an image of learning: the philosopher at his desk.

In this promissory note of an essay, I seek to trace the ways in which those of us who sit within twenty-first century universities and colleges, in the centres of empire, negotiate our complicities and bear witness to flickers of resistance. As professors and teachers within, "we" have inherited the living legacies left behind by that "philosopher at his desk," steeped in those Enlightenment logics of categories, rationalities, and, indeed, "the violence of reason" which underwrote the atrocities of plantation slavery and Indigenous genocide.

These are complicities (Patel, 2016; Patel, 2022)—complicated, layered, and paradoxical complicities—but complicities nonetheless. I contend that this is what needs to remain primary in "our" explorations of the central question posed in this symposium, and now this book.

The task is massive. It is full of tensions and contradictions. It is replete with the excesses that can both defy and reify "the violence of reason" which is so engendered by this: the writing, the text, this language. The only way is to begin somewhere, with trepidation, gingerly, with some fear. This is what it means to privilege affect, push against the supremacy of reason.

So, I thread out my own "politics of location" (Rich, 1994, pp. 210-31), precise and mindful of the pronouns "we" and "our," and how I situate myself within them. At the risk of narcissistic solipsism, I centre my academic training as a historical anthropologist and as a Bengali brahmin feminist scholar from India whose journey within the imperial academy is vitally shaped by the history and confluence of brahminical-caste and white supremacies.

In naming this structural and historical privilege, I am indebted to Shaista Patel's interventions about South Asian descent—and especially dominant caste and *savarna* ("of caste") complicities—within settler colonialism in the United States and Canada (Patel, 2016). In following her call for a scholarly and pedagogical reckoning, I underscore that my/our complicity is consistent and enduring. It rests alongside any claims I make about anti-colonial feminist work from within the US academy. The musings in this essay are not intended to establish any kind of "settler innocence." Additionally, and following Dia Da Costa's important intervention about brahminical and dominant caste complicities in the US academy, naming my brahminical status is also not a quick gesture toward "caste innocence" either (Da Costa, 2018).

These brief reflections are not meant to operate as a confessional or an eloquent disavowal. They will be interrupted to signal the always-unfinished reckonings within these clear scripts of power and privilege.

(Not-so) academic complicities *here* are equally intertwined with complicities *there*. My specific trans/national class and caste privileges that shape all aspects of the political economies of global knowledge production are steeped in the ethnographic research that I have conducted in the tea plantations of eastern India. As I negotiate my relationships with primarily *Adivasi* (Indigenous) and oppressed-caste and Dalit women workers (from diverse ethno-racial backgrounds) in the production of knowledges about tea plantation labour cultures and organizing, I remain, then, always a *memsahib* (colonial term for high-status woman)—from the *burra bungalow*, the "big house," of the plantation (Chatterjee, 2001).[1]

Plantation Framings

The plantation, then, is not just a metaphor or rhetorical framing device through which I understand my formation as an elite settler-immigrant, brahmin, bourgeois, racialized woman academic in the imperial academy. It is absolutely vital that I recognize, with you, the confluence and impact of two supremacies in my formation as a teacher and producer of anthropological knowledges.

The plantation frames the landscape of the university. In 1995, starting my first job as an assistant professor at the University of California, Riverside (UCR), I was given a quick tour through the campus, straight from the airport. I remember vividly that hot, dry day. I remember being driven past citrus groves, perfectly linear arrangements of orange bushes that immediately brought back memories of the bonsai perfection of tea bushes. It was surreal: the heat, and this familiar rationality inscribed onto the landscape that surrounded my new workplace. I learned, later, that citrus farming built on Mexican im/migrant labour formed the political economy of this region from the 1920s. UCR was established as a public-land grant institution in the 1950s. I still remain unaware of Indigenous claims and usage of this land prior to its settlement into citrus stations that then shaped the university. Such are the terms of settler-immigrant ignorance and privilege.

In 2012, when I left my UCR position to join Scripps College in the Claremont Colleges consortium just an hour west from Riverside, where I live, I entered a landscape of verdant and immaculate beauty, worlds away from the more functional architecture and spread of UCR's landscape. Here, beautiful Spanish mission–style buildings surround manicured lawns and old olive trees. At the centre of the small campus, a corridor of trees along a stretch of lawn connects a chapel on one end and what was then the president's residence on the other. I walked daily across that corridor from my office to a classroom to teach a course called Plantation Empires. It did not escape my attention the irony of teaching about the hemispheric connections between plantation histories within this particular arrangement of buildings, trees, and space. The aesthetic meeting point of these histories of conquest, genocide, and the plantation remains surreal. Scripps and the University of California, Riverside (despite the huge differences of scale and the terms of private and public capital) remain haunted by both settler colonialism and the plantation.

Working to "Bear Witness"

How, then, can I navigate such intimate, historical layers of complicity within my pedagogies and scholarship? How can I both create and hold space for liberatory work within such landscapes of power? Is it possible, following bell hooks's lead, to "cultivate the margins" while simultaneously reckoning with such profound, interwoven complicities? Are there conceptual openings through which I (as a teacher fully mired within the terms of imperial academic power) can ethically, and honestly, speak to radical hope, vulnerability, and possibility within and outside the classroom?

These questions are just beginnings. I hold them close as I step through this minefield with anxiety and trepidation. The fault lines of history and the politics of identity that traffic through many colonialisms and shape any and all of the utterances that reach toward liberatory politics. One must—I must—take care, be vigilant. In this specific historical moment, pro-Palestinian students across US campuses are campaigning for divestment and being attacked by militarized police unleashed upon them by administrators, the very people who pay my salary from those very endowments that are the target of these campaigns. I can only be aware of the ethical fragility of any claims that I can make toward "the anti-colonial," or the liberatory, in the face of an ongoing genocide of an Indigenous people enabled by my livelihood and the taxes I pay to the US state.

I can do a few things which many of us, as faculty, are doing: I can follow the lead of student-organizers and learn from them, work in coalition to build solidarities, and also "bear witness." The act of witnessing, of bearing witness, is most often used in works of theology and philosophy.

There is much that I need to continue exploring about its usage in Western thought. For now, it makes intuitive sense because it contains an ethical charge. It is a tool that helps me work a path with, and through, the paradoxes. It helps me anchor myself in these choppy waters and the jagged shoals which lie close under their surface. Again, this is a tentative anchoring, a floating buoy. Clutching onto it, I can reflect, with a passionate detachment, the claims I make toward a liberatory politics. The business of witnessing is an imperfect labour.

In what follows, I share a few autoethnographic moments as brief snapshots of resistance to academic, institutional, and capitalist power. These are observations that cannot be seen as "ethnographic" in a disciplinary and scientific sense. They defy discipline. They narrate a few incomplete stories and lessons I learn from some of my students in the "margins" of the imperial academy—and, briefly, from radical hope enacted by Indigenous women teachers on the edges of tea plantation hinterlands, far from the imperial metropole. Together, these brief stories will mark the jaggedness of affect. They will trace the emotional economies of grief and anger about an academic violence that is, indeed, not academic at all. They will also include interruptions which embody the tensions and irreducibilities of my own positionings within the enduring scripts of caste and class dominance. They also underscore the paradoxes and illegibilities of my racialized and transnational experience within the US academy.

Witnessing Student Organizing During a Pandemic

In early April 2020, barely a month after our classes had been moved to Zoom and students were scattered across the United States and the world, I heard about some students mobilizing a campaign for a universal pass at the college. I was in a fog of grief as I had just lost my beloved *baba* in Kolkata that month, was unable to be with my family, and was trying to be present to students from three classes on the computer screen.

The pandemic had thrown open a Pandora's box about the ongoing crises in higher education—and all of us, students and teachers, were trying to meet each other across the surreal mix of alienation and connection that the Zoom platform was providing. Suddenly displaced, thrown back into varied family and home environments, and worried for the health of their loved ones (especially those on the front lines of health care), diverse students, faculty, and staff were navigating their own deep anxiety and despair.

With the immeasurable kindness and assistance of former student Justin Joseph, who was my research assistant and who had been house-sitting for me, we started to enact Zoom pedagogies which tried to centre affect, and psychological well-being, into the classroom experience. In significant ways, we were all witnessing for, and to, each other. Indeed, I had no choice but to bring my own grieving into the space because there were moments when I did not think I could carry on teaching and functioning— and could not find reprieve institutionally (to take a leave). I was fortunate that Justin was living in my home, and as a recent Pomona College alumnus, he was able to advise me about what might work for his peers and co-created these new pedagogical strategies with me. Across the screen, my students met Justin's and my collaborative pedagogical efforts with immense compassion and concern. It was such a relief to not be teaching alone.

We were already starting to retool the syllabus, and the terms of evaluation, when the student campaign began to emerge. Students, and some faculty, had been sharing stories of housing and food insecurity for some students and the intense stress that particularly low-income, disabled, and international students were experiencing.

As the campaign emerged, I was somewhat aware that a few students in my classes were principal organizers, but their restraint around calling out individualized leadership was my first lesson about the generosity and wisdom of their deeply collective—and underground—ethos.

I will present their campaign through their own words because they were brilliant in documenting their rationale through surveys, research, and social media. I refrain from offering some seamless narrative or analysis about these efforts because my "witnessing" was itself jagged, and I have not reached out to interview some of the students who were more involved than others. I offer a framing of a meticulously organized effort that emerged into two phases: the universal pass campaign and then a very successful mutual aid fundraising effort that lasted into the summer.

The first phase for universal pass involved lobbying the Faculty Executive Committee of the college, which was already considering various grading options, and then shifting their strategy to push toward a full faculty vote. In a public document, "Arguments for a Universal Pass Grading Policy for Spring 2020," campaign organizers presented careful and fully researched arguments for their position—including student surveys, comparable institutional decisions around the same, and highlighting the predicaments of their most vulnerable peers:

The grading policy as it stands rewards students who have greater resources to complete coursework during a time of extensive health, social, and economic devastation which is disproportionately affecting FLI, BIPOC, disabled, immunocompromised, and international students. This global crisis is both revealing and exacerbating the deep inequalities in our society and within our Scripps student body. (Nobody Fails at Scripps Coalition, 2020, p. 3; hereafter, Arguments)[2]

The report then detailed the current grading policy, why proposed changes by the FEC were inadequate, and addressed potential student and faculty concerns. They argued that the "current policy fails students" for the following reasons:

Very few of our lives, students and faculty alike are operating as usual; however we are not equally burdened. **Students of color (particularly Black, Hispanic, and Indigenous students), first-gen students, low-income students, students who are immunocompromised, students whose parents have lost their jobs, students who are now key caretakers in their families, and students whose mental health issues have been worsened at this time are *particularly vulnerable* to the consequences of an inequitable grading system.** (Arguments, 2020, p. 4; bold and italics, sic)

Furthermore, they note that "At the Claremont Colleges, 1 in 4 low-income students doesn't have a stable living situation, and half as many low-income students as non-low-income students have access to a quiet workspace (26% vs. 50%). We have worked to collect more updated and Scripps specific data to understand the differential effect of the current grading policy on students who identify as belonging to the aforementioned groups." In addition, updated surveys of their peers showed that 747 Scripps students (71.3 percent of the reported student body) completed the survey, and "we have done both quantitative and qualitative analyses of those responses. While our consent protocol allows us to share the results of our quantitative analysis, we will not be making qualitative responses publicly available; those have been sent only to faculty members for confidentiality purposes" (Arguments, 2020, pp. 4–5, 6).

They also add that "noteworthy, socioeconomically disadvantaged students…were particularly supportive of such measures" (p. 5). They quote, and repeat the argument at several points, that "comparable prestigious institutions like Yale, MIT, Wellesley" have instituted a universal pass policy, demonstrating "through precedent that Scripps would not be at risk of losing its accreditation by changing to a universal grading policy, but would instead take our place among peer institutions" (p. 6).

After cogently noting how a universal pass policy would meet the needs of diverse students and faculty, the report then offers answers to several FAQs to respond to specific faculty and student concerns with strategic clarity. Some of these excerpts are telling:

> **Faculty Concern:** "What if students stop putting effort into their classes?"
>
> **Response:** "In general, students at the Claremont Colleges are motivated and place a strong value on their education. Students who are in the position will likely still participate and learn the material of the class. At this point, there is not much new material to be learned anyhow....Students who are not in a position to maintain their class participation should be able to focus on their health, and supporting their families and communities. For many students, maintaining their previous levels of class participation is simply not possible—it is not a matter of incentive." (Arguments, 2020, p. 10)

> **Faculty Concern:** "I'm being very accommodating to my students. Why do we need a universal grading policy if faculty understand that many students are in difficult situations?"
>
> **Response:** "We recognize that professors have put in enormous amounts of work to transition their classes online....At the end of the day, we hope to collaborate to discuss protection for students in difficult situations in such a way **that this burden lies on the institution/our larger community, rather than on each individual student.**" (pp. 11–12; bold, sic)

> **Student Concern:** "What about students who worked hard for their A's? Doesn't this policy unfairly penalize them?"
>
> **Response:** "It may be a comparative disadvantage for these students to receive a Pass instead of an A on their transcripts. **In fact, this comparative disadvantage is exactly what renders an opt-in**

policy inequitable: pass/fail and letter grades are inherently unequal. However, many students have worked equally as hard or harder for their grades, and now through no fault of their own are no longer able to achieve at the same level during this pandemic. Students in easier situations do not have a right to higher achievement than students in more difficult situations. It is also our belief that grades attained during this time will be more reflective of access to certain resources than of hard work, intelligence, motivation. Our contemporaries comprise prestigious institutions with extremely high achieving students; many, like Harvard and MIT have instituted universal grading policies. They would not have done so if they were concerned about implications of a 'pass' for the future of their students." (pp. 13–14; bold added)

Because the report is a "living" political campaign document, the authors then outline actionable items for both student and faculty constituencies. They ask students to "(1) Participate in the photo campaign on the Instagram @nobodyfailsatscripps; (2) Send a letter to a faculty member you know; (3) Fill out the anonymous survey; and (4) Follow us on IG and Twitter and share our Graphics and Process" (Arguments, 2020, pp. 20–21). The report also asks faculty to "(1) Email us with your concerns/thoughts/feedback!!! We want to be in collaboration with you; (2) Support a motion to bring this issue to a full-faculty vote at a special meeting; (3) Vote for the amendments at the special meeting; and (4) Advocate for the policy to your colleagues" (p. 21) The report concludes with a compilation of powerful testimonies from students about various pandemic hardships and an assertion of their organizing and their coalitional efforts with other peers across the consortium.

As an open collective of 140+ Scripps students,[3] we are constantly striving to achieve the policy that is the best option for all students' livelihood, first and foremost prioritizing those who are experiencing the greatest harm at this time. (p. 21)[4]

Despite this expansive and meticulously researched campaign, which involved numerous conversations within peer groups and with faculty, the motion did not pass at a full faculty meeting. On April 30, 2020, the campaign registered their disappointment and anger at this vote and also expressed gratitude to all who supported them. Their own analysis about institutional power and opacity rests powerfully alongside a sense of powerful collective, coalitional solidarity with other peer groups.

> We are incredibly disappointed and frustrated to announce that Scripps faculty did not pass a universal policy, but instead maintained an opt-in policy for Spring 2020. With a vote of 45% in favor, 54% opposed, and 1% abstaining, faculty ultimately voted the motion down....
>
> Numerous comparable institutions from Pomona and Pitzer to Wellesley, Barnard, Smith and Harvard have adopted universal policies. This is not a matter of academic honesty or a matter of stepping out of line with comparable institutions. Scripps seeks to stand equal to these schools but has proven itself *inferior*. Scripps' support of equity is performative and any claims that the school protects and fights for its students remain unfounded. Above all, Scripps refuses to listen to data and the voices of its students. We will not forget this.
>
> As a historically but not exclusively women's college, **Scripps claims to provide an environment built on the premise of supporting communities facing systemic oppression. We found that much of the hostility we received from the community—especially a minority of faculty members—a testament to how passionate women and non-binary individuals (especially womxn of color) are often received as aggressive, regardless of the methods and language they choose to use. We expected better of our institution and community. Yet, once again, we must take Scripps' claims and promises with a grain of salt: it continues to use low-income, POC, and disabled students as tokens of diversity for admissions campaigns without actually providing for the needs of many of its most vulnerable students.** In this decision, Scripps has refused to prioritize the needs of the collective student body who lack the resources, time, space, and support they would otherwise have on campus to succeed academically *during a global pandemic*.... [italics in original; bold added]
>
> We want to thank everyone...who have [*sic*] tirelessly fought for a universal grading policy and worked to accommodate the needs of all students....We are especially grateful for Nobody Fails at CMC, Nobody Fails at Pitzer, and folx at Occupy Pomona for their advice, support, suggestions, and extensive advocacy. We are so proud of you

all, regardless of the policies enacted at your respective schools. As for Scripps students, we could not have done a thing without your support, your questions, and all of your kind messages...

This decision has revealed how inequities are upheld and how marginalized students—even when their concerns are shared by a majority of the student-body—continue to be relegated to the margins. Our experience as organizers has also elucidated that Scripps administration has consciously chosen to make the process of student-led change as opaque and difficult as possible...

Our fight hasn't ended, and we will continue to do everything in our power to cultivate the relationships we've built with students and faculty to protect the students that our institution has failed to listen to. **We are not disbanding, this group plans to be a force at Scripps College for many years to come.** (Nobody Fails at Scripps, 2020d; bold, sic)

I include the campaign document and letter in detail because the analysis about faculty/institutional politics offered by the students is abundantly clear. I remember email conversations in which student campaigners underscored the core logic of this campaign was to centre the struggles of their most vulnerable peers. In admirable ways, this coalition—which also included classed and racially privileged women and non-binary folx—was radically pivoting to recognize, in Patricia Hill Collins's words, the "outsiders within" (Collins, 1986). While I would like to expand my conversations with the alums who worked on this campaign and to look over emails and other records from this time, I simply want to express—in this promissory note—my admiration for an extraordinary collective effort that took place within, and against, the dislocations and despair caused by a global pandemic.

What is remarkable is what followed as a second phase of this student-led social movement (Yarduman, 2020). More than twenty organizers went on to create a mutual aid campaign, announcing on their website that "We began as a collective of 140+ students advocating for a Universal Pass....We have since refocused our efforts to mutual aid, and continue to act as a student advocacy collective prioritizing community care, solidarity and transparency" (Nobody Fails at Scripps, 2020b). They state their collective values as including "an explicitly antiracist, abolitionist, anti-capitalist, feminist, queer and transpolitic that centers work against white supremacy and anti-Blackness in our current time"; a belief in "the transformative power of care, mutual respect, and community"; and that they "work from a place of empathy and act in solidarity, not charity" (2020b).

Following the campaign playbook, the mutual aid planning used a similar thoughtful and carefully researched process of gathering information, creating an equitable application process that was fully transparent, collecting funds beginning with GoFundMe and then carrying on with their own accounts. They defined mutual aid as an "act of redistributing your wealth in the practice of solidarity as opposed to charity." They offered a succinct background to why they decided to shift to mutual aid work:

> After the Spring 2020 semester, Scripps students were offered little to no financial support. Many had no way to pay their rent through the semester and faced debilitating personal and familial bills. After conversations with Occupy Pomona and sas [Scripps Associated Students], we had initially planned on hosting the mutual aid fund through sas. However, the faculty member advisors for sas were against the idea, so student organizers had to independently organize a GoFundMe and Venmo effort. We started on May 21st and reached our goal of $52,000 on June 7th, and spent the following weeks distributing funds to the 36 students who had applied for them. After this effort, we put together a Mutual Aid 101 Guide to offer what we learned to student organizers at other campuses. This mutual aid guide has been used by students at colleges across the country including ucla, Colby College and Colorado College to start their own mutual aid efforts. (Nobody Fails at Scripps, 2020c)

I remember, in those hazy months of May, that the mutual aid campaign had been highly successful and raised an enormous amount of funds within a very short period of time. Given that May was also commencement month, and we were still in the first throes of the pandemic, I was frankly amazed at the amount of work that these still anonymous students had done to pull this off—pivoting quickly from the Nobody Fails at Scripps campaign to organize such a successful fundraising campaign (Sherman, 2021).

This admiration was coupled with a profound disappointment at what the students had clearly defined as a lack of institutional financial support for their most structurally vulnerable peers. I don't know if the college ultimately stepped up and assisted students in more individualized ways, and this is something to follow up with further research. I suspect that most of that information will be protected by legal-privacy issues. What is clear, though, is that these student organizers were not going to wait for the institution to step up—and they created a model of solidarity work that was impressively transparent, well-researched, and democratic. They were able to then create a "tool kit" that became useful to their peers in other institutions.

There is so much layered into these stories of generosity, wisdom, and political smarts that I would like to explore. For one, I am interested in the ways that this coalition of predominantly women, femme, and gender non-binary organizers forwarded an explicitly anti-racist feminist vision. Because I teach in feminist studies at this predominantly white institution, I know first-hand how difficult it is to shift the conversations, let alone actions, within the dominant political culture of racial and class entitlement at Scripps. I am also aware of other quasi-unionizing efforts in years past that centred labour and racial equity issues—that are obscured as organizers graduated from the college.

There are also some important ways in which Scripps's women's college status—and the primary gendered nature of this organizing—tends to get marginalized in the annals of student organizing at the Claremont consortium. Intuitively, I know this is a sexist erasure of visionary anti-racist and coalitional feminist organizing. For now, I leave these speculations and curiosities aside and simply underscore how these student organizers created through their praxis another way to do and "be" within the imperial academy. They modelled, through their compassion and political acumen, a kind of radical futurity for all of us, wherever we are placed, in the structures of power in higher education.

Witnessing Radical Hope in the Plantation and Beyond

In fall of 2022, I was finally able to go on a sabbatical and return to East India, the first time after my baba's death. The tea plantations were not really on my radar at this time. But, through a series of mysterious synchronicities, I ended up connecting to two organizers in North Bengal who have been working with a cooperative movement there: Rupam Deb and Bebika Khawas. Between 1999 and 2007, I had been involved in grassroots organizing efforts with plantation women in the central Dooars. Because of the politics of formalization—which is another long story about caste and class dominance—I left this organizing work and had not been back since. I remembered the earlier work, which involved plantation women building small literacy circles, using a feminist-Freirean approach—where women and children were both teachers and learners. But that is another story.[5] I also remember how they named their own classroom circles with words like *asha*, hope.

Now, as my new friends and I scouted for land to create an organizing base, they introduced me to a teacher who had started a small school by using land that was officially "owned" by the plantation. We met Renuka Dhanwar in the two-roomed school and heard the story of their struggle with the plantation managers and police who demanded that they return this tiny portion of land on which they had built their school. Renuka and her fellow teachers were not going to give up their claims to this land, which had been "settled" for tea plantations a century ago by the British. They fought both the police and the tea planters, and essentially "squatted" on the land—claiming it and their right to education on their terms. For the conference, I screened a small video of Renuka Dhanwar speaking (with Bebika Khawas) about their strategies to counter these powerful forces and their tenacious resistance. In this small video, Renuka outlines their struggles to claim the tiny plot of land upon which they built the two-room schoolhouse. Among their strategies was to claim it as a sacred space for ritual. Even then, planters and police did their best to evict them from what the management claimed to be their property. So far, the teachers have prevailed.[6]

It was so inspiring to be connected back to that militancy, radical hope, and creative praxis again.

It is now May 2024 as I finally finish writing this essay. Since that brief meeting about the school in Madhubagan, I have bought some land. I am dreaming of an antiviolence health centre where Adivasi women's voices and lives are centred, of helping with the cooperative movement, and of other translations of what my students at Scripps were calling "mutual aid." The political landscape, underwritten by caste supremacy in India, is also colonizing, feudal, and deeply violent. Who knows what kinds of radical futurities can be built there? I move through the complicities, with the imperial dollar, daring to hope through careful coalition building, transparency, and some honesty. Let's see.

On this end of the planet, a few days ago, I visit the Pitzer College student encampment built in solidarity for Gaza. Many fellow faculty are donating food and supplies and are working hard on coalitional divestment organizing. When I meet some of the folks at the encampment, I notice a sense of joy and togetherness—no one seems particularly scared. This visit was before the violent counter-protest at UCLA at the end of April. I am struck by the calm, and a deep sense of solidarity. I know that the mutual aid ethos is sutured into what these young people are imagining and fighting for.

The year 2024 promises to be another of increasing chaos and polarization in the middle of empire, and in its colleges and universities. After three decades of teaching in the US academy, I am not sure "what universities are for," especially as I witness the full brute force of militarized police being unleashed on my students. But what I do know is that in the face of both covert and overt marginalization and violence, in the face of ongoing genocide and a pandemic, my students were/are carving out possibilities, and futurities, that I think we can co-create with them. I know that in the middle of my individual grief, it was witnessing their collective, underground organizing labour, brilliance, and compassion that brought some light and meaning into my own brokenness and sense of alienation, isolation, and despair.

Now, they are offering us pathways paved with a profound ethical clarity about what matters. Eyes on Gaza, they insist, Eyes on Gaza. They, too, are acting on their witness of genocide and our imperial complicities.

I am more than aware that "bearing witness" here—and there—is enabled by the very terms of power and complicity that I/we are trying to understand, negotiate, and dismantle. They show us, perhaps, what Saidiya Hartman ends her remarkable essay on—an exhortation to the "undoing of the plot"—to challenge that overwhelming "plot of her undoing": "The undoing of the plot begins when everything has been taken. When life approaches extinction, when no one will be spared, when nothing is all that is left, when she is all that is left….The undoing of the plot begins with her drifting from the course, with an errant path, with getting lost to the world" (Hartman, 2020, p.5).

It seems particularly apt to honour, and end, these small meditations about both collective and individual witness with the words of the great national poet of Palestine, Mahmoud Darwish, who said, "without hope we are lost." On the edges of all the plantations, and in the witnessing of "bare life," it is perhaps all that we can cling to, reach for, create. Perhaps, this—this—is what universities are for.

References

Chatterjee, P. (2001). *A time for tea: Women, labor and post/colonial politics on an Indian plantation.* Duke University Press.

Chatterjee, P. (2009) Transforming pedagogies: Imagining internationalist/feminist/antiracist literacies. In J. Sudbury & M. Okazawa-Rey (Eds.), *Activist scholarship: Antiracism, feminism, and social change.* Routledge.

Collins, P.H. (1986) Learning from the outsider within: The sociological significance of Black feminist thought. *Social Problems,* 33(6), S14–S32. https://doi.org/10.2307/800672

Da Costa, D. (2018). Caste-ignorant worlds of progressive academics: Academically-transmitted caste innocence. RAIOT. https://raiot.in/academically-transmitted-caste-innocence/

Hartman, S. (2020). The plot of her undoing. *Notes on Feminisms* 2. Feminist Art Coalition. https://feministartcoalition.org/essays-list/saidiya-hartman

Nobody Fails at Scripps. (2020a). Universal pass. https://nobodyfailsatscripps.wordpress.com/universal-pass/

Nobody Fails at Scripps. (2020b). About. http://nobodyfailsatscripps.wordpress.com/about

Nobody Fails at Scripps. (2020c). Mutual aid. http://nobodyfailsatscripps.wordpress.com/mutual-aid-2

Nobody Fails at Scripps. (2020d). Statement on grading policy vote [Letter]. Google Docs. https://docs.google.com/document/d/1fL2eEv7Ru6WxwFSmVkgGpBjVr8imz1E3i9IAsBrOg-M

Nobody Fails at Scripps Coalition. (2020). *Arguments for a universal pass grading policy for spring 2020* [Live document]. Google Docs. https://docs.google.com/document/d/1xS5yz4IMmlaqYfKKr_UTBs5DxDZb6sz90B3qtJxaeAg

Patel, S. (2016). Complicating the tale of "two Indians": Mapping "South Asian" complicity in white settler colonialism along the axis of caste and anti-Blackness. *Theory & Event,* 19(4). http://muse.jhu.edu/article/633278

Patel, S.A. (2022) Talking complicity, breathing coloniality: Interrogating settler-centric pedagogy of teaching about white settler colonialism. *Journal of Curriculum and Pedagogy,* 19(3), 211–30. https://doi.org/10.1080/15505170.2020.1871450

Rich, A. (1994). *Blood, bread, and poetry: Selected prose.* W.W. Norton.

Sherman, G. (2021, January 24). Nobody Fails at Scripps has met extraordinary need during the pandemic. What comes next? *The Student Life.* https://tsl.news/nobody-fails-legacy/

Yarduman, M. (2020, May 29). After faculty votes against universal pass, Nobody Fails at Scripps looks to the future. *Scripps Voice.* https://scrippsvoice.com/after-faculty-votes-against-universal-pass-nobody-fails-at-scripps-looks-to-the-future

Notes

1   I first began to explore this during my fieldwork in the early 1990s. However, in *A Time for Tea*, I don't explore enough how my caste power (inextricably linked to my class power, which I am more clear about) operated during fieldwork and the ethnographic text.

2   Please see this document online for the full details of the campaign, including surveys and additional research that have been included in hyperlinks throughout it.

3   It is important to note here that the entire student body of Scripps comprises about nine hundred students.

4   They elaborate, "We know from these responses that we, as organizers are not alone in our experiences of intense hardship and suffering. We know that we have the support of the Scripps community from the endless outpouring of love and gratitude that we have been receiving, including endorsements from SAS and the Scripps Store. We know we are not alone because Pitzer and CMC students have built their own collectives modelled after ours which stand in solidarity with us, along with Occupy Pomona who have inspired us immensely, as well as countless affinity groups and individual students from across the five colleges" (Arguments, 2020, p. 21).

5   I have rarely published about our organizing efforts for many ethical reasons; however, for some earlier insights, see Chatterjee, 2009.

6   See Dooars Daily Official. (2024, June 20). *Indigenous community in Indian tea plantation fight for quality education* [Video]. YouTube. https://www.youtube.com/watch?v=moKJsuh-TTo&ab_channel=DooarsDailyOfficial

CHAPTER 11
WHEN SHOULD UNIVERSITIES TAKE A STAND?

Shannon Dea

"To seek truth and advance understanding in the service of society."[1] For years now, in the context of my scholarship on academic freedom, I have used this phrase to characterize the academic mission of the university. It is a good starting point for answering the titular question on which this volume is based—What are universities for?—but the tidiness of my usual formulation does not do justice to the complexity of the modern university as that complexity is revealed in the current contestations over Israel and Gaza. As I wrote this chapter, Harvard University released a faculty working group's "Report on Institutional Voice in the University." The report was Harvard's response to a call for it to adopt an official policy of institutional neutrality in the wake of its response to Hamas's October 7 attack on Israel and the events that followed. The report finds that "the university has a responsibility to speak out to protect and promote its core function," but that "the university and its leaders should not…issue official statements about public matters that do not directly affect the university's core function" (Institutional Voice Working Group, 2024).

In this chapter, against the backdrop of campus responses to Israel and Gaza, I consider the mission of the university and whether that mission is served by institutional neutrality. In my view, it is not so easy (and may be impossible) to prise apart universities' core functions and "public matters." I argue that institutional neutrality is at best a useful fiction and at worst a way of concealing universities' commitments and reinscribing the status quo. Along the way, I offer a primer on academic and expressive freedoms in the context of universities, and on the importance of articulating and balancing core university values, including the duty of care. I conclude by offering advice on when universities should take a public stand on socio-political matters, and what that approach tells us about what universities are for.

Academic Freedom and the Duty of Care

I initially started researching academic freedom because I was deeply concerned about the ways in which the media, the public, and indeed university personnel (who should know better) were conflating academic freedom with freedom of expression—or even wilfully supplanting academic freedom with freedom of expression—in the culture wars that were rekindled by the 2016 election of Donald Trump. A particular catalyst for me was the discourse surrounding then-Wilfrid Laurier University graduate student and teaching assistant (TA) Lindsay Shepherd, who had become a free speech cause célèbre for the flak she received for showing a Jordan Peterson interview in a tutorial without the professor's permission. Most of the discussion of the case focused on expressive freedom, with very few commentators remarking upon the academic freedom of the course's instructor, Nathan Rambukkana, to design and oversee teaching and learning in the course.[2] At the time, even the Canadian Association of University Teachers—plausibly, the primary guardians of academic freedom in Canada—defended Shepherd and remained silent about Rambukkana's academic freedom (Jaschik, 2017). I took the case on in various popular venues, sometimes obliquely and sometimes more directly. The main point that I sought to drive home was that the freedom proper to universities is academic freedom, not freedom of expression, and that when we privilege the latter over the former, we do so at our peril.

Here is the main argument to that effect: the purpose of universities is to seek truth and advance understanding in the service of society. To serve that purpose, university personnel need to be able to engage in risky or controversial scholarship. To ensure that they are able to do so, universities in various ways defend academic freedom. Academic freedom is not an innate and inalienable human right. Rather, is a purposive freedom; that is, it was devised to serve a purpose. It is conferred on the highly qualified personnel who are charged with performing that purpose to support them in that work. Academic freedom comes with corresponding responsibilities that more or less boil down to seeking truth and advancing understanding with sincerity and integrity. Of course, professors get things wrong, but they are supposed to try to get things right. By contrast, freedom of expression is a freedom extended to all persons, irrespective of their roles or credentials, and carries with it no particular responsibilities. Freedom of expression permits people to yell lies in the town square, provided that those lies do not violate the law (as, for instance, threats or defamatory speech do).

Students in Canada do not have formal academic freedom protections.[3] Thus, on my view, the proper framing for the Shepherd case should have balanced Rambukkana's academic freedom to design and oversee the teaching and learning in his course with Shepherd's freedom of expression to share her perspective. In Canada, within the classroom, only the former freedom is protected. Academic freedom is enshrined in every faculty association collective agreement across the country. However, Canadian courts have not found Charter of Rights and Freedoms protections for freedom of expression to apply within university classrooms.[4] In general, constitutional protections, like those in the Charter, place limits on what the state may do, not what other institutions or individuals may do. A McDonald's employee does not have a protected freedom to promote Burger King to a customer while at work; they can be disciplined for doing so. Similarly, students—whether enrolled in a course or TAing it—do not have protected expressive freedom within the course. In short, professors have every right (and again, in Canada, that right is enshrined in collective agreements) to direct how their courses are run.

Recall that academic freedom was established and is today defended in order to support the academic mission of universities to seek truth and advance understanding in the service of society. Just as the search after truth requires that professors are able to pursue their best scholarly judgement unhindered, so the advance of understanding requires that professors are able to plan and direct courses according to their expertise without constraints imposed due to prevailing opinion—including the opinions of students. For instance, a professor should be able to teach evolutionary biology without making accommodations for creationist students.

That said, professors and universities should be cautious about too quickly drawing on academic freedom to overrule other freedoms, including expressive freedom. It is very often wise pedagogy and mentorship to permit students (including TAS) considerable expressive freedom to support them in their intellectual, professional, and moral development. I am much persuaded by Emmett Macfarlane's argument that even where Charter rights do not apply, there are good reasons to defend "Charter values" (Macfarlane, 2022a). Universities and professors do not have a positive duty to provide students with freedom of expression in the classroom—and certainly academic freedom is and ought to be more strongly protected than expressive freedom in academic contexts. However, insofar as both expressive freedom and universities are essential to democracy, there are good reasons for universities to honour and be guided by expressive freedom as a value. Indeed, we might extrapolate from Macfarlane and argue that since students and other non-professorial academics—such as post-docs, teaching centre staff, research officers, and other highly qualified personnel—play a part in the academic mission, they, too, have a claim to academic freedom as a value, even if they are not entitled to de jure academic freedom protections by way of their collective agreements. In practice, this means supporting the expressive and academic freedom of non-faculty university personnel, including students, so long as doing so does not violate the academic freedom of faculty. As more and more scholarly personnel occupy contract and non-faculty positions, defending the value of academic freedom for all scholarly personnel is increasingly important for the good-functioning of the university and the performance of the university's academic mission in the service of society.

Focusing on the academic mission of universities helps to make clear why academic freedom is important to defend in all its complexity. However, when we focus on the academic mission of the university, we see that academic freedom is only one of the freedoms or principles that is essential to that mission. I hew closely to the view championed by Scholars at Risk (SAR) that the academic mission hinges on a cluster of core values that must be carefully balanced (Scholars at Risk 2019/2020).[5] SAR lists several core university values—equitable access, accountability, social responsibility, institutional autonomy, and academic freedom. However, according to the SAR view, core values vary from one university to the next. SAR recommends that universities establish a practice of ongoing internal reflection and communication in order to identify their animating values and to learn how to balance those values when they come into tension with each other, as they often do.

In my role as a senior university administrator, one such principle of which I am acutely aware is the duty of care that universities owe to their students, employees, and community members. I often describe this as the duty to ensure that universities are safe workplaces for their employees and safe homes for their residents. Employers and landlords need to ensure employees' and residents' physical safety from such things as toxic chemicals and unstable building structures. Employers also bear moral and legal duties to prevent harassment in the workplace. The latter can be tricky at universities because some public and academic debates (both in and out of the classroom) can touch on members' identities in ways that they experience as harmful.[6] Further, I have argued elsewhere that universities owe a particular duty of care to Indigenous and other equity-denied members due to higher education's unjust, exclusionary past and present and the educational system's central role in enacting colonialism and cultural genocide (Dea, 2023).

It is crucial to note that the duty of care is not only a moral and legal duty. It is also essential to the academic mission. If universities do not provide safe workplaces and homes for their personnel, they will be less able to recruit and retain highly qualified personnel to participate in the academic mission. If universities do not provide safe workplaces and homes for equity-denied personnel, the personnel they are able to recruit and retain will bring a narrower range of perspectives and expertise to their scholarship, teaching, and learning.

Notice that my earlier characterization of academic freedom marks it as a negative freedom—a freedom from interference—not a positive duty that the state or the university owes professors. A negative right is a right not to be prevented from doing something, whereas a positive right is a right to be enabled to do something. Unlike academic freedom, the duty of care relates to a positive right. Insofar as universities owe a duty of care to their personnel, it is not enough for them to avoid interfering with those personnel; rather, they have a positive duty to ensure that universities and their members are safe.

Many contestations relating to academic and expressive freedom on campus precisely concern the challenge of balancing academic or expressive freedom with the duty of care. Let us return to the Shepherd example. One of the reasons that Rambukkana and others objected to Shepherd screening a Peterson video in a tutorial is that they regarded the video as making the learning environment less safe for trans students. There are myriad such examples.[7] While the responsibilities that accompany academic freedom are often illustrated using such examples as flat-Earth theory,[8] Shama Rangwala notes that the flat-Earth theory example is a red herring and a distraction (Rangwala, 2024).[9] The disputes that get the most uptake in both social and conventional media tend to be conflicts between the academic or expressive freedom to engage in putatively hateful, exclusionary, or harmful scholarship or speech and the duty to ensure that universities are safe places for trans, BIPOC,[10] and other equity-denied people to live and work. A decade ago, this debate often centred on safe spaces and trigger warnings. Today, as universities struggle to respond to Israel and Gaza, the debate increasingly centres on institutional neutrality.

Institutional Neutrality

In the first week or so after Hamas's October 7 attack on Israel, many universities worldwide issued statements condemning the attack and expressing sympathy for the victims of violence in Israel and (less frequently) Gaza (Anderson, 2023). Many of them were soon accused of failing to take a strong enough stand, either in support of Israel or in condemnation of it. In the December 2023 US Congressional hearing on antisemitism on college campuses, then-president of Harvard Claudine Gay was taken to task for Harvard's refusal to fly the Israeli flag on campus following October 7, even though it had flown Ukraine's flag after the invasion by Russia (Quilantan, 2023).[11] At the University of Amsterdam, over 1,200 PhD candidates signed an open letter strongly condemning the university's response to the crisis for having euphemistically characterized genocide as a "situation" and for its silence about the "75 year occupation of Gaza" (Connick et al., 2023). At my then-institution, the University of Regina, a motion to recommend to the president that the University publicly call for a ceasefire in Gaza was vigorously debated before ultimately being tabled and, weeks later, withdrawn. These are just three of many examples, but they illustrate the range of ways in which university administrations were called on to respond to Gaza.

At the same time, universities were reacting to statements by student organizations, academic departments, and other groups. At York University, the university condemned three student unions and threatened to remove their official recognition following the groups' joint statement of solidarity with Palestine, which characterized the October 7 Hamas attack as a "strong act of resistance" and throughout referred to "so-called Israel" (York Federation of Students et al., n.d.). At the University of British Columbia, the administration asked the Department of Anthropology to take down a statement on its website that expressed concern with "genocidal violence in Gaza," and other departments were directed not to post any statements that could be interpreted as political (Paling, 2024). Meanwhile, worldwide, universities continue to undergo political and media scrutiny due to allegations that pro-Palestinian protests and activities on campus make some Jewish students and employees feel unsafe. As the pressure mounts for universities to take a stand or to take a different stand than they are currently taking, many scholars and administrators argue that the right approach is not to take a stand at all but to maintain institutional neutrality (Robinson & Shah, 2024).

Indeed, I recently argued for just this. In January 2024, in response to a request from a faculty member, I circulated an opinion to members of my then-Faculty that included the following passage:

> Universities should be very cautious about adopting a particular disposition on behalf of the institution. Universities are constitutively pluralistic institutions. By design, they bring together scholars and learners with a range of positionalities and perspectives across a range of disciplines and methods. When universities rather than the individuals who constitute them adopt a particular disposition on a matter, particularly on a matter of controversy, they risk creating inhospitable working and learning environments for some of their members and chilling those members' academic and expressive freedom. (Dea, 2024)

I still think that this account is more or less right, but even as I circulated the above opinion, I knew that it was oversimplified. In my capacity as a senior university administrator, I have conveyed direct and indirect support for a range of positions. My email signature includes my pronouns and a land acknowledgement. I don't need to include either of those things, but I do because I wish to model gender-inclusiveness and commitment to Truth and Reconciliation. What, if anything, makes statements about Israel and Gaza any different? Why shouldn't I add a Palestinian or Israeli flag to my email signature too?

The classic expression of institutional neutrality occurs in the 1967 Kalven Report (formally, "Kalven Committee: Report on the University's Role in Political and Social Action"). The Kalven Committee was a faculty committee struck by the university's president. It is worth observing that by 1967, US universities were the sites of vigorous activism and protests on a range of issues, including civil rights for Black people, women's rights, and the Vietnam draft. The main argument of the Kalven Report is that universities should challenge society's established beliefs and values, but that they should do so through the free inquiry of their members. When the university as an institution weighs in on social or political issues, it risks interfering with "the fullest freedom for its faculty and students as individuals to participate in political action and social protest" (Kalven Committee, 1967, p. 3). The Report concludes that the university "can perform greatly for the betterment of society," and therefore should not be "diverted from its mission into playing the role of a second-rate political force or influence."

The Report does admit of two classes of exceptions to the principle of institutional neutrality. First, when there arise in society threats to "the very mission of the university and its values of free inquiry," the university must vigorously oppose those threats. Second, with regards to "university ownership of property, its receipt of funds, its awarding of honors, its membership in other organizations…these corporate activities of the university may appear so incompatible with paramount social values as to require careful assessment of the consequences" (Kalven Committee, 1967, p. 3).

According to the co-chairs of the Harvard faculty working group that produced its May 2024 "Report on Institutional Voice in the University," the report's conclusion that the university should not "issue official statements about public matters that do not directly affect the university's core function" (Institutional Voice Working Group, 2024) "rests on different principles and has some different implications" than Kalven (Feldman & Simmons, 2024). The report provides three reasons for its conclusion. First, university leaders are expert in university administration and not public affairs. Second, pressure on university administrators to make public statements distracts them from supporting the university's core purpose. Finally, university statements on public matters "can undermine the inclusivity of the university community" (Institutional Voice Working Group, 2024, p. 2). According to the report, "The best way for the university to acknowledge pressing public events is by redoubling intellectual engagement through classes, conferences, scholarship, and teaching that draw on the expert knowledge of its faculty" (p. 2).

In a January 2024 reflection on academic freedom in the time of Gaza protests, Jacob Levy leans heavily on the Kalven Report but anticipates some of the central ideas in the Harvard report. Characterizing the core mission of the university as "the discovery, transmission and preservation of knowledge," Levy argues that it is crucial for universities to remain neutral in order to avoid interfering with that mission. He writes: "If academic freedom is the ability of scholars and scholarly communities or disciplines to work without having an orthodoxy imposed on them, institutional neutrality is the commitment not to declare an orthodoxy in the first place" (Levy, 2024). Levy argues that over the years universities have let institutional neutrality slip through a series of "declarations and symbolic statements affirming that the university is on the side of all good things when it's not the job of a university to be on a side at all." In his view, these slips made universities vulnerable to external political attacks and made it harder for them to adopt a consistent and appropriate stance on Gaza. Levy urges that universities must reaffirm institutional neutrality in a range of ways that include avoiding "adopting institutional political platforms on foreign, political or social policy" in order to better "provide the site and space for students and faculty alike to study, explore, discuss and debate, to celebrate, mourn and protest, even the most divisive questions in political life."

Dutch political theorist Eric Schliesser finds Levy's account too absolutist. He lauds Levy's characterization of the mission of the university as the discovery, transmission, and preservation of knowledge, and agrees with his argument that universities should avoid taking dispositions that threaten this core mission. However, Schliesser argues that that core mission is locally inflected by each university's specific mission.[12] Universities are not one-size-fits-all. A liberal arts university has a specific mission to support the discovery, transmission, and preservation of knowledge in the liberal arts. A Jesuit university has a specific mission to support the discovery, transmission, and preservation of knowledge in the Jesuit tradition. A technical university has a specific mission to support the discovery, transmission, and preservation of knowledge in support of technology and technical training. And so on. On Schliesser's account, it would not be reasonable to demand that universities adopt institutional neutrality about their own special missions. On Schliesser's view, "universities and colleges should interpret academic freedom in light of their particular corporate identity which involves the general commitment to discovery, transmission and preservation of knowledge" (Schliesser, 2024).

In short, both Levy and Schliesser advocate for the importance of institutional neutrality. But Levy takes an absolutist approach, and Schliesser takes a context-sensitive approach. I want to push Schliesser's account still further. In my view, institutional neutrality is not just context-dependent; it is incoherent. Institutional neutrality is incoherent because neutrality is incoherent. As feminist philosophers of science, among others, have been arguing for years, there is no "view from nowhere." The ideal of objectivity is unattainable not merely because it is difficult to bracket one's biases and perspective but because it is impossible to do so. Further, the ideas, positions, and persons that are viewed as neutral or objective are so viewed not because they do not adopt a perspective but because they constitute the dominant perspective. Universities routinely adopt and convey particular institutional dispositions in a range of ways—from flying the national flag to welcoming various dignitaries to sending out holiday greetings to awarding honorary degrees for certain kinds of achievements. We read these dispositions as neutral because they are familiar.

It is important to make salient that familiar, dominant positions are nonetheless positions. In a 1966 address to Illinois Wesleyan University, Martin Luther King Jr. argued that racial equality would never be achieved through patience and the passage of time because "time itself becomes an ally to the forces of social stagnation" (King, 1966, p. 4). According to King, systems of power are inertial; so, change requires direct action and legislation. In much the same way, the invisible dispositions of universities will remain operative unless those universities start to convey countervailing dispositions. Both speech and silence can convey views. If, as King noted, patience and time favour the status quo, so often does silence. As I observed above, universities have both a moral obligation to address their exclusionary pasts and present and an epistemic duty to widen the pool of scholars who participate in the academic mission. Pretending that historically dominant (and still very much present) university values are neutral and objective because they are not salient sets up obstacles to universities carrying out those duties.

My view, then, is that institutional neutrality is not just an unattainable ideal but a fiction. As a fiction, it can be deleterious (as we have just seen) or useful. At bottom, the motive behind the useful fiction is the university administration's duty to, so far as possible, enable rather than interfere with the free inquiry, teaching, and learning of its personnel. This duty is of paramount importance. Even though the concept of viewpoint neutrality doesn't bear close scrutiny, adopting institutional neutrality as a defeasible heuristic can help remind administrators to be very cautious about conveying dispositions because doing so can be detrimental to the pursuit of the academic mission. At the same time, emphasizing that it is merely a defeasible heuristic can help to destabilize the myth of neutrality and empower administrators to judiciously express views that align with the mission and core values of the university.

Princeton University's tradition of institutional *restraint* is a helpful model of how universities can strike this balance.[13] Former Princeton president William Bowen, who coined the term "institutional restraint," held that Princeton "is a value-laden institution, and it is for that reason that I avoid using the word 'neutrality' to describe its aims....But the University's core values emanate from its character as a university. In this setting, the unrelenting, open-minded search for truth is itself the highest value; it is not to be sacrificed to anything else" (Eisgruber, 2022). For over half a century, Princeton's senior leaders have in various ways threaded the needle between exercising restraint and speaking up for the values of the university. For instance, in 1963, when students hosted a racist speaker on campus, then-president Robert Goheen both defended the visitor's right to speak and condemned the invitation as out of step with Princeton's commitment to equality.

In 2023, following recommendations by a faculty committee, Princeton adopted new guidelines for official department communications. At issue was whether departments or other units could or should issue statements on socio-political matters. The approach is a model of prudence and balance. Before a department or a departmental administrator may issue a public statement on an extramural matter, the unit must first have a written set of procedures regulating the issuance of such statements. Any statements that are issued must contain the following disclaimer: "This statement has been issued by [unit name] following its policy for issuing statements [link to policy] and does not represent the position of Princeton University" (Office of the Dean of the Faculty, n.d.). While many universities discourage administrators from making public statements, Princeton is clear that they may make public statements on their own behalf so long as they include a disclaimer that their statement represents their view, not the University's.

Princeton's new guidelines are very much in the spirit of SAR's approach to university values. As I discussed above, SAR recommends that universities conduct ongoing conversations about their core values so that when those values are put to the test, university members are ready for the complicated balancing work that follows. Similarly, by obliging departments and other units to develop their own procedures regulating public statements, Princeton ensures that any statements issued in times of controversy are not hasty and reactive but are guided by forethought. Transparent departmental procedures for issuing public statements also help to ensure consistency and provide a ready reply when the media or the public ask "Why this statement at this time? And how is this statement consistent with your last statement/silence?"

It is worth observing that the Princeton approach also uses the model of distributed risk to provide greater flexibility for individual units to develop and articulate their own public positions.[14] As was particularly evident in the US Congressional hearing on antisemitism on college campuses, any time a university office or official makes (or doesn't make) a public state-ment, there is a risk that the university as a whole will receive criticism for it. Princeton's approach more or less confines the risk associated with public statements to the units making them by making explicit where the decision-making resides for such statements. This frees the Arab Studies Department (for instance) to make a public statement on Gaza without having to go through the university's communications department with the inevitable watering-down of the message that would result.

Princeton's new guidelines still leave unanswered the question of under what circumstances an academic unit should make a public state-ment about a socio-political matter. I will conclude by offering some reflections on that question.

When Should Universities Speak Up?

Due to the power universities wield—internally over their members, and externally within society—they have a duty to use that power responsibly, both in their speech and in their silence. As we have seen, when universi-ties take a stand on socio-political matters, they risk interfering with the personnel charged with pursuing the core academic mission. However, complete silence on socio-political matters can reinscribe injustices that are or ought to be misaligned with universities' values and missions. Princeton's tradition of institutional restraint, combined with its guidelines on official department communications, offers a model to strike a balance between speech that interferes with scholarship and silence that slows progress. However, that model does not offer nuts-and-bolts advice on when units or administrators should speak up. Surprisingly, the Kalven Report may help to fill in that gap.

Recall the two exceptions to institutional neutrality carved out in the Kalven Report: (1) the university may oppose threats to "the very mission of the university and its values of free inquiry," and (2) the university may need to carefully assess the consequences of "university ownership of property, its receipt of funds, its awarding of honors, its membership in other organizations" when these activities are "incompatible with paramount social values" (Kalven Committee, 1967, p. 3).

With the first exception, the Kalven Committee no doubt had in mind resistance to state or similar interference in university autonomy. However, the exception can be easily repurposed to extend to resistance to broader socio-political threats to the university's ability to recruit and retain a diverse pool of scholarly personnel in support of the academic mission. Consider the two examples I offered earlier in this chapter of the pronouns and land acknowledgement that I use in my decanal email signature to model gender-inclusiveness and commitment to Truth and Reconciliation. The university's mission is compromised by its history of exclusionary practices and values that reduced participation by Indigenous peoples, women, and gender non-conforming people. Public statements in support of Truth and Reconciliation and gender-inclusiveness can thus help to support the academic mission.

The second exception is a little different. In that case, the emphasis is on the formal and material supports that the university lends to various individuals, organizations, and activities and the duty to ensure that those activities meet the highest ethical standard. For instance, in 2023, my then-university rescinded an honorary degree it had conferred on Mary Ellen Turpel-Lafond following plausible allegations that Turpel-Lafond had misrepresented her Indigenous ancestry (University of Regina, 2023). An honour conferred by a university carries enormous weight. Universities need to be accountable for those conferrals. Likewise, university investments and partnerships should meet the highest standards. That doesn't mean that the whole university community will ever agree on conferrals, rescissions, investments, etc. But the university has a duty to be answerable for all such activities.

In combination, the two Kalven exceptions provide the foundation for a new model for university statements that I term the "proximity model."[15] Public statements by universities should be undertaken with considerable restraint since they risk interfering with the academic mission. Thus, it is not helpful for universities to regularly issue statements about a wide array of socio-political issues. Since they need to be sparing about public statements, they should reserve them for proximate matters—that is, matters in which they are morally or materially implicated. For instance, public statements about Truth and Reconciliation are appropriate for universities that are located on treaty territories or unceded Indigenous land because those universities are morally implicated in settler-colonialism on that land.

Notice that my proximity model mirrors Schliesser's context-sensitive account of institutional neutrality. As Schliesser argues, universities have the right to pursue specific missions. On the proximity account, though, those specific missions bring with them specific moral entanglements and duties, which can behoove institutions from time to time to take a particular stand. For instance, a Jesuit institution has a stronger duty than a secular university to make a public statement about child sexual abuse by priests. Similarly, an agricultural college may be more strongly compelled than a liberal arts college to make a public statement on the human rights violations experienced by migrant farm workers. Geographical location, history, operations, and investments, *inter alia*, can similarly ground proximate moral duties.

Change is hard. Since time and silence favours the status quo, universities will often need to be called to their proximate duties by way of advocacy and protest by their members. We can see this happening in the case of the pro-Palestinian encampments that sprang up on university campuses in the spring of 2024. Most or all of the encampments were established at least in part to put pressure on universities to divest from organizations that directly or indirectly support Israel's war on Gaza and its human rights abuses in Palestine. Whatever one might think of the encampments, they are focused on the activities in which the universities are implicated and for which they are therefore answerable.

Some current university administrators who in their youth participated in campus protests about South African apartheid or similar see the current encampments as importantly different from the movements they belonged to. Perhaps that is true, but it is worth remembering that the legitimacy of campus protests is often only discernible in retrospect. In 1969, students occupied a computer lab at Sir George Williams University (now Concordia University) to protest the university's mishandling of anti-Black/Caribbean racism by a professor. The protestors were ultimately expelled by riot police, who injured several students with batons. Students were variously arrested, incarcerated, and deported. Black protestors were subject to appalling racism by the police and the public. Media denounced the student protestors as a "gang of hooligans," "rampaging criminals," "anarchists," and "thugs" (Palmer, 2009, p. 286) and blamed the protests on outsiders (Irwin, 2020, pp. 35–68).[16] In 2022, following the report of the President's Task Force on Anti-Black Racism, Concordia University apologized for its unjust treatment of the protestors and for its half-century of silence on the matter (Carr, 2022).

If time is an ally to social stagnation, so may be complexity. Proximity is relative, if anything is, and universities are large, complex organizations that are implicated in many activities. Must universities take stands against factory farming or in favour of veganism in virtue of their food services operations? At what point does the connection become so tenuous that a public statement is no longer appropriate? What is to be done in the case of sincere disagreement among members? Unsurprisingly, there are no simple answers to these questions. One size does not fit all, either between universities or even within a single university as time passes and things change. Here, again, SAR's model of balancing core values is helpful. In times of complexity, as universities work to maintain tricky balances among their core values, answerability for what I am here terming proximity is one of the values that ought to be brought into the mix. In the face of the trickiest challenges, we will almost inevitably get this balance wrong, but a sincere effort to balance core values will save us from the worst errors, and, if we're lucky, it will help us do a little better next time around. In the end, taking responsibility is less about achieving perfection than about moral repair.

The messy picture I am painting of university personnel engaged in difficult, ongoing, overlapping conversations about their animating values through controversy, change, and injustice—often across deep disagreement—may be unsatisfying or even frustrating for some readers. For me, though, it gets to the heart of what universities are for. Universities are for seeking truth and advancing understanding in the service of society, and for a million other things. In addition to seeking truth and advancing understanding, university personnel use their scholarly, artistic, and technical expertise to challenge, critique, create, curate, build, fight, ridicule, resist, and even destroy. The university is always constitutively in a state of change. So its values and how they are performed are constitutively under negotiation. Along the way, we make and remake the university. Along the way, we make and remake society.

References

Anderson, N. (2023, October 21). University leaders search for the right words amid Israel-Gaza war. *Washington Post*. https://www.washingtonpost.com/education/2023/10/21/dc-colleges-universities-israel-hamas-statements/

Bartram, M. (2024, May 22). The right to avoid medical advice in mental health care: Open access as an alternative to professional gatekeeping. Alternatives to Legal Prohibitions and Bans for Morally Controversial Behaviour [workshop]. McGill University.

Carr, G. (2022, October 28). Concordia's apology. Concordia University. https://www.concordia.ca/provost/initiatives/task-force-anti-black-racism/apology-1969.html

Connick, E., el Khannoussi, S., et al. (2023, October 15). UvA support for Palestine, end occupation [Letter]. Google Docs. https://docs.google.com/forms/d/e/1FAIpQLSf6RKwGVBgni-r5Te8SOeBBRBAoFqnmXNoRCjRlGoyMBNjS7Q/viewform?pli=1

Dea, S. (2021a). The evolving social purpose of academic freedom. *Kennedy Institute for Ethics Journal*, 31(2), 199–222. https://doi.org/10.1353/ken.2021.0012

Dea, S. (2021b, September 15). The high price of donations. *University Affairs*. https://universityaffairs.ca/opinion/dispatches-academic-freedom/the-high-price-of-donations/

Dea, S. (2023). Academic freedom and the duty of care: Reframing media coverage of campus controversies. In C. Fox & J. Saunders (Eds.), *Routledge handbook of philosophy and media ethics* (pp. 56–68). Routledge.

Dea, S. (2024, January). Dean's report. Faculty of Arts Council, University of Regina.

Eisgruber, C.L. (2022, November 7). Princeton's tradition of institutional restraint. *Princeton Alumni Weekly*. https://paw.princeton.edu/article/princeton-president-christopher-eisgruber-tradition-institutional-restraint

Feldman, N., & Simmons, A. (2024, May 28). Harvard should say less. Maybe all schools should. *New York Times*. https://www.nytimes.com/2024/05/28/opinion/university-statements-harvard-kalven.html

Institutional Voice Working Group. (2024). Report on institutional voice in the university. Harvard University. https://provost.harvard.edu/sites/g/files/omnuum3356/files/provost/files/institutional_voice_may_2024.pdf

Irwin, A. (2020). *Debasing dissent: The role of the news media in the devaluation of Black Canadian activism*. [Doctoral dissertation, University of Waterloo]. https://uwspace.uwaterloo.ca/bitstream/handle/10012/16478/Irwin_Ashley.pdf?sequence=1&isAllowed=y

Jaschik, S. (2017, November 21). The interrogation of a TA. *Inside Higher Ed*. https://www.insidehighered.com/news/2017/11/22/university-faces-uproar-over-recording-showing-how-teaching-assistant-was-questioned

"Kalven committee: Report on the university's role in political and social action" (1967, November 3). *The University of Chicago Record*, 1(1), 2–3. https://campub.lib.uchicago.edu/view/?docId=mvol-0446-0001-0001

King, M. (1966). Dr. Martin Luther King , Jr. speech at Illinois Wesleyan University [1966 convocation speech]. Illinois Wesleyan University, (1–6). https://www.iwu.edu/mlk/

Levy, J.T. (2024, January 13). Lessons in free speech; Universities have shifted away from the principles of academic freedom, Jacob T. Levy writes. Oct. 7 brought to a head problems that have been developing on campus for years. *The Globe & Mail*. Retrieved April 29, 2024. https://link.gale.com/apps/doc/A779240446/CIC?u=ureginalib&sid=bookmark-CIC&xid=b594c105

Macfarlane, E. (2022a). Beyond the hate speech law debate: A "Charter values" approach to free expression. *Review of Constitutional Studies/Revue d'études constitutionnelles*, 26(2)–27(1), 145–68. https://www.constitutionalstudies.ca/wp-content/uploads/2023/12/06_MACFARLANE.pdf

Macfarlane, E. (2022b). Hate speech, harm, and rights. In E. Macfarlane (Ed.), *Dilemmas of free expression* (pp. 35–55). University of Toronto Press.

nescio13. (2024, May 14). Academic and political freedom, social safety, and frustration intolerance (with some Spinoza). Digressionsimpressions's Substack. https://digressionsimpressions.substack.com/p/academic-and-political-freedom-social

Office of the Dean of the Faculty, Princeton University. (n.d.). J. guidance and policies pertaining to official departmental communications. In *Guidebook for chairs, directors and managers*. https://dof.princeton.edu/guidebook-department-chairs-and-managers/chapter-iii-other-administrative-information/j-guidance-and-policies-pertaining-official-departmental-communications

Paling, E. (2024, February 7). After Selina Robinson met with UBC president, Gaza statement disappeared. *The Breach*. https://breachmedia.ca/selina-robinson-met-ubc-president-gaza-statement-scrubbed/

Palmer, B.D. (2009). *Canada's 1960s: The ironies of identity in a rebellious era*. University of Toronto Press.

Quilantan, B. (2023, December 5). 5 takeaways from college antisemitism hearing. *Politico*. https://www.politico.com/news/2023/12/05/college-presidents-testifying-campus-antisemitism-00130277

Rangwala, S. (2024, March 22). Academic freedom and state power. Academic Freedom Under Erasure [Roundtable], University of Toronto.

Robinson, T.R., & Shah, N.H. (2024, February 23). "This has to stop": Harvard set to consider institutional neutrality. *The Harvard Crimson*. https://www.thecrimson.com/article/2024/2/23/institutional-neutrality-feature/

Schliesser, E. (2024, March 22). On academic freedom and institutional neutrality. *Crooked Timber*. https://crookedtimber.org/2024/03/22/on-academic-freedom-and-institutional-neutrality/

Scholars at Risk (2019/2020). *Promoting higher education values: A guide for discussion*. https://www.scholarsatrisk.org/wp-content/uploads/2020/05/SAR_PHV_DiscussionGuide_v20_ONLINE.pdf.

UAlberta Pro-Life v. Governors of the University of Alberta, 2020 ABCA 1 (CanLII).

University of Regina. (2023, February 13). University of Regina rescinds honorary degree awarded to Mary Ellen Turpel-Lafond. https://www.uregina.ca/news/2023/university-of-regina-rescinds-honorary-degree-awarded-to-mary-ellen-turpel-lafond.html

York Federation of Students, York University Graduate Students' Association, & L'association étudiante collège Glendon. (n.d.). Statement of solidarity with Palestine. https://static1.squarespace.com/static/534d4d15e4b0458a1fec3b4e/t/652872b0a266b0042143437f/1697149616600/Statement+of+Solidarity+with+Palestine.pdf. first

Notes

1   My thanks to Rens Bod, Sarah Bracke, Samantha Brennan, Eddie Brummelman, Emily Eaton, Marieke de Goede, Annelies Moors, Sean Tucker, and audience members at SPUI25 (University of Amsterdam) and the Council of Ontario Deans of Arts and Science for help in thinking through some of the ideas in this chapter. Special thanks to Alice MacLachlan and Eric Schliesser for helpful conversations and comments on earlier drafts of this paper. Endless gratitude to Marc Spooner and James McNinch for their generosity and patience, and to Whitney Blaisdell for her empathy and well-timed pep talk. I gratefully acknowledge funding support from the SSHRC Insight Development Grant program. Finally, I am grateful to have done this work as a white settler scholar and uninvited guest first on Treaty 4, the territories of the nêhiyawak, Anihšināpēk, and Dakota, Lakota, and Nakoda, and the homeland of the Métis/Michif Nation , and then in Mi'kma'ki, the ancestral and unceded territory of the Mi'kmaq People..

2   Rambukkana was opposed to Shepherd's having shown the video and was one of three Wilfrid Laurier university personnel who met with Shepherd afterward to raise concerns.

3   Globally, academic freedom protections for students are comparatively rare. Students in Latin America have stronger academic freedom protections than

students elsewhere due to the important role that the student movement played in the Córdoba Reform. The "Joint Statement on Rights and Freedoms of Students" adopted in 1967 by the American Association of University Professors and various student and professional associations characterizes students as having academic freedom but doesn't offer any robust protections to underwrite that freedom. Some Canadian universities have policies extending academic freedom to all members, but they are similarly toothless (see Dea, 2021a).

4   A landmark 2020 Alberta Court of Appeal decision was the first to find that Canadian universities have Charter obligations. However, it found those obligations to apply in the quad, not the classroom. (See *UAlberta Pro-Life v. Governors of the University of Alberta*.) Legal challenges related to the pro-Palestine campus encampments that were active as I wrote this chapter could well see this precedent spread to other provinces.

5   See also Dea, 2021a.

6   See Macfarlane, 2022b, on the difficulties of empirically establishing the harms of hate speech. See also nescio13, 2024, on the vexed question of "social safety" in the campus context. (Eric Schliesser blogs as nescio13.)

7   Indeed, several examples involve Shepherd. Having become a minor free speech champion, she formed a student club that organized events with controversial speakers—including an anti-trans speaker, white supremacist and anti-immigration speakers, and a speaker who challenged the view that Indian residential schools were harmful to Indigenous Peoples. (See Dea, 2023.)

8   I did this with young Earth creationism! (See Dea, 2021b.)

9   Rangwala says that the ubiquitous flat-Earth example in discussions about academic freedom is "a red herring and a distraction" because flat-Earth theory has nothing to do with state/ruling class ideology. According to Rangwala, critiques of state/ruling class ideology are where the rubber hits the road for academic freedom (Rangwala, 2024).

10   The acronym for Black, Indigenous, and people of colour.

11   Gay was forced to resign shortly thereafter, ostensibly for plagiarism early in her career, after a politically motivated search for any excuse to force her resignation uncovered the plagiarism.

12   While Schliesser is responding to Levy, and I am here contrasting their views, Levy has once or twice on social media remarked that he is in broad agreement with Schliesser's view.

13   Thank you to Marieke de Goede for telling me about Princeton's approach.

14   Bartram 2024 helped me to see the Princeton model as exemplifying risk distribution.

15   Sincere thanks to Alice MacLachlan for helping me to develop and refine my "proximity model."

16   Similar tropes were commonly used about the 2024 encampment protesters.

SECTION IV
IMAGINING OUR COLLECTIVE FUTURE AND THE FUTURE OF UNIVERSITIES

In this last section, authors detail creative new departures and reimaginings for the university of tomorrow.

CHAPTER 12
THE UNIVERSITY'S FOUR FUTURES
OR, THE REAL HUMANITIES CRISIS AND ITS CURES

Christopher Newfield

W E ARE ALL TIRED OF THE WORD "CRISIS" IN RELATION TO both the university and the humanities. It's depressing, and it's also distracting from the work of reconstruction we need to do. This is especially true when the crisis lasts so long, for so many years and decades, that it convinces us that there's no solution. Or, we think maybe there *is* a solution, but it has too many moving parts and we won't live long enough. Using a standard matrix for mapping interactions among a couple of variables, in our sorrow this

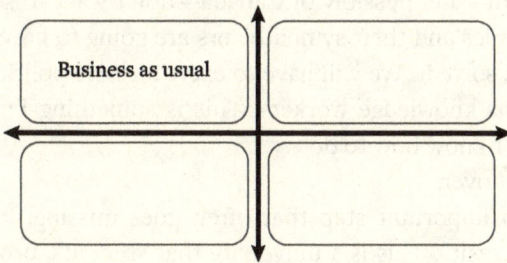

Business as usual

Figure 12.1a. Standard matrix for mapping interactions

turns into *this*.

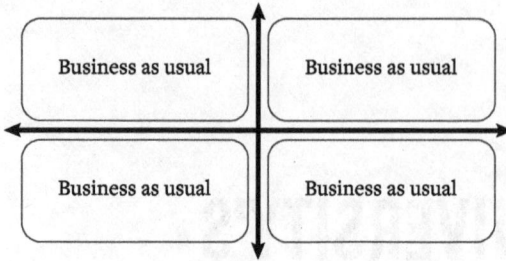

Figure 12.1b. Standard matrix for mapping interactions: Business as usual

And we can auto-populate each domain with familiar content—it takes no thought.

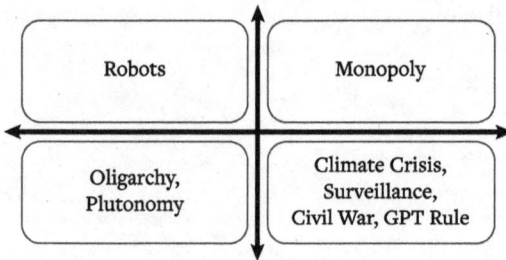

Figure 12.1c. Standard matrix for mapping interactions: Auto-populated

I understand these feelings and impulses, and I often share them. But my main point here will be that solutions can be achieved through collective effort. The higher education crisis is readily solved conceptually, in large part through decolonized philosophies of teaching and research as public goods. And yet the political systems of the United States and United Kingdom—and possibly of Canada—don't want to solve it. So all types of academics and their sympathizers are going to have to make the system want to solve it. We will have to exert massive political agency, as professionals, as knowledge workers. This is something I'm pretty sure academics don't know how to do—yet.

So let's start over.

There is an important step that often goes missing: imagining the post-crisis university. This is a university that students, professors, staff, and communities actually want and would work toward together. They would build it with confidence rather than with our well-honed defensive reflexes. Many groups are happy to anoint themselves authors of the future on our behalf. The technology sector is one. Finance is another, which as we speak is asserting ownership of the energy transition and other ecological transformations. Where is higher education in this scramble? Where are educators?

I'm going to drop us into the middle of the current struggle for higher education through the heuristic of its four futures—and suggest we need to give the best of these futures a massive push. We need to do this for teaching and research but also for society, to address our post-truth conditions; to address the paranoid style that has recaptured politics in many countries; to address the anger, projection, splitting, and hatreds that result; *and* to address the deep need for a non-technological imagination of the future of our societies. This must be an imagination at least as powerful as that coming out of current research on digital currencies, military drones, or machine learning.

So: here's our futures scenario matrix. Four worlds are generated by a spectrum of possibilities on two issues—education on the x-axis (horizontal), and governance on the y-axis (vertical), with funding modes folded into governance.

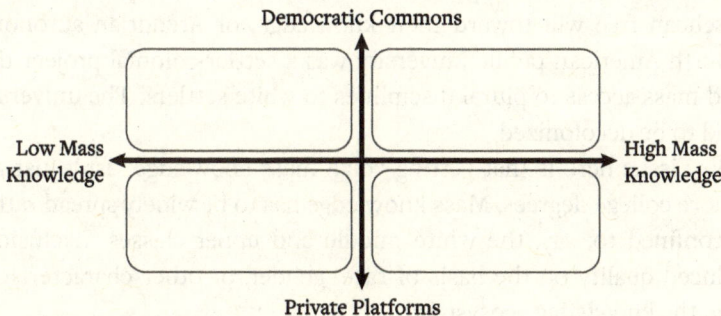

Figure 12.2. Futures scenarios matrix

The x-axis represents a dominant storyline of higher education in Western societies, and that is massification—more access but on condition of economies of scale. In North America and Europe, high school was for a small elite and then became common. Later, bachelor's degrees were for a small elite and then became more common. The movement is in theory from left to right on the axis. The same is true of access by gender and by race, ethnicity, and Indigeneity—first more common for whites, then for people of colour. There's no linear progress here but often delay. Different groups arrive at different speeds, and there's a lot of back and forth. So we can wind up in various places on this axis and even go backward or get stuck.

We normally measure level of education as the share of a population that has a particular degree, like the BA. My phrasing is meant to suggest something else—the amount of general learning in the population. This is very difficult to measure but not to define. The idea of "mass knowledge" is that knowledge has to be widely available—there is spillover from the student to the family, to friends, to one's wider community and society. Mass knowledge also appears in the results of novel research that circulates directly into society rather than entering the commercial patenting and licensing pipeline. Mass knowledge is always a mix of different disciplines (so it isn't only literary or economic or technological but a combination). Mass knowledge is always multidisciplinary knowledge—public higher education was to cover every subject the population wanted to study, and in the nineteenth century North American colleges started to *require* students to distribute some coursework outside their major.

In addition, people have to be able to *use* knowledge, so mass knowledge includes cognitive capabilities. Students are to acquire a certain Nietzschean free will toward their knowledge, or Arendtian autonomy. The North American public university was a settler-colonial project that offered mass access to plural disciplines to white settlers. The university has had to be decolonized.

A key issue here is that getting "high mass knowledge" isn't just getting more college degrees. Mass knowledge has to be widely spread rather than confined to, say, the white middle and upper classes. Exclusions or reduced quality on the basis of race, gender, or other characteristics weaken the knowledge ecosystem.

In addition, knowledge is a function of quality and intensity, not just quantity, which can be spread very thin. Massification has generally meant limiting learning by routinizing knowledge acquisition and testing. In the United States, the explicit goal of the post–World War II period was to get hundreds of thousands of veterans into classrooms by creating the large lecture and TA system and running them through it, giving them a decent general education for generic, even nondescript, white-collar work.

But the next stage—more *intense* learning for all, *deeper* learning for all, through small class sizes, more personalized teaching, special support for the less prepared—never arrived. It got a little way along and was then defunded by most states and provinces. Widening the circulation of knowledge to communities of colour coincided with a thinning out of funds for instruction. There's a strong inverse correlation between the increase in the shares of student bodies that are persons of colour and the flattening or decrease in per-student state funding (Newfield, 2020).

White UG Enrollment % Versus UC General Funds as Share of State Adjusted Gross Income

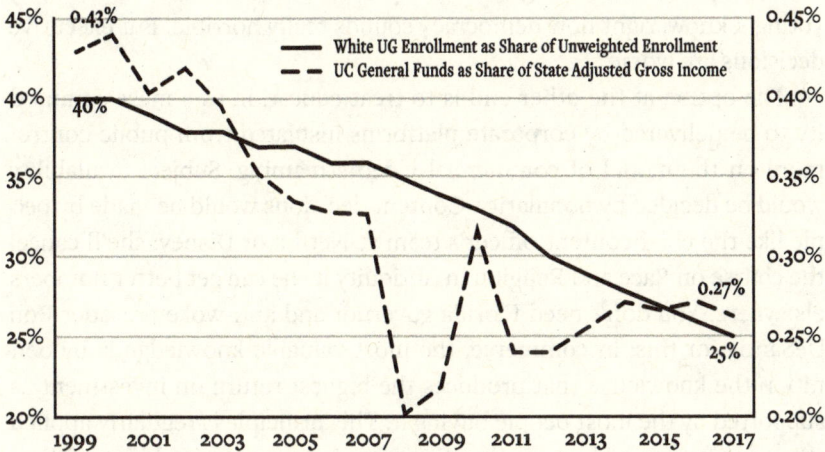

Figure 12.3. White UG enrollment % versus UC general funds as shares of state adjusted gross income

As the share of white students falls (top line), so does state funding (bottom line) as a share of the money state residents actually have in their pockets. Intentionality is hard to prove, but the correlation is clear. Around the time people of colour were admitted in larger numbers, universities became far more focused on reducing costs than on continuously improving learning.

In colleges with high shares of Black and brown students and low-income students, standardization, commodification, and passive learning remained the norm. Companies selling educational technology have devoted themselves for decades to automating learning even further, always promising "personalized" learning that never quite arrives. Technologies like GPTs, though great technical feats, are unlikely to reduce the pacifying effects of massification and *are* likely to make them worse. In short, society moves back and forth on our horizontal axis between less mass knowledge and more—and less.

The y-axis (vertical) expresses how knowledge is governed and provisioned. There are many mixtures, but let's just look at the simple cases. One is that a given level of mass knowledge is treated as a public or social good, funded by everyone who pays tax (at different rates reflecting their incomes), with funding allocated through democratic decision-making. "Democratic commons" can be summarized as common needs funded by common provision, through the tax system, with allocations decided by voting. I know, right now democracy sounds really horrible. But executive decisions are worse.

The option at the other end is to treat education as a mass commodity to be delivered by corporate platforms insulated from public control, more on the model of commercial video streaming. Subject availability would be decided by popularity. Content decisions would be made by people like the chief content officer's team at Netflix or Disney: she'll cancel the course on Race and Religion in Antiquity if she can get better numbers elsewhere. You don't need Florida governor and anti-woke crusader Ron DeSantis for this: in commerce, the most valuable knowledge is by definition the knowledge that produces the highest return on investment as supported by the most people buying it. This principle is regularly applied to many aspects of higher education, as when resources shift to follow changes in undergraduate majoring. That's the platform end—and it has a good start in our current systems.

Let's look at the future that these factors, education and governance, can develop over the next thirty years. Future 1 is business as usual—I call it the Four Ds.

The Four Ds stand for Decline (in learning and research that have no monetary return), Defence (as in "defending the humanities," where we focus on not getting any worse rather than on building something great), Deference (so defence stays within the narrow parameters of appeasement of our funding masters), and Denial (of the fact that the current model, no matter how repeatedly tweaked, locks in decline). Another D word is democracy. But democracy is scarce in this future, having been shredded by privatization (Figure 12.4).

Democratic Commons

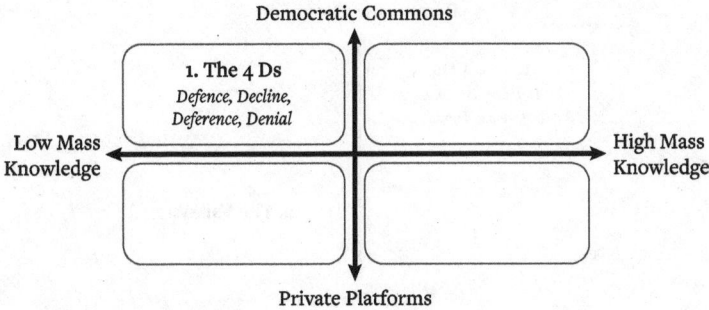

1. The 4 Ds
Defence, Decline,
Deference, Denial

Low Mass
Knowledge

High Mass
Knowledge

Private Platforms

Figure 12.4. Future 1: The four Ds

The public systems have been driven by two major quantitative pressures since World War II: first to increase in size to handle enrolment booms, and second to decrease in cost to handle budget cuts. Although most students in this Four Ds world attend public universities, the entire system has been neoliberalized, meaning, most simply, that the main metric is pecuniary or financial return on investment—wages by major for students, patent revenues from research, gifts logged for the development office, and so on. Another major metric is degree output: how many BA degrees did you produce in a designated year, and at what rate?

The easiest way to increase output is to lower standards—fewer distribution requirements, fewer required courses in a major, no second language requirement for English majors, etc. This world has been halfway privatized and has a funding model that's a conceptually incoherent mixture of public goals and missions with private revenues and cost-per-unit metrics. This incoherence weakens university finances, advocacy, and activism all while confusing the public. Decline is a continuous tendency. Defence tries to slow it down. Deference speeds it up. Denial diverts attention from the reality of the trend.

Next, Future 2, I'll call the Valley (Figure 12.5).

The Valley is driven by tech-based entrepreneurial capitalism. Its core trend is the continuation of the master plot of nineteenth-century industrial capitalism, which is first to Taylorize or routinize individual skill (Frederick W. Taylor developed time-motion studies of industrial labour), and then to replace as many skilled individuals as possible with technology. Big Tech provides this world's vision of the future, which doesn't *break* with nineteenth- and early-twentieth-century capitalism's embrace of routinized skill but intensifies it.

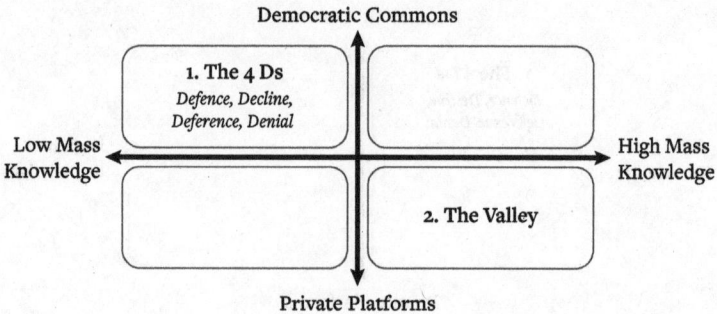

Figure 12.5. Future 2: The valley

The assumption in this future is that to increase the technological level of the society—which is equated with progress—the society must itself move from broadly public and egalitarian institutions managed democratically by government to the allegedly superior concentration and efficiency of a private sector driven by returns on investment. In this future, higher ed continues to charge high tuition and extend its one-sided emphasis on wage outcomes, employability, and STEM degrees. In the Valley, most public and non-elite private universities convert to majority online content and test-based credentialing, with adjunct labour providing course assistance.

The spread of online and hybrid training systems does support higher mass knowledge of some kinds—hence its position on the right-hand side of the chart. But this knowledge has three features we should take into account.

First, knowledge is very unequally distributed, and the Valley's inequalities mindlessly track historic disparities of race and class and other salient identities.

Second, professional knowledge is controlled by managers and the organizations for which they work. We would see the continuation of the trend in which even tenured professors have lost much of their ability to determine teaching and research policy or to speak to the public on behalf of the university, responsibilities now largely controlled by non-academic administrators. As part of this, adjunctification of academic labour continues. Attacks on institutionalized expertise expand.

Third, the Valley extends the radical underfunding of arts and humanities research. Currently, the US National Endowment for the Humanities' funds for research receive one-tenth of 1 percent of the federal research total. In this future, that ridiculous figure gets even worse (Executive Council, 2022).

However, Future 2, the Valley, isn't stable either. It is marked by an inefficient, unjust, and also infuriating concentration of resources, which continues to fuel social unrest in rich countries as well as poor. Addressing climate disorder requires more than technological fixes, as it needs people to change behaviour and governments to support large-scale collective action. Social and environmental conditions never really improve in the Valley, though asset owners maintain returns far higher than the growth of wages, dampening incentives to earn a living through knowledge labour. Those who can afford to wall themselves off from the majorities of their societies focus on doing so.

A root problem of Future 2 is that it is grossly deficient in the cultural knowledges of diverse communities. It assumes journalist Thomas Friedman's 1990s paradigm of "the Lexus and the olive tree," in which Indigenous or local or spiritual or philosophical or anthropological knowledges are relegated—lip service aside—to a backward past (Friedman, 1999). In the Valley, we don't know how to steer technology with culture, politics, and society, all those things that disruption gurus going back to Joseph A. Schumpeter and his concept of "creative destruction" define as burdens to innovation (Schumpeter, 2008). Political turmoil prevents technology platforms from working as predicted. Of course, local creativity flourishes, but it does so on a scale that is too limited to increase democracy, general learning, and systemic effects. Instability isn't necessarily a *good* thing, but at least it prevents the Valley from ruling the planet.

Since Future 2 maintains instability, a likely political and corporate response will be to increase systems of social control. This gets us to Future 3, which I'm calling the Long Gig (Figure 12.6).

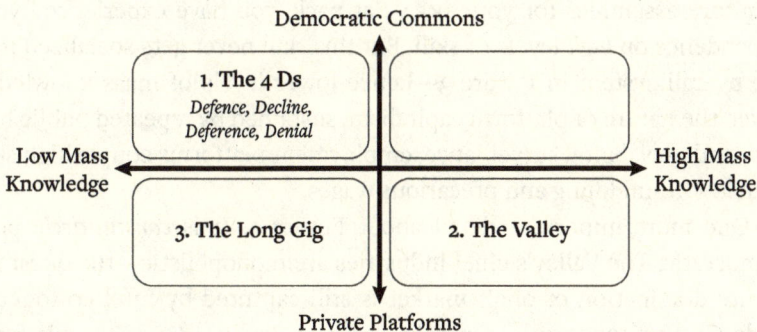

Figure 12.6. Future 3: The long gig

It's a gig economy, and gigs don't lead to jobs or careers for knowledge workers outside of a small elite, and an increasing share of knowledge jobs are "gigified." This is a "task rabbit" world.

In this future, society's dominant groups decide that the advancing state of programming and automation systems means they don't have to pay taxes to support the cost of pretty good mass higher ed. They had invested in four decades of discrediting both government regulation of business and the Keynesian focus on achieving economic health through continuously rising wages. Regulation and wage rises are dismissed as old school: these groups are then ready to cast off the remnants of their partnership with the progressive political forces that had supported Future 1.

The Long Gig's denizens long ago tired of paying professional salaries, health costs, and retirement packages, even to privileged white-collar workers. As we move through ever more elaborate applications of machine learning, they decide they can automate nearly all white-collar work outside of the super-elite service professionals who work directly with executives and owners in finance, tech commercialization, software engineering, and property investment. This allows the intensification of the *rentier* version of capitalism, where returns from asset ownership grow far faster than those from labour income, which makes basics like student housing in college towns less and less worth the high cost. In the United States, 5 percent of college enrolments stay in a combination of blue-chip private research universities, elite liberal arts colleges, and public flagships. Everyone else prepares for various membership levels in the cognitariat.

Note that the gig economy only works because of the high skill of its employees—if you ever hired, say, a stone mason who apprenticed in Guatemala working for a local Anglo contractor, or a Mechanical Turk furniture assembler for your IKEA flat pack, you have experienced your dependence on *high* levels of skill. But this skill never gets socialized into the overall system in Future 3—hence lower levels of mass knowledge. Given the nature of platform capitalism, sustained by repeated public bailouts and easy digital surveillance, employment platforms couple high skill with low-to-middling and precarious wages.

One more important detail about Future 3. It is *constitutively* post-democratic. The Valley's chief industries are monopolistic—the quest for secure domination of one's market is still captured by Intel co-founder Andy Grove's 1990s title, *Only the Paranoid Survive.*[1] Once the platform structure reduces and unevenly distributes knowledge, this world loses most of its remaining ability to coordinate disparate groups in a diverse society and engage in collective action regarding large-scale problems. This future is at a *cooperative disadvantage* in relation to the planetary challenges that require levels of mutual respect and coordination like we have never seen.

In addition, tech platforms are increasingly capital intensive. They already started to struggle when interest rates were raised meaningfully above zero in 2022. In feeding a now-bottomless appetite for capital, tech leaders will bend the knee to absolute monarchies and other stripes of authoritarian rulers with large markets (like the United States) or large reserves of petro-dollars (Kinder & Hammond, 2023). A company like Uber will be even less likely to support driver unionization when significant capital comes from sources like Saudi Arabia's sovereign wealth fund, as began to happen in 2016 (Kinder & Hammond, 2023). In the Long Gig, the peoples of the countries of OPEC+, in the Middle East, Africa, and elsewhere, find their democracy campaigns opposed not only by their national elites but by venture capital and its tech allies in the Global North.

Okay, Three Futures, and none of them good. We'd better not screw up Future 4.

Let's take stock of where we are. The Four Ds is our future inherited from post-war welfare-state capitalism. It had deep flaws, race-based exclusion being one, but it had a coherent budget model and a set of modest social aims: the public benefits of general higher learning were to be increasingly widely spread and were therefore *not* to be rationed by market forces. Education was not to be commodified: one effect was that public college tuition was free. This model has been half-dismantled and then kludged together with its opposite. The outward-facing public mission was retained because it is politically popular, but the inner workings came to depend more on private funds and were hollowed out.

We might be tempted to keep trying to make it work. It's familiar to us, and we have a lot of work-arounds. But both the educational quality and the fiscal solvency of this world's public universities are unstable. In Future 1, quality for students and researchers and solvency for universities *will* decline.

Here I won't lay out the reasons why I say this. I've written three books and literally hundreds of blog posts about the budget logic and won't browbeat you with them. Suffice to say that in a book called *The Great*

Mistake, I summarized the logic as a devolutionary cycle, a doom loop in which each step unwittingly feeds the next (Newfield, 2016). The doom loop sequences pretty much everything people don't like about today's university on the US version: the deep confusion about public benefits, the underfunding of all non-STEM research, the hidden and unjust cross-subsidies, the high tuition and the student debt, the ever-growing exploitation of contingent labour, the constant cost-cutting in the educational core, the chasing after tech solutionism, the persisting barriers related to race and sexuality, the growing food and housing insecurity of full-time students, the widening gulf between rich and poor colleges, the unevenness of student learning, the managing of future debt by students working way too many hours during school terms, and the squeezing of the joy and the transformative power of learning and of becoming an intellectually capable person through the insistence, by universities' own senior officials, that learning is for earning.

The loop has pulled higher education away from democracy and down toward the private government of platform capitalism. Universities mostly model autocratic governance, in which the highly educated have as little voice as all other regular folks. The absence of shared decision rights among faculty, staff, and senior managers has stifled open dialogue and innovation. Information feedback loops have been suppressed, and this lack of input from the whole university is one reason why its organizational learning is rare, and the negative loop persists.

The original sin that launched the Future 1 loop was university leaders cooperating with political and business figures in backing away from education as a public good (including multiracial and anti-colonial practices as goods). The effect has been to hide from everyone the non-monetary benefits at the heart of higher education—the intellectual and indirect benefits both personal and public. Since the 1980s and 1990s, universities have been scared to educate the public about our radically intellectual functions and their social benefits. Most of the public just does not know why they should care when public funding is cut. Nor do politicians of all major political parties, none of whom will even discuss major increases in public funding that would be spent on campuses according to internally determined academic priorities. It saves them money—Democrats, Liberals, Labour—to go with the right-wing charge, theorized in public-choice economics, that academics pursue their own self-interest and must never run their own affairs.

As I said at the start, I know for a fact, on the basis of this research, that *all* these problems can be fixed. But a necessary if not sufficient condition is much more public money. The most promising pressure in the United States today, even after Donald Trump's return to the White House, is coming from academic unions, where strikes are modelling the prerequisite of real improvement, which is collective action. And yet the structural fixes take public *money*. In the United States, there's a race between decline and unionization. Under our current model, with public funding capped, decline will win. Democratic contestation will continue, but if we stick with Future 1, the society's limited level of mass knowledge will not meet society's needs.

The default alternatives are Futures 2 and 3. The biggest difference between them lies in the level of mass knowledge, which will be higher in the Valley than in the Long Gig. The United States is currently moving from Future 1 to Future 2 for exactly this reason: elites think, "Well, in the Valley at least there will be enough smart people to do the technical work." In neither Future 2 nor 3 is knowledge properly connected to democratic governance or correctly distributed.

In both, US higher education stays as stratified as its economy. Premium universities will still lavish funds on their hand-picked students, delivering them to elite professional services where the median salary for an early-career financial analyst, say, is four to ten times the median college salary for that stage. The next tier of US universities, including public flagships, would be forced to spend the next thirty years trying to square the circle of doing more with less, just as they have for the last thirty years. The vast majority of higher ed institutions (in the United States, the 3,800 or so open access colleges) will become quasi-automated, offering a combination of ed-tech hybrids of "AI"-powered online courses managed by a shrinking army of adjuncts. College will be intellectually disappointing for most students, feeding public hostility to the sector. Learning will be limited, sustaining a post-truth society. Elites give up on democracy because it seems an exercise in angry ignorance (to which they of course have contributed money). The dream of a democratic, racially-egalitarian knowledge society is, in Futures 2 and 3, a distant memory.

This is very bad. I'm not saying it will happen. I am saying it *can* easily happen. And the best way to increase the chances of this post-knowledge, post-democratic technocracy is that we in universities do nothing to seize the policy discourse and control our working conditions. In other words, we can cruise into Futures 2 or 3 simply by carrying on the passive stance that we academics widely adopted in recent years.

However, we still have Future 4. It is defined by a combination of a fully democratic commons and high levels of mass knowledge. Is this fantasy? Well, I call it the Culture after the vast intergalactic system in the late Iain M. Banks's science fiction series ("Culture series," 2025) (Figure 12.7).

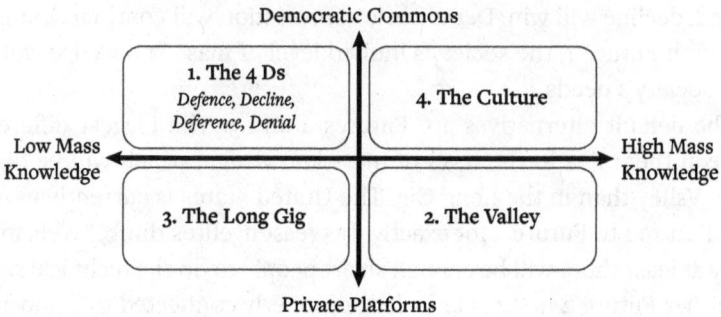

Figure 12.7. Future 4: The culture

Banks was a prodigious world-builder, and his series assumes the complete repudiation of the "two cultures" divide codified by British writer C.P. Snow in the late 1950s, which haunts us to this day (Snow, 1964). The Culture combines highly advanced technology with equally superior cultural knowledge. There are true AI entities with superhuman cognitive powers, there is travel faster than the speed of light, *and* there is equally advanced *cultural* knowledge. Advanced cultural knowledge is the *only* thing that allows the Culture's coexistence of millions of disparate civilizations. It is a universe of abundance, a quasi-automated luxury communism. Life in the Culture is oriented toward achieving personal and collective pleasures in post-scarcity economies. People feel the usual range of shame, hatred, conflict, and the urge to start large-scale wars. But, to repeat, this universe functions at an extremely high level because it has achieved massive increases in *cultural* intelligence, in which high technology is entirely embedded.

It's risky to tie the attainment of very high levels of mass knowledge in a collective-goods democracy to a science fiction series. But I do this to imply how great it will be rather than how unlikely it is. The conditions for democratically managed conjunctions of advanced tech and cultural knowledge are neither science fiction nor utopian. We can find this combination described in mid-twentieth-century documents like the US Truman Report (1947) that among other things called for the massive expansion of the community college system, while also calling for a new emphasis on the humanities and social sciences for the sake of democracy. We can find the Culture's combination in the US *Report of the Commission on the Humanities* (1964), which recommended the creation of a national humanities research infrastructure to spread literature, philosophy, history, and the rest into the daily lives of the whole population (The Commission on the Humanities, 1964). We can find this combination in nearly every document of the feminist, civil rights, Indigenous, and queer movements of recent decades, all of which try to reorient common life on the basis of greatly upgraded cultural knowledge.

This future has an actual history in our own world. The concepts here are basic: first, that cultural and social knowledges are put on equal footing with technical knowledges; second, that various racial, cultural, and linguistic standpoints are put on equal footing with each other; and third, that the *entire* population, *everyone* willing and able, receives this arts *and* sciences higher learning. The historical foundation was mainstream social democracy coupled with what we'd now call epistemic justice in the relations between technological and cultural disciplines (that part is still in the future).

The Culture can have this combination because it has repudiated the neoliberal doctrine of privatization—it has repudiated, that is, the false promise that services where *everyone* needs a high general standard of care—like health, housing, energy, education—can *ever* be furnished by private firms looking for returns on market investments. We tried this model in everything for forty years. The results are in: it has failed to produce equitable outcomes (which was never its actual goal).

Collective institutions in Future 4 are funded with our shared national finances, which turns out to be both cheaper and more efficient than private goods production at the scale of society. Future 4 adds a higher education baseline of sixteen years of school and offers tertiary education to all for *free* as parts of the United States and Canada started doing for high school in the nineteenth century. Future 4 also eliminates today's grotesque inequality of per-student funding across US campuses, in which the best-prepared students at a place like Stanford receive ten to twenty times the resources of students at the local two-year college. So in the

Culture, access-oriented public colleges, starting with tribal colleges and Historically Black Colleges and Universities, see their per-student funding increased to the level of average private colleges (about $20,000 per student in 2020 dollars, or three to four times more than the current rate) (Newfield, 2021). Divisions by race and class and immigration status have by 2050 come closer to disappearing than at any time in North American history (even as the identities are retained and strengthened). The Culture hasn't yet achieved egalitarian justice, but it has over thirty years eliminated today's common assumption that racial equality will never happen, which supports widespread and ongoing work toward it. Future 4 has created the conditions for an economy led by public investment, producing for the full spectrum of human knowledge needs (Benanav, 2023).

Another positive mechanism is the mass understanding of budgets in a society that routinely combines arts and sciences education. Future 1 was hampered by the lack of common understanding of educational underfunding or its effects. The very numerate residents of Future 4 grasp that higher and universal educational standards aren't very expensive once properly shared. In the 2010s, a small group of faculty activists had calculated that California's public colleges and universities could be made tuition-*free, and* their per-student funding increased to higher 2000 levels, for a cost of $66 per year to the median state taxpayer (in 2018 dollars). In Future 4 this kind of thing becomes common knowledge. The society updates and expands this research and adopts tax-based "66 dollar fixes" across the country. Colleges still have different mixes of educational aims, subjects, and students, but their *funding* is equalized, so that poor students no longer disproportionately attend poor colleges.[2]

The much better funding allows non-elite education to become deeper and more diverse. By 2050, the "two cultures" divide is a distant historical memory, and qualitative and quantitative knowledges continuously interact. The result is that huge world problems—climate chaos, mass poverty, hardened borders, continuous warfare—are addressed by a much wider proportion of the public than is the case today, which can bring to bear more powerful combinations of knowledge—and collective agency.

Three other features of Future 4 are worth pointing out.

All its levels of education are much better at linking learning to practice. In universities, that means combinations of liberal and practical arts. Graduates have direct experience with implementing ideas collaboratively with other people. By 2050, this common participation in intellectual self-governance gives tens of millions of people concrete experience with building and governing large knowledge institutions, which in turn helps make hard ideas a reality.

Another feature: the interaction between formal and informal knowledge overcomes the "ivory tower" image of higher education and heals today's divide between college and non-college people. The Culture, by bringing nearly everyone into *some* kind of contact with higher ed, has figured out how to keep culture wars from taking over political life.

Finally, organizational life has been democratized. Future 4 recognizes this elemental fact that our backward Four D's world denies: *intelligence is* the equitable interaction of *all* of the *many* minds in a given system. Equality doesn't reduce intelligence by dragging the really smart people down to our level. In reality as grasped by Future 4, intelligence—mass knowledge—*is* a collective product of all of the people under egalitarian conditions of open exchange.

Let's take stock of where we are. I've described four stylized futures. The first three are backed by powerful minority interests. Each of them has been destabilized by those interests' own policy decisions and the models' internal contradictions. Each produces very uneven results—suboptimal results for the great majority. Each of them will continue to function for their minority interests, while devolving slowly and producing suboptimal results for everyone else, to the point of dystopia.

There's then Future 4, the Culture (Figure 12.8).

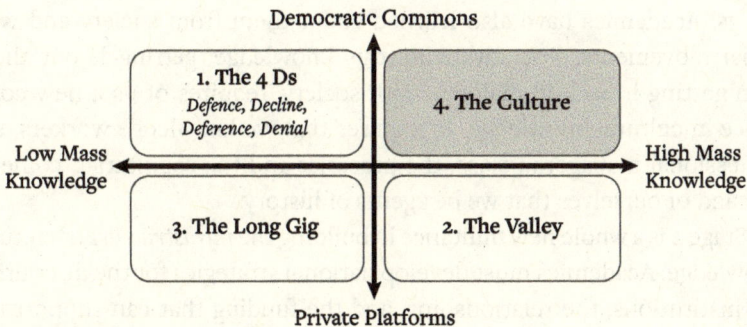

Figure 12.8. *The four futures*

I've claimed that it is not utopian and that its basic elements are lying around us waiting to be used. But that does leave us with the question I'll end with: How do we get a process started for moving from a stuck culture to this better one?

The Culture obviously won't get built in a day—or a decade. But it does have to be *built.* I suggest these first two stages of the construction plan.

Stage 1: we need to identify and then respond systematically to *society's existing demands* for cultural knowledge. Large segments of the people of North America and elsewhere want universities to help provide the knowledge that will realize the following ideals:

- a non-lethal West in the world that can take direction from and collaborate equitably with other nations;
- life not defined and limited by economic goals;
- the mutual recognition of diverse identities, causing a major reduction in the incessant arguments about whether this or that type of person has the right to exist;
- a working democracy, one liberated from its most regressive forces;
- shared control over all new technology;
- rigorous reading and interpretative methods for understanding complex materials that are riddled with spin, propaganda, deep fakery, text generated by sequence-completion algorithms, and every kind of bullshit in the philosophical sense; and
- the legitimation—the rightness and the glory—of the pursuit of happiness and fulfillment.

The arts, humanities, and social science disciplines are about all these things. Academics have also learned about them from society and with social movements. But advancing this knowledge, getting it out there, then getting it back in dialogue with society, requires of us a new confidence in cultural knowledge. It requires that we knowledge workers, the professional-managerial class, the precariat and the cognitariat, come to demand of ourselves that we be agents of history.

Stage 2 is a whole new militance in building the *infrastructure* of cultural knowledge. Academics must develop national strategies for the discourses, the institutions, the relationships, and the funding that can support the creation and dissemination of cultural knowledge.

Any national strategy should have at least the following elements: One is developing and disseminating detailed analyses of the damage to research as well as teaching that adjuncting has done. A second is a loud breaking of the silence about grotesque funding inequalities among different kinds of universities and different subjects (Newfield, 2025). These are inequalities that put sociocultural knowledges and their most diverse practitioners at the bottom. Another is setting funding targets for socio-cultural research over a ten-, twenty-, and thirty-year period. A fourth is to develop the large-scale circulation of cultural research knowledge. One model is the National Bureau of Economic Research—we need a National Bureau of Cultural Research. A fifth is setting targets for the reversal of adjuncting, year by year by year.

This combination of practices, with others, will lead to a system that will allow us to respond to the social demands for knowledge I've mentioned. It will remove the widespread precarity that unjustly subordinates workers in cultural fields.

The irony of the current predicament of cultural fields is that the world will *not* move forward unless it makes much better use of the knowledge these fields produce. There are *no* strictly technological solutions to climate change; economic stagnation; the debt crisis; mass poverty; the wars in Ukraine, Gaza, and Sudan; species extinction; police violence; continuing injustice toward Indigenous Peoples; migration; transphobia; the renewable energy transition; or any other challenge. We will not move ahead an inch without massive new doses of cultural intelligence.

The problems with the first three futures reflect the fact that our mode of development has reached its limit: capital-intensive, energy-intensive technology-driven change has reached its limit. The way forward now is through a "reversal in ordinary common sense" (Hall, 2017). The way forward now is through a revolution in culture. The cultural disciplines have to be autonomous, strong, funded, confident, and their workers securely employed so that they can contribute to building the future as we all now must.

We, we academics, engage the forces that create the world. If we also do our institutional work, the outcome will be Future 4, the Culture, in 2050. In the words of Renuka Dhanwar, an activist bringing higher education to communities near the Madhu Tea Estate in West Bengal, "as long as we fight, we will not lose."[3]

References

Benanav, A. (2023). A dissipating glut? *New Left Review*, 140/141. https://newleftreview.org/issues/ii140/articles/aaron-benanav-a-dissipating-glut

The Commission on the Humanities. (1964). *Report of the Commission on the Humanities*. American Council of Learned Societies. https://www.acls.org/wp-content/uploads/2021/11/Report-of-The-Commission-on-the-Humanities-1964.pdf

Culture series. (2025, July 5). In *Wikipedia*. https://en.wikipedia.org/wiki/Culture_series

Executive Council. (2022). Statement on research funding in the humanities. Modern Language Association. https://www.mla.org/Resources/Advocacy/Executive-Council-Actions/2022/Statement-on-Research-Funding-in-the-Humanities

Friedman, T.L. (1999). *The Lexus and the olive tree: Understanding globalization*. Farrar, Straus and Giroux.

Dooars Daily Official. (2024, June 20). *Indigenous community in Indian tea plantation fight for quality education* [Video]. YouTube. https://www.youtube.com/watch?v=moKJsuh-TT0&ab_channel=DooarsDailyOfficial.

Grove, Andy. (1996). *Only the paranoid survive*. Doubleday.

Hall, S. (2017, February 10). Stuart Hall: Gramsci and us. *Verso*. Excerpt from *The hard road to renewal: Thatcherism and the crisis of the left* (Verso, 1988). https://www.versobooks.com/en-gb/blogs/news/2448-stuart-hall-gramsci-and-us.

Kinder, T., & Hammond, G., (2023, April 11). Silicon Valley vcs tour Middle East in hunt for funding. *Financial Times*. https://www.ft.com/content/567ca518-b138-4273-bfe6-0712ef31e01d

Newfield, C. (2016). *The great mistake: How we wrecked public universities and how we can fix them*. Johns Hopkins University Press.

Newfield, C. (2020, June 28). When are access and inclusion also racist? *Remaking 11: Long Revolution*. https://utotherescue.blogspot.com/2020/06/when-are-access-and-inclusion-also.html

Newfield, C. (2021). Budget justice: Addressing the structural racism of higher education funding. *Academe Magazine*, 107(2), 57–64.. https://www.aaup.org/article/budget-justice

Newfield, C. (2025). Humanities decline in darkness: How humanities research funding works. *Public Humanities* 1, e31. https://doi.org/10.1017/pub.2024.39

Schumpeter, J.A. (2008). *Capitalism, socialism, and democracy* (3rd ed.). Harper Perennial Modern Classics.

Snow, C.P. (1964). *The two cultures and a second look: An expanded version of the two cultures and the scientific revolution*. Cambridge University Press.

Waters, R. (2023, April 14). Can Intel become the chip champion the US needs? *Financial Times*. https://www.ft.com/content/8fd0bb2b-429d-4699-a6d4-aac20e01641f

Notes

1   Grove wasn't wrong about his industry of microchip design and manufacturing. See, for example, Waters, 2023.

2   In the United States, this will involve targeted subsidies for less wealthy private colleges and universities.

3   Research video courtesy of Piya Chatterjee, Scripps College.

CHAPTER 13
IS HOPE PRACTICAL?
REMAKING UNIVERSITIES
IN AN ERA OF CLIMATE CRISIS

Tom Sperlinger

Introduction

USED TO TEACH A TWO-HOUR SEMINAR, DURING THE FIRST half of which I asked, "Why would someone speak in class?" and, in the second half, "Why would someone be silent?" The students were aged eighteen to over seventy and were studying on a foundation year, often returning to education after a long gap. We started by talking about urgent forms of speech, for example if someone spotted danger and shouted "Fire!" One of the wider debates that emerged was between those who felt pressure to speak, for example to end an awkward silence, and others who only ever spoke when it was clear nobody else needed the space. This point was critical to how students subsequently reflected on their own participation and that of others.

We live in a moment in which many people within universities have cause to shout "Fire!" Bryan Alexander (2023) cites the example of Pacific Union College (PUC), in Angwin, California, as a microcosm of the sector's future (p. 41). Fire is now a routine threat at a campus that is on the front line of California's deadly wildfires, which are becoming more frequent. There are firebreaks and conservation easements between the campus and the most likely fire paths, while staff also serve in the fire department. Students are pursuing degrees in first response or conservation technology. There are new forms of urgent speech emerging, within and outside the classroom.

The discussion about why someone would be silent in our seminar was always fascinating. We spoke about the difference between having something to say and being able to put it into words. Crucially, we spoke about positive forms of silence, such as making space for others or listening. The discussion always turned to another form of silence: the question of who was not in the room and therefore did not have an opportunity to speak. This idea had particular resonance in a context in which students said that the one thing they had in common was that they had not imagined a year earlier being at university.

Many voices are not heard within universities, with increasingly stark consequences in the Anthropocene. One of the choices we face is between futures of greater collective action or of unimaginable inequity. Alexander's survey assumes that global temperatures will rise by around two degrees Celsius by the year 2100. But in one chapter, "Best Case and Worst Case," he goes further. In the best-case scenario, temperature rise is controlled to one degree through collective action and innovations in science and human behaviour, in which higher education plays a pivotal role. In the worst-case scenario, higher temperatures "trigger a runaway sequence of events," habitable areas retreat closer to the poles, nuclear war erupts, and the work of academia all but ceases: "The undergraduate curriculum shifts to a disaster mode, teaching practical skills for survival: medicine, agriculture, basic industry" (pp. 177–78).

Facer (2020), like Alexander, sees collective action as one of the areas where universities could play a critical role in avoiding the potential worst-case scenarios ahead. Facer emphasizes "reinvigorating the civic role of institutions…to build ecologically and socially resilient communities" as one of four areas of activity. The other three priorities she sketches for higher education, which overlap with Alexander's analysis, are redesigning the day-to-day operations of universities, shifting toward interdisciplinary complexity in "knowledge structures" to address the challenges ahead, and supporting students to "live well with each other and the planet" (pp. 7–9).

In this chapter, I reflect on two experiments in rethinking the current model of higher education, with an eye to how the world may be different in 2050 or 2100. My first case study explores my experience working on a new campus development at the University of Bristol, a research-intensive institution in South West England. The campus was first initiated in 2016, and I have been academic lead for (civic) engagement for it since 2018. The second case study is Black Mountains College (BMC), a new institution in Wales. It was first conceived in 2016 by the writers Ben Rawlence and Owen Sheers, and it welcomed further education students in 2021 and undergraduates in 2023. I have worked as chief academic officer for BMC since January 2021, combining this role with my job at Bristol. The college positions itself as the first UK institution dedicated specifically to education at a time of climate emergency.

I am not seeking to replicate the larger, sector-wide surveys that Alexander, Facer, and others offer. Instead, I explore the difficulty of enacting significant structural change at a local level and suggest wider lessons. As Alexander and Facer show, if we are to face the urgency of the climate crisis, we will need to remake higher education (and much more than that). But the climate crisis is also a challenge because we understand what action is needed; yet achieving it is difficult because of entrenched economic and social systems, a huge variety of competing crises and demands, and the seductive quality of denial. This makes it timely to reflect on how change happens or fails.

Case Study 1: The University of Bristol's Temple Quarter Enterprise Campus

Context
The main building of Bristol's Temple Quarter Enterprise Campus (TQEC), currently named Cattle Market 1 or CM1, was originally due to open in 2021, and it is sketched tentatively on A-Z maps of the city. It is now due to open in 2026, due to delays especially related to COVID-19. CM1 was modelled partly on Cornell Tech in New York, which opened in 2012 and is a graduate campus that aims to "develop the leaders and technologies of tomorrow." TQEC is due to be the home of the university's new Business School (which launched in 2022), the "tech" end of the Faculty of Engineering, and a smaller Centre for Innovation and Entrepreneurship. The university footprint in the area is expanding in the meantime: the Dental

School relocated to a converted office building nearby in September 2023. Ultimately, CM1 will be home to nearly 5,000 students (some of whom will live in accommodations nearby) and 650 staff, plus co-located industry, civic, and community partners.

TQEC is part of a major expansion of the university since 2012, prompted by changes to funding and the regulatory climate in higher education in the United Kingdom, which has allowed a university like Bristol to increase the volume of UK and international students it recruits, having for a long period received a high volume of applications per place. One aim of the campus is to create space to increase teaching activity to help the university remain financially sustainable, especially involving high fee-paying international students. But if that were the only aim, the university might have built a new campus more quickly and cheaply in other parts of the city. The location opens up other opportunities and brings particular responsibilities at a time of HE expansion more generally. The expansion of both universities in the city—the University of the West of England (UWE) has also increased in size in the same period—has created ongoing tensions with local communities, including related to rising living and housing costs.

CM1 is directly adjacent to Bristol Temple Meads, the city's main railway station. But the station is not at the centre of the city. In fact, historically this site often marked a boundary; in a much longer history, it was monastic land, outside the city walls. It was the site of a burial pit for those who had died of cholera during epidemics in the 1800s. For nearly a hundred years it was a cattle market (hence "Cattle Market 1"), and there are stories of bulls escaping and marauding through nearby streets (and people avoiding the area on market days). Most recently, it was a post office sorting site, which received an estimated 75,000 items of mail each week from around the world in the 1950s.[1] The campus is adjacent to areas to the east and south of the city that experience high levels of economic deprivation and in which rates of progression to higher education are low: one in eleven eighteen-year-olds in Hartcliffe, in south Bristol, progress to university, versus nearly 100 percent in Clifton, where the university's existing campus is based.

The wider area around the campus is also a site for planned redevelopments over the next thirty years. The university has emerged as a key anchor tenant in an area that could reshape the city in radical ways. The whole development is emerging in half-spoken tension with a significant flood risk associated with the land. The Environment Agency indicates the site could see flood depths of 1.84 metres by 2080, while King (2022) notes that government maps "show the site is at a medium or high risk of flooding, which means there's anywhere between a one in 30 and one in 100 risk of flooding in any given year." Flood mitigations are in place but it remains to be seen how they will withstand a changing climate.

Successes

When I joined the TQEC program, it had a newly established "Engagement Board," alongside two similar committees exploring research and education. The scope of "engagement" was not fully defined. I applied for the role because I thought the location created a unique opportunity to rethink the role of the university in the city-region, including by creating relationships with local communities to whom the university is often invisible. I have tried to focus on what the university, and wider world, might be like in fifty years' time. Inevitably, it has been difficult to maintain that focus consistently amid the competing demands of the present moment, including during COVID-19. It is one success that this strand of activity has survived in what has been an extremely volatile large capital project. It has won support internally and externally, and it has influenced the University adopting "the global civic university" as one of three pillars of its refreshed strategy in 2021.

I articulated in 2018 that I wanted to focus on three areas (see Figure 13.1). The first two were to build meaningful connections with a very wide range of partners and communities and to create the infrastructure (on and off campus, hard and "soft") to sustain engagement across all university activities. In an early challenge, I was told by a senior colleague that engagement would not happen at the campus itself but in the community. The third is where it felt like we could try to do something new. Too often, when universities "engage," at the end of the process "we" are still the university and "you" are still the community or the partner. We wanted to change that and create opportunities for a different range of people to be part of the university community.

Some of the critical successes have been in the first two areas, while it is in the third that the promise of this work is, as yet, incomplete. We have built meaningful connections with a wide range of community partners, whose voices have influenced the project. For example, we engaged early on with Women of Lawrence Hill, a project initiated by Bristol Women's

Voice to explore local women's empowerment within the wider Temple Quarter area. Their recommendations supported an emphasis on employment opportunities for local people, linked to high-quality child care and flexible study opportunities.[2] We have also engaged regularly since 2018 with groups of stakeholders convened by Eastside Community Trust, who drafted a best- and worst-case scenario for the campus in 2018, which we have regularly revisited with them (Eastside Community Trust, n.d.; also, see Appendix). In 2019, we initiated the Temple Quarter Engagement Fund, financially supported by alumni and donors, which over the next three years funded forty collaborative projects involving partners working with staff or students, with projects drawn from all six academic faculties. This created a wide range of new relationships and a spirit of partnership working way beyond the core academic schools to be located at TQEC.

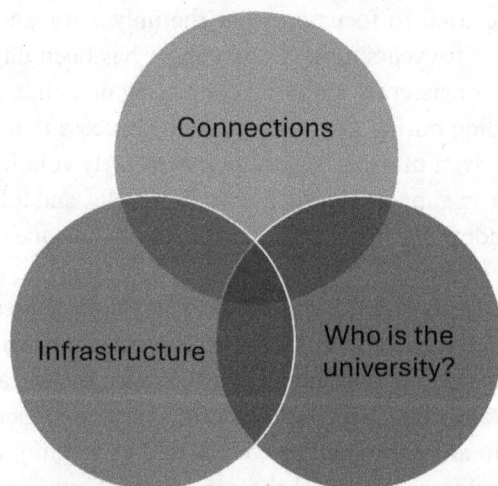

Figure 13.1. Three areas of focus for building a university community

In terms of infrastructure, we lobbied successfully for the creation of two key engagement spaces in prime locations on the ground floor of CM1. The first is the "Bristol Rooms," which will be adjacent to the main reception area. We argued that if industry and enterprise partners would be co-located on-site, it made sense to create a space for civic and community partners. We will work with community infrastructure organizations to curate this space, which will be home to a very wide range of partners from civic and community organizations, local government, and those doing corporate social responsibility work in larger organizations. This will be one large room divided into three "zones" (a circular seating area; a long table adjacent to a kitchen; and a flexible space), with an interactive map of Bristol on one wall, which can be changed to show various kinds of data and to display other cities or regions. We are planning this as an area where university staff and students can work with partners on shared challenges, including as the city-region seeks to adapt to the deeply unpredictable local effects of climate change. Nearby is the "Story Exchange," a round space that will seat approximately twenty-five people, and which we anticipate being used for conversations of various kinds in which different voices and forms of expertise can speak on equal terms.

Through imaginative work by the architects, and careful planning, these spaces have gradually fed into a wider civic plan for the ground floor of the building as a space open to the public. This includes a large entrance hall, named the Exchange Hall, which can also be a space for events. One of the teaching spaces adjacent to the Bristol Rooms, meanwhile, can be adapted as a crèche, with suitable toilet facilities located in an adjoining room and capacity to make the area private to meet statutory requirements.[3] This will be a new facility for the university and will make open days, research focus groups, various kinds of teaching, and other activities accessible to parents and carers in new ways.

When the campus opens, the Bristol Rooms will form the focal point of a network of spaces on and off campus. In 2018, the university was invited by a community organization, the Barton Hill Settlement (subsequently renamed the Wellspring Settlement), to join a new micro-settlement project, housed in old shipping containers on their site. The Settlement is a community organization that offers a range of services and activities itself, but which is also home to a wide range of other organizations: health services, a theatre company, an organization supporting carers in the South Asian community, and more. Barton Hill is about twenty minutes' walk from TQEC, is one of the most economically "deprived" areas of Bristol, and is home to many of the city's recent migrant communities, with over seventy languages spoken there. The Settlement has a long history with the university: it was founded as the "university settlement" in 1912, and university staff continued to be involved with it—some even living on-site—until the 1970s, when it became an independent community organization (see Meller, 2021).

In 2021, the "micro-campus" opened, with the university as tenants in the micro-settlement development alongside the charity Bristol Refugee Rights. The micro-settlement opened in the midst of COVID-19 and put the university at the heart of a community organization that was central to coordinating support during lockdowns in that period, and this led, among other things, to a research project looking at community aspirations during the pandemic (Brown et al., 2020). There is now a full program of activities there every week, including evening classes, a law clinic in which students offer free legal advice, and a "little library" that offers a day for drop-in and book-borrowing service for local parents and children. This last activity came from a direct request by local residents because of a gap in local library services in this area and is provided by the university library staff.

These spaces are all important in moving toward the third "circle" of activity I mentioned, the task of rethinking who is the university, who gets to be part of its community, and in which communities it participates. We have had some successes in this area. We have scoped a program of activity called Twilight Temple Quarter, a series of evening and out-of-hours activities that will bring together enterprise and community partners, local residents, and students to learn, innovate, and collaborate. We have worked with colleagues in human resources to rethink staff recruitment, leading to the creation of a two-person community engagement team; the launch of an outreach initiative called "Join us!" that seeks to prepare and support potential applicants to employment; the creation of a target of 1 percent of the university's employees being apprentices by 2025; and the sharing of a significant percentage of unspent apprenticeship levy with partners in the city-region, creating eighty-nine apprenticeships within around thirty-six small- and medium-sized enterprises. As well as creating a crèche in CM1, the university is now exploring options to convert a building nearby as a nursery, which will serve the needs of staff and students but also (critically) provide support to those wishing to become students or staff at the university, or returning to employment nearby, including via an apprenticeship.

One critical aim of the engagement strategy was always to rethink what educational provision the university offered to local people, acknowledging the deep educational inequalities in the city. Although the university was founded as a university college for local people in 1876, initially providing night classes, this aspect of its mission has waned. We had some successes in this regard, winning support to explore the creation of a more flexible degree and lobbying, as part of the refreshed university strategy in 2021, to double the number of students recruited from the city-region from 7.5 to 15 percent, an increase of around two hundred new students per year, with emphasis on those communities in which participation is lowest. But there have been challenges putting these aspirations into practice.

Challenges

One setback in this work so far has been with a proposed flexible undergraduate degree aimed at local people who would not otherwise enter higher education. We commissioned feasibility work in 2018, which reported considerable need and enthusiasm locally for a degree of this kind, and ran focus groups in 2020, via community partners, with groups of young people not planning to enter higher education. Drawing on the focus groups, we designed a structure for a new type of degree at Bristol that would be open access—no prior qualifications or particular knowledge requirements at the point of admission. Students would take two accredited modules as short courses, at low cost, prior to entry into the full degree, which could be completed over four years part-time, attending one day per week. Year three of the program would be a work placement or work-based learning project. At an institution with high entry requirements, this structure represented a substantial change.

There were concerns that such a program could only justify the scale of system and process change required to deliver it if it were established at scale. I worked with professional services colleagues across the university to scope the changes required and produced a business case for a version of the program with around two hundred students per year on it and multiple pathways, including all the TQEC anchor schools. The proposal, which was due to be based in the Business School, went through the university approval processes three times, but was not approved. I remain very excited by it: such a program could transform who gets to study at the university and who has a voice and a say in major growth industries in South West England (and farther afield), including in the digital, creative, entrepreneurial, and health sectors. It had already generated significant enthusiasm among employers and industry partners, who wanted to work with us to co-design the degree. For example, one CTO of a major global organization told me that "there are missing people in our industry" and that he thinks this absence of experience of "what it takes to make something valuable to someone else" has a direct impact on the lack of commercially successful companies in the United Kingdom.

Why was the proposal not approved, and what lessons come from it? Possible answers to this question would point to nuances of university politics, competing priorities (such as international student recruitment), as well as the tensions that arise within a major project, for example whether it is a "change" project or an expansion of existing activity. But a more interesting question is: Why was the proposal not approved when there was general enthusiasm and support for it? Or, to put it another way: What makes it hard for an institution to launch a program of this kind, even when there is a conscious commitment to it? What would make that easier?

Longer histories and sector-wide policies are relevant. As Sowula (2023) writes, reflecting on universities across the globe,

> There's very little incentive for established institutions to be disruptively innovative. Serious competition is only for students and research funding. The communities that might benefit most from major disruption tend to have the least influence on an institution's leadership. There's great fear of failure and great rewards for basically standing still; replicating or preserving the past, including past inequities.

A major question for any government is how to create incentives (financial and otherwise) for universities to innovate in different ways, beyond competition for students or research funding. This needs to include those "communities that might benefit most from major disruption," shaping both policy and the direction of individual universities. It also needs to include rewards for taking risks and doing things differently rather than (inadvertently) rewarding homogeneity or stasis. What would sector-wide incentives look like to create change in this area, analogous to the shift prompted by the emphasis on impact in research within UK universities since 2010 (see Smith et al., 2020)? They might include a "social mobility premium" in relation to the percentage of students institutions recruit from low-income areas (see Adia, 2024), a grant to Further Education and Higher Education institutions to work collaboratively on adult education as part of devolved powers for lifelong learning in each region (with some "horizontal" accountability, where institutions report to regional as well as local government), and a new target of 75 percent of adults aged eighteen to thirty participating in higher education but across a much broader range of provision (short courses, professional development, apprentice-ships, and degrees). Answering this question more fully falls beyond the scope of this chapter, although I am pursuing it in parallel work.

An Unfinished Story

TQEC is not yet the best- or worst-case scenario sketched by Eastside. There remain opportunities to utilize the new campus to catalyze inter-disciplinary learning and student real-world projects as well as to rethink the operations of the university. In the civic space, too, we are looking for new opportunities. We are exploring the creation of a second "micro-cam-pus" in Hartcliffe, in south Bristol, aligned to a "micro-degree" offer, co-designed with the community employers, and designed to be a route into work or further study.

There are ongoing questions about how the community in CM1 will function in practice. It will be a complex building, in which some dynam-ics and perspectives may dominate and in which the civic spaces we have created may still feel marginal. This is part of the irony of, and limitations inherent in, some strategies of inclusion: the risk of perpetuating an expe-rience of marginalization. In a best-case scenario, however, this could still be a very exciting place with a genuinely wide range of people, organiza-tions, communities, and voices speaking, and having opportunities to do so on equal terms.

If I were starting a new job on a similar project now and had the power to change anything, what would I do differently? I would make one struc-tural change. I would create a single academic School for Shared Futures, Innovation and Technology for the new campus.[4] Schools are imperfect vehicles, but they are the currency by which Bristol, at least, organizes itself at present. This school would combine similar academic elements to TQEC but would organize them in a single administrative function, which would have a single externally facing goal: to mobilize the widest possible range of stakeholders to work together on shared futures, emphasizing themes of equity, innovation, and technology, and putting the complex-ities of climate change at its centre. There would be three related inter-nal goals. The school would be asked to create the structures that would enable its university to recruit a broader range of students (local and inter-national), offer them a truly interdisciplinary education (and an analogous research environment), and emphasize real-world projects and contacts as part of studies at all levels. I do not yet know whether the alternative

I am imagining would get to a similar place as TQEC by 2026, albeit via a different route, or if it is a substantially different vision.

Case Study 2: Black Mountains College

Context

Black Mountains College is based in Talgarth in South Wales and in the wider Bannau Brycheiniog (formerly the Brecon Beacons National Park), with which it has a close partnership. The college's main campus, Troed yr Harn, is a 120-acre upland hill farm, which is being renovated and converted. The college is unusual in the United Kingdom, as a new institution in a rural setting. It was inspired by the similarly named Black Mountain College, an experimental college founded in the 1930s in North Carolina and known for the many artists who emerged from it and for the anti-fascist energies that catalyzed it, including from the refugees from Europe who found their intellectual home there. The new Black Mountains College (BMC) is inspired by the great crisis of the present: the climate and ecological emergency.

A number of principles underpin BMC's work. One is accessibility. The kind of futures that will emerge out of the climate crisis may hinge on who has a voice. The college is trying to create a community that is genuinely diverse and that influences the range of programs offered (further and higher education, plus short courses) and the admissions and recruitment policies for them, which are largely open access.

The second is place. The specific location and relationship to nature is vital; all of the college's programs emphasize learning outside as well as indoors, and with the whole body and all of the senses, as well as with the mind and emotions. This is also a proudly Welsh institution, working closely with the principles of the pioneering *Well-being of Future Generations Act* in Wales, which requires all public bodies to consider the well-being of future generations in their work (Future Generations, n.d.).

The third is urgency. The climate emergency is happening now, and some of its consequences are unavoidable. But, as Alexander (2023) shows (pp. 161–81), there remain major things that we do not know about the scale of what awaits us and about the possibilities within our human responses. This daunting moment requires an urgent adaptation and reimagining of how we live individually and collectively. All of the college's courses are practice-oriented for that reason. Climate is also not the only urgent crisis.

The degree program, in particular, is oriented around sustainable futures and systems change, considering the intersection of different challenges, including the different futures technology is opening up, challenges to the future of democracy in a digital age, mass migration, and a need to rethink our economic systems.

Successes

The existence of BMC, in challenging times, represents a significant success in itself. It has required complex funding and other support to initiate it. As of September 2023, the college has fifty-one students enrolled across three further education courses (National Vocation Qualifications in Nature Recovery, Coppicing and Greenwood Trades, and Regenerative Horticulture) and thirteen students in the inaugural cohort of the undergraduate program, a BA in Sustainable Futures: Arts, Ecology and Systems Change. The further education courses are validated by the local NPTC Group of Colleges, and they have a shared core program, Change in Practice, looking at the skills and practices that can help to build sustainable futures. The undergraduate degree is validated by Cardiff Metropolitan University. The short course program is wide ranging. For example, the college offers an annual climate careers fair aimed at young people, acknowledging that climate is now relevant to almost all careers; courses in composting toilets, botanical drawing and painting, dry stone walling, tool sharpening, and sustainable cooking; and courses for key audiences to help them make a difference, including a course for parish and town councillors and another for shareholders.

In some respects, the college already mirrors aspects of both the best- and worst-case scenarios that Alexander (2023) sketches. For example, it acknowledges a need for a fundamental reorientation in what skills we prioritize, in order to live differently, with an eye to the likelihood of food and water scarcity, unpredictable weather, disrupted supply chains, and a need to live closer to Earth and to one's community.

BMC has, thus far, been successful in creating interdisciplinary knowledge structures, with some limitations. The undergraduate degree is interdisciplinary in design, although it was not validated (as initially hoped) as a joint Arts/Sciences degree, as this was not available via Cardiff Metropolitan; it is thus an arts degree with a heavy flavour of relevant sciences. The program takes an interdisciplinary approach to systems change, drawing on frameworks from the arts, ecology, and sociotechnical systems but also casting the net more widely. There have been opportunities to rethink the day-to-day operations of a college, including in the use of a rural location and the decision to work across the usual boundaries of further/higher/adult education. This remains a work in progress, and there is a continual interplay between (for example) radicalism and the regulatory requirements imposed by accreditation (and the funding it brings with it).

I will focus especially on the undergraduate degree, with which I have been most involved, as an example of what has worked well, and what remains work in progress. The degree is open access—no prerequisites for admission—and is taught primarily over three days per week in "family friendly hours" (9:30 a.m. to 2:30 p.m.), to improve accessibility, and will also be available part-time in the future.

Each year of the program is structured around a question. Year 1 is "How can we learn in a changing world?" Year 2 is "How can we address some of the world's most urgent challenges?" Year 3 is structured around a question that each student designs themselves, and which they pursue through both a research project and a "change in practice" module, which may be a work placement, civic engagement project, or new venture creation project. So, for example, a student's question might be "How can we feed the next generation?" and could combine a research project with work placement in an organization supporting sustainable food production in Wales. Creative practice is knitted through the whole degree program at BMC, although it does not aim to train its graduates specifically to become artists or practitioners. Instead, creative practice is positioned as a way of learning to see and know. As Raymond Williams, who himself grew up in the Black Mountains, writes (1961/2001),

> Art is ratified, in the end, by the fact of creativity in all our living. Everything we see and do, the whole structure of our relationships and institutions, depends, finally, on an effort of learning, description and communication...Thus the distinction of art from ordinary living, and the dismissal of art as unpractical or secondary (a "leisure-time activity") are alternative formulations of the same error...The arts, like other ways of describing and communicating, are learned human skills, which must be known and practised in a community before their great power in conveying experience can be used and developed. (p. 54)

To adapt Williams's formulation for the present moment: creative practice can help students to imagine alternative futures—and all of the relationships, institutions, communication, and ways of living that they depend on—and, in Facer's terms (2020), learn to "live well with each other and with the planet."

It is worth emphasizing that, for a program principally concerned with futures, the degree starts early in the first year with a module called "How can we understand the past?" which allows students an opportunity to think about how the past is narrated—and by whom—and how we have arrived at the current moment of crisis. The focus is on pluriversal histories; in how our current predicament arises partly out of the particular stories we have told ourselves about how we arrived at this moment, and whose voice has been heard.

Implications

The original Black Mountain College in North Carolina opened in 1933 and closed in 1957. It has a long legacy and is still well known, including because of the influence of many of its faculty and students in the arts (see Fortini 2022). But it had a drastically reduced number of students by the 1950s and was in debt. Josef Albers, who led the school, left for Yale in 1949 to direct its first design school.

BMC is at an early stage. But the College has shown what can be achieved by starting from scratch and responding to the urgency of the times, and some limitations in doing so. It is hard to get started without accreditation, which brings limitations and an element of conformity (for example to the assessment strategy for the degree, which is less radical than originally envisioned). There are also questions of size and scale. The college ultimately aims to recruit forty students per year to the degree, and the further education and short courses continue to grow. But there is a ceiling on its scale, partly due to its location and also due to the constraints of funding. There is a perennial question about whether projects of this kind can or should be scaled up or replicated or are important because of their more human scale and their rootedness (in BMC's case) in a particular place. With the earlier BMC in mind, it is worth remembering that scale and longevity may not be the only test and that such interventions are sometimes important because they are human-sized and intervene in the challenges of their times; they shape and change the wider culture, which then needs new forms of intervention to change it again. The scale of BMC may in itself be instructive as we face a future in which we experience the planet-wide implications of climate change in increasingly local ways, and in which the communities of which we are part shape our responses. BMC offers one model in which it is possible, at a local level, to live differently and to learn with others, and from the Earth.

Conclusions

I finish with a few general reflections:

- The conventional university (for all its imperfections) remains, as Adrienne Rich (1979) argues, a "vital spot" and a "place where people can find each other and begin to hear each other" (p.127).

- It is also a source of certain kinds of power, as Rich acknowledges, and universities do not currently mobilize that power effectively, as Sowula (2023) and others argue, including to unlock the structural and other adaptations climate change now requires. Established universities have the resources to contribute on a much larger scale, yet they lack the incentives—and, sometimes, the imagination—to do so.

- We have relied too heavily on a single model of higher education in the United Kingdom (and in many other places too): the residential, full-time model developed hundreds of years ago for a small number of privileged young men who went on to careers for life (see Sperlinger et al., 2018, pp. 35–49). Meanwhile, we have scaled back the extramural tradition, which offered opportunities to people across their life course and kept universities much closer to the communities of which they are part. This choice may prove especially problematic as we move into an era shaped by an ageing population, an urgent need for retraining adults as technologies change rapidly (including in the energy industry) and new challenges emerge, and a need to organize ourselves collectively.

- There is a real space and need for alternative forms of higher education to provoke and challenge conventional universities and to offer alternatives in themselves. These alternatives are also vital because of the increasing risk in the UK context of homogeneity in what universities look like and in the perspectives they and their graduates speak from (see Sperlinger, 2020). Existing universities also need more support to differentiate themselves (or retain their distinctive qualities).

- Interventions such as BMC show just how much is possible by transforming the higher education sector, but they cannot achieve it alone, including because of the challenges of scale.

- There are also challenges in how to create such models that are genuinely inclusive and which retain their potency as interventions while also conforming to regulatory and funding regimes.

- Universities should not be places of harmony (including with the findings of Saguy et al., 2009, in mind). But there are challenges in putting this into practice, including in mission-led organizations like BMC, which also strive to be inclusive. One challenge I'm interested in with BMC is whether its curriculum can be inclusive of someone who disagrees radically with its mission and how to include those who do not yet know about the climate emergency…

- And in larger, more conventional, universities, the question of who speaks will continue to be fraught—and some of the power differentials among different stakeholders will sway what is possible and whose voice is heard.

Alexander (2023) closes his chapter on best- and worst-case future scenarios with "another choice." On one hand he suggests a future that "starts with the Industrial Revolution and shoots past *Star Trek*," and two more centuries of material progress and innovation: "Think of humans in 2300 living two hundred years of age." On the other hand, Alexander echoes McKibben (2019) and others who see rapid human progress as a cause, rather than the solution, of our major ailments and suggests in fact we need to live differently: "On the other hand, for the next centuries we could instead commit ourselves to repairing the earth and restoring the balance between our species and its planetary home." (Alexander, p. 180)

The gap between these visions is vast. The role of higher education is
staggeringly different. The choice between them is one we make by
how we conduct ourselves for the next two to three generations. That
choice may be unconscious and emergent or deliberate, open and strategically made. Academia can play a role in that species-wide decision.
(Alexander, p. 181)

The Temple Quarter Enterprise Campus assumes a "shoots past *Star
Trek*" framework, in which universities are part of a trajectory of ongoing progress. Black Mountains College, on the other hand, is committed
to repair and restoration. I cannot predict which of these projects will
have greater longevity or greater impact beyond itself. I don't know, in
Alexander's terms, which decision we will make. But we urgently need
models for *how* we might make "species-wide decisions," or trans-species
ones, and also local decisions that are society-wide, which may become
increasing critical in a time of climate crisis.

In order to face these futures, a capacity for collective decision-
making is critical, and higher education institutions can play a distinctive role. Even to decide between the contrasting visions that Alexander
outlines, for example, we need to be able to hold them both in mind and
grasp the realities of the work they each demand.[5] That requires expertise
of many different kinds speaking across disciplinary bounds and perspectives from across society being heard. One of the reasons I find the vision
of BMC so compelling and continue to see such potential in the Bristol
Rooms and the Story Exchange is that higher education has not fulfilled
its promise to be a meeting point for expertise and experience from across
society. Perhaps that future lies ahead of us.

Raymond Williams (1980) wrote at the conclusion of an essay on
nuclear disarmament that

to build peace, now more than ever, it is necessary to build more than
peace...Unless protest can be connected with and surpassed by significant practical construction, our strength will remain insufficient. It is
then in making hope practical, rather than despair convincing, that we
must resume and change and extend our campaigns.[6]

There are inherent challenges, now as when Williams wrote, in moving from critique to action; from a diagnosis of what is wrong in higher

education, to creating structures that can help us to glimpse alternative futures. To build a sustainable future, it is necessary to build more than that. As Read (2023) argues, the acts of protest that have been so necessary in mobilizing for "system change" instead of climate change need now to be connected with and surpassed by significant practical construction. One task is to create truly ecological universities, responsive to the complex human and earthly ecosystems around us. The challenge of making hope practical remains daunting. We need new ways of finding and of beginning to hear one another.

Appendix

These are the "best case" and "worst case" scenarios for TQEC that Eastside Community Trust (formerly Up Our Street) presented to the university in 2018:

> **Best-case scenario:** A central meeting place bringing diverse groups together to learn from each other. A leisure, commercial, service, and educational offer which reflects the needs of the local population. A sense of ownership from local young people to raise aspirations. An inclusive route which connects communities which are geographically close but currently feel disconnected.

> **Worst-case scenario:** A student enclave that excludes local people and responds only to the needs of affluent international students. A cold urban form lacking natural features which dominates the area and adversely impacts local identity. A gated/inaccessible space which is closed to the local community.

References

Adia, E. (2024, February 26). The next government should introduce a social mobility premium. *Wonkhe.* https://wonkhe.com/blogs/the-next-government-should-introduce-a-social-mobility-premium/

Alexander, B. (2023). *Universities on fire: Higher education in the climate crisis.* Johns Hopkins University Press.

Bristol Women's Voice. (n.d.). Women of Lawrence Hill. https://www.bristolwomensvoice.org.uk/project/women-of-lawrence-hill

Brown, G., Jones, N., & Kibuye, J. (2020). *A Wellspring Settlement report: The changing needs and aspirations of the Lawrence Hill community in the* COVID-*19 crisis—March–July 2020*. University of Bristol. https://www.bristol.ac.uk/media-library/sites/law/research/Final%20WS_%20UoB%20Report%20for%20publication%20(1).pdf

Eastside Community Trust. (n.d.). Home. https://eastsidecommunitytrust.org.uk/

Facer, K. (2020). *Beyond business as usual: Higher education in the era of climate change* [HEPI *Debate Paper 24*]. Higher Education Policy Institute.

Fortini, A. (2022, July 7). Why are we still talking about Black Mountain College? *New York Times*. https://www.nytimes.com/2022/07/07/t-magazine/black-mountain-college.html

Future Generations. (n.d.). *Well-being of Future Generations Act 2015*. Future Generations—Commisioner for Wales. https://www.futuregenerations.wales/about-us/future-generations-act/

King, A. (2022, August 5). The issues bubbling beneath the Temple Quarter development. *The Bristol Cable*. https://thebristolcable.org/2022/08/the-issues-bubbling-beneath-bristol-temple-quarter-redevelopment

McKibben, B. (2019). *Falter: Has the human game begun to play itself out?* Wildfire.

Meller, H. (2021). *Hilda Cashmore: Pioneering community worker and founder of Bristol's Barton Hill Settlement*. Bristol Radical History Group.

Read, R. (2023, November 8). Extinction Rebellion's future is far less radical than its past. *The Guardian*. https://www.theguardian.com/commentisfree/2023/nov/08/extinction-rebellion-future-less-radical-unite-positive-action

Rich, A. (1979). *On lies, secrets and silences: Selected prose 1966–1978*. W.W. Norton.

Saguy, T., Tausch, N., Dovidio, J.F., & Pratto, F. (2009). The irony of harmony: Intergroup contact can produce false expectations for equality. *Psychological Science, 20*(1), 114–21. https://doi.org/10.1111/j.1467-9280.2008.02261.x

Smith, K., Bandola-Gill, J., Meer, N., Stewart, E., & Watermeyer, R. (2020). *The impact agenda: Controversies, consequences and challenges*. Bristol University Press.

Sowula, T. (2023, November 28). Eight years and eight thoughts…LinkedIn. https://www.linkedin.com/pulse/eight-years-thoughts-tim-sowula-z2nxf?trk=public_post_feed-article-content

Sperlinger, T. (2020, November 6). Tear down the fences. *London Review of Books*. https://www.lrb.co.uk/blog/2020/november/tear-down-the-fences

Sperlinger, T., McLellan, J., & Pettigrew, R. (2018). *Who are universities for? Re-making higher education*. Bristol University Press.

University of Bristol. (2018, December 12). *The history of the Temple Quarter Enterprise Campus* [Video]. YouTube. https://www.youtube.com/watch?v=pFk5pxrUmZc

Williams, R. (1980). The politics of nuclear disarmament. *New Left Review, I/124*. https://newleftreview.org/issues/i124/articles/raymond-williams-the-politics-of-nuclear-disarmament

Williams, R. (2001). *The long revolution*. Broadview Press. (Original work published 1961)

Notes

1   For further details of the history of the site, see a film summarizing staff and student projects: University of Bristol (2018).

2   For more details of the Women of Lawrence Hill project, see: Bristol Women's Voice (n.d.).

3   This involved creating a space that can be enclosed and private, has accessible outdoor space nearby, and has some smaller toilets adjacent to it. On three separate occasions, I was in a meeting, in which this idea came up, and a male colleague (who was not affected by the idea and whose role did not require him to comment on it) spoke with considerable anxiety: "Will there be children here? In the building?"

4   The closest example to what I have in mind is the Edinburgh Futures Institute, although it does not foreground equity or engagement in the same way: https://efi.ed.ac.uk/ [last accessed 31 July 2025].

5   *Star Trek* may offer a more compelling model than Alexander acknowledges. For example, in an episode of *Star Trek: The Next Generation*, "The Inner Light" (Season 5, episode 25, 1992), the crew of the Starship Enterprise encounters an alien probe, which causes Captain Jean-Luc Picard to pass out and—within a matter of minutes on the Enterprise—experience forty years in the lifetime of Kamin, an ordinary man with scientific leanings, on a planet threatened by the nova of its sun. The episode encapsulates both of the futures Alexander posits for humankind, and in the shadow of which we are living: a technological future of ongoing progress (represented by the Enterprise) and a humanoid people facing the dawning reality of catastrophic environmental change in their own lifetimes. The story has extra poignancy because Picard experiences family life and fulfillment as Kamin, which he has not tasted himself, producing a different kind of investment in future survival or oblivion. We must learn to live, like Picard, with intimate knowledge of a potentially long future and, simultaneously, with the possibility of environmental catastrophe unfolding sooner than we think. Universities can be a space in which to navigate that fraught reality.

6   This passage may be the source of a quotation commonly attributed to Williams: "To be truly radical is to make hope possible, rather than despair convincing" (in which case the oft-quoted line is a corruption). If Williams used both formulations, I have not been able to identify the source for the more popular version.

CHAPTER 14
TE WHARE WĀNANGA O AWANUIĀRANGI
WHAT ARE UNIVERSITIES FOR[1]

Linda Tuhiwai Smith

I WANT TO REFLECT ON WHAT WE HAVE LEARNED BY DEVELOPING alternative institutions to the university. At the same time, I want to write about what we have done to try and reform and change universities. My entire academic career and my everyday life when I was in universities was engaged in trying to change them. I look back on that and I am quite proud about some things, but I've also come over time to realize what a complex machine and what a complex idea the university is.

When my colleagues say, "Yes, we've got to decolonize the university!" I say, "Off you go. Get on with it; I'm going to put my feet up." What I have learned since I first started, is a university is not a singular thing. It's not a unitary idea; it's a grand idea. But when you're in it, there are multiple ideas, some of which are really contradictory. It is a place of great hope and possibility where you meet, if you're lucky, wonderful teachers who inspire you.

But it can also be a place that is the exact opposite: a place full of denigration and hopelessness and exclusion. It is a place that has lots of "mean-spirited" people in it. It is a place that encourages a particular way of learning that can damage one's spirit, let alone one's hope that we can do the things that we might have set out to do. So universities are not easy places to change.

I want to start though by referring a little bit more to where I have come from.[2] First, there is my great-great-grandmother. The timescale is important when we are looking at the New Zealand context. My great-great-grandmother was a Chief; a chiefly woman who married a Chief because that is what they did back then.

She had the task of supporting our tribe after the confiscation of our land. She had to rebuild a community that had lost 90 percent of its land through confiscation because we were seen as being in rebellion against the (British) Crown. She was an amazing woman whose story you won't read about in New Zealand history. She had to rebuild families. She went to court all the time to try and get land back.

The next woman is my great-grandmother, who was the daughter of someone who was seen as a rebel, a follower of two rebels who were imprisoned for supporting a pacifist group who lived deep in the forest, but that was still seen as a threat to the Crown. She raised my father until he was about eight years old. Another important person is my grandmother. There is a picture of her standing beside her son, my father. My father was an anthropologist who did his PhD in the [United] States. Subsequently he was at McMaster University and then at UBC before returning to New Zealand. That is my dad's side of my family. There are no pictures of men because most of them died. I never knew my grandfathers on that side of the family.

On my mother's side of the family is another great-grandmother and a great-grandfather. On the mantelpiece in our family homestead, there are photos of our grandparents and my aunts, and now of my mother who has died. In the sitting room, every time we go home, we love looking at these photos. These are our ancestors, and they give us the sense of who we are.

My father, as I said, was a professor. If my mother had had the opportunity to go to university as a young woman she would have excelled; she was an amazing woman. She directed our lives and believed in the value of education. In a way, the story of colonization in New Zealand is a different educational story to the story I hear in Canada. Some of that is about what the British learned over hundreds of years of being in other countries.

Our treaty with the Crown was signed in 1840. A Native school system started in 1867; it was a day-school system where our communities owned half the school. The Māori had to provide the land and part of the salary and firewood for the head teacher. Our people embraced literacy really quickly; there was a time when Māori people were more literate than the non-Māori who happened to be mostly sailors, whalers, and traders in the early part of the nineteenth century. The Māori embraced schooling because they saw in it some kind of promise.

They also embraced Christianity: the kind of Christianity we got was under the Missionary Society, that is, Evangelical Protestant missionaries from England. But we also got French Catholics. The competition between France and England motivated letters written to England to hurry and organize a treaty before the French asserted their sovereignty over New Zealand. And there were other nations there as well. Participation in education played a big role in our experiences and shaped our fundamental belief that even though we understood and experienced education as damaging, there was this idea that education was also promising.

My family on my mom's side are farmers, so the confiscation of lands was on my father's side. My parents come from different tribes. My father had no land; it was taken by the Crown. But on my mother's side our land was the land of my ancestors. We are on a site of many hundreds of years of direct descent to us. It is green, hilly, mountainous, isolated, and rural.

Another important image I hold close to me is part of an ancestral house, but to us it contains representations of our knowledge. One of the interesting things that missionaries were fascinated with was that Māori had theories of knowledge and many stories about knowledge: philosophies, for example, about the connection between knowledge and our humanity. To be humans, our early godly ancestors, if you like, had to search for and find knowledge and bring it back for humans to be able to live. That connection between knowledge and our humanity is really embedded in our cosmologies and our customs.

Those stories are in most of our carved meeting houses. This particular ancestral meeting house is special because it has a story. It was borrowed by the Crown and taken to England as part of one of the world exhibitions. The Crown then forgot to give it back; for over a hundred years it journeyed and went to other exhibitions. During these times the carvings were put on the outside of the house; they turned it inside-out so the people could see the carvings.

This meeting house went to the Sydney Exhibition and then it was given to the Otago Museum, which is down at the other end of the country. The

246 • Tuhiwai Smith

return of this house was seen as absolutely essential to the treaty settlement that our tribe had negotiated. There were lots of arguments from the museum and from all the people who had loved this meeting house that it should not come back to us. They argued first that we didn't know how to look after it and that we had no conservators and nowhere to put it. And when they asked our negotiators (and my dad was the chair of the negotiators) "What are you going to do with it?" they said, "We're going to use it for what it was built for: it is a house."

And they said, "But the carvings are old." We said, "In our houses all our carvings are old; we are all conservators; we are all guardians." It took twenty-five years of negotiations, but when they finally came home, the carvings had had their feet cut off because they couldn't fit in the museum. The feet came home in separate boxes, and a team of carvers then did what they had to do to restore it and recreated it as a modern meeting house, which now stands alive, a living entity.

Our relationship with the house, the carvings, the weavings, the paintings, the people who did that, who conceptualized it, the people who planned our understanding of our universe, all of that is encompassed in this house, as a house of knowledge, a house of learning. So when we think about the university as a house of knowledge and a house of learning, our expectation is that it would know quite a lot about us and that should be a good thing. But obviously our experience was that they knew nothing about us, and what they did know we thought were lies and misrepresentations.

The experience of education ended up being disappointing. Māori, for example, who graduated from university at the end of the nineteenth century were lawyers and doctors who were sent to the United States. But that was not the intention of government policy. The intention of education policy at that time was that schools should teach Māori boys to be good farmers and Māori girls to be good farmers' wives.

It came to the attention of the Department of Education that there were some Māori men and a couple of women, through the church boarding schools, who had been prepared for university. An inquiry in 1906 occurred and punished those schools for allowing this to happen. The Department of Education instructed them to stick to the vocational curriculum for Māori students.

You can see for Māori peoples the importance of policies. Contrast the juxtaposition of our own knowledge system and values about knowledge against what we were experiencing in schools through education, and also politically through the confiscations and loss of our land, and the disruption of and antagonism to our language and culture, and the social disruption to our families. All of this had to come to a head, and it did in the 1970s. By then I was at university and was part of a generation of political activists, and that experience has shaped my career.

What happened to Indigenous knowledge through colonization? Basically it was smashed. Actually, even that is too obvious in the sense of what it once was: the original shape of it was an egg. But it was smashed so badly that you could not even recognize it was an egg. It became fragmented, just like our meeting house. It was confiscated, put in museums and hidden. Much of it was lost through people abandoning it. The critical thing is actually not the shell of the egg. What holds the shell together is a soft membrane; that is important because it holds the parts together; it is the membrane that makes everything fit and make sense.

And then all of this—our knowledge, our language, our way of being— got boxed up and given back to us in a curriculum of representations like dancing and art—the soft parts people think about as culture. In other words those aspects of our knowledge and culture that were seen as palatable: the performance parts. This approach avoided the deep philosophical logic that made all of our culture make sense.

The challenge for us Māori when we are thinking about education in the context of thirty years of language revitalization is to ask how do we restore our knowledge? How do we put the egg back together again? The first point was to ask universities whether they could help, but actually they couldn't because they had caused a lot of the fragmentation. The linguists took the language; the biologists and botanists took the animal and plant sciences; the geographers took the land; the historians ruled a line and said, "Everything before we arrived is not history": history starts with the arrival of the British.

Academic disciplines that have studied Māori have created their own language for studying other people. They've created theories and methods for how you begin to do this. They have coded it to such a point that you can sit in a class about Māori and not recognize who or what they are talking about. So, if traditional academic disciplines can't help us, what do we do to restore our knowledge? We have to do it ourselves. I mean that is what we must do. This is my work. And I have been doing it for thirty years.

We began in prefabricated buildings that were borrowed and left over from other old redundant schools and were brought onto the site. This institution was actually started by my tribe. It was a vision of the tribe, and it was a vision, obviously, that my father carried and articulated because he was a scholar. And in our tribal governance minutes is a law passed by the tribe to establish a whare wānanga (meaning the provision of an Indigenous tertiary education).

The term *whare wānanga* is ancient. It means house of learning, a house of higher knowledge. We already had those ideas about knowledge, but it's a modern whare wānanga, obviously. It has modern buildings, students, staff, and we teach a range of degrees, diplomas, certificates, all the way through to doctorates. We had three doctoral programs, two international ones in Hawaii and one in Washington State with Indigenous students in them.

Once again, there was this commitment, if you like, of us, of our tribe, of our people to the idea of higher education, and to the idea that it is important to pursue qualifications. Each of those things were actually debated. The Elders debated. Did we want an institution that required and granted qualifications? Obviously, that was not what we had in the past. But the reality for our people is they need to feed themselves. To feed themselves they need employment, and qualifications were the means for them, in their view, to legitimate what they were learning, but also to give them something that they can take into the job market. It was a qualification they could carry outside the tribe.

So now we have degrees in teaching, nursing, humanities, and environmental studies. Our reach extends to isolated rural communities; most of our teaching is actually outside of the main campus in the communities. The teaching that happens here is what we call wānanga-style, so not classes on a weekly schedule but an intense one-week semi-residential program. Students come from all over the country and they sit in wānanga; there is a process and a pedagogy of being in wānanga together. They eat together, talk together, they sleep together and meet in-house for a week, and then they go back home. And they have work that they have to do, and then they come back in.

Most of our students are mature students. Many of them have qualifications from other institutions, but they are seeking Māori experience and knowledge. They feel it as an absence in their lives. Many of them are also second chance learners whose experience of education was terrible and who felt like failures. They have come to the wānanga expecting that they will be looked after. I talked earlier [in the symposium] about manaakitanga, the value of the institution has to be one of generosity and reciprocity and hospitality to our students.

To return to the metaphor of the egg, the broken egg, I want to give an example of what I mean about disciplines and genres and trying to put it all back together again. In the British Museum is the only surviving example of a traditionally made sail that was made in New Zealand. They have analyzed the genetics on the plant material used to weave the sail, so its origin is known. Many people have gone to the British Museum to see it, and of course we all want our artifacts back and of course they don't want to give them back, even if it is the only example in the world of something our people produced. It is under lock and key, and when you do go to visit that sail they really watch you like a hawk.

A group of my colleagues travelled to the British Museum. In the group was a weaver, who weaves in the traditional style as well as being a contemporary weaver. Another colleague was a navigator of ocean-going waka (canoes). The third person was a Māori astronomer who is actually very famous in New Zealand at the moment. The weaver looked at the sail and saw the weave and some holes, and she was so excited. "I don't know how they did this. We don't do that anymore. I haven't seen this before." She was absolutely fascinated by the weave and the fabric and the complexity of it.

The navigator looked at the sail and at the holes in it and said, "Oh, that's obviously for the wind, and there's a flex in the sail when you look at the shape; it's worn." The astronomer and the navigator were looking at it and realized it couldn't have been an ocean-going sail. It must have been for close to shore, or maybe for rivers, not oceans, for in-shore, not off-shore travel.

So three different skill sets looked at that piece of knowledge, and the three of them needed to work together to build a story about the sail. A lot of our knowledge is like that. We need lots of different people with different expertise to construct and reconstruct meaning because many of these artifacts have been separated from us and the context of other surrounding elements that made them make sense.

But we are also intrigued, for example, about who made it and where it was made. If you think knowledge revitalization is just about thinking about the past, you are mistaken. Now you can do genetic research that sources where that material was grown. So we need to find someone who can search for such a place.

There is another point I want to make about revitalizing Indigenous knowledge: it isn't just about the past. It is very much about using all knowledge to help us do the job we want to do. This means being intrigued and curious about new technology, being interested in science because we want something from it. We want it to tell us something we can't figure out for ourselves. So we see the usefulness of these things to answer our own questions.

We are interested in re-looking, if you like, at what universities offer, but having universities meet our needs for building our knowledge. I know people think about Indigenous knowledge as "traditional"; but we don't use that term because *traditional* implies a number of things such as dead, old, useless, and done by people who were primitive, and this old knowledge has no future.

Whereas, we look at such knowledge and we see a future. We see relationships; we see wonder. It's like, "We made that?!" Every day, when we look at what our ancestors produced, we see something wondrous. And that is what knowledge should do. That is what universities should do: make you feel wondrous about what you are learning and about the possibilities of where it can take you.

At our new institution, the Wānanga, one of the big tensions we had was about graduation. The universities also have what they call Māori graduations, which are ceremonies outside of our meeting houses where our students are able to wear the university regalia and their Māori regalia, which are the cloaks. When we were designing the Wānanga, we had to think carefully and critically about every element: every course, every design of a classroom, the role of teachers, every detail. Do we want to do it how universities do it, or do we want to redesign something that suits us that is modern? Or do we want to use something from the past?

The graduation issue is an interesting one and it is gloriously colourful. What our students wanted was academic regalia, and what our communities wanted was their Māori regalia, so our ceremonies have both. The university and the Wānanga have to hire the traditional regalia. And then on top of the academic gowns, graduands put on all their traditional jewellery, cloaks, headgear, the whole nine yards.

Another thing we had to discuss was, "Do you want a ceremony where somebody reads your name and you walk across the stage?" Yes, they wanted that too. It is an interesting process when thinking about decolonizing institutions. Often you target the medieval component of a university and say,

"Yes, we're going to get rid of that." But we also like to dress up: we like ritual, we like ceremony, and we like borrowing other people's good ideas.

But in our community, we also like to mark important occasions with prayer and with welcoming ceremonies. We have a parade down the main street of our town, and all the local schools come out and perform on every street corner. (There are only about four street corners, the town is so small.) The villagers come out to celebrate with huge welcomes.

One thing the students didn't like about university graduation is you could only invite two people. So for ours, honestly, the entire community turns up. The whānau, the children, the grandchildren, the in-laws, the friends; so, it's a noisy affair. My father is quite old and used to be chair of the council. They used to say, "You know, no more singing," because after every person has their name called their whānau stand up and perform and sing and do the haka. And that means the ceremony used to go from morning into the late afternoon or early evening.

As a council now we really need to finish by three o'clock. We started at 8:00 a.m., and the staff have to be there at 6:30 to get ready. We've got all these elements. It is an interesting negotiation, trying to develop a different institution, but one that reflects our community. They want to see it have some elements of a university, but still feel, be, and practise the values of Māori.

It is a fine balance: We had a conversation recently about being celebratory. One of our Elders said, "We are āwangana: we are humble, we are a humble people." That was his subtle message to us. Our younger generation want to express this joy through dressing up, celebrating, and being noisy, but then we get this pullback. We are humble and education is serious, but our ceremonies are important and integrated into graduation to reinforce our knowledge about knowledge.

One of those ceremonies is actually a prayer, an incantation that confirms the knowledge one has learned. So tohunga, a traditional practitioner or priest, at the end of the ceremony does this very ancient karakia that used to be heard in the traditional whare wānanga. And the purpose of this karakia, or prayer, is to fix the knowledge you have learned in your mind, but also to set you free, free from the spiritual significance of your study. So it means, "Phew!": Go and celebrate. You can be in the world and be proud of what you have achieved.

That is just one small example. Every detail has had to be thought through and negotiated with our communities, our tribe, our Elders, and our students. Our new-generation students have new ideas about what they want to do and how they want to learn. They are into technology, and they want to travel the world. We have no scholarships to give them; we would love to do those sorts of programs, but we are still constrained.

We are not allowed to call ourselves a university because in New Zealand the Education Act specifically protects the term *university* for the seven settler colonial institutions. They translate the term *university* into the Māori language. Guess what term they use? Te whare wānanga. We are not allowed to translate our term into the English language using the word university. So, we make gains and then we lose them. We make three steps forward, and then we go two steps back.

We have to make a decision: Do we put our energy into fighting that, or do we need to put up these other courses? Do we need to make sure our students are able to finish their programs? Where, if you are a small institution, do you put your energy to fight? We are absolutely in a political environment where everything is weighted against us. What we have in buckets full is complete self-belief in our knowledge, complete belief in the rightness of revitalizing it, and complete belief in our capacity to do so.

Decolonizing the university is an intergenerational exercise; I don't think we can do it in ten years. Even if we built a brand new university, simply by calling it a university we've already framed it in its history and its expectations. But a university is also more than just an institution. Universities don't necessarily control accreditation in the professions such as engineering, law, and medicine. Those are controlled by powerful professional organizations and disciplinary bodies. Most disciplines taught in universities are international disciplines where scholars themselves determine what is taught. We have learned it is really hard to change a single department in a university. It is really hard to change a 100-level compulsory course.

We have learned those are the ones you have to go after: the gatekeeping courses. They often occur at the 100 and 200 level. The 100 level is the "Come, come, all. We love you," and then we get you and say, "No, we don't love you. You've got to comply and learn the rules." The 200-level courses are, "Get out, we only want a few of you because we're going to invest in you." And the 300-level courses are, "Okay, you're the chosen ones. You can write an essay with the word 'I', or the term 'I think.'"

That is my cynical approach to the undergraduate curriculum and a bachelor's degree in New Zealand. So, it is piece-by-piece work. We've worked at it constitutionally through the Treaty of Waitangi. Every university in New Zealand has to honour the Treaty of Waitangi. It's like everyone used to have the picture of Queen Elizabeth hanging in council rooms while they also had the Treaty of Waitangi hanging too. But doing those things is often simply symbolic and they're not implemented into practices.

Every university vice-chancellor or president has it in their employment contract that they will honour the Treaty of Waitangi. Every university teaches the Māori language. Every job in a university has a preamble which says, "Our institution honours the Treaty of Waitangi." Now, don't get me wrong, those little things took decades to get into the system, but on their own they don't change practice.

For example, to me the best writers in New Zealand in the English language are Māori, and it took decades to recognize Māori literature in the English language. I remember a conversation with the Head of English who said, "Look, I want to talk to you. We need a Māori person in the English Department." I said, "Yes, that's a great idea!" He said, "I've got a position coming up, but they need to have a PhD." I said, "Yes, we've got a lot of them." He said, "In English." I replied, "Okay, the number was just cut down, but I know a few." And then he gave me the kicker: "But we really need someone who can teach seventeenth-century English literature." And I said to him, "If you want a Māori literary specialist, don't you think they should be teaching Māori literature?" And he said, "Well, I don't think we are ready for that."

So there are so many levels of change: curriculum, pedagogy, governance, the scholarly community. And while we might talk about universities, countries have science systems. The science systems are better funded in terms of research and how tightly that is controlled and how it controls publishing. That all has to be transformed.

One of the things I've done is start four journals just so that our scholars could publish somewhere. The first was a feminist one; we were complete amateurs. I had to get my brother-in-law to do the design of the cover. I didn't know how to cost it; we were stapling the pages together. It was an awesome publication, but it was completely unsustainable. And now there's a PhD student writing her dissertation about those journals because the articles in them were what we needed at the time: writings by Māori women.

We restarted another journal, and I had learned a few more skills about how to produce a journal—we had an editorial board. It was really posh;

they were all academic writers, and we even had a patron. And then I had to go to our board and argue for some money. They said, "Well, do you have a business case?" I said, "Well, I've got a vision." They said, "No, can you put up a business case?" And I said, "What am I supposed to do?" And they said, "Value, you know, you've got to have a value proposition."

I thought, "Well to me, the value of revitalizing our knowledge is something you cannot put a dollar figure on." And the board kindly looked at me and said, "Linda, it's a good idea to do a business case so we can assign some dollars. About how many dollars do you think you need?" And I just plucked a number out of the air: "Oh, about $100,000?" They nearly fell off their chairs. "Well, tell us how that $100,000 will be used." And I really had to think about it. "Okay, we need reviewers, we need a system for review, and we need people who can coordinate the reviews so we get them on time. So that means we need a pretty hot commercial editor. Then we need an editorial board to do some work. Then we need some principles about what we're going to publish and what we're not going to publish. Then we need to decide if we're going to put it in the Māori language, English language, and other Indigenous languages."

So, my $100,000 grew really quickly. And the good thing is we got the money to start a journal called *AlterNative*, which is still going.[3] But then we thought we needed a journal for our doctoral students to help them to start publishing. So we created the MAI *Journal*, an open access journal that publishes multidisciplinary peer-reviewed articles around Indigenous Knowledge and development in the context of Aotearoa, New Zealand. It has developed into an early career journal which is online.

We can do all we like in our curriculum, but if our scholars and our researchers cannot get their work published that means they are often not seen as credible. They can't win research grants because they have no track record, and the track record in New Zealand consists of money granted, publications, and the ability to show you can manage a contract.

So the systems that bind the university and that run through it like veins, are really complex systems. To me the decolonizing agenda is an intergenerational program. If you look at it like that, there is room for everyone to contribute, but you've got to bite off the chunks that you can. I thought I'd solved it when I wrote *Decolonizing Methodologies* (1999), but no. Because the other thing, at every turn of the corner, is the possibility it will all fall over in a minute. Universities are really good at re-forming themselves. The power dynamics within a university and the hierarchy within a university are just somethings to wonder at.

References

Smith, L.T. (1999). *Decolonizing methodologies: Research and Indigenous peoples.* Zed Books.

Notes

1   This chapter is based on my presentation at the symposium that took place on May 6, 2023. It has been edited for readability and accuracy.
2   In my address to the symposium I was able to refer to a several photographs of my ancestors.
3   *AlterNative: An International Journal of Indigenous Peoples* is an international peer-reviewed interdisciplinary journal published online as well as in quarterly print issues.

CHAPTER 15

SÎPÂ WASKWÂHK (UNDERNEATH THE BIRCH TREE)

Ê-ISKOCÊSIHKÊHK (CREATING SPARKS FOR A FIRE)—THE NEED FOR INDIGENOUS KNOWLEDGE IN UNIVERSITIES

Tammy Ratt

Introduction

> *In the last half a century, a growing number of Indigenous scholars have successfully passed through the conventional educational systems in almost every profession and in every disciplinary tradition, and while most have not had Indigenous Knowledge systems embedded in that education, there are growing efforts to include Indigenous Knowledges, perspectives, and communities in various forms and under various theories, such as culturally responsive curricula, infusion and integration in conventional disciplinary knowledges and methodologies.*

—BATTISTE & HENDERSON,
"Indigenous and Trans-systemic Knowledge Systems"

I ATTENDED THE SYMPOSIUM IN REGINA, SASKATCHEWAN, CAN-
ada, *What Are Universities For?*, in May 2023. This event was one of the
most beneficial educational experiences I have had; I attended every
session and enjoyed it! I reflected on and truly connected with the topic.
What are universities for anyway? Why do I continually bring myself
back to this space, "the university"? Why do I want to spend my life here?
What do I expect and what can I offer? What do previous and current
scholars bring to the table?

Because I use an Indigenous theoretical framework and see things
through an Indigenous lens, that someday I want embedded in all things
academic, I see value in the places where I have come to know and
understand epistemology, including literature, oral stories, and personal
knowledge that I have gained through experience. It feels holistic and I
think I am sometimes naive about situations in other environments or
institutions: I have always been a part of the First Nations University of
Canada and the University of Regina. Now I teach an Indigenous language
here, primarily with my Indigenous peers. I am surprised when people
do not know the value of Indigenous knowledges and do not have the
same views as I do. I have never been questioned about my right to use, or
the rationale for, Indigenous frameworks for research. My first professor
in the doctoral program did not focus on Indigenous content or ways of
knowing as the primary epistemology to teach from; they were included
or referenced in some areas but were not the focus. My second instructor, on the other hand, focused on Indigenous knowledge and Elder and
knowledge keeper teachings and taught through this lens. The class (of
mostly non-Indigenous students) was defensive about this. They talked
about how this perspective did not apply to them, and they could not
apply this approach in their research. This was the first and only time
in my university education where I felt out of place, and I worried about
what my peers might say. I have had peers who have not been so lucky or
successful within this institution, so I do not want to say that problems
do not exist. University is hard, and some people do not do well because
these are colonized spaces. I have had friends who have had to give pieces
of themselves that they were not comfortable giving and also keep pieces
of themselves, so as to not overstep their own boundaries, but then lose
out on opportunities.

awîna niya—Situating Self

Tammy Ratt nitisiyihkâson. oskana kâ-asastêki êkwa minahik wâskahikan ohci niya. What does the university do for me? I originally just wanted to get my degree, so I could have a better life, and I relied on the university to get me there. After completing my BEd in secondary Indigenous education, I was inspired and wanted to do more: I want to create positive educational experiences for others. My passion is Indigenous languages, and I want to create community learning opportunities for anyone who wants to learn Indigenous languages.

When I was in elementary school, I wanted a PhD so I could write self-help books, but as I got older that dream vanished with my lack of success in the public education system. I was told I talked too much, I was too silly, and I needed to know my place. But I never wanted to know my place in that system if it was not fun and not respectful of me. I never felt smart or that I was actually capable of doing anything until I attended my first year of university. I did not feel as invested in completing my MEd degree; I just wanted to receive it so I could be accepted into a PhD program. I consistently scored lower than the class average. In this setting I still did not feel as smart or capable as my peers. I always came up with a different analysis, so I thought I was in left field and felt like an outsider. The first class of my master's was heavy. It taught me about anti-racist and anti-oppressive education, and I came to learn that all these things I have experienced were real and they happened to other members of the BIPOC (Black, Indigenous, and people of colour) group. After finishing my master's degree, however, I thought I would not apply to the doctoral program. For over a year I had bouts of relief some evenings when I would lay in bed, thankful I had nothing to read or write. In time, I saw a poster that stated First Nations University of Canada was offering an Indigenous Language Master of Education program. I thought, "Now this is something that would be fun," and I wanted to learn more about teaching Indigenous languages. Fast forward five classes in: I decided "I love this and am inspired." If I could research language and art, then I wanted more education. With the support of many wonderful academics, I applied and was accepted into a PhD program in the Faculty of Education. I feel sheltered in the university setting because I am confident and feel cared for by so many mentors.

Listening to the Voices at the Conference

kihci-kiskinwahamâtowikamik is the word for university in nêhiyawêwin. During the symposium, Knowledge Keeper Joseph Naytowhow broke the word down: kihci, meaning sacred, kiskinwa is guiding, mato is cry, and wikamik is building. He said, "You are guiding somebody, and there will be tears in this space." This felt like a personal reflection of my university experience: I cried a lot. I sometimes would sit on my bed, on the phone with my sister with a pile of things to do scattered all over the bed, and I would cry. She would not say much; she would just listen. I do not remember how I came out of the crying, but I have the degrees, so it passed, and I passed. Many of the academics at the conference described the university's role as being for the good of society and to bring diverse groups of people together to discuss ideas and to inspire and make things better. There was also talk about diversity and inclusion. Many scholars believe that work needs to be done in order to decolonize the university space and be more inclusive of other ways of knowing.

Dr. Gloria Ladson-Billings (2023) introduced the world to culturally relevant pedagogy. She quoted Jonathan Haidt, who said universities are the "arena where truth is sought, discovered and explored" (https://bigthink.com/thinking/jonathan-haidt-campus/). I learned that European universities started out as church schools and that is why we still wear robes at graduation. This is so interesting to me, I wished it had something to do with wizards. Ladson-Billings said universities have often been the centre of social conflict and change, but they have also been places of elitism and exclusion. She asked a few deep critical questions: "Can we have diverse thinking without diverse peoples? Can we have democratic ideas with a censored curriculum? And can we learn about democratic ideas without academic freedom?"

Dr. Sheila Cote-Meek (2023) focused on the pursuit of truth and knowledge that universities have been associated with. She introduced me to the word *debwewin*, which is an Anishinaabe word meaning *true*. She explored the questions: "What is truth? Whose truth are we talking about? How can universities confront difficult truths? How can the university ensure diversity when so many people are excluded? And how can it be truthful? Who decides which knowledge systems are valued?" She noted the lack of Indigenous people in the academy and insisted representation does matter, particularly when you are the lone voice in the room or when

you are questioned if you don't respond to issues of Indigenous authen-
ticity. Cote-Meek makes me think about how there is not just one way
to be Indigenous. An example might be, some Indigenous people dance
powwow, some people are part of Indigenous ceremonies, some bead and
make Indigenous art. Some Indigenous people grew up on reserves, but
some were raised in cities. However, "we" are Indigenous, even if "we" do
not bead, or dance powwow; we are all different. How have universities
contributed to the ongoing colonization of Indigenous Peoples and how
does it continue today? Cote-Meek understands that the university is full
of contradictions—good things are created for the betterment of society,
but the roots are also deeply colonial, and systemic issues of oppression
need to be addressed. She quoted Murray Sinclair who said, "Education got
us into the mess; education will get us out." She continued talking about
the violent and ongoing impact of colonization on the land. It creates
extreme inequalities which in turn affect access to education, to adequate
resources, to employment, and to decision-making and self-determination.
The history of colonialism, oppression, and racism creates structures and
systems that influence what is taught, how it is taught, and who teaches it.
She commented on how complacent universities are and that they need to
re-examine how they provide education. Universities should lead change
in education that promotes awareness, understanding, and, importantly,
integrates Indigenous histories, knowledges, and pedagogies in the classroom. She continued to ask, "How do we recognize longstanding colonial
practices that remain deeply entrenched within the educational systems
and how do we do this without further supporting colonialism?"

Dr. Linda Tuhiwai Smith is an icon. She is wonderful, smart, and passionate and paved the way for Indigenous research in an academic setting.
Dr. Smith (2023) talked about the university being a contradictory space
that serves multiple purposes and has been layered over the years. She
says it is a "men's place," where whiteness exists and where men are not
good at letting go of some ideas and not good at letting new or radical
ideas in, which is contradictory to what the purpose of a university was
and should be. A university can be a place to inspire, to meet others, to feel
lucky and be fortunate, but it could also be the exact opposite: fostering
hopelessness, meeting mean people, and encouraging a particular way of
learning that may damage one's spirit. Universities are not easy places to
change. She says we should make universities more attractive to young
people. Universities are behind where students are. Institutions of higher

learning need to rethink some of their fundamental objectives. She notes that we are in a great social transformation. She talked about what we can learn from institutions that have developed different kinds of spaces for learning. She asks how universities can clean up the mess they have created. She says they can't; we must do it ourselves. When Linda Tuhiwai Smith says "we," I assume she is referring to Indigenous groups, and in this specific case she is referring to her people, the Māori.

For her, the Māori must reclaim the languages the linguists took, and the land the geographers took, and the history the historians took. In New Zealand, the Māori have created their own school of higher education; it cannot be called a university, but it is higher education. Most of the teaching occurs outdoors and in the communities. She calls the students "second chance learners" because their first educational experience, like mine, was not good. She says when we look at something that our ancestors produced, "we feel wondrous" and that is what universities should do, make us feel wondrous about what we can do.

Dr. Piya Chatterjee (2023) described universities as imperialistic spaces of knowledge-making. She talked about radical dreaming and about the "possibilities of a more liberating education." I love this idea of radical dreaming. Most interesting was Dr. Chatterjee speaking about the feminist reading circles in India and the women's desire to learn how to read in English. The reading circles use Western schooling as an inspiration. This made me wonder why we always put value on Western ways of knowing. Dr. Chatterjee explained that it does not have to be a choice—it does not have to be only one way or the other. We can learn both ways of knowing, all ways of knowing, and it is not up to 'us' to decide what 'they' should learn or value. Let the community decide in every situation.

Dr. Liz Morrish (2023) asked how the university can fulfill its obligations if the government does not value its contributions. Universities should be rooted in "civic content." When Dr. Morrish says civic content, she is talking about universities being for the good of all people in the area, including, specifically, people outside the university setting. She questioned what universities do for people who do not attend them, and I thought this was a powerful statement. If the university's goal is for social good and improvement, what does it do for the people who are not there? How can it positively affect the community as a whole?

Similarly, Dr. Kevin Kumashiro (2023) questioned what it means to succeed in education and noted that "success often means assimilation" for individuals. He suggests that usually means that you become better than most at "playing the game" (of being a student). This reflects my own experience in elementary and high school: if the system doesn't succeed at breaking "the other" down, then we are stronger for it.

Dr. Jonathan R. Cole (2023) spoke about the university having three basic functions: discovery (research), dissemination of knowledge (teaching)—both of which will change lives—and building citizens with a sense of civic responsibility. I find the concept of "building citizens" to be troubling. I have found that people who are different and do not follow the rules are cut out from being treated fairly in a classroom. I appreciate that what he meant by civic responsibility is creating a desire and obligation to help others and to build a just and more equitable society for everyone. However I think we need to be aware that while we are building these specific people, others are lost because quite frankly they do not fit into this narrative—it is just not as easy as that. The public education system is not made for everybody.

Administrative Views

During the 2023 symposium, the president of the University of Regina, Dr. Jeff Keshen, suggested that the university creates something better. Dr. Jerome Cranston, former dean of Education at the University of Regina, spoke about how whiteness exists within the university and how it continues to be unchallenged. Dr. Joel Westheimer, University of Ottawa, commented that we need students who think differently and ask critical questions. Dr. Malinda Smith from the University of Calgary spoke of universities as spaces for imagination and possibilities for lifelong learning. They tackle social problems and challenges through innovation and can enhance the quality of life, but they also maintain the status quo.

There was also a panel of presidents representing the Canadian Institutes of Health Research (CIHR), the Natural Sciences and Engineering Research Council (NSERC), the Social Sciences and Humanities Research Council (SSHRC), the Canadian Association of University Teachers (CAUT), and Universities Canada. It was wonderful to have all these people in the same space, at the same table, considering I had just applied for an SSHRC fellowship. I could not help but notice the lack of diversity among the leaders of funding agencies and higher education associations. Each white male talked about how he was committed to diversity in the university and funding projects with Indigenous people and how the agencies all do their part. But I wonder how this lack of diversity affects their decision-making in the important roles they fill. How do they know the benefits for each community if they are not from here or have likely never visited the communities the First Nations University serves? For my SSHRC application I had to check a box that said I was Indigenous. How many of the people who submitted applications for SSHRC fellowships were Indigenous? How many non-Indigenous? And how many of those Indigenous people received one? I heard most of them talk about the importance of valuing Indigenous people and the foundational knowledge they provide for specific disciplines such as medicine and health, but they only showed this value through the percentage of funds they put aside for Indigenous research and equity hiring.

First Nations University Voices: Indigenous-Led and Culturally Responsive Education

I was lucky enough during the symposium to be on a panel on the importance of Indigenous-led and culturally responsive education. (This session was held in the teepee-shaped glass atrium at First Nations University.) I was so nervous because "what do I know?" But I was also excited to sit with so many "big deals": Cadmus Delorme, former Chief for Cowessess First Nation; Lori Campbell, associate vice-president Indigenous engagement at the University of Regina; Dr. Blair Stonechild, professor emeritus at First Nations University; and moderator Dr. Angelina Weenie, associate professor, Indigenous Education, First Nations University. I shared my own views based on what I learned from the presenters through the week of the symposium and based on my experience teaching Indigenous and non-Indigenous youth in the public school system for thirteen years, as well as completing Indigenous education and language degrees.

Indigenous people have been educating their own from time immemorial, and this education was successful. Our knowledge kept us alive and kept many early settlers alive too. In my doctoral studies, I have been reading a lot about epistemology and ontology and how we come to know. I have considered what kind of knowledge is valued in the academic world. Indigenous people have always valued critical thinking, art, transformation, women, and diversity. These elements for some time in a Western world view were not valued. Indigenous people were engineers, farmers, hunters, doctors, and teachers. Many Indigenous values and ways of coming to know have been undermined by Western knowledge systems, but recently they are being acknowledged as "real" ways as coming to know (even) by non-Indigenous people. Indigenous epistemology represents all the things that I expect the university to provide to me and the community I want to live in. When I think about Indigenous education and Indigenous pedagogy, I understand now how it has always been for the civic or public good. It has been about transformation. It honours the gifts you have and how you fit into the community. It does not try to change the way you are to fit into society. From a knowledge keeper, I have learned about "backward" people in Indigenous societies. These people are at ceremonies and are respected even though they dance in the opposite direction and throw things in the fire that you are not supposed to. In contrast, students in the classroom who do not follow the rules or who think differently are often removed and not valued or respected. I think about how the backward or different people have a place in society. This makes me think of students who think differently, and I wonder how much better off they would be in an Indigenous society. Indigenous epistemology makes me realize that anything is possible—like Dr. Chatterjee said, "dare to dream." Within this dream, I believe that Indigenous languages should be embedded in all education and that Indigenous people need to lead the way. Elders say teach the way we used to teach, and I believe this is through authentic, experiential, and artistic teachings out on the land.

My own educational experiences as an Indigenous woman included dropping out several times, not graduating, and becoming pregnant, but in my heart I knew I needed to get my education. I eventually showed up at the First Nations University as a mature student. I did not know what I wanted to study; I did not have grade 12, and I was pregnant. The man who met with me ended up being my academic advisor for my whole degree. He helped me to apply and to register for classes. He never questioned me; I think he just knew I needed help getting started. The influence of two teachers in my first year helped me decide that I needed to become a teacher who would help students succeed in the public school system. I wanted to make students feel the way those two teachers made me feel: smart enough to be successful.

When Joseph Naytowhow described the kihci-kiskinwahamâtowikamik as a sacred place, where people are guiding and crying will happen, I connected in such a way. Part of the application process is an interview with the faculty and Elders. One question they asked was how I handle stress, and I said, "I cry" (I had already cried during this interview). One of the instructors said, "Oh you might need a new way to handle stress." But an Elder then said, "No, that is exactly how you should handle stress, because crying is cleansing." I am happy to have received this piece of knowledge, and I share it with people so they know that crying is okay.

Later, when I left university after that degree, I already knew I wanted to come back to that space to teach. I heard somebody once say that the education system is okay having many students not be successful, but I am not okay with that.

Engaging with the Community

During the symposium, I understood that everyone in the university has different priorities. There were concerns, for example, from librarians about resources, from Indigenous programs about not receiving funding, and from those creating safe spaces for 2SLGBTQ+ people. Every faculty has their own agenda. Everybody is doing what they think will make this community a better place, a better space—somewhere that they would want to be.

I know the university works in communities where it has relationships and partnerships. Student services invite high school students to come to campus and participate in events as a transition into university. Drouin-Gagné (2021) says that "Indigenizing the academy also requires engaging with Indigenous communities, especially the community in territories [where] universities are situated" (p. 60). But I would take this further, like Liz Morrish, and question what the university can do for people who are in our communities that have no relationship with or intention of coming to university. What does the university do for them if indeed the university is for the public good?

Scholars also suggest considering the importance of hiring an Indigenous person with community connections to "provide funding and time for community visits outside of research agendas" (Louie, 2019, p. 804). Louie also writes that "a potential workload for honouring community obligations is to provide course releases for faculty members who have responsibility in traditional societies" (p. 805). Another important aspect in engaging with the community is to ensure that there is an "equitable relationship between the non-Indigenous researcher and the Indigenous community" (Gewin, 2021, p. 317).

Inclusion of Indigenous Knowledge Systems

Willie Ermine (1995) says that the Western school system is damaging to Aboriginal epistemology, and Indigenous youth are forced into a system that "promotes the dogma of fragmentation and indelibly harms the capacity of holism" (p. 110). He writes "it is imperative that [we] take up the cause of our languages and cultures because therein lies Aboriginal epistemology, which speaks of holism" (p. 110). Battiste and Henderson (2021) say "Indigenous Knowledges are distinct and different from Eurocentric or western knowledge systems, though they are still not being fully appreciated by Eurocentric scholars as knowledge systems with their own languages, protocols, ethics, ontology, and epistemologies" (p. ii). Gaudry and Lorenz (2018) write that "Western approaches to knowledge production will need to be pushed back while Indigenous approaches to knowledge production are simultaneously being strengthened in the center. The goal is to enable Indigenous world views to take up more space throughout the entire academy" (p. 222). It is important to address knowledge hierarchies within the institution. Drouin-Gagné (2021) states that "Indigenizing the academy means reclaiming and validating Indigenous epistemologies, methodologies, and research questions" (p. 47). Louie identifies "critical elements of achieving and maintaining Indigenous Knowledges may include spending time on the land, maintaining relationships, honoring our responsibilities in ceremony, and holding roles in traditional class or societies" (p. 802). Louie (2019) also says the university's responsibility is to form a "potential framework…to establish criteria to ensure…an environment that fosters Indigenous Knowledges" (p. 802). Gaudry and Lorenz (2018) suggest forming course requirements within different faculty degrees, such as required courses in Indigenous history, languages, and epistemology.

I would include land-based teaching in all of this because the land is the foundation of Indigenous epistemology. It only makes sense that to decolonize university settings that the teaching space should change. Gaudry and Lorenz (2018) say that "moving sites of research and learning off-campus also involves a recognition that universities as they now exist may not necessarily be the key sites of decolonial Indigenization" (p. 225). Drouin-Gagné (2021) says that "land-based pedagogy has emerged in Indigenous higher education systems, since at least the 2000s. Aiming at re-establishing the relationships between Indigenous peoples and their territories, this pedagogy is part of the movement of Indigenous knowledges resurgence" (p. 55). When Drouin-Gagné (2021) says that "by centering on relations to land, resurgence offers a new way to engage with Indigenous rights and knowledges" (p. 56), academically, this means to move from talking about the land within conventional classroom settings to studying instances where we engage in conversations with the land and on the land in a physical, social, and spiritual sense. I have imagined sitting with and on the land and writing letters to the land in nêhiyawêwin. This is something I want to do so that I can reclaim and renew a deeper relationship with the land.

Inclusion of Indigenous Languages

I have heard for many years that our languages as Indigenous people are central to our ways of being and if we lose our language, we lose our culture. It is important that the university does what it can to support the implementation of Indigenous languages in the institution. Battiste and Henderson (2021) say that "each Indigenous Knowledge system is distinguished by its own language, and in Canada at least 11 language families exist with over 60 Indigenous languages currently being spoken. When discussing Indigenous Knowledge, it is important to note when one is referring to a singular language knowledge system or the many Indigenous Knowledge systems" (p. ii). Gaudry and Lorenz (2018) say that "prayer, speaking your language, [and] honoring your ancestors, are the foundation of resurgence" (p. 224). Battiste and Henderson (2021) say that "the more speakers of Indigenous languages who enter the academy, the more scholarship will move closer to new methods and ethics of trans-systemic approaches and will unpack meanings in knowledge systems based on verbs and being-ness, as distinct from knowledge systems based on nouns or objects" (p. xiii).

Linda Tuhiwai Smith talked about universities learning from Indigenous organizations that have creative programs in higher education. Drouin-Gagné (2021) agrees that "mainstream universities could learn lessons from existing approaches in Indigenous higher education programs and institutions" (p. 46). They say this because Indigenous people have had to exist in multiple knowledge systems and adapt to them for a long time.

While ignoring Indigenous perspectives, society demands that we either achieve within the Eurocentric model of education or live a life of poverty and welfare as the uneducated and unemployed or unemployable. Thus, in one way or another, we are regularly forced to validate the colonialists' mythology. We are being forced to sacrifice Indigenous worldviews and values for norms outside traditional cultural aims. (Hart, 2010, p. 4)

Scholars have confirmed that decolonizing the academy is of great importance and needed in order to accommodate and adapt to different learners. To do this would be what Gaudry and Lorenz (2018) define as "decolonial Indigenization [which] envisions the overhaul of the academy to fundamentally reorient knowledge production based on balancing power relations between Indigenous peoples and Canadians, transforming the academy into something dynamic and new" (p. 219). The University of Regina's Aboriginal Advisory Circle defines the goal of Indigenization as

the transformation of the existing academy by including Indigenous knowledges, voices, critiques, scholars, students and materials as well as the establishment of physical and epistemically spaces that facilitate the ethical stewardship of a plurality of Indigenous knowledges and practices so thoroughly as to constitute an essential element of the university. It is not limited to Indigenous people, but encompasses all students and faculty, for the benefit of our academic integrity and our social viability. (Quoted in Pete, 2016, p. 81)

I feel grateful that I attend the University of Regina. I believe it is leading the way in Indigenizing the institution. I am not saying that this work is done, or people have not had negative experiences within this institution. I know Indigenous faculty who have left as a result of their own negative experiences, but those same people made my experience here more positive. I know students who have felt isolated and alone. I cannot assume, based on my experiences, that problems do not exist here. However, I can say that I have experienced great support and comfort in this institution. Gaudry and Lorenz (2018) state that "research shows, Indigenous faculty and allies tend to already be ahead of administration and invested in new transformation approaches to a decolonial academy" (p. 226). This is promising, but administrations must be on board to dismantle current structures that stand in the way of real change in all universities.

The Future of the University and Me

As I participated in this week-long international symposium I wondered, "What are my expectations of the university? Why do I continue to come back to this institution? And why have I always dreamed about working here?" I want my knowledge, as a student, as an educator, and as an Indigenous person, to be valued. I want experiences that inspire me. I want to meet people who inspire me. And I want to believe that anything is possible. I am lucky enough to be in a situation where knowledge from Indigenous people is valued and respected and sought after. I never feel doubted or questioned by my supervisor or my committee or other academics who teach and guide me.

I want to feel that the knowledge I come with is valued. I want to feel important and that the people who teach me care about how I do. I want to know that they think that my ideas are good, but I also want to know when my ideas are incomplete and for them to teach me how to navigate this and that they care enough to help me analyze my thoughts. My knowledge comes through my experiences with my ancestors, through kinship, and through community. Indigenous epistemology values all these ways of coming to know, and I want the university to acknowledge these ways of knowing.

I want the university to provide me with opportunities that inspire me. These experiences and opportunities will add to my learned knowledge. An example of this occurred when a professor devised a plan to help those interested in working on an article for publication. This was a huge thing for me. The Faculty of Education organized a mentorship program with published academics who had the same interests as graduate students like me and helped to edit our papers. This was how I got my first publication, "*miskasowin askihk*." I still print it off, sign it, and gift it to people to be funny, but I am actually so proud of myself. Definitely one of the coolest things I have ever done. Similarly, the First Nations University of Canada is always providing me with opportunities to learn the most amazing things, such as hide work and colouring porcupine quills with natural dyes. They also allow me to attend and provide funding for events where I get to learn nêhiyawêwin.

Inspired by the *What Are Universities For?* symposium, I want the university to provide experiences where I can continue to meet more Indigenous people who will inspire me. Whenever I attend any academic or social events, I look for brown faces. If I see brown faces, I know this is an environment I want to be in and that I have allies. Dr. Marc Spooner taught a research class I was in. It was amazing. I have learned so much about "research"; I learned that I wanted to research "research" itself. He did not focus on Indigenous methodologies, but he taught different theoretical frameworks in a sequence that made sense. Then he invited people into the space who would do a better job than he to teach us. Then he organized this conference and invited the most amazing scholars: Indigenous and non-Indigenous people who have written articles I have read. I knew I wanted to be in this space and around all the people who attended. This symposium is a strong example of what a university should be.

I want university to make me feel and believe that anything you can dream of can be done. This is why I applied for a PhD: because I was made to believe that, one, I could do it, and two, I could research Indigenous languages and art. I want to buy land and start a culture camp where we will create art and learn nêhiyawêwin. As an educator, my goal is to ensure that the students I teach believe all things are possible. I think that Indigenous epistemology opens that door to endless possibilities, and I hope that the university lets me fulfill these possibilities with its guidance. I want the university to honour me and guide me to learn more about Indigenous epistemology so that I can be successful in my studies, in my research, in my teaching, and in the communities I am part of.

Conclusion

The symposium has confirmed for me that the way forward on my own path is to articulate, live, and teach from a perspective of nêhiyaw onto-epistemologies. During the 2023 fall semester, I completed my comprehensive exams for my PhD, and through the process I created a nêhiyaw onto-epistemology which I would like to use for the research I do now and in the future. *miskâsowin nêhiyawiwinihk*, which means coming to know oneself through being nêhiyaw (Cree-ness, being Cree), is represented through the birch tree and its surroundings. The theoretical framework is inspired by Indigenous researchers, Elders and knowledge keepers, friends, teachers, and personal experiences through life. Within this framework the methodology is represented by the trunk, the leaves, and the branches. The trunk has vascular tissues that carry materials throughout the tree. The mistikowat (trunk) represents the knowledges (ancestral/spiritual/

experiential/literary which were formed in the roots (epistemology) and carried to the rest of the tree. The nipiya (leaves) attract sunlight and convert it to the sugars that feed the tree for growth (photosynthesis). This represents the process of the project, from data collection to data analysis, referred to also as meaning-making. The watihkwana (branches) hold the weight of the leaves on the tree. They grow, they change, they break. This represents the self, which includes self-preparation, -healing, -change, and -reflection. I hope this description of the birch tree will help in understanding how this approach to knowledge, including language revitalization, will add to current research and conceptual understandings and strengthen Indigenous cultures (see the Appendix below for a summary of this imagery).

Marc Spooner sees the university as a lighthouse pointing the way to safe passage and new knowledge. But the university can also be viewed as a fire, which is another use of the birch tree. Birch bark is the best to start fires, and birch wood burns hot and clean. Just as fire provides light, warmth, safety, and protection, it is also used to heat the ancestral rocks in Sweat Lodges for healing. The university can be a place to explore and strengthen the critical holistic and inclusive concept of wâhkôhtowin (that is, the understanding that we are all connected very deeply spiritually, physically, emotionally, and mentally).

If the scholars at the symposium agree that we are in a time of transformation, and decolonization needs to happen, I hope my reflections in this chapter help people think more deeply and search more thoroughly about what needs to happen within the university setting and about our own individual roles in the institution. I am inspired by what I have learned from others who already work to make the university a space for all people to benefit. I believe that the university is a place where we learn to embrace a space within ourselves to help the greater good beyond ourselves.

Appendix

miskâsowin nêhiyâwiwinihk

My mom's friend calls the birch tree a medicine tree. This connects to the idea that the birch tree is a sacred tree. The Ojibwa, Odawa, and Blackfoot—and many more, I am sure—have sacred stories about the birch tree. Some believe that the birch tree was a gift given to them. This is because the birch tree offers so much.

Figure 15.1. waskway—birch bark tree

Source: Digital image by Danaya Stevenson (2023), property of the author.

Onto-epistemology

Ontology is the nature of existence, reality.

Epistemology—how we come to know.

Indigenous research tends more toward the idea of onto-epistemology.
The whole tree and environment of the tree represent this world view.

watapiyak—roots
The roots spread under the ground, and they anchor the tree. They extract moisture and nutrients from the ground.

- ancestral/intergenerational/community knowledges
- spiritual knowledge (dreams, visions, magic, prayer), which is the foundation of my ways of knowing

This is where my knowledge rests, it is stored here, it is from here that new knowledge is grown.

Environment
The environment affects the tree and the way the tree responds to the environment it is in (pîsim/sun, yôtin/wind, kimiwan/rain).

- knowledge I gain from experiences
- literature, teachings, storytelling, stories, *âtayôhkêwin* (sacred stories)

This knowledge does not come from the roots, it comes from my experiences moving through this world, as well as the knowledge I gain from my relationship and interaction with extant knowledge and wisdom (literature, story, etc.). I experience it as a living, thinking person.

wayakêsk—bark
Axiology—ethics and morals—the sacredness of the tree.
The bark is the protective layer for the tree.
I view this as the ethics and morals within Indigenous onto-epistemology.

Reciprocity atamiskaw—asonamakêwin
Ermine (2023) teaches the word *atamiskaw* in many of his presentations, in all his encounters. He says that atamiskaw, the word, tells us that that when we meet people, we need to enrich them. He says it is in our language how we should live. asonamakêwin is a word in Cree that I have learned along the way, it means that it is our responsibility to pass on knowledge that we learn.
The tree provides

- buds—medicine salve
- chaga grows on this tree
- sîwâkamisikan—water—syrup—as a syrup for cooking and baking, but as a water for medicine (it helps kidneys and liver, but you can only drink it once a year because you can only get it in the spring when the nights still freeze, and days are above 0; the water must be drunk within a few days before it goes bad)
- oxygen
- basket making and other artistic uses—birch bark biting, birch bark canoes, fire
- The tree also reduces erosion and moderates climate, removes carbon dioxide from the air.

From outside the tree,

- shade
- home
- shelter
- fire
- smoke
- habitat for many species

There is no question that the tree gives back more than it receives from the humans. I think as a researcher I should give back more than I receive. The research should give back so much more than it takes. This brings to mind the notion of care that figures prominently in Indigenous research.

Methodology: How knowledge is gained
"MISTIKOWAT"—TRUNK
The trunk has vascular tissues that carry materials throughout the tree.

The trunk represents the knowledges that are carried throughout the research, the literature knowledge, the ancestral knowledge, experiential knowledge, carried from the roots to the rest of the tree. It is put into practice.

NIPIYA—LEAVES
The leaves attract sunlight and convert it to sugars that feed the tree for growth (photosynthesis). The leaves represent the project, and the

process of information gathering and meaning making (data, data collection, and data analysis) represents photosynthesis.

WATIHKWANA—BRANCHES
The branches bear the leaves—they grow, they change, they break. They hold up the leaves.

Self (preparations), healing and change over time, reflexive.

References

Battiste, M., & Henderson, S. (2021). Indigenous and trans-systemic knowledge systems (ᐃᓯᑕᐧᐃᐧᓇᐣ ᐧᓇ ᐧᐅᑕᐧᐃᐧᑕᐧ ᐊᐧᐸ ᐟᐸᐊᕑᐣᐣᐟᐧᓬᐟ ᐧᓇ ᐧᐅᑕᐧᐃᐧᑕᐧ ᐣᐟᐧᐅᑕᐧ). *Engaged Scholar Journal*, 7(1), i–vi. https://doi.org/10.15402/esj.v7i1.70768

Chatterjee, P. (2023, May 3–6). *Within and beyond the plantation: Imagining anti-colonial feminist pedagogies, otherwise* [Presentation]. What Are Universities For? International Symposium. Regina, SK, Canada.

Cole, J.R. (2023, May 3–6). *What are universities for? Pre-symposium, expert panel, May 3, 2023—Darke Hall, University of Regina*. [Video]. YouTube. https://www.youtube.com/watch?v=DgnwIO4DVGM

Cote-Meek, S. (2023, May 3–6). *Reimagining the pedagogy of truth*. [Presentation]. What Are Universities For? International Symposium. Regina, SK, Canada.

Drouin-Gagné, M.-E. (2021). Beyond the "Indigenizing the Academy" trend: Learning from Indigenous higher education land-based and intercultural pedagogies to build trans-systemic decolonial education. *Engaged Scholar Journal*, 7(1), 45–65. https://doi.org/10.15402/esj.v7i1.69978

Ermine, W. (1995). Aboriginal epistemology. In M. Battiste & J. Barman (Eds.). *First Nations education in Canada: The circle unfolds* (pp. 101–11). UBC Press.

Gaudry, A., & Lorenz, D. (2018). Indigenization as inclusion, reconciliation, and decolonization: Navigating the different visions for Indigenizing the Canadian Academy. *AlterNative: an International Journal of Indigenous Peoples*, 14(3), 218–27. https://doi.org/10.1177/1177180118785382

Gewin, V. (2021). Respect and representation: Indigenous scientists seek inclusion for their knowledge and for themselves. *Nature*, 589, 315–17. https://biogeoscapes.org/wp-content/uploads/sites/33/2021/02/How-to-Include-Indigenous-Researchers-and-Their-Knowledge.pdf

Hart, M.A. (2010). Indigenous worldviews, knowledge, and research: The development of an Indigenous research paradigm. *Journal of Indigenous Voices in Social Work*, 1(1), 1–16. https://scholarspace.manoa.hawaii.edu/bitstream/handle/10125/15117/v1i1_04hart.pdf

Kumashiro, K. (2023, May 3–6). *Higher education must step up, as must academics.* [Presentation]. What Are Universities For? International Symposium, Regina, sᴋ, Canada.

Ladson-Billings, G. (2023, May 3–6). *Closing the marketplace: Restriction, repression, & retrenchment in US higher education.* [Presentation]. What Are Universities For? International Symposium, Regina, sᴋ, Canada.

Louie, D.W. (2019). Aligning universities' requirements of Indigenous academics with the tools used to evaluate scholarly performance and grant tenure and promotion. *Canadian Journal of Education, 42*(3), 791–815. https://journals.sfu.ca/cje/index.php/cje-rce/article/view/3903

Morrish, L. (2023, May 3–6). *From neoliberalism to authoritarianism: Universities, metrics, regulation and surrender to governmental control* [Presentation]. What Are Universities For? International Symposium, Regina, sᴋ, Canada.

Pete, S. (2016). 100 ways: Indigenizing and decolonizing academic programs. *aboriginal policy studies, 6*(1), 81–89. https://doi.org/10.5663/aps.v6i1.27455

Smith, L.T. (2023, May 3–6). *What we can learn from developing different institutions of higher education?* [Presentation]. What Are Universities For? International Symposium, Regina, sᴋ, Canada.

CONCLUSION
A CALL TO HOPE

James McNinch and Marc Spooner

> *I passed a Chinese takeaway; a discount furniture warehouse, an attack-dog kennels and a grim housing estate like a partly rehabilitated prison camp. There were no cinemas, churches, or civic centres and the endless billboards advertising a glossy consumerism sustained the only cultural life.*
>
> —J.G. BALLARD, *Kingdom Come*

> *The suburbs dream of violence. Asleep in their drowsy villas, sheltered by benevolent shopping malls, they wait patiently for the nightmares that will wake them into a more passionate world.*
>
> —J.G. BALLARD, *Kingdom Come*

In J.G. Ballard's dystopian vision of twenty-first century life, *Kingdom Come*, such a landscape adjacent to a motorway is a bleak symbol of a culture bereft of spirituality or morality. The only truth here is a burnt-out stub end of consumerism, materialism, and technology where the populace is passively "waiting for a crime to be committed" (Ballard, 2006, p. 7). In short, it is a landscape where the question "What's a university for?" makes no sense because there are no universities and no one sees the need for them.

Our first edited volume, *Dissident Knowledge in Higher Education* (Spooner & McNinch, 2018) contained a foreword by Zeus Leonardo and an afterword by Peter McLaren. Both contributions assessed the impact of the election in 2016 of Donald J. Trump as the forty-fifth president of the United States. Both men despised, lamented, and feared Trump's racism, misogyny, and xenophobia and the imminent threat to democratic principles and the rule of law in the United States. At the time, we did not fully appreciate just how prescient had been both Leonardo and McLaren. We also did not anticipate that the American people and world would once again be facing the impact of a now more emboldened, maddened, and vindictive Trump as forty-seventh president. Already, he openly muses invading Greenland, Panama, and annexing Canada among a number of other grim policy orders, including mass deportations, immigration and border lockdowns, climate change denial, a variety of economic sanctions, and the blanket pardon of January 6 insurrectionists.

When Marc and I were editing that first volume, we were both attracted and repelled by what we saw as the static tranquillity and the privileged security of an academic life built on a feudal hierarchy ranging from lowly undergraduates to full professors and serviced by various ranks of administrators, technicians, tradespeople, and labourers. At the very least, this was an academy kept all too domesticated with busy-work under an all-encompassing audit culture to participate in its own governance, let alone to lift its collective head as witness to the world.

The ivory tower seemed a perfect symbol of academia remotely at a distance from and above the truck of ordinary life. However, numbingly spinning the academic wheel, shuttering one's doors, or insulating oneself in privilege was never a viable option, but even less so now; nor will it offer any long-term safety or comfort as democracy and the rule of law are once again tested. This time on shakier ground as the traditional pillars of democracy—the free press, an impartial judiciary, the legislature, and the university—have all been weakened.

In Arthur Miller's classic melodrama *Death of a Salesman* (1949), planting a garden that will never grow, Willy Loman keeps sounding the alarm—the post-war world is changing: "The woods are burning! The woods are burning!" Such desperation embodies the fear, anxiety, and stress of impending doom. It is now time for all of us to extinguish such flames, to find a way through the smoke, and to initiate necessary action starting with characterizing hope as a form of defiance.

Now in 2026, we are still asking, with just as much concern and urgency, "What are universities for?" Indeed, the authors of the chapters in this book have made earnest and insistent attempts to propose a variety of answers to this all-encompassing question; looking to the future with them we find hope. The contributors have stated clearly and unequivocally that universities have an urgent role to play in revitalizing a desire for justice and equity in a more truly democratic society. The university must be a place where scholars, students, and the public continue to ask questions, to engage and endeavour to reach further, to see more clearly, to better understand the universe, ourselves, and, perhaps more importantly, beyond ourselves, to things and beings that are comprised in complex nested systems bigger than ourselves and our greatest imaginations…

Collectively walking the balance beam between such optimism and pessimism makes the question of what universities are for existentially difficult to answer in the face of unwelcome truths. As members of the academy, we are all implicated and conflicted because universities are deeply embedded in the societies they serve. The seductive image of the ivory tower is a mirage and a ruse.

Despite all of the progress humanity has made over thousands of years, we still endure incredible suffering at one another's hands. In 1785, Scottish bard Robbie Burns included this verse in *Man Was Made to Mourn: A Dirge*:

> Many and sharp the num'rous Ills
> Inwoven with our frame!
> More pointed still we make ourselves
> Regret, Remorse and Shame!
> And Man, whose heav'n-erected face,
> The smiles of love adorn,
> Man's inhumanity to Man,
> Makes countless thousands mourn!

This lament is not just about the constancy of wars and human suffering across the ages. It is about how our societies and our institutions are structured. As academics, we are wittingly and unwittingly complicit in exacerbating greater and greater inequity between the general population and the "mega-moguls" and "techno-feudalist bros" who see themselves entitled to a new imperial world order in which they believe they are not bound by the rule of law or democratic institutions and for whom the rest of us are mere impediments to their tyrannical dominion (Rushkoff, 2023).

Hauntingly, Davis and Monk (2007) observe how in our neoliberalized times a "winner-take-all ethos is unfettered by any remnant of social contract and undisturbed by any ghost of the labor movement, where the rich can walk like gods in the nightmare gardens of their deepest and most secret desires" (p. ix).

This nightmare is epitomized in US Defense Secretary Pete Hegseth's introduction of President Trump to the troops at the American base in Qatar in mid-May 2025. He revealed what is really meant by "Make America Great Again" (MAGA): "We are restoring a warrior ethos: No more political correctness, gender pronouns, DEI, CRT, or climate change. We are in the business of war-fighting." He told those assembled they should only be focusing on four things—"accountability, standards, warriors and lethality...to defeat the violence unleashed by wokeness and weakness" (*Times of India*, 2025).

The official erasure of the identity of transsexual and transgender individuals through a presidential executive order (there can be only two sexes: male and female) is the epitome of a callous disregard for human rights and the dignity and respect every person deserves. Such explicit and intentional erasure of a population is just one infamous signature of fascist regimes.[1] Other examples follow to demonstrate the desperate need for institutions of higher education across the globe to counter this dangerous assault.

Across social media, the acronym DEI is now, in the war on woke, hurled as an insult to demean queer people, people of colour, and indeed anyone who might object to the ruthlessness of Christian nationalists and the Republican right (Hasan 2025).[2]

In this collection, Liz Morrish reminds us such a strategy is designed to deliberately "deflect questions about inequality, power and representation" such that, in just one ludicrous example, "Florida schools are attempting to teach the story of Rosa Parks without mentioning her race."

As we saw at Trump's inauguration, he surrounded himself with some of the world's richest tech oligarchs who adhere to a narrow range of beliefs and values that reinforce his own narcissistic authoritarianism. David Weitzner (2025) calls these people "algorithmic supremacists" who disdain the messiness of mere ordinary people in favour of the numerical and almost other-worldly sterility of artificial intelligence.

Influenced by the founders of "the Dark Enlightenment," American software engineer Curtis Yarvin and British philosopher Nick Land, "adherents advocate for hierarchical, authoritarian systems of governance, enabled by technological innovation led by hybrid CEO-meets-monarch-like figures" (Collins, 2025). Others in the broader MAGA circle "have identified universities as primary ideological enemies, with Mario Rufo helping to remake New College of Florida in the image of Christian nationalism" (Wilson, 2024). This ideological position is accompanied by sneers at the "excess of empathy": soft-hearted liberalism that has become "toxic" and will destroy civilization (Wong, 2025).[3]

It is clear that Trump has always been a man without scruples or ethics. By constructing empathy as a weakness, his coterie of supporters and entourage of sycophants can justify brutality as a sign of strength. This includes defunding anything affiliated with DEI and CRT, mass deportations of immigrants, cuts to domestic and foreign aid, reducing funding to organizations that support women, including recriminalizing the reproductive rights of women (Levine, 2025) and supporting the forcible displacement of Palestinians from their homeland to turn Gaza into the "Riviera of the Middle East" since now there seems to be "nothing there" (*All Israel News*, 2025).

This thick-skinned toughness also covers the anti-vax stance of Robert F. Kennedy Jr: vaccines are alien dangers; illness only affects the weak; death acts as a necessary cull to strengthen the herd. Survival of the fittest willfully ignores social determinants of health and well-being. It becomes mixed with policies to support unbridled capitalism and the racism inherent in the white nationalist "great replacement theory." Elon Musk, the father of thirteen or more children himself, advocates for pro-natalism by challenging himself to help "seed the earth with more human beings of high intelligence" (Beres, 2025). The connections between such eugenic thinking and racism and political action is exemplified in the Trump regime paying to bring white South African Afrikaners to the United States as "refugees from genocide" despite any evidence to support such an allegation (Bowden, 2025).

Such dangerous thinking and actions chart the critical role schools and universities must play to challenge such insidious new orthodoxies and counter them with humane and ethical alternatives for the sake of our very humanity.

In accepting the freedom to publish prize at the British Book Awards in May 2025, Margaret Atwood remarked that she "could not remember another time when words themselves have felt under such threat." Looking back over her sixty-year career she noted:

> Those years included the Soviet Union, when samizdat was a danger-
> ous method of publishing. Hand-produced manuscripts were secretly
> circulated and bad luck for you if you were caught. They've also
> included the recent spate of censorship and book banning, not only
> in the oppressive countries around the world, but also in the United
> States. They have included too the attempt to expel from universities
> anyone who disagrees with the dogmas of their would-be controllers.
> (Atwood in Knight, 2025)

Gathered in this volume are diverse and thoughtful voices from institutions of higher education. These voices insist that strong counter narratives
exist to oppose the dangerous state of affairs facing liberal democracy and
human rights. There are vital and useful alternatives with which to chart a
course away from these dangerous elements of fascism in the world today.

And so, we must say that this unwelcome truth requires that universities work much harder to defeat the tyrants of this world, trumped-up bully
boys who are embedded in every aspect of societies around the world and
in all ranks of the military, government, business, and industry. They are
the twenty-first-century equivalent of the robber barons of the nineteenth
century who believed that the goal of the expansionist colonial enterprise
was to ensure their own incredible wealth and privilege at the expense of
others, both mere lesser individuals and entire civilizations. This is a race
and class struggle that universities must address.

There can be no reconciliation with the past if there is not first an
understanding of truth even if it is differentiated, complex, and contested.
Universities must help us to come to terms with this past. If we don't,
as the old adage goes, we are doomed to repeat it. Specialization, and an
increasingly labour-market-focused higher education, means that fewer
and fewer of today's university students study other cultures, histories,
languages, and literatures, in other words the humanities and arts. This
lack contributes to societies deficient in understanding and knowledge
that would better enable them to fight for themselves and for others.

If we don't know about the unbelievable harm authoritarian strong-
man tyrants of the past have done, we will be helpless in the face of ruth-
less tyranny. "The banality of evil," so eerily exposed by the Nuremberg

Trials of Nazi war criminals and the reportage of philosopher Hannah Arendt (1963) serves to remind us of this truth.

Former Justice of the Supreme Court of Canada and visiting professor of law at Harvard University, Rosalie Silberman Abella has a passionate commitment to international law and the protection of human rights. Born in 1946 into a Jewish family where her two-and-a-half-year-old brother and her father's side of the family all died in the Treblinka extermination camp, Abella despairs that we have forgotten the hard truths of the Holocaust.

> We're at the edge of a future unlike any I've seen in my life-time. The extremes have occupied the middle and the middle is polluted by bombastic and demagogic incivility from the extremes....Everyone is talking and no one is listening except in their own ideological silos. It's a moral quagmire, a moral free-for-all and a moral vacuum. How did we get here? The truth is, we let it happen by tolerating the intolerable for far too long, sacrificing principle for political pragmatism, substituting political accountability with moral lassitude, and replacing moral clarity with moral laissez-faire. (Abella, 2024)

The great Canadian socialist politician Tommy Douglas, along with those of his generation, experienced the rise of fascism, Nazism, and totalitarianism; Canada fought with allies in wars against these dangerous "isms." Douglas understood that

> fascism begins the moment a ruling class, fearing the people may use their political democracy to gain economic democracy, begins to destroy political democracy in order to retain its power of exploitation and special privilege. (Douglas, n.d.)

Up against such hard truths, what can a university be for? It seems to us that this question is almost as protean as asking about the meaning of life. If there were a simple answer, if only truth were that easy, then perspectives as different as hedonism and puritanism might be easily reconciled in an understanding that nuance and subtlety are lost if we seek easy short-cuts to the truth. Mark Kingwell (2024) has argued that "intellectual inquiry should not offer comfort or affirmation of what we already believe. It's not even about social justice either, unless we individually choose that path." Most of the authors collected in this volume would dispute that last sentence. Working to make a better world is not merely an individualistic endeavour; a world that is more just and equitable requires the commitment of entire institutions, particularly schools and universities.

If the woods are figuratively and literally burning out of control, if the ivory tower is in flames, how else might we imagine the university and its purpose? Fire is a powerful symbol, both an image of death and destruction and of life and rebirth (as the phoenix rises from the ashes). Fire is at once a weapon and a defence as well as a provider of warmth and light. Louis Menand (2024) commenting on the political and economic intrusion of politicians and donors into university affairs summarizes in "Academic Freedom under Fire": "Politicians despise it. Administrators aren't defending it. But it made our universities great—and we'll miss it when it's gone." If someone is "on fire," they have been sparked and are burning with energy; but if someone is "under fire," they are being attacked. To be "burnt in effigy" means someone's image is set on fire to symbolize that person's demise.

Educators over the years have been warmed and inspired by the quotation attributed to Plutarch: "The mind is not a vessel to be filled, but a fire to be kindled." Surely that is what, at least in part, a university is for. Do these conflicting images of fire capture the contradictions inherent in today's university where knowledge is under siege?

We have valued highly the image of the lighthouse to represent the university; ancient lighthouses of course were once giant bonfires, signalling and warning of dangers below. The iconic image of the lighthouse, used for the symposium that instigated this publication, captures the glow of a light that guides us in new and safer directions, helping to safely navigate difficult waters. A beacon is a comfort to those who have lost their way, and the constancy of the lighthouse evokes the vigilance of standing on guard.

Piya Chatterjee, in her chapter speaks of an "ethical charge [that] helps me anchor myself in these choppy waters and the jagged shoals which lie close under their surface." This ethical charge is her own personal lighthouse as she navigates the dangers of researching "others" from her own privileged yet compromised position.

Tammy Ratt, in her chapter calling for the need for Indigenous knowledge in universities, draws on the image of waskwây, the birch tree, and its many uses in traditional cultures to represent the concept of all things being interrelated. The birch provides sap and shelter and medicines and, of course, hardwood to build with and to make fire. Trees have been potent symbols of life in cultures, mythologies, and religions across time. The roots, trunk, branches, and leaves of a tree provide a vivid image of the connectedness of all things, making much more than just the sum of its parts.

The Athabaskan peoples of Alaska and Yukon understand that trees are aware of their surroundings and communicate with one another (Milne, 2022). Research has shown this to be true on a scientific level, thanks to the mycorrhizal networks that connect trees underground (Simard, 2021). For many, the symbol of the tree "represents harmony and balance in nature, rebirth and a connection of the earthly and the spiritual" (University of Strathclyde Glasgow, n.d.).

Perhaps the tree can be an inspiration, in its longevity. "Nothing evokes the future's potential like planting a tree that could live a thousand years," writes environmentalist Arno Kopecky (2024).

> Thinking about this quickly becomes a meditation on the precarity of our historical moment. Disaster is everywhere. Between the turbo-charged wildfires and droughts of a heating climate, breakneck urban development, geopolitical mayhem and the bottomless appetites of industry, it's hard to imagine any piece of earth being left in peace for 10 years, let alone 10 centuries.... To put it another way, we'll either change our ways and learn to live sustainably, or we won't....Either we'll succumb to our addictions, or we'll get over them. (Kopecky, 2024)

The tree is a symbol that challenges us in our institutions of teaching and learning to ensure that such magnificence can, should, will, and must continue into the future. That is the threat and the inspiration, and that is the truth the academy must nurture and seek.

Let us not take for granted the precarious freedoms scholars in universities in democratic nations currently, though imperfectly, access as tools to complete their work, for it has not been long the case. In fact, it has only been a little more than a century that it has existed in higher education as it is currently conceptualized in North America. Academic freedom is most succinctly defined as "freedom of inquiry and research; freedom of teaching within the university or college; and freedom of extramural utterance and action" (AAUP, n.d., p. 292).

As the chapters in this collection have explored, the threats universities and scholars face are many and include, among others, a creeping authoritarianism and democratic backsliding; growing adaptation of artificial intelligence, anti-intellectualism, and seeping post-truth rot. Other threats include shrinking funding and ongoing government attempts to repurpose higher education as only an individual benefit and strictly to service the labour market and industry. Ever-present, too, is resistance to and resentment of change and initiatives that champion equity, diversity, and inclusion.

In parting, we wish to leave you with this slightly updated Greek proverb: "A society grows great when old folks plant trees in whose shade they shall never sit." A properly functioning, reimagined, and fully aspirational university is, then, just that: an investment in the world's collective future.

References

AAUP. (n.d.). Appendix 1. 1915 Declaration of principles on academic freedom and academic tenure. https://www.aaup.org/NR/rdonlyres/A6520A9D-0A9A-47B3-B550-C006B5B224E7/0/1915Declaration.pdf

Abella, R.S. (2024, June 1). What happened to the legacy of Nuremberg and the liberal democratic values we fought the Second World War to protect? *The Globe and Mail*. https://www.theglobeandmail.com/opinion/article-what-happened-to-the-legacy-of-nuremberg-and-the-liberal-democratic/

All Israel News. (2025, May 15). President Trump reiterates plans to take over Gaza Strip, turn it into 'freedom zone.' *All Israel News*. https://allisrael.com/president-trump-reiterates-plans-to-take-over-gaza-strip-turn-it-into-freedom-zone

Arendt, H. (1963). *Eichmann in Jerusalem: A report on the banality of evil*. Viking Press.

Ballard, J.G. (2006). *Kingdom come*. Fourth Estate.

Beres, D. (2025, May 4). Maga's era of 'soft eugenics': Let the weak get sick, help the clever breed. *The Guardian*. https://www.theguardian.com/us-news/ng-interactive/2025/may/04/maga-soft-eugenics

Bowden, J. (2025, May 12). Trump repeats disputed claim that white farmers suffering 'genocide' in South Africa as first 'refugees' are flown in to US. *The Independent*. https://www.independent.co.uk/news/world/americas/us-politics/south-africa-refugees-white-farmers-trump-b2749416.html

Collins, C. (2025, May 19). Anti-democratic 'Dark Enlightenment' ideas have spread from Silicon Valley to Washington. *The Globe and Mail*. https://www.theglobeandmail.com/opinion/article-anti-democratic-dark-enlightenment-ideas-have-spread-from-silicon/

Davis, M., & Monk, D.B. (Eds.). (2007). *Evil paradises: Dreamworlds of neoliberalism*. The New Press.

Douglas, T. (n.d.). Tommy Douglas quotes. AZ Quotes. https://www.azquotes.com/author/4101-Tommy_Douglas

Hasan, M. (2025, February 11). What Republicans really mean when they blame 'DEI.' *The Guardian*. https://amp.theguardian.com/commentisfree/2025/feb/11/dei-trump-republicans-racism

Kingwell, M. (2024, January 5). There was no halcyon age of university excellence. *The Globe and Mail*. https://www.theglobeandmail.com/opinion/article-there-was-no-halcyon-age-of-university-excellence/

Knight, L. (2025, May 12). Margaret Atwood says she cannot remember another time 'when words themselves have felt under such threat.' *The Guardian*. https://www.theguardian.com/books/2025/may/12/margaret-atwood-words-under-threat-freedom-to-publish-british-book-awards

Kopecky, A. (2024, April 22). Where do you plant a tree with a 1,000-year lifespan? *The Globe and Mail*. https://www.theglobeandmail.com/opinion/article-where-do-you-plant-a-tree-with-a-1000-year-lifespan/

Levine, J. (2025, May 20). Trump is using his assault on government to retaliate against women. *The Guardian*. https://www.theguardian.com/commentisfree/2025/may/20/trump-retaliation-women

Menand, L. (2024, April 29). Academic freedom under fire. *The New Yorker*. https://www.newyorker.com/magazine/2024/05/06/academic-freedom-under-fire

Miller, A. (1949). *Death of a salesman*. Viking Press.

Milne, B. (2022, June 16). Symbolism of trees: Spiritual meanings scross history. *Better Place Forests*. https://www.betterplaceforests.com/blog/symbolism-of-trees/

Rushkoff, D. (2023, November 25). "We will coup whoever we want!": The unbearable hubris of Musk and the billionaire tech bros. *The Guardian*. https://www.theguardian.com/books/2023/nov/25/we-will-coup-whoever-we-want-the-unbearable-hubris-of-musk-and-the-billionaire-tech-bros

Simard, S. (2021). *Finding the mother tree: Discovering the wisdom of the forest*. Allen Lane.

Spooner, M., & McNinch, J. (2018). *Dissident knowledge in higher education*. University of Regina Press.

Times of India. (2025, May 16). Pete Hegseth's astounding speech for US Troops in Qatar. https://timesofindia.indiatimes.com/videos/international/full-wokeness-weakness-pete-hegseths-astounding-speech-for-us-troops-in-qatar/videoshow/121199196.cms

University of Strathclyde Glasgow. (n.d.). Why our symbol is a tree. https://www.strath.ac.uk/studywithus/ourcampus/whatsoncampus/faithspiritualitysupport/whyoursymbolisatree

Weitzner, D. (2025, May 9). We must fight back against the rise of 'algorithmic supremacists.' *The Globe and Mail*. https://www.theglobeandmail.com/opinion/article-we-must-fight-back-against-the-rise-of-algorithmic-supremacists

Wilson, J. (2024, December 21). He's anti-democracy and pro-Trump: The obscure 'dark enlightenment' blogger influencing the next US administration. *The Guardian.* https://www.theguardian.com/us-news/2024/dec/21/curtis-yarvin-trump

Wong, J.C. (2025, April 8). Loathe thy neighbor: Elon Musk and the Christian right are waging war on empathy. *The Guardian.* https://www.theguardian.com/us-news/ng-interactive/2025/apr/08/empathy-sin-christian-right-musk-trump

Notes

1   According to US census statistics, this affects a "mere" 1.6 percent of the American population. But that translates into more than five and a half million people in the US (a significant minority). Also note that 5 percent of young adults (18–29) identify as trans or non-binary. https://www.pewresearch.org/short-reads/2025/02/26/americans-have-grown-more-supportive-of-restrictions-for-trans-people-in-recent-years/

2   Hasan gives examples of how DEI is the "new N word." Obama's press secretary, a Harvard graduate, was derided as a DEI appointment. Kamela Harris as vice-president was called a "DEI hire." The 2024 Super Bowl half-time show, starring Kendrick Lamar, was dismissed as just "total DEI." The helicopter crash with a plane in Washington, DC, in January 2025 was blamed on DEI hiring and training initiatives implemented by Democratic secretary of transportation, Pete Buttigieg, an openly gay man.

3   Wong notes that toxic empathy is a concept attributed to Gad Saad, a professor of Business at York University in Toronto, for whom Elon Musk has a "public bromance."

THE FUTURE OF UNIVERSITIES, KNOWLEDGE, AND DEMOCRACIES

NAVIGATING POLYCRISIS AND AUTHORITARIANISM

Malinda S. Smith

"When democracy falters, it takes the institutional autonomy of universities down with it," Daniels, Shreve, and Spector argued in *What Universities Owe Democracies* (2021). To support their case, Daniels et al. cited obvious examples of the Taliban's closure of the American University of Afghanistan and Viktor Orbán's expulsion of the Central European University from Hungary. Then, we might not have anticipated that a mere four years later we would add to this list what some describe as the United States government's "aggressive" and "extra-lawful" actions toward its most prestigious universities, including Brown, Columbia, Cornell, Harvard, Northwestern and Princeton (Romine and Mascarenhas, 2025). Universities, long recognized as bastions of free inquiry and social betterment, now face intensifying political, economic, and ideological pressures. This moment signals a reconfiguration of universities' role as democratic pillars, particularly in addressing global challenges and planetary polycrises.

What is the role of higher education in democracies confronting poly-crises, where multiple, interconnected crises—political, social, economic, environmental—occur simultaneously, amplifying and creating a complex, systemic threat that exceeds the sum of its parts? The chapters in this volume are an important contribution to critical university studies, rein-forcing interventions, like Daniels et al. (2021), who urged universities to return to four foundational functions: fostering epistemic and intellec-tual pluralism, providing civic education to sustain democracies, enabling knowledge production and the stewarding of facts through academic freedom and free inquiry, and enabling socioeconomic mobility to ensure productivity, prosperity, and sustainability. These roles are needed now, more than ever, to navigate polycrises, counter global authoritarianism and right-wing populism, and sustain a healthy democracy.

This Afterword to *Knowledge Under Siege: Charting a Future for Univer-sities*, takes as one of its intellectual starting points the September 2023 CBC Ideas panel, "What Are Universities For?," hosted by Nahlah Ayed at the University of Regina (CBC Radio, 2023). Broadcast nationally, the panel featured distinguished scholars—Linda Tuhiwai Smith (University of Waikato), Joel Westheimer (University of Ottawa), Jonathan R. Cole (Columbia University, joining virtually), and me (University of Calgary)—who critically examined the evolving role of universities in democratic societies. Our dialogue with Ayed addressed foundational questions: What is the purpose of universities? Where have they faltered? What are they doing well? And what do they owe the public?

The panel explained the university's scientific, intellectual, moral, and civic responsibilities, its role in free enquiry, in the pursuit of knowledge and in sustaining democratic pluralism. It also discussed how corporatiza-tion, audit culture, and backlash against equity and social justice, among other areas, contribute to undermining the universities' public mission, threatening academic freedom and institutional autonomy. In my own contribution to the Idea's show, it was productive to think alongside Westheimer, Cole, and Smith. I argued that universities must be spaces of the imagination, public institutions that are central to sustaining democ-racy and addressing complex global challenges, including the enduring leg-acies of settler colonialism, slavery, and systemic oppression. Universities have a distinct public mission: to educate to address "wicked problems," educate for democratic citizenship, foster creativity and innovation, and pursue knowledge for the public good. While universities are perceived as inherently liberal institutions, most North American institutions were founded within colonial, patriarchal, and exclusionary contexts. Expressed commitments to inclusion are obstructed by contemporary universities' tendency to conserve existing traditions, which can make them conservative in structure and culture. This tendency to conserve rather than change limits possibilities as it tends toward maintaining the status quo. The social sciences, humanities, and the liberal arts disciplines are indispensable both to defending public universities and sustaining democracies. I argued for a pluri-university, which can be a transformative academic model that challenges monocultural knowledge systems by embracing diverse epistemologies, ontologies, and ways of knowing to advance democracy, justice, and inclusive excellence within and beyond the academy.

Knowledge Under Siege rigorously pursues these and other intellectual threads, confronting the historical and contemporary forces shaping and reshaping the contemporary university. Amid a polycrisis—political polarization, debates over academic freedom, external interference, funding cuts, and skepticism about higher education's value—this Afterword argues that universities must navigate these challenges while upholding foundational principles. Defending institutional autonomy and academic freedom is essential for free inquiry, the pursuit of knowledge, and the health of democratic societies.

In a historical moment defined by deepening polarization, authoritarian resurgence, and the destabilizing effects of recent political interventions in American universities and democratic norms, higher education, along with the free media and independent judiciary, remain indispensable to democratic renewal and to confronting the forces that threaten the fabric of free and open societies. Rather than retreating into the comfortable, but false, refuge of neutrality, universities must actively defend democratic ideals, foster critical thinking, nurture civic capacities, and cultivate critical inquiry—all essential to sustaining democracies. As John Dewey emphasized over a century ago in *Democracy and Education* (1916), education is not merely a transfer of information but a transformative process that equips individuals to question, debate, and participate meaningfully in democratic life. These capacities and skills are now indispensable to resisting disinformation and populist rhetoric, and to countering polarization.

The university's democratic role is under increasing threat. Funding cuts, attacks on scientific integrity, and restrictions on academic freedom are converging pressures that represent existential threats to higher education's mission. These disruptions—whether through budget reductions that stifle and censor research, assaults on climate science that undermine truth-seeking, or visa restrictions that sever global ties—impede universities' ability to function as independent sites of inquiry and democratic engagement. In this context, institutional autonomy and academic freedom are not merely aspirational values but essential tools of resistance against authoritarian encroachment.

We are reminded of Wendy Brown's anticipatory critique in *Undoing the Demos: Neoliberalism's Stealth Revolution* (2015), where she warned that authoritarianism often cloaks itself in neoliberal policies that commodify education and redefine it as a private good rather than a public trust. Brown argued that universities must reject this hollowing out of their purpose and erosion of democratic values and, instead, reclaim their democratic function by promoting critical inquiry, dissent, and public dialogue. This resistance must be deliberate and public, requiring universities to confront the forces of authoritarianism head on, and to safeguard the freedoms that sustain the university as a space for contestation, open discourse, scientific discovery, and collective goals.

This commitment to higher education's indispensable role in sustaining democracy also requires investment in the moral and imaginative capacities—as advanced by Martha C. Nussbaum in *Not for Profit: Why Democracy Needs the Humanities* (2010), where she argues that the humanities—through fostering empathy, global awareness, and critical reasoning—are essential to preparing citizens capable of resisting authoritarian overtures. Universities must be inclusive, pluralistic spaces, where diverse voices are amplified and students are equipped to engage across difference in pursuit of justice. Such spaces directly challenge authoritarian tendencies that feed on ignorance, division, obedience, and conformity. In such a moment, higher education is also called upon to cultivate global alliances, research partnerships, and scholarly exchanges that reinforce and expand shared democratic values. In doing so, higher education can recentre knowledge as a public good in which the defense of intellectual freedom becomes an act of civic resistance and a safeguard of democracy itself.

Charting a Future of Possibilities for Higher Education

Marc Spooner and James McNinch's *Knowledge Under Siege* arrives at a pivotal moment. With this volume and their earlier works, Spooner and

McNinch have emerged as critical voices challenging neoliberal restructuring of higher education, especially their earlier edited volume, *Dissident Knowledge in Higher Education* (2018). Their work critically examines the multiple ways that uncritical encroachment of audit culture, market logics, and settler colonialism can narrow the university's public mission by marginalizing non-dominant epistemologies and suppressing dissent, democratic engagement, and scholarly autonomy. One consequence is the narrowing of what constitutes legitimate knowledge, with market-driven metrics increasingly privileged over critical, community-engaged scholarship.

Spooner's work also draws attention to the conflation of academic freedom with broader notions of free speech and expressive freedoms. Academic freedom is a professional competency of academics, and this is distinct from the unrestricted, including ill-informed, everyday opinion expressed by citizens in democratic societies. The erosion of academic freedom poses a threat to the integrity of research and scholarship and the role of universities as spaces of critical inquiry and dissent. Both Spooner and McNinch emphasize that the university must reclaim its historical role as a space for the promotion of epistemologies that are inclusive, decolonized, and enabling of social justice. These themes, among others, weave through *Knowledge Under Siege*, as universities face new encroachments under rising authoritarianism and what Timothy D. Snyder cautions against in *On Tyranny*, "anticipatory obedience" and the tendency to comport oneself with the prevailing order, and to "obey in advance" (Snyder, 2017).

Higher education stands at a crossroads. While the university is one of the most enduring institutions in modern civilizations, its identity and social function remain in flux. As this collection reveals, the university always has been a site of contradiction and potentialities—a simultaneously enabling and contested space. It illustrates how universities are under pressure, yet their role in sustaining democracy and knowledge remains incomparable and irreplaceable. The chapters collected here engage critically with the university's evolving social contract and offer insights into its contradictions and potentialities. Together, they prompt a re-examination of what the university is, whom it serves, and how it might resist instrumentalization in pursuit of a more inclusive, democratic and just future. In the analysis that follows I briefly reflect on these chapters and the university's contested role and possibilities at a moment of global recalibration.

The first contributions to this collection underscore the university's multifaceted roles as a site of discovery, democratic participation, and cultural expression. Jonathan R. Cole offers a foundational defense of the university as an engine of innovation that has long served as "incubators of independent thought." However, they now confront intensified threats from political instrumentalization, epistemic exclusivity, managerialism and audit culture in which market-based governance replaces social trust with surveillance and performance metrics. Cole's contribution is complemented by Joel Westheimer's comparative lens on the civic functions of universities in democratic and authoritarian contexts. Westheimer's argument that universities must serve democratic purposes finds intellectual lineage in Dewey's *Democracy and Education*, where he insists that education is fundamental to a functioning democracy. Westheimer's advocacy for the free exchange of ideas, student activism, and engagement with the idea of the public good builds on a rich tradition of the critical pedagogical lineage of Paulo Freire (1970/2018), who saw education as a praxis of freedom. Both Cole and Westheimer highlight the university's responsibility not merely to transmit knowledge but to cultivate critical citizenship.

Whitney Blaisdell's research examines play, art, accessible spaces, and "playspaces." It enriches the volume with a metaphoric reading of the university as "playspace"—a space of tension and imagination where contradiction is generative. We are reminded that beyond the infrastructure of labs and lecture halls, the university is an affective, social, and symbolic environment. Blaisdell's dual lens—utopian and dystopian—recalls for us Lefebvre's conceptualization of social space as simultaneously produced, lived, and contested (Lefebvre, 1991). Such spatial multiplicity also echoes Edward Soja's theory of "Thirdspace," one where the real and imagined intersect in pedagogical possibilities (Soja, 1996). This framing invites us to consider the university not as a static institution but as a living, contested site shaped by ongoing social and epistemic conflict. Together, these authors affirm the university's need to balance competing commitments—between autonomy and accountability, tradition and innovation, critique and a duty of care. These perspectives collectively underscore the university's essential functions in democratic society.

The second section of this volume engages the structural reconfigurations of neoliberalism, critique of geopolitical contestations, and domestic forces shaping universities. The chapters confront the systemic challenges that threaten the role of the university, particularly the encroachment of neoliberal and authoritarian tendencies. The chapters also build on concerns previously raised by Philip Mirowski's (2011) *Science-Mart* about the neoliberal university becoming a market-driven epistemic regime. Simon Marginson traces the global entanglement of science and nationalism, warning against the erosion of transnational collaboration. The analysis of global university science highlights a paradigmatic shift. The empirical findings—namely, China surpassing the United States in citation indices—signals a realignment in global academic hegemony. He warns of the potential dangers of "technonationalism" and commodified science, which could foster an overly competitive, zero-sum global environment, limiting global collaboration and innovation.

Liz Morrish analyzes the United Kingdom's audit cultures, performance metrics, and bureaucratic logics that instrumentalize and marginalize critical disciplines, insurgent and subaltern knowledges, and ways of knowing—fostering a culture of uniformity and conformity. The critique of metrics and regulatory cultures in the United Kingdom academy underscores how New Public Management (NPM) techniques, originally theorized by Christopher Hood (1991), have undermined the autonomy of knowledge production. Morrish's documentation of the decline of the humanities amplifies Martha Nussbaum's *Not for Profit: Why Democracy Needs the Humanities* (2010), which argues that democratic societies are imperiled by the erosion of critical, humanistic inquiry.

A decolonial and Latin American perspective is advanced by Consuelo Chapela, who anchors knowledge production in the university in the long history of colonial epistemic violence and emancipatory resistance. Chapela's reference to "universities for hope" invokes the legacy of decolonial thinkers such as Enrique Dussel (2011) and the liberation pedagogy of Orlando Fals Borda who, in April 1995, offered salient insights for critical researchers: "Do not monopolise your knowledge nor impose arrogantly your techniques, but respect and combine skills with the knowledge of the researched or grassroots communities, taking them as full partners and co-researchers." Fals Borda goes on to say, "Do not trust elitist versions of history and science which responds to dominant interests but be receptive to counter-narratives" (Fals Borda, 1995). Chapela, like Borda and Boaventura de Sousa Santos (2014), calls for the decolonization of knowledge and the revalorization of epistemologies of the South.

Peter McInnis chronicles the erosion of collegial governance and academic freedom, calling for renewed faculty engagement and activism.

Focusing on Canadian universities reveals how the neoliberal entrench-
ment constrains academic freedom and collegial governance. McInnis
echoes Bill Readings's warning in *The University in Ruins* (1997) that the
university's telos has been evacuated by vitiating evolution of holistic
conceptions of excellence and merit in favour of excellence as an empty
signifier. McInnis, like Sheila Slaughter and Gary Rhoades (2009), con-
tends that the managerial and audit university can become instrumental-
ist, reductionist and, in the process, undermine the critical public role of
higher education in democratic societies. These chapters converge around
a central insight: the university is not immune to global shifts in governance, ideology, and political economy. The critiques presented in this
section also illuminate the structural forces compromising the university's autonomy, academic freedom, and critical functions. The analysis
moves beyond critique to envision countervailing practices of resistance
rooted in solidarity, labour organizing, and epistemic dissent.

The next section in *Knowledge Under Siege* explores potential pathways for reimaging and revitalizing the university's mission in response
to these challenges, and by reframing the university as a transformative
site. Focusing on renewal, this third section argues for alternative imaginaries and institutional practices. Kevin Kumashiro urges a break with
technocratic visions of higher education, calling instead for universities
that foreground collective struggle and transformative justice. Kumashiro
asks us to interrogate the university's complicity with empire and injustice
echoing the work of Gayatri Chakravorty Spivak, who illuminated the role
of elite knowledge systems in sustaining imperial logics (Spivak, 1999).
Kumashiro's proposition that universities must cultivate an "imaginary of
what could be" also aligns with Maxine Greene's idea of "wide-awakeness"
in educational visioning (Greene, 1995).

Sheila Cote-Meek draws on Anishinaabe pedagogies of relational
truth-telling to advance a decolonial and affective approach to teaching and
governance. Cote-Meek's chapter draws on the Anishinaabemowin word,
"Debwewin"—truth-telling from the heart—which is one of the Seven
Grandfather Teachings in Anishinaabe culture. This work also resonates
with the writing of other Indigenous scholars in the volume, such as Linda
Tuhiwai Smith (1999), whose *Decolonizing Methodologies* insists that reclaiming Indigenous knowledge systems is an act of intellectual sovereignty.
Cote-Meek joins a growing movement toward epistemic justice, including
the decolonial scholarship of scholars like Leanne Betasamosake Simpson.

Student activism is linked to transnational feminist resistance by Piya Chatterjee, offering a powerful model of witnessing and action within and beyond the university. Chatterjee's reflections on complicity and mutual aid invoke Eve Tuck's (2009) concept of "desire-based research"—which seeks not only to explore "damaged-centered research" and harm but to foreground aspirations, wisdom, resistance, and hope for the future. Chatterjee's comparative lens—from United States campus protest to Indian plantation worker literacy—illuminates the transnational dimensions of academic activism and solidarity, while resisting what Tuck refers to as the damaged and depleted narrative of hegemonic research on Indigenous, disenfranchised, and marginalized communities.

Shannon Dea's nuanced interrogation of university neutrality directly challenges the "view from nowhere" epistemology recalls Donna Haraway's insights in "Situated Knowledges," the scientific gaze "that makes the unmarked category claim to see and not be seen, to represent while escaping representation" (1988, p. 581). The university is not an impartial observer with a single point of view that is objective. In contrast to this mythical view, Haraway's "situated knowledges" advances a specific, partial, and local nature of perspectives that aims to foster critical inquiry and accountability. In this feminist epistemology tradition, Dea's analysis of the concept of "institutional neutrality" calling for principled stances in moments of social crisis places an emphasis on institutional responsibility and repair. Their reflection also recalls for us Eve Sedgwick's vision of reparative reading and critical hope. Contributions in this section offer a vison of the university as an active participant in societal betterment and transformation in all spheres. Together, the essays in this section provide us both conceptual and practical guideposts for institutional navigation, and for prioritizing justice, relationality, and public accountability over singular and myopic market logics and metrics.

The final section of the volume delves deeply into imaginative frameworks for co-constituting equitable, inclusive, and decolonial futures. Contributors explore how to navigate the polycrisis, pathways toward reimagining the university amidst planetary and democratic crises, and the future of the university. They share speculative but grounded imaginaries for the future. Christopher Newfield's "Four Ds" concept offers a diagnosis of the structural malaise impacting universities, especially the decline of the humanities and creative arts, and the urgency of decolonial knowledges, and calls for reinvestment in public institutions. Newfield's diagnoses captures the recursive loops of decline and stasis impacting the humanities, but he counters this with a call to build a "knowledge commons" beyond privatized models of education. Newfield's work, which should also be read alongside Wendy Brown's *Undoing the Demos* (2015), articulates the deep structural deformation of public education under neoliberalism.

Tom Sperlinger explores Black Mountains College (BMC), arguing that it shows how it models, or can model, an experimental, climate-responsive university that unsettles and transforms dominant institutional logics. Sperlinger's experiments in alternative education, including BMC, suggest sustainable paths forward. His ethos is echoed in earlier research such as Ivan Illich's *Deschooling Society* (1971) and Giorgos Kallis and Hug March's decolonial "imaginaries of hope," well-being, and ecological education for planetary futures (Kallis & March 2015).

Finally, Linda Tuhiwai Smith and Tammy Ratt round out the volume by making the case for Indigenous-centred epistemologies, pedagogies, and methodologies. Individually, and collectively, they articulate visions of the university that are land-based and culturally grounded. These works stand within a broader shift toward "ontological pluralism" in higher education, as advocated by scholars like Arturo Escobar (2018) who called upon universities to recognize multiple ways of knowing and being in the world. These incisive interventions unsettle Eurocentric frames and offer transformative pathways for institutional reconstitution.

In an historical moment of authoritarian resurgence, universities must stand as guardians of free inquiry, fostering inclusive communities that reflect the diversity of our world, knowledges, and ways of knowing. As Daniels (2021) reminded us, "no democracy can prosper without independent universities." By fulfilling their democratic obligations, universities not only safeguard knowledge but also ensure that the promise of pluralistic, equitable, and free society endures. This collection refuses nostalgia for a mythical golden age of the university and a surrender to dystopian determinism. Instead, it offers rigorous critique, visionary speculation, and a call to collective imagination and action. The university, if it is to endure as a public good, must be continually reclaimed.

The deeply reflective chapters in this volume are a call to a reassertion of values and meaningful action. The essays connect the past with the present and provide a guidepost on future-focused actions. By way of closing out I would like to extrapolate five key takeaways for future-focused transformative actions.

1. **The University is a Contested Terrain of Power and Possibility.** The university is not a neutral container with a view from "nowhere," but a space produced through contestation. Its mission in democratic societies must be constantly and actively negotiated. Dea, Cole, Westheimer, and Blaisdell variously highlight how universities are indispensable pillars of democracy and play an important role in fostering independent thought, critical inquiry, and civic engagement that are vital to the intersections of universities and democratic societies.

2. **Managerialism, Neoliberal Metrics, and Intellectual Autonomy.** McInnis and Morrish highlight how managerialism, audit cultures, and single-focused commercial imperatives reshape universities in the idealized image of the market, marginalizing the social sciences, humanities, and creative arts—and critical thought—so urgently needed to resist authoritarianism and sustain academic freedom and democracy.

3. **Global Shifts in Academic Power Demand New Epistemic Alliances.** Marginson on scientific competition through citation and Chapela's decolonial critique reveal the urgent need to disrupt and transform Euro-American academic hegemony, guard against one form of hegemony being replaced by another, foster equitable global knowledge collaborations, and co-constitute decolonial futures.

4. **The Urgency of Indigenous and Decolonial Epistemologies.** The university of the future needs to integrate decolonial epistemologies—Indigenous epistemologies, epistemologies of the South, plural knowledges and diverse perspectives and ways of knowing. Smith, Cote-Meek, and Ratt argue that the recovery and integration of Indigenous knowledge is not ancillary but central to decoloniality and to reimagining the university's ethical and epistemic possibilities.

5. **Reimagining the University, Critical Imagination and Civic Purpose.** The university of the future must include innovative models that prioritize meaningful community engagement and well-being, social justice, and sustainability to revitalize higher education. Kumashiro, Chatterjee, Sperlinger, and Newfield remind us that universities should be loci for democratic engagement and building models for alternative futures.

Reclaiming the University as Sites of Hope and Possibility

Across time and space, the university has been many things: a space for seeking truth, knowledge creation and innovation, a crucible for debate and dissent, and a contradictory vehicle for both domination and emancipation. As institutions of higher education face increasing pressure to conform to reductive models of merit, utility, and identity, the challenge is not simply to defend existing structures but to reimagine and repurpose them. The chapters in *Knowledge Under Siege* provide a layered, transdisciplinary, and often contradictory portrait of the university as it navigates intensifying political, economic, epistemic, and ecological pressures. The chapters in this volume importantly converge on a powerful argument: the future of universities is inseparable from broader struggles for democracy, justice, epistemic pluralism, and ecological sustainability. The chapters affirm universities' indispensability to democracy, civic engagement, and public good, yet warn of threats from polycrisis, neoliberalism, and authoritarianism. With "knowledge under siege," universities must reclaim their public mission—not through nostalgia for a liberal past, but by embracing their role as sites of struggle, imagination, human flourishing, and collective possibilities. To reclaim the purpose of universities in democracies necessitates reorientation beyond market value and epistemic hierarchy. As bell hooks (2003) reminds us, "To be truly visionary we have to root our imagination in our concrete reality while simultaneously imagining possibilities beyond that reality."

References

Alcoff, L.M., Mendiello, E. (2000). *Thinking from the Underside of History: Enrique Dussel's Philosophy of Liberation.* (2nd ed.) Rowman & Littlefield Publishers.

Brown, W. (2015). *Undoing the demos: Neoliberalism's stealth revolution.* Zone Books.

CBC Radio. (2023, September 5). Universities: What's the Point? Ideas with Nahlah Ayed. https://www.cbc.ca/listen/live-radio/1-23-ideas/clip/16007535-what-universities-for

Daniels, R.J. (2021, September 28). Why authoritarian regimes attack independent universities. *The Washington Post.* https://www.washingtonpost.com/opinions/2021/09/28/why-authoritarian-regimes-attack-independent-universities

Daniels, R.J., Shreve, G., & Spector, P. (2021). *What universities owe democracy.* John Hopkins University Press.

de Sousa Santos, B. (2014). *Epistemologies of the South: Justice against epistemicide.* Routledge.

Dewey, J. (1916). *Democracy and education.* Macmillan.

Dussel, E. (2011). *Filosofía de la liberación [Philosophy of liberation].* Fondo de Cultura Económica.

Editor Ed News. (2020, April 20). Student researcher concerned with accessibility to play. *Education News* [Blog]. https://www2.uregina.ca/education/news/student-researcher-concerned-with-accessibility-to-play/

Escobar, A. (2018) *Designs for the pluriverse: Radical interdependence, autonomy, and the making of worlds.* Duke University Press.

Fals Borda, O. (1995). *Research for social justice: Some North-South convergence.* Plenary Address at the Southern Sociological Society Meeting, Atlanta, April 18.

Freire, P. (2018). *Pedagogy of the oppressed.* Bloomsbury. (Original work published 1970)

Greene, M. (1995). *Releasing the imagination: Essays on education, the arts, and social change.* Jossey-Bass.

Haraway, D. (1988). Situated knowledges: The science question in feminism and the privilege of partial perspective. *Feminist Studies, 14*(3), 575–599. https://doi.org/10.2307/3178066

Hood, C. (1991). A public management for all seasons? *Public Administration, 69*(1), 3–19. https://doi.org/10.1111/j.1467-9299.1991.tb00779.x

hooks, b. (2003). *Teaching community: A pedagogy of hope.* Routledge.

Illich, I. (1971). *Deschooling society* (R.N. Anshen, Ed.). Harper & Row.

Kallis, G., & March, H. (2015). Imaginaries of hope: The utopianism of degrowth. *Annals of the Association of American Geographers, 105*(2), 360–68. http://www.jstor.org/stable/24537850

Lefebvre, H. (1991). *The production of space* (D. Nicholson-Smith, Trans.). Blackwell.

Mirowski, P. (2011). *Science-mart: Privatizing American science.* Harvard University Press.

Nussbaum, M.C. (2010). *Not for profit: Why democracy needs the humanities.* Princeton University Press.

Readings, B. (1997). *The university in ruins.* Harvard University Press.

Romine, T., & Mascarenhas, L. (2025, April 16). Harvard's president rejected Trump's demands. Here's how other university leaders have responded to the White House. CNN. https://www.cnn.com/2025/04/15/us/universities-responses-investigations-funding-freeze

Slaughter, S., and Rhoades, G. (2009). *Academic capitalism and the new economy: Markets, state, and higher education.* John Hopkins University Press.

Smith, L.T. (1999). *Decolonizing Methodologies: Research and Indigenous Peoples.* Zed Books.

Snyder, T. (2017). *On tyranny: Twenty lessons from the twentieth century.* Penguin Random House.

Soja, E.W. (1996). *Thirdspace: Journeys to Los Angeles and other real-and-imagined places.* Wiley-Blackwell.

Spivak, G.C. (1999). *A critique of postcolonial reason: Toward a history of the vanishing present.* Harvard University Press.

Spooner, M. and McNinch, J. (2018). *Dissident knowledge in higher education.* University of Regina Press.

Tuck, E. (2009). *Suspending damage: A letter to communities.* Harvard Educational Review, 79(3): 409–28. https://doi.org/10.17763/haer.79.3.n0016675661t3n15

SUBJECT INDEX

Includes subjects as well as book titles cited in the text and listed in the References. Information contained in Figures (f), Tables (t), or Notes (n), is indicated accordingly.

China First initiative, 73

China University Geoscience, STEM research ranking, 71 (t4.4)

civic engagement, by universities, 11, 26, 42–44, 223, 234, 301–2

Claremont Colleges consortium, 163, 167–68, 173

Clarivate Analytics, 64

Clark Kerr Lectures, 7

climate crisis: assaults on climate science, 294; calling for innovative adaptation, 223, 227, 231–32, 236; flood mitigation around U of Bristol, 225; need for broad decision-making, 237–39; possibility of environmental catastrophe, 241 (n5); relevant to all disciples, all careers, 233

Closing the Marketplace: Restriction, Repression, & Retrenchment in US Higher Education (G. Ladson-Billings), 37

Colby College, 172

Cole, Jonathan R., xxix, xxxvi, 24, 292, 301

colleges: admission policies, 15, 114; alternative models of, 8, 12; dependence on AI-powered courses, 213; effects of COVID on, 120; funding support for, 205, 212, 216; liberal arts curricula in, 6–7, 84, 210; polarization, chaos at, 175; research procedures at, 118–19. See also futures, of higher education; private colleges/universities; public colleges/universities; students

colonialism/colonization: affects on Latinoamerican universities, 88; genocide of Indigenous Peoples, 156, 162, 164, 183, 191, 261; legacies of in universities, 154–55, 157, 258, 261, 269, 292; origin of academic disciplines, 27; settler-immigrant ignorance, privilege, 162–63; suppressing democratic engagement, 295; university complicities in, 162, 164, 174, 183; violent, ongoing impact of, 156, 261. See also reconciliation

Colonized Classrooms: Racism, Trauma and Resistance in Post-Secondary Education (S. Cote-Meek), 150, 158

Colorado College, 172

Columbia University, 6, 8, 11, 291–92; high-citation science papers, 62 (t4.2)

Complaint! (S. Ahmed), 35

Concordia University: strike action at, 131 (n7); Task Force on Anti-Black Racism, 193

Conservative Political Action Conference, 107

Contingencia, hegemonía, universalidad. Diálogos contemporáneos en la izquierda (J. Butler, etc.), 92

contract academic staff (CAS). See faculty

Córdoba Reform, 196 (n3); promoting democratic universities, 88

Cornell University, 291; Cornell Tech campus, 223; high-citation science papers, 62 (t4.2); STEM research ranking, 71 (t4.4)

Cote-Meek, Sheila, xxxviii, 261, 298, 300–301

COVID pandemic: effects on students, student test scores, xxxviii, 43, 147, 169, 228; effects on universities, university teaching, 90, 137, 165–67, 170–71, 175, 223; need for academic service, 120; opportunity for change in aftermath, 104, 106, 138, 140. See also activism

AUTHOR INDEX

Includes authors cited in the text and/or listed in the chapter references. Information contained in Figures (f), Tables (t), or Notes (n), is indicated accordingly.

ABOUT THE AUTHORS

Whitney Blaisdell is an award-winning PhD candidate in the Faculty of Education at the University of Regina. A former public-school teacher and current instructor with SUNTEP, she also serves as co-chair of the Regina and Area Early Childhood Network and executive director of Project Play YQR, a non-profit organization founded on her graduate research. Whitney's research focuses on play, education, ethics, and design. Her scholarship has contributed to art exhibits, community-based organizations, park designs, conference presentations, peer-reviewed articles, podcasts, public journalism interviews, urban revitalization efforts, and more.

Consuelo "Coni" Chapela. Mexican. Currently a professor-researcher in the Health and Society research area at the Universidad Autónoma Metropolitana Xochimilco Campus in Mexico. Her scholarship reflects her concerns with the relationship between knowledge and society, its intimate connection with justice, human dignity, the ways of knowing the world to transform it, and the impact of all this on the conditions of individual and collective bodies. She trained as a medical doctor at the National Autonomous University of Mexico, has a master's in Community Medicine at the University of Edinburgh, and a PhD in Social Sciences from the IoE at the University of London. She is ex-president of the International Association of Qualitative Inquiry and active in associations enhancing community power through critical dialogue, research, and planning.

Piya Chatterjee teaches in feminist studies at Scripps College. She is completing thirty years in the US academy, which she also writes about. Her publications include A *Time for Tea: Women, Labor and Post/Colonial Politics on an Indian Plantation* (Duke University Press, 2001); *States of Trauma: Gender and Violence in South Asia* (Zubaan, 2009) as co-editor; and *The Imperial University: Academic Repression and Scholarly Dissent* (University of Minnesota Press, 2011). Piya is now working in solidarity with grassroots organizing and cooperative building with tea plantation communities in the Dooars, West Bengal, India.

Jonathan R. Cole, is the John Mitchell Mason Professor at Columbia University. He was provost and dean of faculties at Columbia from 1989 to 2003. His scholarly work includes the development of sociology of science: see *Smoother Pebbles: Essays in the Sociology of Science* (Columbia University Press, 2024). Much of his recent work has discussed aspects of higher education: see *The Great American University* (PublicAffairs, 2009) and *Toward a More Perfect University* (PublicAffairs, 2016), among other books and essays on the subject. He has written extensively on academic freedom and free inquiry. He is an elected member of the American Philosophical Society, the American Academy of Arts and Sciences, and the Council of Foreign Relations.

Sheila Cote-Meek is Anishinaabe from the Teme-Augama Anishnabai. She is currently director and professor of Indigenous educational studies at Brock University. She was the inaugural vice-president of equity, people and culture at York University where she led the development of the Decolonizing, Equity, Diversity and Inclusion (DEDI) strategy and York's Black Inclusion Strategy. She was the inaugural associate-vice-president of Indigenous and academic programs at Laurentian University where she developed the Indigenous Sharing and Learning Centre, the Maamwizing Indigenous Research Institute, and the Master of Indigenous Relations. Dr. Cote-Meek is author of *Colonized Classrooms—Racism, Trauma and Resistance in Post-Secondary Education* (Fernwood Publishing, 2014) and three co-edited books: *Decolonizing and Indigenizing Education in Canada* (Canadian Scholars, 2020), *Critical Reflections and Politics on Advancing Women in the Academy* (IGI Global, 2020), and *Perspectives on Indigenous Pedagogy in Education: Learning from One Another* (IGI Global, 2023).

Shannon Dea (she/they) is a professor of philosophy, and provost and vice-president, academic and research at St. Mary's University in Halifax,

Nova Scotia. She is the author of *Beyond the Binary: Thinking about Sex and Gender* (Broadview, 2016 and 2023) and of numerous articles and book chapters. Her recent research spans classic American pragmatist philosophy, social and feminist philosophy, and topics related to higher education, academic freedom, and freedom of expression. Between 2018 and 2022, she was the author of Dispatches on Academic Freedom, a regular *University Affairs* column. Shannon lives and works on the ancestral and unceded territory of the Mi'kmaq People.

Kevin K. Kumashiro (kevinkumashiro.com) is an internationally recognized expert on educational policy, school reform, teacher preparation, and educational equity and justice, with a wide-ranging list of accomplishments and awards as a scholar, educator, leader, and advocate. He is the former dean of the Schools of Education at the University of San Francisco and Hofstra University; the founding chair of the national network Education Deans for Justice and Equity; and the award-winning author or editor of ten books, including *Bad Teacher!: How Blaming Teachers Distorts the Bigger Picture* (Teachers College Press, 2012) *Against Common Sense: Teaching and Learning Toward Social Justice* (Routledge, 2015), and, most recently, *Surrendered: Why Progressives Are Losing the Biggest Battles in Education* (Teachers College Press, 2020).

Gloria Ladson-Billings is the former Kellner Family Distinguished Professor of Urban Education in the Department of Curriculum and Instruction and faculty affiliate in the Department of Educational Policy Studies at the University of Wisconsin–Madison. She is a fellow of the British Academy, the American Academy of Arts and Sciences, and the Hagler Institute for Advanced Study at Texas A&M University. She was the 2005–2006 president of the American Educational Research Association (AERA) and from 2017 to 2021 served as the president of the National Academy of Education (NAEd). Ladson-Billings's research examines the pedagogical practices of teachers who are successful with African American students. She also investigates critical race theory applications to education. She is the author of several critically acclaimed books and numerous journal articles and book chapters.

Simon Marginson is professor of higher education at the University of Bristol and emeritus professor of higher education at the University of Oxford, joint editor-in-chief of *Higher Education*, honorary professor at Tsinghua University in China, and professorial associate at the University of Melbourne in Australia. He is a fellow of the British Academy, the Academy of Social Sciences in the United Kingdom, and the Society for Research into Higher Education, and a member of Academia Europaea. Simon's research is focused on global, international, and comparative higher education; global science; higher education in East Asia; and the contributions of higher education to the common good. He publishes three books with Bloomsbury Academic in 2025: on UK higher education and Brexit (authored with Vassiliki Papatsiba), on academic mobility and immobility (edited with Aline Courtois, Catherine Montgomery, and Ravinder Sidhu), and on global higher education in times of turmoil.

Peter S. McInnis is a member of the Department of History at St. Francis Xavier University and teaches North American social history. Research interests include labour and working-class history, deindustrialization and public memory, film history, and the evolution of academic freedom in Canadian universities. McInnis has been active in faculty unions for twenty-five years. He has served on the executive committee of the Canadian Association of University Teachers since 2014 and was elected to three terms as CAUT president.

James McNinch is an emeritus professor and a former dean of the Faculty of Education at the University of Regina. He served as the founding director of that university's Teaching and Learning Centre. Previously, he was the director of the Gabriel Dumont Institute of the Métis peoples of Saskatchewan. His research and writing has focused on gender and sexuality, racism and white privilege, and tenets of masculinity. He helped to bring *fYrefly*, a leadership and resiliency camp for queer youth, to Saskatchewan fifteen years ago. He serves on the editorial board of the *International Journal of LGBTQ+ Youth Studies* and the *Journal of Men's Studies*. He continues to work with provincial school divisions negotiating their way through diversity, equity, and inclusion initiatives. He can be reached at james.mcninch@uregina.ca.

Liz Morrish is an independent scholar. She is also an honorary visiting fellow at York St John University, UK. For over thirty years she taught linguistics at Nottingham Trent University, UK. Since leaving academia, Liz has found it easier to reclaim academic freedom, and she continues to research and write in the areas of higher education policy and critical university studies. Her most recent book, co-authored with Helen Sauntson, is *Academic Irregularities: Language and Neoliberalism in Higher Education* (Routledge, 2020). In 2019, Liz wrote *Pressure Vessels*, a paper for the UK think tank, the Higher Education Policy Institute, on the epidemic of poor mental health among university staff (https://www.hepi.ac.uk/2019/05/23/pressure-vessels-the-epidemic-of-poor-mental-health-among-higher-education-staff). Liz also writes a blog: *Academic Irregularities* (https://academicirregularities.wordpress.com).

Dr. Christopher Newfield, Director of Research, Independent Social Research Foundation, London, UK, and Distinguished Professor Emeritus, University of California, Santa Barbara. He has written a trilogy of books on the university as an intellectual and social institution: *Ivy and Industry: Business and the Making of the American University, 1880–1980* (Duke University Press, 2003); *Unmaking the Public University: The Forty-Year Assault on the Middle Class* (Harvard University Press, 2008); and *The Great Mistake: How We Wrecked Public Universities and How We Can Fix Them* (Johns Hopkins University Press, 2016). He is also co-editor of *Limits of the Numerical* (University of Chicago Press, 2022) and co-author of *Metrics That Matter* (Johns Hopkins University Press, 2023). His current projects involve literary and cultural knowledge, the future of higher education, and the culture of equality.

Tammy Ratt is a nēhiyaw, ēkwa Scottish iskwêw. minahik waskahigan ohcīyiwa wiya okāwiya (her mother is from Pinehouse Lake, Saskatchewan), and her mother tongue is nēhiyawēwin. ohtâwiya Swift Current ohcîyiwa wiya (her dad is from Swift Current Saskatchewan). namôya kî-nêhiyâw (he didn't speak Cree). Tammy is a beginning speaker of nēhiyawēwin. She is a mother, wife, daughter, sister, auntie, teacher, and a student. minahik waskahigan, Swift Current, êkwa oskana kā-asastēk ohciw. Tammy has a secondary Indigenous education degree, a Master of Education, and is currently working on her PhD, which examines Indigenous language education using art as a method of transmission. She is currently the program coordinator for the Indigenous Languages program at First Nations University of Canada where she also teaches Beginner Cree courses.

Malinda S. Smith is a professor of political science and an associate vice-president research at the University of Calgary, where she leads initiatives to advance inclusive research excellence. She is a member of SSHRC Governing Council and Executive, and vice-chair of the Scarborough Charter Inter-Institutional Forum. She is a co-author of *The Equity Myth: Racialization and Indigeneity at Canadian Universities* (UBC Press, 2017), and editor or co-editor of seven books, including *Critical Concepts: An Introduction to Politics* (Oxford University Press, 2023), *Nuances of Blackness in the Canadian Academy* (University of Toronto Press, 2022), and *Securing Africa: Post-9/11 Discourses on Terrorism* (Routledge, 2010). Dr. Smith is a recipient of numerous awards and honours, including a Doctor of Laws (honoris causa) from Simon Fraser University, a P.E. Trudeau Foundation Fellowship, and an ISA-Canada Distinguished Scholar Award.

Linda Tuhiwai Smith is a renowned scholar with an international reputation for her contributions to Indigenous education grounded in the cultural revitalization of the Māori Peoples. She was the founding co-director of the Māori Centre of Research Excellence, the Pro-Vice Chancellor Māori and dean of the School of Māori and Pacific Development at the University of Waikato in New Zealand, and now a distinguished professor at Te Whare Wānanga o Awanuiārangi. Smith's academic work is about decolonizing knowledge systems. The recipient of many awards and honours, she became the first Māori scholar to be elected into the American Academy of Arts and Sciences in 2021. Smith's groundbreaking book *Decolonizing Methodologies: Research and Indigenous Peoples*, first published in 1999 and available in many translations, continues to be a major influence on the research, teaching, and scholarship of decolonization.

Tom Sperlinger is a professor at the University of Bristol and chief academic officer for Black Mountains College, a new institution dedicated to education at a time of climate emergency. He is author of *Romeo and Juliet in Palestine* (Zero Books, 2015), a teaching memoir about a semester he spent at Al-Quds University in the West Bank, and lead author of *Who Are Universities For?* (Bristol University Press, 2018), which imagines a higher education sector in which the whole of society participates. He is currently preparing a co-edited *Companion to Dangerous Books*.

Marc Spooner is a full professor in the Faculty of Education at the University of Regina. His research interests include audit culture, academic freedom, and the effects of neoliberalization and corporatization on higher education, as well as social justice, activism, and participatory democracy. He has published in many venues, including peer-reviewed journals, book chapters, government reports, and a wide variety of popularizations. He is the co-editor of the award-winning book *Dissident Knowledge in Higher Education*, the current *Knowledge Under Siege: Charting a Future for Universities* (both from University of Regina Press, 2018 and 2026), and is oftentimes a social/political commentator who can be followed on Bluesky at @drmarcspooner.bsky.social.

Joel Westheimer is professor of democracy and education at the University of Ottawa. He is also an education columnist for CBC Radio. An elected member of the National Academy of Education and a fellow of the American Educational Research Association, Westheimer is an expert in civic education and the role of schools in democratic societies. His last two books are the award-winning *What Kind of Citizen? Educating Our Children for the Common Good* (2nd ed., foreword by Gloria Ladson-Billings, Teachers College Press, 2024) and the edited volume *Pledging Allegiance: The Politics of Patriotism in America's Schools* (foreword by the late Howard Zinn, Teachers College Press, 2007). He has delivered more than 350 keynote speeches, nationally and internationally, and is a regular contributor to newspapers and magazines, including the *Washington Post*, the *Globe and Mail*, the *National Post*, and the *Toronto Star*. Find out more at joelwestheimer.org.